CAPTORS AND CAPTIVES

A VOLUME IN THE SERIES

Native Americans of the Northeast:
Culture, History, and the Contemporary

EDITED BY

Colin G. Calloway and Barry O'Connell

CAPTORS AND CAPTIVES

THE 1704 FRENCH AND INDIAN RAID ON DEERFIELD

EVAN HAEFELI AND KEVIN SWEENEY

UNIVERSITY OF MASSACHUSETTS PRESS   AMHERST AND BOSTON

Printed in the United States of America
LC 2003009016
ISBN 1-55849-419-7

Designed by Dennis Anderson
Set in Dante by Graphic Composition Inc.
Printed and bound by The Maple-Vail Book Manufacturing Group

Library of Congress Cataloging-in-Publication Data

Haefeli, Evan, 1969–
    Captors and captives : the 1704 French and Indian raid on Deerfield / Evan Haefeli and
Kevin Sweeney.
        p. cm. — (Native Americans of the Northeast)
Includes bibliographical references and index.
    ISBN 1-55849-419-7 (alk. paper)
    1. Abenaki Indians—Wars. 2. Indian captivities—Massachusetts—Deerfield. 3. Indians
of North America—Wars—1600–1750. 4. United States—History—Queen Anne's War,
1702–1713. 5. Deerfield (Mass.)—History—Colonial period, ca. 1600–1775. I. Sweeney,
Kevin, 1950– II. Title. III. Series.
    E99.A13 H34 2004
    973.2′5—dc21

                                                                        2003009016

British Library Cataloguing in Publication data are available.

For our parents,

Richard and Nancy Haefeli

and

Michael and Beatrice Sweeney

CONTENTS

ILLUSTRATIONS

MAPS

ACKNOWLEDGMENTS

OVER THE course of ten years that involved research in three countries and seemingly endless drafts of a manuscript, you incur many debts. Here we gratefully acknowledge them and reserve to ourselves the burden of failing to heed proffered advice or, worse yet, the inadvertent failure to acknowledge someone or someplace that has assisted us.

Many individuals helped us learn about the histories of the various communities into which our research took us. In our project's earliest stages we were assisted by three historians who had already written about the events of 1704: Geoffrey E. Buerger, John Demos, and Rick Melvoin. Alice Nash, Harald Prins, and James Spady generously shared their thoughts as well as then unpublished research with us. Angela Goebel-Bain, Suzanne Flynt, Don Friary, David Proper, Amelia Miller, Tim Neumann, and other current and former members of the staffs at Historic Deerfield, Inc., and the Pocumtuck Valley Memorial Association provided assistance and encouragement at the outset and since. We also learned from the staff and outside consultants for the Web exhibition, "The Many Stories of 1704," sponsored by the Pocumtuck Valley Memorial Association. In particular, our participation in this undertaking brought us into contact with Patrick Côté, Curator-Conservator of the Musée des Abénakis in Odanak, Huwennuwanenhs Stéphane Picard, and Louis-Karl Picard-Sioui from Wendake, Village des Hurons, and Kanatakta and Brian Deer, the current and former executive directors of the Kanien'kehaka Onkwawén:na Raotitiohkwa Cultural Center at Kahnawake. They helped us see things we might have missed. Brian Deer also gave the entire book a close reading. Along the way, we benefited from the criticism of members of the Five College Social History Seminar, the fellows of the Charles Warren Center at Harvard, and the participants in Amherst College's Atlantic World seminar who read and commented on early versions of our work. Portions of this work were also presented at the Algonquian Conference, the French Colonial Historical Society Conference, and the New England American Studies Conference.

The staffs of many libraries aided this project immeasurably. First and foremost were members of the staff at the Memorial Libraries in Deerfield, David Bosse, Sharmon Prouty, and Martha Noblick, who maintain this institution's remarkable collections. The reference staff and the interlibrary loan staff at Amherst's Frost Library helped locate and obtain hard-to-find publications in French and unpublished master's and doctoral theses. And we thank the libraries that loaned them. The need for such requests was significantly reduced by the large collection of publications on New France at the Neilson Library at Smith College that was nurtured by Marine Leland and maintained by a generous endowment set up in her memory. We also found assistance and critical materials at the Massachusetts Historical Society, New York Historical Society, The Historical Society of Pennsylvania, Princeton University's Firestone Library, and Harvard University's Widener Library. The staffs of the public library in Boucherville, the Archives du Séminaire de Trois-Rivières, Archives du Séminaire de Nicolet (especially Marie Pelletier), Archives Nationales de Quebec in Montreal, the Canadian National Archives in Ottawa, and the Archives Nationales in Paris were extremely accommodating, helping us obtain documents and illustrations, while patiently negotiating occasionally difficult crossings of linguistic boundaries. Staff members at Fort Chambly and Patrick Coté also went out of their way to help locate critical plans. Individuals at the Archives départementales de la Gironde in Bordeaux, Bibliothèque Nationale de France in Paris, the Beinecke Library at Yale University, the Canadian National Archives in Ottawa, the McCord Museum in Montreal, Montreal Central Library, the Newberry Library in Chicago, and Department of Rare Books and Special Collections, Princeton University Libraries assisted us in obtaining illustrations.

An important component of the book's illustrations are the maps produced by Kate Blackmer. They are in fact more than illustrations. They elegantly tell their own stories of colonists' aspirations, Native dispossession, and imperial warfare that complement the stories in the text.

We are grateful to the many people who read the book at various stages and made helpful suggestions. The series editors, Colin Calloway and Barry O'Connell moved the project forward. Dan Richter helped us re-envision our book through the correct end of the telescope. Don Friary, for many years the Executive Director at Historic Deerfield, Inc., gave it a close reading informed by his unique familiarity with Deerfield's history. Rick Melvoin also drew upon his work on Deerfield's history to reassure us when we needed it most. Three colleagues, Gerald McFarland at the University of Massachusetts, Neal Salisbury at Smith, and John Servos at Amherst, generously shared with us their perspectives on the project. We owe an especial debt of gratitude to two scholars of New France, Jay Cassel and Sylvie Dépatie, who helped guide us through the historigraphic thickets of the French colony. Sylvie went beyond the usual bounds of scholarly generosity and proofread our French.

As novices in matters of book publishing, we were fortunate to have the support of the staff at the University of Massachusetts Press. Our editor, Clark Dougan, gave us a title and a deadline, without which we may never have finished the book. Carol Betsch guided the manuscript through the publication process. Deborah Smith's painstaking copyediting saved us from embarrassing errors and made the book read better. Our thanks to Nairn Chadwick for his excellent index.

Financially, this project is indebted to several institutions. At an early stage, assistance came from a Hampshire College Threshold Grant and the American Philosophical Society's Phillip's Fund for Native American Research. Princeton University provided money for a subvention. Amherst College's H. Axel Schupf '57 Fund for Intellectual Life also provided funds for a subvention and paid for Kate Blackmer's maps. A grant from Tufts University helped pay for illustrations and the indexing.

Finally, we owe debts that go beyond the usual acknowledgments of family members and friends for emotional and material support. Margaret and Michael Sweeney proofread parts of the book, while Jamie assisted with illustrations. Maggie's proficiency in French was of assistance at critical points in the project. Without the hospitality and enthusiasm of the Coburn family of West Springfield, Massachusetts, especially Tom Coburn, Marie Coburn Gill, the late Phil Coburn, and the late Bob Gill, our collaboration would have been impossible. The same must be said for the steady support of Richard and Nancy Haefeli and Michael and Beatrice Sweeney over these many years, and to them we dedicate this volume.

CAPTORS AND CAPTIVES

INTRODUCTION

WAR AND CAPTIVITY

A s the northwesternmost town of New England, Deerfield, Massachusetts, found itself in 1704 at the forefront of a clash of peoples and empires in northeastern North America. On the morning of February 29, 1704, a joint French and Indian raiding party attacked this English village where some 275 inhabitants and 20 garrison soldiers slept. In a surprise assault, 250 to 300 Abenakis, Frenchmen, Hurons, Mohawks, Pennacooks, and Iroquois of the Mountain penetrated the village's stockade and killed 50 and captured 112 of the residents. By evening half of the village's population was gone, men, women, and children. Many homes lay in ashes. The English killed 11 of the attackers and wounded at least 22, some of whom never made it home. The death toll and the number of captives taken made it one of the most devastating assaults on a colonial village anywhere in New England, New York, or New France. Ever after, Deerfield has had a special place in American history.[1]

In 1704, Deerfield was not a particularly important place. Nor was the village or any of its inhabitants a special target, merely a convenient one given the town's location. Still, it was not exactly the "unoffending hamlet" seen by Francis Parkman, the famous nineteenth-century New England historian. As a New England town, Deerfield embodied the cutting edge of an aggressive and expansionist culture, one whose social and economic survival depended on securing ever more land for its increasing number of children to farm. That land could only be gotten from the region's Natives, who had been resisting English expansion since King Philip's War in the 1670s. They continued to do so even after King Philip's War displaced them from their southern New England homelands. For the Abenakis and the Pennacooks living in what is today northern New England and neighboring Canada, the raid on Deerfield offered an opportunity to strike back. For the French empire, the raid was part of an effort to curb the growth of the English empire in North America. But lacking the large population of New England, New France had to depend on Native alliances much more than New England did. This meant that when the French went to war in the Northeast, they called upon Native communities in Canada for support. In 1704 these included the Hurons of Lorette, the Iroquois of the Mountain, and the Mohawks at Kahnawake (see appendix A).[2]

1

Deerfield in February 1704 thus became a point of convergence for struggles that had both trans-Atlantic and local origins. Fighting had begun in the Northeast in 1703 as part of a major European war, the War of the Spanish Succession. This conflict, which would continue until 1713, would be remembered by later generations of New Englanders as Queen Anne's War, but its origins owed more to the actions of another monarch, France's Louis XIV. On the Continent, the war was ignited by Louis's decision to support his grandson's claim to the Spanish throne. King Louis hoped to bring not only Spain but also its vast overseas empire into the strategic and economic orbit of France. Natives in the Northeast hesitated to involve themselves in this contest between the rival empires. They were still recovering from a long series of wars that had ended only a few years before. Despite long-standing problems with the English, many of the Abenakis and Pennacooks wanted to remain "Neuters," but the strategic plans of the French and the fears and provocations of the English made neutrality impossible. Influenced by imperial strategy and colonial trade, officials in New France precipitated the fighting by pressuring Eastern Abenakis and Pennacooks to attack English settlements in Maine in August 1703. But throughout the war, the less than enthusiastic Native allies of the French often hung back from fights in which they had nothing to gain. Thanks in part to their efforts, peace always threatened to break out in the Northeast long before the War of the Spanish Succession had ended in Europe.[3]

Those Natives who chose to attack Deerfield did so only after they had made a series of individual and collective calculations. The French could start a war on their own, but they could not finish it without help from their Native allies and they could not dictate the terms of Native participation. The autonomy of Indian communities, even those in Canada, meant that every warlike undertaking involved constant negotiations. Natives still had specific cultural, economic, and political interests of their own, and they were quite astute about pursuing them. For the Abenakis and Pennacooks, the raid came during the third in a series of conflicts with the English going back to 1676. For these Natives the Deerfield raid could therefore be seen as an integral part of the Third Anglo-Abenaki War, an overlapping war fought to resist English invasion of their lands. But when the Hurons of Lorette, Iroquois of the Mountain, and Mohawks of Kahnawake attacked Deerfield, they were not fighting an overlapping war against a traditional foe whom they saw as a specific threat to their lands. They were waging what the Canadian historian Peter MacLeod has called a "parallel war," a war within an imperial war for personal goals rather than national interests. The aims of these personal wars paralleled but remained quite distinct from the goals of their French allies. "In parallel warfare, Amerindians went to war in search of prisoners, scalps, and matériel; Europeans attacked or defended forts." In

February 1704, 200 to 250 Natives from five communities chose to join with 48 French soldiers and militiamen to attack Deerfield.[4]

The size and character of the Deerfield raid offers a variety of opportunities and challenges for a historian. Its fame helped make it a memorable event. For this reason, it has received an extraordinary amount of attention from historians, genealogists, and archivists, rendering it an excellent entry point into the histories of Native, French, and English peoples of the colonial Northeast. To explain in an inclusive manner how and why the raid happened, we have found it necessary to situate it in a context that is both broader and narrower than that of previous accounts. We cast our net widely to pull in Native and French as well as English perspectives. In an effort to create a single story that moves beyond the generalizations and stereotypes of national and communal histories, we have chosen, whenever possible, to focus on individuals. By building our account of the raid around their stories, we have found ourselves putting into practice what has been called the new "frontier history." Whereas frontiers used to be seen as a thin line between settlement and wilderness, "civilization" and "savagery," they are now recognized to be territories or zones of interaction between different cultures. In recognition of this change, many scholars now follow the lead of the historian Richard White and speak of a "middle ground" rather than frontiers.[5]

At present scholars probably see middle grounds in too many places. White originally coined the phrase to describe the particular dynamics he discovered at work in the Great Lakes region. There, individuals from different communities sought to pursue their own ends according to their particular cultural heritages and interests. The ambiguous result, the "middle ground," was shaped by the inability of any group, French or Native, to impose its will on another. The Great Lakes were a special case. Beyond the effective reach of either the French or the English empire, it was a region where well into the eighteenth century the cultural traditions and political agendas of Natives continued to have as much influence as, probably more than, those of the contending imperial powers. Inspired by White's work, many scholars now see the frontier experience as characterized by "kinetic interactions among many peoples which created new cultural matrices distinctly American in their ecclectism, fluidity, individual determination, and differentiation" that led to "social diversity, innovative cultural adaptations, and political mutability." But this was not true of all early American frontiers. By 1704, the Northeast was not such a place, for reasons that we make clear. The pull of European as well as Native cultural traditions and identities remained strong. Boundaries and barriers did exist, and, as the historian James Merrill has pointed out, there was a barrier between Native and English peoples that "they could not, would not, tear down."[6]

We do believe that where a "middle ground" did exist it was fundamentally about relations between individuals. It could move around but it usually did not last long—no longer than the relationships that created it. However, this fluidity also means that one can find something of a middle ground in unexpected places—the military expedition against Deerfield, the retreat to Canada—as well as in more obvious places such as at French missions and in Native villages. Although we do not use the term "middle ground," White's attention to the agency of Native Americans and to the subtlety of cross-cultural relations has influenced our approach to creating a new history of the Deerfield raid. In our book we add to images of clashing cultures and empires more complex stories of cultural accommodation and conflict between individuals and communities.

By following individuals across frontiers, we have found that the Atlantic empires of England and France played crucial roles in shaping their lives. Tracing out the causes and consequences of the 1704 raid on Deerfield, we have found unexpected strengths and weaknesses in both empires. At the edge of empire, solutions become problems and problems become possibilities. In the case of New France, military strength reveals political weaknesses. In the case of New England, domestic divisions reinforce imperial power. Usually portrayed on maps as solid blocks of color—blue for the French and red for the English—these colonial empires were in reality more like diaphanous spiderwebs connecting individual places and people. These empires were based on networks of relationships and allegiances that ran from London and Versailles into the interior of North America. Without them, officials in Europe could not project power and influence into places and onto peoples they often poorly understood. With them, colonists and Natives were able to strengthen communities that otherwise would have been destroyed in the turmoil unleashed by European imperialism.

We have also learned that the course of empire in North America often depended on the deeds of rather obscure people. Projects formulated in Europe depended not only on the cooperation of colonial officials in New France and New England but also on the aspirations of family farmers in Deerfield, the pursuit of profits by merchants in Boston, the economic calculations of Canadian fur traders, the missionary zeal of priests, the diplomacy of Pennacooks, the fears of Abenaki warriors, and the grief of Mohawk women. All at various times supported and subverted the aims of officials in London and Versailles. Their everyday hopes and fears created relationships and allegiances that both extended and limited the reach of the French and English empires in America. By looking at individual people from all the communities involved in the Deerfield raid, we have found that there was a surprising amount of contact between people living in and around the two empires and across cultures in the Northeast. To a certain degree war and peace were extremes on a continuum of on-going interactions. As a result we have written a book that is as much about the connections between peoples as it is about the conflicts over resources, religion, and politics that drove them apart.

Our pursuit of connections flowed naturally out of the experience of the Deerfield captives. Later generations in New England would remember the raid as the Deerfield Massacre, but for contemporaries, the significance of the attack was defined by those taken captive, not those who were killed. For French and Native raiders as well as the English survivors, captivity gave the event its military, economic, and spiritual meaning. The captives left behind a variety of legacies in texts, notarial records, and oral traditions. Like contemporaries and other researchers before us, we too have been drawn to the captives' experiences.[7]

Without an understanding of captivity, the whole raid and its aftermath cannot be comprehended. Taking captives had ancient cultural roots among Native peoples and was part of their traditions of warfare. Taking captives was the primary motive for many of the Native raiders who participated in the raid. French officials and soldiers knew this and used the promise of captives to ensure their allies' participation. In this way, the taking and sharing of captives played a fundamental role in the ongoing negotiations of French-Indian alliances. At the same time, other French colonists—members of religious orders, devout and wealthy merchants and nobles—wanted to gain control of English captives to turn them into good French Catholics. Their efforts to ransom captives from Natives put a strain on military alliances and inhibited the French soldiers' chances of launching another successful raid on the scale of the attack on Deerfield. Competition for captives thus helped drive the war and undercut it.

Captivity preoccupied the English as well. Protestant New Englanders feared for the souls of captives who stayed with French or Native Catholics. Tales of captivity gave the Deerfield raid a prominent place in early American history. The first and most influential account of the raid was written by a captive, the Reverend John Williams, Deerfield's minister. His narrative, *The Redeemed Captive Returning to Zion,* recounts in detail his flock's captivity and sufferings in Catholic New France. Its publication in 1707 helped save a royal governor, galvanized the colonial war effort in Massachusetts, and played a role in reconciling the colony's residents to the new British imperial order founded on liberty, private property, and anti-Catholicism. Williams's narrative was repeatedly reprinted, exposing subsequent generations of readers to the story of the raid and becoming a classic of early American literature in the process. The text's narrative of suffering, testing, and triumph remained at the core of subsequent New England and American accounts of the raid and has kept the memory of a clash of cultures alive to this day. Its legacy in the United States has helped perpetuate images of conflict between Indians and colonists, between "savagery and civilization," between Catholics and Protestants.

Alternative stories of the raid and captivity are found in Abenaki, Mohawk, and Canadian communities descended from Deerfield's one-time attackers. In many ways they draw on the legacy of the other famous Deerfield captive, John Williams's daughter Eunice. Adopted into the Mohawk family of her captors, Eunice lived out the rest of her life as a Mohawk, giving birth to children who continued the Williams family name in the village of Kahnawake, where her descendants still live. While New England stories, drawing on John's legacy, are preoccupied with the defense and preservation of tradition and boundaries, the stories of Eunice's experience confront the tremendous changes brought by the expansion of New England. Adoption, assimilation, and adaptations to situations not of the captives' own choosing are the usual themes of these narratives. Recently, this story has been brought to a wider audience by the research of John Demos in his book *The Unredeemed Captive: A Family Story from Early America*.

Our research has drawn us to other individuals whose experiences of crossing between cultures tend to complicate the seeming polarities defined by the experiences of John and Eunice Williams. We have found their cases to be unusual and rather unrepresentative of the experiences of the majority of Deerfield's captives. For example, most of those who remained in Canada lived with the French, not the Indians as did Eunice. This pattern resulted from the distinct histories of the Native and French communities. It involved both individual choices and the actions of French men and women who preferred to turn English captives into French Catholics, not Native American Catholics. There are also the stories of the Kelloggs, who returned to New England after living in Canada for several years. Joseph, who had learned several Native languages, served the Massachusetts colony as a well-regarded interpreter and soldier. His brother Martin, a somewhat more questionable character, became involved in disputes that rocked the English mission to the Mahicans at Stockbridge, Massachusetts. Their sister Rebecca lived at Kahnawake over twenty years before returning and serving as an interpreter at Stockbridge and elsewhere. Yet other returning captives became enthusiastic participants in scouting and scalping parties launched against their former captors.

Because we came to believe that the diversity of individual stories makes a detailed study of the Deerfield raid particularly valuable, we strove to uncover the names and identities of as many specific individuals as possible. A lack of sources has made it difficult to recover the identities of most of the attackers, especially those from Native communities, for which there are few written records before the middle of the eighteenth century, and oral traditions do not, as a rule, highlight the exploits of individuals from this period. Among the

French, official records tend to report only the names of the elite, and most of the French names that we know for certain are those of officers, who were members of the nobility. Because of the nature of the existing records, we can say more about individual English captives. We often have had to rely on them to take us into Native and French communities. And when we have been able to uncover the name of a French enlisted man in the colonial regulars or a Huron or Pennacook attacker, the particular fates of individual captives have usually led us to them. This situation creates an undeniable bias that we have worked hard to overcome.

As we dug deeper we discovered that captives and others who crossed and re-crossed cultural boundaries were part of the story before the raid as well as af-ter. Among the visitors to Deerfield during the 1690s were Indians from south-ern New England who at one point had been captured by the English and put into servitude. John Williams would meet one of these individuals when he ar-rived at the Abenaki village of Odanak in Canada. French leaders of the Deer-field raid were the sons of men who had lived in Native communities, one in-voluntarily as a captive of the Iroquois. The position of their families, and their own facility with Native languages grew out of these experiences. Two of the people killed during the Deerfield raid were captive African Americans, slaves of the town's minister. Another of the men killed in the raid was a former En-glish captive who had lived with the Abenakis. He may have come to Deerfield in the company of three French fur traders who moved to New England to seek their fortune. French traders such as these occasionally employed English cap-tives because of their linguistic skills and contacts. The three Frenchmen would be captured during the attack and returned to New France as prisoners. As the people of Deerfield knew well before 1704, captivity was a fact of life on the New England frontier.

A history of an event like the 1704 Deerfield raid is in part a story of large, im-personal forces at work: demographic trends, social structures, economic crises, and imperial conflict. But, as we try to emphasize, there is also a history of indi-viduals struggling with these forces, trying to carve out an independent course, to cross the dividing lines drawn between French and English, Native and Eu-ropean. That their stories have sometimes been lost to the cultural memory of their communities does not diminish their significance. On the contrary, they formed an important challenge to the colonial and later nationalistic identities based on exclusion and prejudice that remember the raid but do not understand why it happened. Now, three hundred years after the fact, it is time to pay heed to their stories while we study and analyze the forces that overshadowed them.

PART I

CREATING COMMUNITIES

CHAPTER 1

FRONTIER TOWN

I N 1704, Deerfield was the "Utmost Frontier Town" in western Massachusetts. Colonial authorities saw such a place as marking a boundary that had to be defended. Here ended the landscape colonized by the English, their crops, their animals, and their beliefs, and just beyond their fields was land controlled by the Indians. This image of a confrontation between civilization and savagery was inherited by subsequent generations of Americans. In time, Americans also came to see a frontier as a place of a rebirth and of opportunity where "free land" nurtured individualism, democracy, and nationalism.[1]

The actual experiences of Deerfield's residents diverged from this mythic image. The English men and women who moved to Deerfield in the later 1600s were not individualistic pioneers; they migrated as members of families and groups. They took up land on the frontier to provide for their growing numbers of children and to re-create a familiar, ordered way of life, not embrace a wilderness's promise of unfettered freedom. The land itself was not a "howling wilderness" but was in many respects already a garden. No rigid barrier separated these English colonists from the region's Natives. Crops, trade goods, and individuals moved, usually peacefully, but sometimes violently, between peoples living in the area.

Still, the village of Deerfield embodied a claim on the land that denied that of the region's Natives, who in turn contested the colonists' presence. Fuelled by families who produced on average six to seven children, the process of town formation along the New England frontier became, in one historian's assessment, "a land-grabbing engine of growth." Decades before the empires of England and France clashed in the Northeast, Natives fought against the demographically driven imperialism of the New Englanders. At its deepest level the 1704 raid had its origin in this contest.[2]

E NGLISH newcomers saw only empty lands when they looked upon the open meadows alongside the meandering Pocumtuck River in 1670. But what appeared to them to be an ideal natural setting for an English village was, in fact, a human habitat of great antiquity. Natives had lived in the valley lying between the Pocumtuck ridge on the east and the foothills of the Hoosac range on the west for thousands of years. They had purposefully manipulated the local environment, transforming it into a landscape that sustained them physically and spiritually. For hundreds of years, local peoples had relied on hunting, fishing, and gathering to sustain themselves. They had periodically burned over the woods to remove undergrowth and make hunting and gathering easier. Each spring they fished the falls of the Connecticut River at nearby Peskeompscut. Men and women had their own spheres of work. Men hunted and fished, women gathered foods and took care of the homes. At night they probably told stories of Wequamps, the nearby ridge formed by the body of a great beaver, as the Pocumtucks remembered it. Their economy may have been simple, but their lives were never isolated. Those who lived at Pocumtuck were located on an ancient crossroads. They traded with other peoples up and down the Connecticut River and east and west over what is now called the Mohawk trail into the Hudson River valley region. What the English initially saw as a frontier or boundary was, in fact, an intersection (map 1).[3]

Connections to other peoples to the south and west brought the changes that produced the new landscape at Pocumtuck. Sometime in the period between 1100 and 1500 the people at Pocumtuck—or rather the women—began to cultivate corn, beans, and squash. Villages grew larger as people joined together to clear fields for annual planting. By 1600, the village at Pocumtuck had perhaps five hundred to one thousand residents. The new foods women cultivated made it possible to support more people. In terms of nutrition, they produced the bulk of their families' food. Men's work changed less. They continued to fish in the spring and to hunt in the fall and winter. Their efforts met critical needs for animal protein and supplied leather for clothing and tools. Though the Pocumtucks of 1600 were much more rooted than their predecessors of six hundred years before, they preserved many of the ancient traditions of seasonal movement. It was not easy to keep a village in one spot for more than a decade or so. Maize fields lost their fertility, and wood, which was crucial for fuel and construction, was harder to come by as villagers used up the local supply. But in a sense, the Pocumtucks moved around so they could remain where they were. Their periodic mobility allowed them to exploit the region's patchwork landscape of rivers, fields, and woods while cushioning their overall impact on the environment. Other village communities developed up and down the Connecticut River alongside the Pocumtucks. To the south were the Agawams, Norwottucks, and Woronocos; to the north, the Sokokis. They all shared a culture, spoke similar languages, and at times intermarried, but each village had its distinct identity and leaders.[4]

The Pocumtucks' way of life began to suffer shortly after European colonists arrived. As in earlier centuries, great changes followed the trade routes into

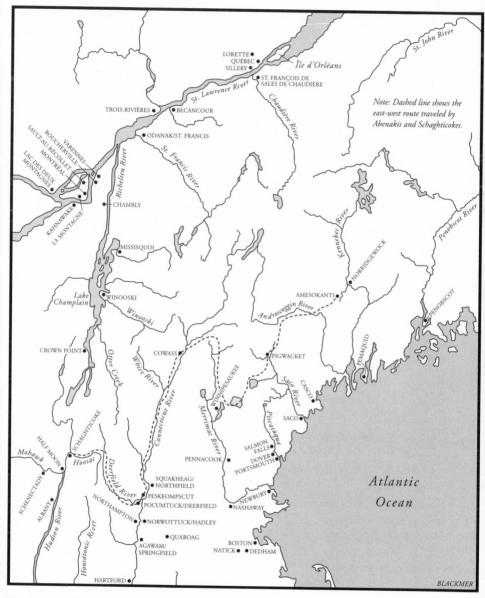

MAP 1. Map of the Northeast, circa 1660–1725.

Pocumtuck. First came deadly new diseases. Between 1633 and 1635 a smallpox epidemic swept up the Connecticut River, killing up to 90 percent of the inhabitants in some villages south of Pocumtuck. Next came English settlers to fill up the recently depopulated land. They established Springfield by the villages of the Agawams and Woronocos in 1635 and Northampton and Hadley by the villages of the Norwottucks in 1654 and 1659. English traders traveled up to Pocumtuck bearing cloth and iron tools to exchange for maize and furs. This peaceful and mutually profitable trade was not destined to last. As English farms developed, their need for Natives' corn diminished. As Native men focused more intently on the fur trade, beaver began to disappear. Pocumtucks soon found themselves indebted to English merchants eager to take their land as repayment. Similar entanglements had undermined the land bases at Agawam, Norwottuck, and Woronoco, providing the English with room to set up their own villages. Despite these pressures and mutual fears, the Pocumtucks resolved to keep "the old league of friendship betwixt the English and our selves."[5]

The disruptions produced by European colonists also caused problems with the Pocumtucks' neighbors to the west. Across the Hudson River were the Mohawks, the easternmost nation of the potent Iroquois League. In the late 1640s, the Five Nations of the Iroquois League—Mohawks, Oneidas, Onondagas, Cayugas, and Senecas—entered into a series of wars with the French and their Native allies in Canada that proved far more destructive than any war in recent memory. When it was over, whole villages and nations had been wiped out and uprooted—including Pocumtuck. In the 1640s, the Pocumtucks were allied with the Mohawks and Narragansetts, who lived in what is now Rhode Island, against the Mohegans living in Connecticut. This alliance was linked to the wampum trade between Narragansett Bay and the Mohawk valley. Mohawk furs, often gained in the wars with the French and Natives in Canada, moved through Pocumtuck to the Narragansetts in exchange for wampum, carefully polished shell beads of great value in Native cultures and political economy. For the Mohawks, alliance with the Pocumtucks helped protect the trade in wampum and shielded their eastern flank from attacks by the Eastern Abenakis in Maine, who were allied with the French. By the 1650s, Mohawks were also fighting the Western Abenakis in what is today New Hampshire. Among the latter group were the Sokokis, whose main village was less than twenty miles north of Pocumtuck.[6]

Pocumtucks now had to choose their friends with great care. The consequences could be devastating. The Sokokis had been Mohawk allies but had recently developed ties to the French. In December 1663, Mohawks launched a devastating attack on the main Sokoki village at Squakeag. The survivors fled. About thirty took refuge with the Pocumtucks, who now found themselves caught between two conflicting demands. Though giving aid and comfort to their Sokoki neighbors, most wanted to remain at peace with the Iroquois League. But some evidently decided to support the Sokokis and choose war. In June 1664, members of a Mohawk peace delegation were killed while on an embassy to Pocumtuck. No one knows who or what prompted this treacherous act, but its consequences were disastrous. Mohawks returned in force with other League Iroquois the next year. They destroyed the Pocumtucks' fort, killing and capturing many of them and dispersing the survivors. Some Pocumtucks apparently headed south to seek refuge with the Norwottucks. Others may have trekked north to join those Sokokis who had earlier sought refuge in New France. By now, the Iroquois were at war with almost all the other Natives in New England. Fighting continued into the early 1670s, even after English settlers began to arrive at Pocumtuck. But no Pocumtucks were there to greet the newcomers because living near the point where the Mohawk trail intersected the Connecticut River had become too dangerous.[7]

As at Agawam and Norwottuck, the English quickly seized the opportunity to acquire the temporarily vacant Native land. In February 1667, a Pocumtuck living in the Connecticut valley, Chaulk or Chaque, signed a deed that "granted, bargained & sold" to Captain John Pynchon of Springfield "Certain persels of Land at Pacomtuck." Though he supposedly conveyed this land "fully clearly & absolutely," Chaulk reserved the "Liberty of fishing for the Indians in the Rivers or waters & free Liberty to hunt Deere or other Wild creatures & to gather Walnuts chestnuts and other nuts things &c on the commons." For the English the deed was, like so many other land transactions, a transference of an absolute right to possess, use, and dispose of land as they saw fit; for the Natives it was an agreement granting and reserving certain uses of the land in question. Chaulk was identified as a sachem, but one suspects that some Pocumtucks, especially those not privy to this agreement, contested what he had conveyed to the English.[8]

Ironically, the English wanted to take Pocumtuck land because they were actually granting other land near Boston to Natives. The Englishmen for whom Captain Pynchon acted as an agent lived in Dedham, Massachusetts. This rather large English town had been forced by the colony's legislature to surrender some of its acreage to provide land for an Indian reservation at Natick. To compensate Dedham's English landowners, the colonial government authorized the town to select eight thousand acres lying anywhere within the boundaries of the land claimed by Massachusetts. Rights to the land did not go to all of Dedham's residents but only to those sixty-eight individuals known as proprietors who owned shares in the town's land corporation. To lay out the grant, representatives of

Dedham's proprietors chose the rich grasslands and corn fields at the heart of the Pocumtuck homeland.[9]

The purchase of Pocumtuck land reveals the different ways English colonists related to land. For Dedham's proprietors, the land at Pocumtuck was primarily a commodity, an investment that could be sold. It is unlikely that many of them ever intended to settle on it. Large tracts of land still remained within the town of Dedham. But if a new town could be laid out, lands surveyed, and buyers found, the proprietors would have a windfall and potential source of income from the land without having to work it themselves. A speculative market in the sale and resale of proprietary shares in Pocumtuck quickly developed. By the early 1670s, most of the original Dedham proprietors had sold out. Dedham may have acquired Pocumtuck, but Pocumtuck acquired English settlers from elsewhere.[10]

To draw settlers to Pocumtuck, Dedham's proprietors imposed on the site the plan of an ideal English farming village (map 2). They hired a surveyor, or "artist," to transform the local topography into a recognizably English vision of community with home lots and fields, property lines and fences. On top of a plateau that rose about twenty feet above the meadows bordering the river, the surveyor laid out a village street. It was about a mile long and ran south to north through the center of the half-mile–wide plateau. Along this street, the surveyor located forty-three home lots, ranging in size from two to four acres. On these lots, settlers were expected to build their houses, barns, and outbuildings and cultivate plots of vegetables. North and south of these home lots he laid out two ranges of long narrow strips of plowing land for planting such crops as wheat and maize. Meadowlands to the west were divided into strips of mowing lands for cutting hay. In addition to a home lot and strips of plowing and mowing land, each landowner eventually received woodlots located on the ridge just east of the home lots along the town street. This linear plan with home lots strung out for over a mile suggests little concern with providing for common defense and was clearly a product of three decades of peaceful relations between the English and the region's Natives.[11]

Each plot of land was an individually owned property even though they were located in a common field surrounded by a single fence. The English field was "common" only in that the residents of the town collectively managed its use. Each spring, the town as a body decided when it was time to plant and remove from the common field livestock grazing upon the stubble. Each fall it would determine when it was time to harvest and to readmit livestock. Every owner of strips of land in the common field was held responsible for keeping up part of the fence. Eventually it ran for nearly fifteen miles around the common field. The town also regulated the use of the woodlots and controlled the livestock

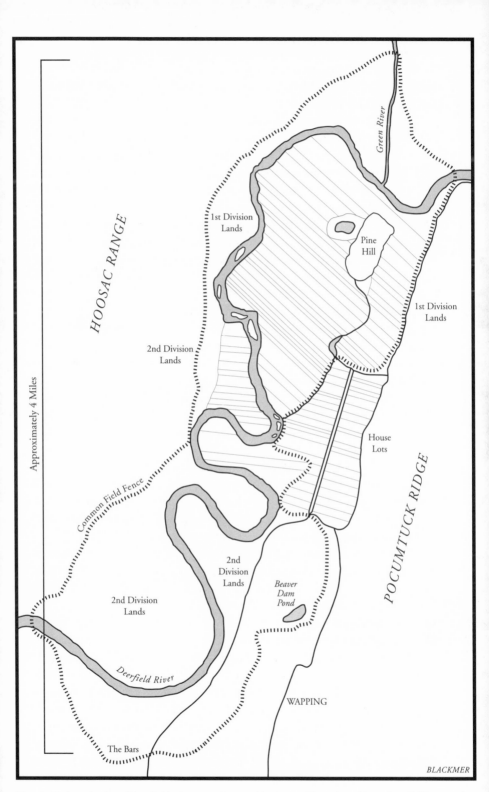

MAP 2. Early town plan of Deerfield, circa 1700. Sources: Fragment of Proprietors' Map, Deerfield, Massachusetts, 1671; "A Plan of the Common Field in Deerfield," December 1793, by David Hoyt (both, Pocumtuck Valley Memorial Association Library); Greenfield, Massachusetts, Topographic Map, U.S.G.S., 1990.

that freely ranged in the woods when the common field was closed. But individuals owned the land.[12]

This particular organization of a landscape with its village street surrounded by commonly fenced, narrow strips of farmland was a conscious revival of a medieval landscape. By the 1600s, only some English immigrants were familiar with such forms of land use. Common field villages were not very common in seventeenth-century New England. But in the Connecticut valley where the broad, rich meadowlands lent themselves to such an arrangement, several such villages had been laid out. The intention was not to promote communal farming of open fields but to promote family farming of individual landholdings.[13]

Seventeenth-century New England towns were made up of families—large families—and the English village at Pocumtuck was designed to accommodate them. People moved in groups even if, as in Pocumtuck, they purchased their lands as individuals from Dedham proprietors. The provisions for implanting the seeds of a community were as important as imposing individual lot lines on the landscape. Settlers expected their new town to have a church, a school, and a local government. Colonial authorities acted to ensure that they did. Not long after the English arrived at Pocumtuck, the Massachusetts legislature ordered people settling new towns to "have respect to neerness and conveniency of habitation for security against enemyes and more comfort for [Chris]tian comunion and enjoyment of God's worship and education of children in schools and civility." Ideally, physical surroundings—one's home, its location, and the land one farmed—reinforced community and provided economic security.[14]

The settlers who eventually secured rights to land at Pocumtuck came from two locations. Twelve families came directly from eastern Massachusetts, seven of them from the Dedham-Medfield area. Among them was the family headed by John Farrington, the only one of the original proprietors to move directly from Dedham to Pocumtuck. Most of the other settlers came in groups from the nearby towns of Northampton, Hadley, and Hatfield. A few joined them from towns farther down the Connecticut River.[15]

At least half of the families had close relatives in the initial community. The Hinsdale and Hawks families embodied the most complex example. Robert Hinsdale had helped found the Dedham church, then moved to Medfield in 1651 and Hadley in the 1660s, when he fell into debt. By 1670 his clan had grown to six families living in Hadley and Hatfield. He brought with him to Pocumtuck five sons, three sons-in-law, one stepson, and his second wife, Elizabeth Hawks of Hadley. Other groupings were smaller. Zecheriah Field of Hatfield and Joshua Carter of Northampton were brothers-in-law. Nathaniel Sutlieff came from Medfield with his father-in-law. John Weller, his young family, and his brother, accompanied his father from Northampton. These relationships wove the community together more tightly than the quilted pattern of the common field that surrounded the village.[16]

These colonists, who shared in the devout Protestantism of New England, came to Pocumtuck searching for economic improvement and security, not religious freedom. The Connecticut valley towns were running out of land for the next generation of farmers. In 1672, some residents of Hadley petitioned the Massachusetts legislature for additional lands. This town supplied a quarter of Pocumtuck's settlers. Northampton petitioned the next year. Generally, families who came to Pocumtuck were young and not well established economically. Heads of ten of the families were in their twenties and eight in their thirties. Fourteen families had fewer than four members when they moved and another five had exactly four, at a time when more established New England families typically had five to seven children. A half-dozen single men in their twenties also moved to Pocumtuck.[17]

The economic backgrounds of these settlers, while varied, generally confirms a picture of younger men seeking opportunity on the frontier, in some instances accompanied by fathers or fathers-in-law seeking to provide it for them. Of nine individuals whose previous landholdings are known, two held inconsequential amounts. Three apparently held no land at all. All of these men increased their landholdings by moving to Pocumtuck, even though initial landholdings were of modest size: no one had less than twenty acres, no one more than sixty acres. In more established towns, the average landholding was sixty acres. There was a certain mediocrity of condition that reflected the similarity of these families' backgrounds and the ability to obtain land at Pocumtuck. They sought only enough land to support themselves, a "competency" as it was often called, not to amass great wealth. The lack of great differences in landholdings was the most obvious influence of a frontier environment on this otherwise typical New England town.[18]

"Free land" on the frontier did not undermine the colonists' need for community. The street on which they lived, the common field that they farmed, and the meetinghouse they had erected by 1675 attested to their desire to recreate a typical New England town. In 1673, the Massachusetts legislature, in answer to a petition from Pocumtuck's settlers, "judgeth it meete to allow the peticoners the liberty of a touneship." The town of Deerfield, as English Pocumtuck came to be known, acquired local political institutions to govern itself. Voters could use this power collectively to pass regulations, manage the common field, grant land to newcomers, and even exclude unwanted settlers. This authority could be greater and more exclusionary than that of the church, and as in most New England towns, it preceded the establishment of ecclesiastical authority. Later in 1673, the town secured the services of Samuel Mather, member of a prominent clerical family, as their minister. In 1674, Moses Crafts obtained permission to keep an ordinary "and sell wine and strong liquor." By 1675 the village of approximately two hundred inhabitants had the necessary institutions to function as a typical New England town. What it did not have was much time.[19]

IN JUNE 1675, a series of clashes over land and law between Wampanoags and English settlers in Plymouth Colony escalated into warfare. Metacom, the Wampanoag leader, called "King Philip" by the English, had confronted diminishing landholdings and growing threats to his leadership from colonial officials and Christianized Natives for several years. Now he turned to armed resistance. Leaders of Plymouth called upon the governments of Massachusetts and Connecticut for assistance. They also sought the aid of Native allies such as the Mohegans—the Pocumtucks' enemies. To elude the English, Philip and his followers followed the paths of the old Narragansett alliance with the Mohawks. Moving northwest, they gained support among the Nipmucks of central Massachusetts and the Pocumtucks and others remaining in the Connecticut valley. Before the fighting ended in fall 1676, a series of bloody battles killed hundreds on both sides, destroyed thousands of homes, and effectively ended the political independence of Native communities in southern New England. This war remains New England's most destructive ever.[20]

The impact of King Philip's War on current and former residents of the Pocumtuck valley was profound. Fighting spread to the banks of the Connecticut River in late summer 1675. It soon drew additional combatants, Native and English, into the valley. In a matter of weeks, four decades of relatively peaceful relations between English settlers and Native residents were replaced by desperate combat. Bonds forged by the trade in furs and English goods proved incapable of holding back demographic pressures, and the resulting contest for land, that pushed the two peoples apart. Both the English and Native populations in the Connecticut valley had been growing since the early 1640s. The amount of usable land, as each culture defined it, was limited and diminishing. In this time of crisis, resentments, particularly those of Natives who felt themselves badly used by the English, quickly rose to the surface. English towns turned into armed camps. Native villages that had stood near them for decades were abandoned.[21]

Because of its relatively isolated location, Deerfield was especially vulnerable. Two attacks were beaten off in early September 1675. On September 18, a column of carts escorted by a company of about fifty soldiers was ambushed while crossing a stream a half-dozen miles south of the village. As the Reverend Increase Mather of Boston sardonically reported, the English had been "so foolish and secure to put their arms in carts and step[ped] aside to gather grapes, which proved dear and deadly grapes to them." Almost all of the New England soldiers died in the battle, along with fourteen men from Deerfield—close to half of the village's adult males—who were serving as teamsters. Among the dead were the inveterate pioneer Robert Hinsdale and three of his sons. A third of the village's families lost their fathers. Three days later, authorities ordered the evacuation of the village, concluding it could no longer be defended. Natives reoccupied Deerfield and planted corn in its fields the following spring.[22]

Deerfield was one of the few villages in western Massachusetts that the Natives regained for themselves. With the assistance of troops from eastern Massachusetts and Connecticut, most English towns were successfully defended. It was, however, a closely fought contest. Springfield was destroyed on October 5. Hatfield and Northampton suffered repeated attacks. In addition to Deerfield, Brookfield, Northfield, and Suffield were abandoned, and during spring 1676 officials seriously considered evacuating Hatfield and Northampton. But the residents of Hatfield, Northampton, and Hadley stayed put. Among them waited refugees hoping to return and restore their devastated farms at Deerfield.[23]

New England's Natives lost the war in part because the Mohawks of the Iroquois League turned on them. Philip had tried to gain their support for his cause, but, at the encouragement of the governor of New York, Mohawks attacked his main force during winter 1675–1676. Tradition claims that several hundred of Metacom's followers died in the battle. Cut off from the west and north and pursued by Mohawk warriors, King Philip and his supporters headed back toward the English settlements. During spring 1676, their attacks on Northampton, Hatfield, and Hadley were repulsed.

In the aftermath of these Native reversals, the English seized the initiative in the Connecticut valley. On May 19, a company of almost 150 Englishmen fell upon a large body of Natives who had gathered at Peskeompscut to fish at the falls. This gathering of Pocumtucks, Nipmucks, Narragansetts, Wampanoags, and undoubtedly others was taken completely by surprise. Most of those present during the assault appear to have been women, children, and the elderly. Two to three hundred were either killed outright or drowned in the Connecticut River. In June, a thousand Englishmen swept up both sides of the Connecticut River, clearing out any remaining Natives. Some time before this operation, surviving Pocumtucks had moved away, seeking refuge to the east among the Pennacooks, to the north with the French in Canada, or to the west, in Schaghticoke, under the protection of their erstwhile enemies, the Mohawks of the Iroquois League. That fall, the English harvested the corn Natives had planted at Deerfield in the spring.[24]

With peace seemingly on the horizon, several English families returned to Deerfield and attempted to re-establish their village. Two of the original settlers, Sergeant John Plympton and Quintin Stockwell returned in spring 1677. They were joined by John Root, who had married the widow of one of Hinsdale's sons, and twenty-two-year-old Benoni Stebbins, who took up a plot of land purchased years earlier by his father, Rowland. In the summer they were joined by Philip Mattoon, who settled on land he rented from John Pynchon, one of the community's largest landholders.[25]

As it turned out, the war was not over, and Deerfield remained contested ground. Fighting continued in the east, in Maine, until 1678. In the Connecticut valley there was one more raid. On the morning of September 19, 1677, a party of approximately two dozen Pocumtucks and Norwottucks, led by a man called Ashpelon, attacked Hatfield. They took several prisoners and moved north to Deerfield to fall upon the unsuspecting settlers. John Root was killed and the rest were captured. Benoni Stebbins subsequently escaped. These Natives had come south from a place of refuge in Canada. Fearing detection by the Mohawks, they took their remaining captives and headed back to Canada. After reaching their northern refuge, they burned Sergeant Plympton to death. With the assistance of French authorities, English negotiators eventually secured the release and return of the remaining prisoners. These captives had become the first New Englanders to make the trek to Canada as prisoners and return. Though they had been driven away from their homes, it was clear that the valley's Natives would continue to challenge the English presence in the region. More important, they now saw Canada as a secure base from which to carry out attacks.[26]

E ARLY in 1682 English settlers returned to Deerfield. As before, growing families and the hope of betterment and economic security drew settlers to take up lands in this exposed frontier village. Proprietary shares could be bought from those who had grown discouraged and from heirs of those who had died in the war. If a man could not afford to buy rights to land, the town granted him twenty acres and a home lot. In return, a recipient had to take up the land and remain for three years. Again, those who were attracted by these conditions tended to be relatively young heads of newly established families. Among the new settlers, two-thirds of the adults were in their twenties or early thirties. Half of the family units contained three people or fewer; a dozen were single males. Overwhelmingly, these men and women were first-generation New England–born. The men came from families in which a majority of the men had had to leave their hometowns to find new land on which to establish their families.[27]

Once more, family connections bound together the men and women who migrated to Deerfield. Forty-five of the sixty-one families belonged to one of eighteen groups of kinfolk. At most sixteen families or individuals appear to have arrived without some kin. Two of these were men who soon married into one of the existing family networks. Reinforcing these ties were those of community. Three-fifths of the settlers came from Northampton, Hadley, and Hatfield. Another quarter came from towns farther down the Connecticut River. Survivors from eighteen of the original settler families increased Deerfield's cohesion.[28]

Among the settlers were seven newcomers whose prominence eclipsed that of the original English settlers of Deerfield. They quickly emerged as the town's leaders. Most were wealthier than the average Deerfield settler, and several were related by marriage. Two brothers from a prominent Hadley family, Thomas and Jonathan Wells, became the community's military leaders. Thomas frequently served as a selectman and often presided over town meetings as moderator. When he died in 1691, Jonathan succeeded him as commander of the town's militia company. David Hoyt of Hatfield, a brother-in-law of the Wellses by his first marriage, also served as a selectman and a militia officer, becoming Jonathan's lieutenant. Members of the church made the pious Hoyt and John Sheldon their deacons, laymen who had responsibilities for administering communion wine and overseeing church discipline. Sheldon, who moved to town from Northampton shortly after his marriage, served on the town's board of selectmen, moderated town meetings, and was also the ensign, or the third-ranking commissioned officer in the local militia company. John Catlin arrived with the title of "Mister," suggesting a status usually conferred by a liberal education, a possibility borne out by his service as both a teacher and town attorney in Newark, New Jersey. After coming to Deerfield in the early 1680s, he also served as a selectman and moderated town meetings. Another newcomer, Thomas French, married Mary, a daughter of John and Mary Catlin, and quickly gained local prominence, serving first as a selectman in 1686, when he was only twenty-nine, and later, in 1695, as town clerk.[29]

Benoni Stebbins, who had escaped when the war partly led by Ashpelon attached Deerfield, was the final member of Deerfield's new circle of leaders. He was a colorful character originally from Northampton, whose life story shows that one did not have to be a devout Puritan to succeed in New England. Spirit and force of personality, not piety or education set him apart. In 1667, at the age of twelve, he had conspired with two other "young lads of Northampton" to "run away to the French" in Canada. During Sunday services, this gang broke into a house and stole "24 shillings in silver and 7 in Wampum" to pay Quanquelatt, a local Indian, to guide them north. The plot was discovered and the participants punished. Authorities gave Quanquelatt twenty lashes; Godfrey Nims, "the ringleader in these villianes" got fifteen on the naked back; Benoni Stebbins and the other boy received eleven each. Stebbins reached his twenties unbowed and still adventuresome. Though he fought in King Philip's War, he was also among a group of men who were prosecuted and fined for wearing their hair too long in 1676.[30]

About five years after his first brush with captivity in 1677, Stebbins returned with his wife, Mary, and their children, Ebenezer and Thankful. Mary appears to have been a kindred spirit. In 1678 she was presented by the county court and fined 10 shillings for "wearing silk contrary to Law" and aggravating the offense "by persisting in it after she was once presented before." With Benoni and Mary came his brother John and his family, and the family of Benoni's old partner in crime, Godfrey Nims. Before he had turned forty, this former juvenile delinquent had served four times as a selectman, was a sergeant in the militia, and had become one of the wealthiest men in town. His house stood on the west side of the street between those of Ensign Sheldon, his brother-in-law, and the local minister.[31]

These were Deerfield's first town elders. Some of them assumed this status at a relatively early age at a time when most New England towns turned to older men. They led the local militia and filled half of the openings on the board of selectmen during the period before 1704. Though great differences in wealth still did not exist in this frontier farming community they were, with the exception of David Hoyt, noticeably better off economically than the other settlers (see appendix B). Voters perhaps assumed that because of their situation, they were in a better position to devote time and effort to overseeing the town. They did not form a local oligarchy nor were they part of a ruling class, being essentially farmers like their neighbors and ultimately dependent on their neighbors' votes for their positions of leadership. But they did command respect among the status-conscious New Englanders, who deferred to their judgment and regularly referred to them by their titles: Captain Wells, Deacons Hoyt and Sheldon, Mister Catlin, and Sergeant Stebbins.[32]

New England towns placed great emphasis on maintaining order and harmony. Ideally, such order and consensus was achieved by voluntary consent. In Deerfield consent was attained by broad participation in government. Almost all of the town's men contributed in some way to managing the community's affairs. In addition to its selectmen, the town annually elected four to six fence viewers, two or three surveyors, haywards, tithingmen, and tax collectors, a town clerk, a constable, a clerk of the market, and a packer of meat. Over two-thirds of the town's sixty or so men were called on to fill some town office during the 1680s and 1690s. In fact, in 1696 the town ordered that "a penalty of one shilling shall be laid upon every legal voter not attending town meeting." In these early years, few meetings failed to attain a consensus. Most of the business considered at the three to four town meetings held during the year concerned local elections, land grants, land management, economic regulations, and live-stock control. Differences of opinion could arise over these matters, but not un-til 1709 is there a record of dissent at a town meeting.[33]

Achievement of consensus was undoubtedly aided by the homogeneity of the community. With the possible exception of Godfrey Nims and Thomas French, who may have had French ancestors, the town's leaders and voters de-scended from English stock. They all farmed the land and shared in the man-agement of the common field that surrounded the village. By contemporary standards most were relatively poor farmers who owned a home lot, a house, some land, some livestock, and not much else. Estate inventories reveal sparsely furnished houses and farms that could lack basic tools. In early Deerfield, men often shared expensive farm implements, such as plows, as well as the heavy work. Landholdings ranged from roughly ten to one hundred acres, amounts that were exceeded by the holdings of poor to middling farmers in more estab-lished towns such as Hadley and Northampton. Most estates carried numerous small debts. With no divisions between rich and poor, creditors and debtors, farmers and nonfarmers, Deerfield lacked the economic basis for the kinds of conflict that affected more established communities.[34]

A shared religious outlook added to the unity and consensus in public affairs. As elsewhere in New England, virtually all residents adhered to a reformed ver-sion of Protestantism historians call Puritanism. Adherents believed that God did not act through rituals, tradition, or church hierarchies but instead acted directly on each individual by an unconditional offer of saving grace. The only effective conduit of this saving grace was God's Word: the Word read in the Bible and the Word preached. Those who considered themselves among the saved or the elect drew together and founded purified, congregational churches of visible saints that banished all reminders of medieval Roman Catholic ritual, sacred im-ages, and episcopal government. Differences arose primarily over the best way of organizing such churches and over the criteria for church membership.

The absence of religious conflict in Deerfield was due to the backgrounds of its settlers and the character of its new pastor. Neither English Pocumtuck nor the resettled village of Deerfield had been established as an expression of reli-gious dissent from another community. People came to Deerfield in search of land, not a better church order. No church had been organized at the Pocum-tuck of the 1670s. Samuel Mather, who preached to the first English residents of Pocumtuck, had never been formally settled in the community and eventually left after its breakup in 1675. Only in 1688, a half-dozen years after the resettle-ment, did Deerfield residents formally gather a church. When they did, they fol-lowed the prevailing pattern of other Connecticut valley churches, which adopted a broader understanding of church membership than many eastern

Massachusetts churches did. They usually extended baptism to most children and full church membership to all adults who sought it except, of course, those who led outwardly scandalous lives. The local congregational church was the spiritual embodiment of the entire community, not an exclusive reserve for a minority of visible saints. Somewhere between one-half and two-thirds of Deerfield's adults eventually joined the church, a very high percentage compared with the more restrictive churches outside the Connecticut valley. Like everywhere else in New England, nonmembers as well as members were required by law to attend Sunday services.[35]

Deerfield's pastor, John Williams, a twenty-two-year-old Roxbury resident and recent graduate of Harvard College, had had the mettle to accept the call to this frontier village where life would not be as easy as it was for ministers in more established towns. Two other candidates had turned down the job before Williams accepted the invitation to settle in 1686. His call came from the town, as well as the church, for it was the town's taxpayers—those outside of the church as well as full members—who paid the minister's salary. As in most other New England towns, the minister's salary was the largest single item in the local budget. Though poor, Deerfield's residents tried to be generous. They agreed to pay Williams a salary of £60 a year, to be raised eventually to £80, which would put him on a par with the ministers of Hadley and Northampton. In addition, they gave him a home lot in the center of town, built him a sizeable house, gave him land in the open fields, and provided him with proprietary shares in future land divisions. The community and John expected that his pastoral relationship would endure for life and that the spiritual growth and well-being of both parties would intertwine.[36]

John Williams was well integrated into the ecclesiastical culture of Massachusetts Bay and the Connecticut valley. He married Eunice Mather, daughter of the late Reverend Eliezer Mather of Northampton and Eunice Warham Mather Stoddard. The match allied John to three prominent New England clergymen: the Reverend Increase Mather of Boston, his wife's uncle, the Reverend Solomon Stoddard of Northampton, her stepfather, and the late Reverend John Warham of Windsor, her grandfather. Eunice Williams proved to be a woman of more than conventional piety and strength. Scriptures formed a part of her daily devotions for "she was wont personally every day," as her spouse later wrote, "to delight her soul in reading, praying, and meditating of and over, by herself in her closet, over and above what she heard of them in our family worship." She also possessed the inner strength needed to confront the trials of a frontier parish. As the daughter of one minister and stepdaughter of another, she had years of personal observations to draw on when facing the challenge of managing the private life of the town's most public figure.[37]

As minister, John Williams was one of the most prominent settlers in Deerfield. His status was reflected in the unusual structure of his household, which included Deerfield's few African-American residents. Like several other New England ministers, Williams was a slave owner. The presence of slaves, who provided household labor, made clear that even frontier Deerfield was connected to the networks of trade and bound labor that defined the economy of the Atlantic world. Williams's first slave, known as Robert Tigo, possibly an Anglicized version of the name Roberto Santiago, appears to have been an African who came to Deerfield from a Portuguese or Spanish colony. In the late seventeenth century few slaves came directly from Africa to New England. Most were transported north from the Caribbean basin to Rhode Island for resale. After Tigo's death, Williams purchased a man and a woman, named Frank and Parthena. Their names reveal little about their possible origin, for which there is no other evidence.[38]

Williams served as Deerfield's primary link to the wider world. The deference accorded him—he too was addressed as "Mister"—acknowledged his position as a community leader whose authority and status extended beyond the parochial boundaries of Deerfield's meetinghouse. Though ordained ministers did not fill civil offices, ministers were expected to speak on matters of public concern and to offer counsel to civil authorities. Accordingly, Williams always took care to "inform himself of the Transactions and Affairs of <u>Europe</u>, and to understand the State and Circumstances of the Province." Towns in western Massachusetts probably demanded more of their ministers than did those in less isolated locations. The residents of Deerfield expected the Reverend Williams, for example, to use his connections in matters of public interest to petition authorities in Boston and Hartford for military protection, tax relief, and other types of assistance. Williams did not fail them during the 1690s, when he and his flock faced daunting challenges.[39]

DEERFIELD'S involvement with the politics of Massachusetts and the empire was limited but increased during the later 1600s as war and political changes touched the frontier. In 1689, Massachusetts overthrew a royally appointed governor in its colonial version of England's Glorious Revolution, and Deerfield sent a legislator to Boston for the first time. From 1685 to 1688, the Catholic James II had ruled England. Besides not sharing the same religion as the majority of his subjects, who were Protestant, James also had a predilection for authoritarian government. He had replaced the original charter governments of the New England colonies and put them all under one governor, creating the unified Dominion of New England. The invasion of England by a Dutch army under William of Orange allowed the English to replace James with

William and his wife, Mary, who was James's eldest daughter. The deposition of King James pulled England and its colonies into war with France. The Glorious Revolution and the resulting war, the Nine Years' War—sometimes called King William's War in the colonies—began the cycle of imperial wars between England and France that would be waged on American soil up through the American Revolution.[40]

In the Connecticut valley fighting began in 1688, a year before the Nine Years' War started, and it owed more to the legacy of King Philip's War than it did to the contest between European empires. That summer, eleven Indians from Canada raided Northfield, killing six of its residents. Included in this party of raiders was at least one Pocumtuck. Micah Mudge of Northfield recognized several others as "formerly belonging to these parts." A couple he knew by name. Most of these raiders were in fact local Natives who had sought refuge in New France in the aftermath of King Philip's War. Their return to the Deerfield area and simultaneous attacks along the Maine frontier signaled the beginning of the Second Anglo-Abenaki War.[41]

After fighting broke out in Europe between England and France the following year, the Second Anglo-Abenaki War came to coincide and overlap with the Nine Years' War. In this new struggle, frontier towns in New England for the first time faced Native enemies supported by the resources of a hostile European power. Ideologically, hostilities took on a new dimension as Protestant New England confronted a Catholic foe. The Connecticut River made the western Massachusetts towns particularly vulnerable to French and Indian raiders operating from bases near Montreal. Raiders could, with relative ease, ascend Lake Champlain, cross the Green Mountains, and descend the Deerfield or the Connecticut River to fall upon Deerfield, Northfield, Hatfield, or Northampton. With the abandonment of Northfield in 1690, Deerfield became the most exposed town in the region, a dubious distinction it would retain for a quarter century.

To defend themselves, Deerfield's residents fortified their village for the first time. They constructed a stockade, or palisade, that encircled ten houses standing in the center of the village. To provide secure housing for residents whose homes lay outside of the stockade the town voted that "such persons shall have habitations provided for them within said fortifications att the Town charg but any prson or prsons that shall provide habitations for themselves shall be exempt from the charges" to pay for such housing. These temporary refuges were small and rather crude. Some were referred to as cellars. Young militiamen were ordered up from the towns down the river to serve as garrison soldiers. They, as well as locals, spent time in "Watchings, Wardings, & Scoutings." There was a lot to keep an eye on.[42]

Much to the colonists' consternation, Deerfield remained a vital crossroads for Natives, who regularly passed by or through Deerfield as they moved back and forth across the expanse of territory bounded by the Native village of Schaghticoke on the Hudson River, Canada, and Abenaki villages in Maine. During the 1690s, Natives came from Schaghticoke to trade or hunt, remaining for days or weeks at a time. The Schaghticokes had maintained their ties with their kinsmen in Canada. Thus, Ashpelon, the Pocumtuck who had led the 1677 raid on Deerfield, now reappeared as a Schaghticoke sachem. This time he attempted to mediate conflicts between colonists and Indians hunting in the area around Deerfield. New York and its allies, the Five Nations of the Iroquois League, had joined the war against the French and raiding parties of Schaghticokes and Mohawks occasionally stopped in Deerfield after attacking villages in Canada. In 1691, approximately 150 Schaghticokes moved to western Massachusetts, claiming that a scarcity of food in New York colony forced them to relocate. They were probably fleeing the war along the New York frontier and saw the Connecticut valley as a safer location than the Hudson River valley. A large French and Native raid had destroyed the village of Schenectady, not far from Schaghticoke, the year before. The Schaghticokes, mostly Norwottucks and Pocumtucks who had fled from the Connecticut valley after King Philip's War, stayed in the Deerfield area for a half-dozen years.[43]

Deerfield's colonists feared the Schaghticokes because they could not control their movements and they doubted their loyalty. As they saw it, "sometimes they dwell at Sratuburk [Schaghticoke], sometime at the eastward and make marriages with the Eastern Indians [Pennacooks and Eastern Abenakis], and sometimes at Canada." Though loyal allies of the English in New York, the Schaghticokes were not necessarily friends of the New Englanders. After all, memories of King Philip's War were just fifteen-years-old. John Pynchon referred to them as "our former Enymy Indians" and warily regarded them as future enemies. Their continuing ties with Eastern Abenakis especially were suspect, for they had joined the war on the French side. Consequently, it did not take much for Schaghticokes to get into serious trouble at Deerfield.[44]

An encounter involving three Natives during summer 1690 revealed how quickly suspicion and animosity could turn a seemingly peaceful visit into a fatal incident. In June, three men claiming to be Schaghticokes arrived in Deerfield apparently intending to trade. They were not all strangers; nor were they all on the best of terms. One of the Natives, Chepasson, berated the English after being compelled to pay a long-standing debt that he owed a Deerfield resident. He said, "they were all boys and would not fight when the Frenchmen came but would cry as the Dutchmen did, and he said further that he saw the Dutchmen cry." This report suggests that Chepasson was present at the attack on Schenectady in February 1690. Relations worsened. Not long after this outburst,

Chepasson threatened to cut off Benjamin Brooks's head and tried to obtain a gun or knife to kill Godfrey Nims. He was confined and placed under guard. But he remained defiant. He asked the "negro that watched him," probably Robert Tigo, "to let him have his gun that he might kill goodman Nimms, and on his [the Negro's] refusal he desired his knife for the same purpose; he attempted to pull away his gun; told him he would not hurt him but only Englishmen." Tigo held onto his gun and knife. The next day, Chepasson tried to bribe a young Englishman who was guarding him. Failing this, he overpowered the youth and ran to the gate but was shot dead before he could escape. His two companions were detained.[45]

Chepasson's behavior had its roots in the resentments sown during and after King Philip's War. Before he succumbed to an illness, another of the trio, John Humpfries, provided the English with more information. Humpfries claimed that all three had been "to the Eastward" and that they had participated in the 1689 attack on Dover, New Hampshire. Both Humpfries and Chepasson spoke English quite well, and Chepasson had, in the past, traded with Deerfield residents. At least one of the trio had been captured during King Philip's War and had spent a period of enforced servitude in an English household. The men had carried the bitter legacy of King Philip's War to New Hampshire, to New York, and finally to Deerfield.[46]

The inhabitants of Deerfield suffered greatly during the Nine Years' War. In 1690 garrison troops arriving from Connecticut Colony apparently brought a "great sickness" that had ravaged the lower valley the year before. Scores fell ill with "agues and fevers." Some died. Sickness and fear kept farmers from tilling their fields and began a cycle of inadequate harvests and scarce food. Constant rounds of watching, warding, and scouting consumed their energy. Lieutenant Thomas Wells died in 1691, depriving the town of an important leader. Caterpillars ate much of the corn crop in 1692, aggravating food shortages. Early in 1693, discouraged residents of Deerfield wondered whether they had "a call to apply ourselves to this Honorable Court [the Massachusetts legislature], for an order to depart the place." Then in June Indians killed three or four residents. Later in the year another was taken captive. John Williams barely escaped from a party lying in ambush. In September 1694, a large force made a direct assault on the town. They were beaten off after inflicting only a few casualties, but Native warriors returned in 1695 and 1696 to ambush those who ventured too far from the stockade. Over the course of the war, twelve residents of Deerfield were killed, five wounded, and five captured.[47]

It seemed as if Deerfield might be abandoned again. Some residents grew discouraged and left. But in 1695 Massachusetts passed a law that designated as a "frontier town or plantation" eleven settlements, Deerfield among them. This act threatened landowners with forfeiture of land and other residents with imprisonment if they moved away from these towns without first obtaining a special license from the governor and council. Despite this law, seven families left in the fifteen years after 1689. However, most of the inhabitants stayed and continued work on a new meetinghouse. Evidently they had overcome their earlier despair. The area remained relatively safe during 1697, when European hostilities ended at the Treaty of Ryswick.[48]

The restoration of peace occasioned the third time Deerfield sent representatives to the legislature in Boston. Even though the town's residents usually did not look beyond their borders for guidance or assistance, war gave rise to one exception. The town depended on the government in Boston for garrison soldiers, tax relief, and subsidies. It also looked for guidance to the commander of the Hampshire County's militia: John Pynchon until his death in 1703 and then Samuel Partridge of Hatfield.[49]

Apart from the legislature, one of Deerfield's most important contacts in Boston was the Mather family, John Williams's in-laws. Increase and his son Cotton were perhaps the two best-known ministers of colonial New England, in part because of their prodigious publishing record but also because of their influence on colonial politics. Increase had gone to England to secure a new charter for Massachusetts in the wake of the Glorious Revolution. But not all colonists were happy with this new charter—some wanted the old charter government back. Their dissatisfaction led later to political struggles that put a strain on Deerfield's—and John Williams's—relationship with the Mathers. For the time being, the Mathers had nothing but praise for the determination of Deerfield's residents in the face of adversity. In 1699, the Reverend Cotton Mather singled out Deerfield as "an Extraordinary Instance of Courage in keeping their Station though they have lived all this while in a very Pihahiroth [a place in the wilderness, Exodus 14:2, 9; Numbers 33:7, 8]." "Their worthy Pastor Mr. John Williams," Mather believed, "deserves the Thanks of all this Province for his Encouraging them all the ways Imaginable to Stand their ground." By staying put, Deerfield's residents had taken the brunt of enemy assaults and shielded other towns.[50]

A degree of prosperity came with the return of peace. The Reverend Williams's family continued to grow, as did his ability to provide for it. During fifteen years of marriage with Eunice, John fathered ten children. Eight survived the usual perils of the first years of life. The oldest boy, Eliezer, was sent to Hadley to continue his studies in preparation for college. By 1702 he felt secure enough financially to acquit the town "from all dues upon the account of Rates from my first Settlement to the Rate of this present year 1701–2." A little to the north of the

Reverend Williams's house, Ensign John Sheldon built a large two-story, center-chimney house with an overhang. Several young men and women in the village married. Joseph Catlin married Sheldon's daughter Hannah in June 1701, forming a new alliance among the town's leading families. Like Joseph and Hannah, most young men and women found their spouses in Deerfield. It was a rather inbred and inward-looking community.[51]

The return of peace did bring a few new residents to Deerfield. William Arms swapped real estate in Hartford, Connecticut, for Thomas Hunt's home lot at the far south end of the town street. After thirteen years of frontier life, Hunt had decided to resettle far to the south in the more secure Lebanon, Connecticut. On May 2, 1700, two of Arms's daughters married two local men, Zebediah Williams (no relation to John) and William Belding in a double ceremony. A new man of distinction arrived, John Richards. An educated man and an heir of one of the Dedham proprietors, he bore the title "Mister" and received the appropriate deference, being elected to the board of selectmen and hired by the town to teach school. Another man from Northampton, Robert Price, arrived and watched his daughter Mary wed local boy Samuel Smead.[52]

By the end of 1703, Deerfield was beginning to mature as a community. It contained about 50 families and about 260 to 270 inhabitants, only slightly more than there had been in 1688. The composition of the community did change, for it was no longer a collection of recently established families and a smattering of young, unmarried men. Younger families and individuals were no longer attracted in such large numbers. There were fewer single men and families had, on average, more children. There were now three rather poor families headed by widows (see appendix B). Four orphans had come to town to live with distant relatives. These children and those in the widows' families would prove to be particularly vulnerable to the threats faced by the residents of a frontier town.[53]

D EERFIELD and similar frontier towns were not formidable military outposts of an expanding English empire. Nor were they dynamic engines of commercial growth that added to the wealth of the empire. They were instead traditional, subsistence farming communities that produced and consumed New England's primary crop: large families with hordes of children. As such, they were an on-going threat to the region's dwindling population of Indians and a source of concern for the far less populous French colony in Canada. Because of Native resistance and French fears, Deerfield began as contested ground and remained so in the early 1700s.

In spring 1702, Joseph Dudley, the new governor of Massachusetts, brought news of England's entry into a new imperial war—the War of the Spanish

Succession. Deerfield was again an endangered frontier town. John Williams, with a mixture of concern and pride, noted:

> [S]trangers tell us they would not live where we do for twenty times as much as we do, the enemy having such an advantage of the river to come down upon us, several say they would freely leave all they have & go away were it not that it would be disobedient to authority & a discouraging to their brethren: The frontier difficulties of a place so remote from others & so exposed as ours, are more than be known.

Not long after the Reverend Williams wrote these lines all of New England would know of Deerfield's difficulties.[54]

CHAPTER 2

NEW FRANCE

T HE French raiders who attacked Deerfield in 1704 were the embodiment of an imperial New France. This was a domain that stretched far beyond the farms of habitants who lived along the Saint Lawrence River three hundred miles north of Deerfield. It extended from Acadia on the Atlantic coast, north to Hudson's Bay, west to Native lands bordering on the Great Lakes, and southwest to Louisiana. Imperial strategy, Native alliances, and the fur trade held together the far-flung components of this expansive and tentative domain. New France loomed large on maps of North America but in reality rested lightly upon the ground. It was an overextended empire that lived in growing fear of the rapidly expanding English colonies. Heavily populated and packed tightly together along the Atlantic coast, these colonies posed a mighty threat to French hegemony, if not French survival, in North America.[1]

It is unlikely that many of the French raiders came directly from working on farms along the Saint Lawrence. Most would have been recruited from among members of the Canadian nobility and young men involved in the fur trade: voyageurs and *coureurs de bois*. They were products of New France's military frontier, which faced the Iroquois League and the English colonies, and its commercial frontier, running up the Saint Lawrence and into the Upper Country around the Great Lakes. All had ties to the colony's Saint Lawrence hearth with its seigneuries, but their interests went beyond those of the habitants, whose frontier experience usually did not extend much beyond the development of family farms. Also unlike the habitants, the raiders' interests converged quite closely with those setting policy in Paris and carrying it out, as they saw fit, in Quebec and Montreal.

Ironically, peace and a plentiful supply of beaver skins, precisely what the French had long been fighting for in the 1600s, caused an economic crisis that threatened the whole colony. During the seventeenth-century wars against the Iroquois League and the English, the French had fought for survival and control of the western fur trade. Now, the European contest to determine the succession to the Spanish throne had produced a new understanding of the place of New France in French policy. Unfortunately for New France, the strategic role of the colony expanded at a critical time when the resources of the colony, and of

France itself, were shrinking. The raid on Deerfield was part of French officials' military solution to diplomatic problems that had their roots in the collapse of the Canadian beaver trade and uncertain relations with their Native allies.

THE particular mission entrusted to the expedition against Deerfield had its origins in a relatively new set of strategic calculations. In May 1701 King Louis XIV informed his officials in Canada that he intended to use New France and the new French colony of Louisiana as a military barrier for blocking English access to the interior of North America and shielding neighboring French and Spanish colonies. This initiative formed part of France's preparations for the war to determine who would be the next king of Spain. Louis, who supported the claims of his grandson Philippe d'Anjou to the Spanish throne, wanted to preserve the integrity of the far-flung Spanish empire. The French viewed the populous and expansive English colonies as the greatest threat to the valuable colonies of France and Spain in the West Indies, and, potentially, even Mexico. Louisiana, supported by New France and its western Native allies, could block English movements into the West and South. Fighting in North America also came to be seen as a strategically useful distraction that might draw English attention away from what the king and his ministers in France saw as the more important, European, theater of the war.[2]

This new understanding of the strategic value of New France depended on close cooperation with Native allies across North America. Since its beginnings, the Canadian colony had been viewed as a base for capturing the fur trade of the North American interior and converting its Native inhabitants to Catholicism. Gradually the underpopulated colony had also come to depend on Native warriors for its defense. As Governor Louis-Hector Callière explained, "The policy of a governor of Canada does not consist so much in taking care of the French who are within the scope of his government as in maintaining a close union with the savage Nations that are his Allies." But officials in France did not realize how crucial the fur trade was to maintain this "close union." Since the 1660s, when Louis XIV made New France a royal colony, his ministers had worked to create a compact colony of settlement along the Saint Lawrence running from Montreal to just beyond Quebec. They felt that such a colony was more likely to be self-supporting and secure and thus less of a drain on the royal treasury. Officials in France viewed trading and military posts in the interior as expensive ventures that needlessly embroiled the colony in Native wars.[3]

Fur traders, military officers, and some Canadian officials recognized the critical role played by the fur trade and engagement with Natives in the interior. They, therefore, tended to encourage expansion of the French presence in the Upper Country. They knew that the surest route to success in New France was to participate in the fur trade and to obtain an office funded by the royal treasury, both of which often depended on intensive involvement with Natives and their conflicts. Their goals led them to act in ways that undermined the ideal of a compact colony. Above all, it led them to produce ever more furs. Matters came to a head in the 1690s, when a surplus of beaver pelts glutted the market and depressed the price of furs on the Continent. This unfavorable market situation destroyed the economic viability of the French firm managing the Canadian fur trade and plunged the colony into an economic crisis. Combined with the French ministers' policy of favoring a compact Laurentian colony and disengaging from the western interior, the crisis in the fur trade led in 1696 to a decision that severely limited access to the Upper Country. All but four of the western posts were slated for abandonment. French traders were denied *congés,* the licenses to trade in the interior. They were prohibited from even traveling into the Upper Country, though scores of them ignored this ban, which went into effect on January 1, 1698. The fur trade was to be limited to Natives who brought their furs to Montreal.[4]

The withdrawal from the Upper Country threatened to undermine French alliances with western Indians. Trade involved satisfying social obligations and meeting cultural needs of the Natives as well as providing utilitarian goods. These needs included French mediation of disputes among Natives. The very kind of involvement in Native affairs in the Upper Country that officials in France wanted to avoid was viewed as critical by many western Indians. Without an active French presence as benefactors and mediators, alliances lost some of their meaning for the western nations. But the French continued nonetheless to look to the western Indians to keep in check members of Iroquois League who had attacked New France repeatedly during the Second French-Iroquois War, which lasted from 1682 to 1701. This calculation remained a centerpiece of French policy even after the Iroquois League entered into a treaty of peace and neutrality with the French and their Native allies in 1701. The active support of the western Indians was also crucial for any design to use New France and Louisiana as a barrier to English expansion westward or as a strategic diversion of English resources.[5]

The 1701 treaty with the Iroquois League—the Great Peace of Montreal—actually complicated French relations with Natives in the Upper Country. Strategically, the agreement added immeasurably to the colony's security by ending the League's hostility toward New France. It marked the beginning of an Iroquois policy of neutrality, which, with a few exceptions, lasted for half a century. Historians have pointed to the treaty as the "crowning achievement of a certain form of colonialism based not on agricultural expansion and settlement, but on alliance with the indigenous peoples." But peace with the Iroquois

League reduced the value of alliance with the French for the colony's Native allies. Members of the league actually embarked on a policy of making alliances with Natives in the West. By insisting that the Iroquois League make peace with France's Native allies, the treaty also had the effect of opening the western fur trade to the Iroquois and the English. As long as the members of the Iroquois League and the western nations were enemies, the route to Albany was closed or ran clandestinely and circuitously through Montreal. After 1701, a direct route to Albany was open and if French merchants could not offer good prices, Iroquois traders linked to Albany could.[6]

Much to the consternation of French officials, English traders and officials seized this opening and attempted to divert the western fur trade to Albany. In this effort English traders were aided by an ability to offer trade goods at cheaper prices and to pay more for beaver. A shift in the fur trade to Albany carried with it powerful diplomatic and strategic consequences that threatened the western design of Louis XIV and the security of Canada. New York governor Richard Coote, Earl of Bellomont hoped that diversion of the trade would frustrate the strategic plans of the French and allow the English "to laugh at all their projects to circumvent us, their new settlement at Mechisipi and Canada and Nova Scotia put together." For their part, French officials recognized the danger and feared that "the savages our friends will become our enemies and the result will be the inevitable loss of the colony, which could never be sustained without them, and much less still if they were against us." The outbreak of the War of the Spanish Succession, which England entered in late spring 1702, made securing the active support of their traditional Native allies even more pressing for French authorities in Canada.[7]

In addition to retaining the support of the western nations in the Upper Country, the French counted on the assistance of the Eastern Abenakis in Maine and Acadia to hold the English in check along the eastern borders of New France. The French believed that the security of Acadia, France's vulnerable maritime colony, depended on open hostility between the English and the Eastern Abenakis. During the Nine Years' War, attacks by Eastern Abenakis and Pennacooks had temporarily driven back the English frontier in Maine and had killed or captured eight hundred to nine hundred colonists. Many officials in New France expected that similar raids would again be necessary to defend Acadia and Canada itself in the early 1700s. But collapse of the beaver trade had weakened French alliances with Natives in the East as well as the West. The inability to supply Native allies with trade goods created opportunities for English fur traders and officials and thus threatened to undermine critical military alliances. Massachusetts Governor Joseph Dudley worked hard to win over the Eastern Abenakis, promising them "trade and everything they want if they will keep off from our English settlements during the war." The governor of Acadia, Jacques-François Monbeton de Brouillan, feared losing the support of the Abenakis "because the French cannot supply them with their needs and no longer seek their furs which are their sole resources."[8]

Louis-Hector de Callière, who governed New France from 1698 to his death in 1703, strove to counter Dudley's diplomatic initiatives. Callière as well as some officials in France originally had favored maintaining a truce with New England that would neutralize any potential problems arising from disaffection among the Eastern Abenakis. But the likelihood of a truce vanished in the face of Governor Dudley's continued activity and of the arrival from France of explicit orders to take the offensive. During summer of 1702, Callière informed the Eastern Abenakis that England and France were at war, and because of this, they had his encouragement and support to attack the English. At a December meeting he appealed to their shared Catholic faith and urged them to remain loyal to France. He also emphasized the economic advantages of war, claiming that the plunder obtained on raids and the gifts provided by the French would enable them to live more comfortably while at war than they did in peacetime. Arms and ammunition constituted the bulk of the annual French gift in 1702. The Abenakis, however, remained unmoved.[9]

Failing to make any headway with the Eastern Abenakis, the French began to plan their own strikes against the New England frontier. Because of the colony's relatively limited manpower of approximately thirty-six hundred militiamen and eight hundred regulars (compared with New England's thirteen thousand to fifteen thousand men capable of bearing arms), such attacks would have to be made with Natives recruited from villages along the Saint Lawrence. The Connecticut valley's proximity to Montreal and a desire to avoid conflict with the Five Nations of the Iroquois League made it an obvious target for raiders. A French raid relying heavily on allies drawn from the villages around Montreal would therefore tend toward Deerfield and its neighbors. As early as summer of 1702, Governor Callière had apparently identified the Connecticut River as a likely destination for raiding parties with Native allies. But the governor remained on the defensive during 1702 because he believed that New France was going to be attacked. A lack of arms, canoes, and other resources also prevented him from doing much offensively.[10]

Governor Callière died early in 1703 and was succeeded by Philippe de Rigaud de Vaudreuil. A military officer by training, the sixty-year-old Vaudreuil had served in Canada for sixteen years and put down roots in the colony, marrying Louise-Elisabeth de Joybert, a second-generation Canadian. He had fought in the war against the Iroquois League and had been appointed governor of Montreal in 1698. As a soldier he had won the respect of his fellow officers and of France's Native allies. As governor of Montreal he was well regarded, even popular. Experienced and confident, Vaudreuil provided the colony with sound and energetic leadership at a critical moment.[11]

The new governor's plans for defending New France continued the strategy outlined by his predecessor. Preservation of peace with the Iroquois League remained the centerpiece of this policy and the colony's defense. To maintain the 1701 treaty of peace and neutrality with the league, the governor foreswore offensive operations against the colony of New York and worked hard to retain the western Indians, so feared by the Iroquois, as French allies. Along the New England frontier he sought to promote war between Eastern Abenakis and English colonists. Fighting would frustrate efforts by Governor Dudley of Massachusetts to secure the Abenakis' neutrality and possibly turn them actively against the French, a remote possibility but a real French fear. Promoting raids by allied Indians living in Canada against New England's frontier would increase the likelihood of triggering war between Eastern Abenakis and the English, who might have difficulty determining the precise identity of Native attackers. In addition, raids against New England would provide Natives suffering from the downturn in the fur trade with profitable employment. These raids and joint operations undertaken with French support would keep the populous English colonies off balance and force them to spend money on fortifications and garrisons instead of offensive operations.[12]

In contemplating raids against New England's frontiers, Vaudreuil also sought to carry out the wishes of his superiors in France and hoped to add to his own reputation. Some colonial officials, most notably the former intendant Jean Bochart de Champigny and Claude de Ramezay, Vaudreuil's successor as governor of Montreal, objected to such raids because they feared that they would only incite English counterattacks. Champigny in particular believed that the English "want only peace, aware that war is contrary to the interests of all the Colonies." But after giving some support for a treaty of neutrality to protect Acadia, officials in France had adopted a more aggressive stance in 1702. They dropped talk of neutrality and encouraged Canadian officials to send out raiding parties against New England, while maintaining a de facto truce with the colony of New York. The comte de Pontchartrain, minister of the marine from 1699 to 1715, would approve of Vaudreuil's decision during the summer of 1703 to send Canadians and Native allies against New England's frontiers to draw the Eastern Abenakis into the War of the Spanish Succession.[13]

THE heritage and experiences of Canadian-born military officers made possible the joint French and Indian raids launched against the frontiers of New England. The Canadians who gathered at Chambly early in 1703 to attack Deerfield came from communities—Boucherville, Chambly, Montreal, and

Trois-Rivières—and from families that were products of a half-century of struggle with the Five Nations of the Iroquois League. This conflict, which began around 1650, had merged in 1689 with an international contest for supremacy in Europe that pitted England against France and Canadians against New Englanders. In the 1680s and 1690s New France had lost six hundred killed and captured out of a population that nonetheless grew from about ninety-seven hundred to about fourteen thousand. During these decades of almost constant warfare, the colony's military establishment and Canadian nobles assumed an importance that rivaled the church and overshadowed that of the colony's merchants.[14]

As in France, the nobles of New France constituted a privileged order whose status was legally recognized and whose membership was based on birth or letters of ennoblement. Like colonial society in New England, colonial society in Canada owed much to Old World institutions and values, which in France were monarchical and aristocratic. Such a regime had a need for nobles to serve as military officers, clergy, and civilian officials. Louis XIV, therefore, supported the development of a Canadian aristocracy. He granted nobles who migrated to New France much of its land in the form of seigneuries, most of the military commissions, and many other privileges, such as fur trading licenses. Since a man who attained noble status passed it on to all of his offspring and the families of Canadian nobles produced an average of nine children, the Canadian nobility expanded rapidly. A visitor from France believed that "in New France there are more nobles than in all the colonies put together." By 1700 the nobles constituted 3 percent of the population, two to four times the proportion in metropolitan France.[15]

Nobles also formed a disproportionate share of the French contingent in the force that gathered at Chambly in 1703. Among the forty-eight to fifty Frenchmen in the raiding party headed for Deerfield were at least ten Canadian-born members of the nobility. The commander, thirty-five-year-old Lieutenant Jean-Baptiste Hertel de Rouville, came from one of the colony's preeminent military families, the Hertels. He had seven brothers serving in the colonial regulars, the *troupes de la marine*. Three or four brothers—most likely twenty-nine-year-old René Hertel de Chambly, twenty-seven-year-old Lambert Hertel, seventeen-year-old Pierre Hertel de Moncours, and possibly nineteen-year-old Michel accompanied De Rouville to Deerfield. Another prominent military family that was well represented among the Deerfield raiders was the Bouchers. Ensign René Boucher de la Perrière was accompanied by two of his nephews, twenty-seven-year-old Jacques-René Gaultier de Varennes and his nineteen-year-old brother Pierre, both cadets in the *troupes de la marine*. Another of the expedition's officers, thirty-two-year-old Ensign François-Marie Margane de Batilly, was related to René Boucher by marriage. Finally, there was twenty-seven-year-old Charles Legardeur de Croisille, a member of another prominent noble family.[16]

Nobles serving as officers and cadets in the *troupes de la marine* played a critical role in offensive operations, and their importance had grown as the numbers of Canadian-born officers increased. Whereas the rank and file of the *troupes* remained native-born Frenchmen, the officer corps of the *troupes* was opened to Canadians. In 1685, Governor Jacques René de Brisay de Denonville began nominating Canadians for commissions as half-pay officers, so-called *officiers réformés*. In France these half-pay commissions served as pensions for retired officers. In New France, *officiers réformés* continued to serve; most were carried on the rolls of particular companies. After reductions in the size of the military establishment in 1689 deprived some officers of their commands, Governor Louis de Buade de Frontenanc expanded the number of *officiers réformés*. Officials in France complained about the expense of so many supernumerary officers, but their numbers only grew. Well-connected Canadian youths of fifteen or sixteen could obtain appointments as cadets and serve for years in the ranks until promotion to ensign. In one historian's opinion, it was little more than a system of welfare for members of the nobility. But as a welfare system it did not pay very well. It could actually cost money to take up a commission. Those who secured such commissions did so primarily to pursue honor and glory for themselves and their families, not riches.[17]

By offering commissions to Canadians, governors obtained a useful core of officers familiar with colonial warfare. The practice also provided them with a limited source of patronage. Governors regularly nominated men for commissions as officers and *officiers réformés*, though the king was free to reject such recommendations. The appointment of cadets and *enseignes en second*, essentially *enseignes réformés*, lay entirely within the governor's power. Governor Frontenac's critics claimed that his desire to preserve a large military establishment with its opportunities for patronage had even affected his fighting of the war against the Iroquois League. The early eighteenth-century historian Father Charlevoix observed that Frontenanc "loved to rule, he had the nomination to most of the military commands, which rendered all the good families absolutely dependant on him, and won him an authority, which it would mortify him deeply to see curtailed." Some charged that he avoided a decisive end to the war with the Iroquois League because removal of the Iroquois threat would have removed the need for so many troops and officers. A reduction in the number of officers was a reduction in the patronage power of the governor-general.[18]

By the beginning of the eighteenth century, the peculiar features of New France's colonial military establishment had become entrenched. Frontenac's immediate successors, governors Callière and Vaudreuil, perpetuated the top-heavy system. While reducing the number of captains and lieutenants *réformés*, they expanded the number of *enseignes réformés*, usually called *enseignes en second*, and cadets. Most of the 28 companies of the *troupes* had 1 or 2 cadets, possibly an *enseigne en second*, an *enseigne en pied*, a lieutenant, and a captain. In addition, half of the companies carried a lieutenant *réformé* on their rolls. In 1701 there were 122 officers and at least 28 cadets for a military establishment with an authorized strength of 840 enlisted men. The ratio of officers to men of approximately 1 to 7 was extremely high, even by the standards of the continental French army, where the ratio was 1 to 9. By comparison, the presidios along the northern frontier of New Spain had ratios of 1 officer to 15 men and the Independent Companies of English regulars stationed in New York had ratios of 1 officer to 33 men. One-third of the officers in the *troupes*, possibly closer to one-half if the *enseignes en second* are included, were native-born Canadians by the early 1700s. All of these noble officers were clearly not needed to lead the *troupes*, many of whom did not even know their officers' names.[19]

Commanding French soldiers was perhaps the least of these officers' responsibilities. On raids against villages of the Iroquois League and the frontiers of New England, they were more likely to be leading Canadian militiamen. Historians who celebrate somewhat uncritically the ability of the Canadian militia often ignore this unusual aspect of New France's military system. Junior officers also functioned as vital liaisons to Native allies, coordinating attacks with Native warriors and serving as shock troops in battle. These responsibilities explain why so many lieutenants *réformés*, *enseignes en pied*, *enseignes en second*, and cadets accompanied comparatively small numbers of French soldiers and militia on raids against New England. Officers and cadets went on raids to learn their trade, to prove themselves, and to win distinction and promotion for themselves and their families. The governor rewarded them with sought-after assignments, promotions, and other favors. They in turn became a constituency favoring a more aggressive posture during wartime. These men readily volunteered to participate in raids such as that undertaken by the army at Chambly.[20]

Despite official favoritism, the period from 1690 to 1715 was difficult for Canadian nobles, as it was for most people and institutions in New France. An Atlantic-wide economic recession held both France and its colony in a stultifying grip. At the same time demographic pressures challenged nobles' efforts to maintain their families' status. Even though only three Canadians were granted letters of nobility between 1690 and 1705, the proportion of nobles in the overall population of New France continued to grow. With opportunities for advancement from the fur trade and returns from landholdings limited by economic conditions, nobles and aspiring nobles grew even more dependent on

state largesse. But here too they met frustration, for the large families of the nobility produced more children than New France could use as military officers,
clergy, and civil officials. Military commissions became harder to obtain. Once
secured, advancement, largely based on seniority, was slow. During the early
1700s, approximately 15 percent of the male offspring of the nobility emigrated,
seeking employment elsewhere. Their departure in turn reduced marriage opportunities for the daughters of the nobility.[21]

T HE situation was particularly challenging for the Bouchers and the Hertels,
    the two noble families that supplied so many men for the Deerfield raid.
Though two of the most famous examples of the Canadian nobility, these families were in fact atypical. From relatively humble beginnings in Trois-Rivières,
the families' founders had risen to prominence through military service. Because of first-hand knowledge of France's Iroquoian enemies and special ties to
the colony's Native allies, they became valued servants of the crown. They
owed much to their skills learned in the forests of New France, but they owed
even more to a system of official recognition and patronage shaped by France's
Old Regime. By the 1690s, the Bouchers and Hertels had joined the ranks of the
Canadian nobility, an achievement matched by only nine other Canadian families during the entire existence of New France from 1608 to 1760. But it was in
both instances an uncertain achievement clouded by questions and dependent
on the continuing recognition and support of superiors.[22]

The Boucher family's tenuous place in the colony's elite had been secured by
the efforts of Ensign René Boucher's father, Pierre, who grew up with the colony
and did much to make it grow. He was born in France in 1622 and brought to
New France in 1635 by his father, a carpenter. The family settled near Quebec,
where the young Pierre came under the tutelage of the Jesuits. In 1637 he
went to Huronia as a *donné*, a lay assistant to Jesuit missionaries. He stayed for
almost four years, during which he learned the Hurons' language and observed
their customs. When he returned, he served the governor as a soldier, interpreter, and Indian agent. He was present when Montreal was established in 1642.
Two years later he took up a permanent post as interpreter at Trois-Rivières, an
early center of the fur trade. The town was also a critical military outpost during the First Iroquois-French War, which began around 1650 and lasted until
1667. In 1649 Pierre married a Christian Huron woman, Marie Ouéadoukoué,
who died later in the year from complications during childbirth. The same year,
Boucher became captain of the town. In 1653, he led forty-five very young and
elderly men in a memorable nine-day defense of Trois-Rivières, beating back repeated attacks by six hundred Iroquois before making peace with the assailants.
After this military and diplomatic achievement, he was appointed governor of

Trois-Rivières. At the urging of the colony's governor, the king conferred letters of nobility on Boucher in 1661.[23]

Pierre Boucher's greatest service to the struggling colony came in 1661 when he was chosen to go to France to plead for increased assistance from the king. The war with the Iroquois continued, the economy of New France was in a shambles, and the existing frame of government appeared incapable of meeting the colony's needs. In France Boucher met with prominent clerics, government ministers, including Jean-Jacques Colbert, the minister of the Marine, and eventually King Louis XIV. According to Boucher's memoirs, the king questioned him "about the state of the country, of which I gave him an accurate account, and His Majesty promised me that he would help the country and take it under his protection." When he sailed for New France in 1662, Boucher came with one hundred soldiers, needed provisions and munitions provided by the king, and one hundred laborers he recruited himself.[24]

The year after Pierre Boucher's return, the king reorganized the colony's administration, transforming a collection of missionary outposts and fur-trading stations into a New France with an agricultural base and a social order resembling that of France. Colbert poured people and money into the colony. He used New France as a laboratory for a rationalized, centralized administration that would be the model for a new and improved France. There would be no entrenched local interests, no lawyers, no *parlements,* no Protestants, and, he hoped, no opposition. He made the colony a royal province with a royally appointed governor-general responsible for defense and diplomacy and an intendant who oversaw justice, police, and finances. In 1665 the Regiment Carignan-Salières arrived from France with one thousand men. This regiment played an important role in persuading the Iroquois League to make peace in 1667. It also supplied much-needed colonists when four hundred enlisted men and thirty officers chose to settle in Canada rather than return to France in 1668. The fathers of Margane de Batilly and of the Gaultier brothers were among these officers.[25]

With the end of the First Iroquois-French War, Pierre Boucher embarked on a new venture, the establishment of what he hoped would be a model seigneury. The granting of large blocks of land as seigneuries to nobles, prominent non-nobles, and ecclesiastical institutions had been envisioned by the colony's founders as an efficient way to settle and develop land. It also laid the economic foundation for a stratified social system of orders similar to that of France: there would be those who prayed, those who fought, and those who worked, the third estate. Ideally, the first estate, the church, and the second estate, the nobility, would secure their economic status by granting habitants land on their seigneuries. The habitants would then clear and farm the land and pay rents and occasional dues to their seigneurs. Additionally, the seigneurs would receive income from directly

farming the lands that they retained, their *domains,* and from economic monopolies, such as operating the local grist mill. Possession of a seigneury, however, would not make one noble: privilege in New France brought economic advantages; economic advancement did not necessarily bring privilege.[26]

As it turned out, possession of a seigneury did not bring with it much economic advantage either. In most instances, the colony's sparse population, a
lack of markets, and the low returns from fixed rents and economic monopolies
provided seigneurs with relatively little income before the mid-eighteenth century. In the seventeenth century seigneurs had little incentive to develop their
lands, which often remained unsettled and uncleared. Many of these early
seigneurs lived much like habitants. Others were absentees. Families retained
their seigneuries hoping to obtain a secure income from the land at some point
in the future. They also retained the land for its prestige value. After all, landed
estates were the foundation of the wealth and status of the elite back in France.
Estates also gave noblemen their distinctive second names; Rouville, Chambly,
and Varennes were all names of seigneuries in New France, none of which supplied a noble-sized income to their owners.[27]

Pierre Boucher, however, because of his energy and enterprise and his
seigneury's location, beat the odds and created one of the most successful
seigneuries in New France. He obtained a grant of land on the south shore of the
Saint Lawrence nine miles down river from Montreal. He laid out thirty-eight
long, narrow lots in two groups or *côtes* along the shore of the river (map 3).
Over a period of six years, Boucher recruited thirty-eight men as settlers, many
of them from Trois-Rivières, three-quarters of them in their twenties or early
thirties. All of them appear to have been born in France and probably came from
urban backgrounds. Like most immigrants they did not come to New France in
family units: at least half of them had arrived in Canada as unmarried servants
or soldiers. Unlike most immigrants, they stayed. The lands they received in
Boucherville offered them an opportunity to establish families and settle permanently. Two-thirds of them did, though finding a wife in Canada could be
difficult, for men outnumbered marriageable women by twelve to one during
the 1660s. The marriageable women were either French-born servants in their
early twenties or Canadian-born daughters of habitants who married in their
mid-teens. Couples had on average seven children. By 1700, Boucherville was
one of the colony's most populous seigneuries with around four hundred inhabitants, and Boucher was one of the few seigneurs who were "quite well-to-do."[28]

Even a seigneury as successful as Boucherville differed significantly from
contemporary villages in France. Pierre Boucher believed that after four or five
years most settlers were "in easy circumstances and well fitted out for persons
of their condition in life." These settlers also came to see themselves as proud,

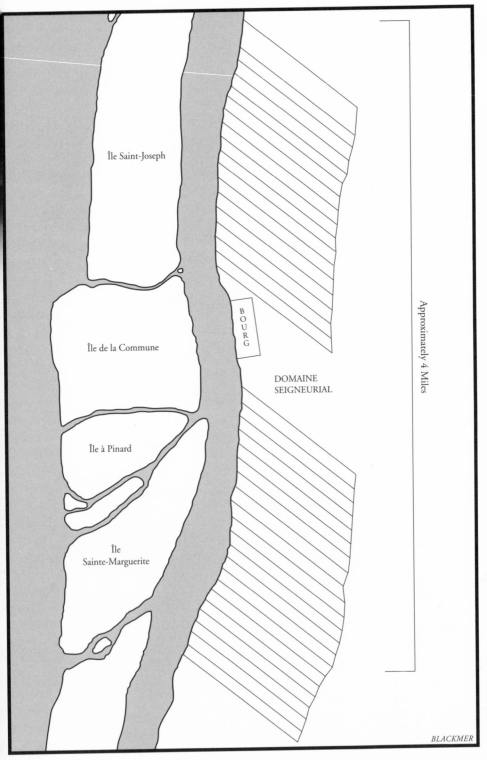

Labels within image:
- Île Saint-Joseph
- Île de la Commune
- Île à Pinard
- Île Sainte-Marguerite
- BOURG
- DOMAINE SEIGNEURIAL
- Approximately 4 Miles
- BLACKMER

MAP 3. Boucherville, 1673. Source: Adapted from "Premières Concessions à Boucherville," map by Jean Gareau, in G. Robert Gareau, *Premières Concessions d'habitations 1673 Boucherville* (Montreal, 1973), 13.

independent-minded habitants, not peasants. They paid no taxes and enjoyed the freedom to hunt and fish where they pleased. Often there was no resident parish priest because the parish system took hold slowly in New France and the tithe paid to the church was half the rate paid in France. Habitants generally preferred to live spread out along the river where they could maintain some household independence rather than living under the eye of a parish priest or their seigneur. More than in France or even Deerfield, the household was the fundamental unit of agrarian production in early Canada. However, there was the seigneur who was the community's local landlord who appropriated some of the habitants' production in the form of rent and fees. Despite his position, the Canadian seigneur was no feudal lord. French officials had consciously sought to limit the political and even economic powers of seigneurs in New France. The seigneury never functioned as a unit of local government. Resistance by residents also limited a colonial seigneur's power, as Boucher learned when he attempted to prevent his tenants from hunting and fishing on the seigneury's commons.[29]

The seigneury of Boucherville embodied Pierre Boucher's desire to establish a landed, aristocratic dynasty, but his position rested ultimately on his ability to establish a family and obtain continued favors from the government. By 1704 Boucher had had difficulties in both realms for several years. He had remarried in 1652, taking as his second wife Jeanne Crevier, who had settled in Trois-Rivières as a child. They had fifteen children; eight sons and five daughters reached adulthood. Two sons became priests. The other six served in the *troupes de la marine.* By 1700 four of the daughters and one son had married into established noble families. But the family's apparent success was threatened in the late seventeenth century by a series of crises. The unexpected deaths of a son and a son-in-law added to Pierre Boucher's economic burdens. Worse, his ennoblement was suddenly, and apparently inadvertently, revoked by a blanket royal decree. By the later 1600s French officials had become reluctant to ennoble Canadian families, making it very difficult to secure new letters of nobility for Pierre Boucher. In 1694 the proud seigneur of Boucherville rejected a suggestion that he purchase letters of nobility, a not uncommon practice in contemporary France. He believed that his service to the crown had earned him the honor. Besides, there were few Canadians, apart from the wealthy merchant Jacques Le Ber, who could genuinely afford to purchase their nobility. There the matter rested in 1704. The Bouchers still carried themselves as members of the nobility. But a favorable resolution of their now ambiguous status came to depend more and more on service to the crown by Pierre's sons.[30]

This burden of service fell increasingly on Ensign René Boucher de la Perrière, the sixth son of Pierre and Jeanne. René had participated in the expeditions against the Iroquois during the 1680s. In his service with France's Native allies he learned Native languages and became familiar with partisan warfare. In 1694 he received a commission as an ensign in the *troupes de la marine*. Three years later he served with distinction under Pierre Le Moyne d'Iberville in his attack on Saint John's, Newfoundland. Though regarded as a "good officer" by his superiors, he was a thirty-six-year-old ensign in 1704, looking for promotion to lieutenant and for legal confirmation of his family's noble status.[31]

The Hertel family's rise closely paralleled that of the Bouchers, though it had not taken them as far socially or economically by 1704. This family owed its position in New France to the efforts of Joseph-François Hertel de La Fresnière, a man his contemporaries nicknamed "the Hero." Born in Trois-Rivières in 1642 to humble parents, Hertel rapidly grew to manhood, becoming at the age of fifteen a soldier in the town's garrison. In July 1661, Iroquois raiders captured him and carried him back to their home village. Adopted by an old woman, he learned the language and customs of the Iroquois. After two years, he escaped and made his way to Montreal, where he married in 1664 Marguerite-Josèphe Thauvent, the daughter of an army officer and heir to the seigneur of Chambly. Joseph-François and his wife returned to Trois-Rivières, where he again served as a member of the garrison and as an interpreter. He also engaged in the fur trade. During the mid-1660s and again during the 1680s he went on four expeditions to Iroquoia and participated in "a quantity of small fights to repel incursions." In recognition of his services, Governors de La Barre and Denonville designated him commander of the Native allies of the French.[32]

In leading French and Indian raiders Joseph-François Hertel established his military reputation. He turned these skills against the English in 1690, when Governor Frontenac launched three raids, on Casco, Maine, Salmon Falls, New Hampshire, and Schenectady, New York. Hertel led twenty-five French volunteers and twenty-five Native allies against Salmon Falls. His three oldest sons, Zacharie-François, Jacques, and Jean-Baptiste, accompanied him and gained on-the-job training as partisan officers. After attacking the New Hampshire village, where his men killed or captured eighty-eight residents, he and some of his men joined the attack on Casco. Later in the same year Hertel and four of his sons participated in the defense of Quebec. For the remainder of the Nine Years' War hardly an expedition was launched or a battle fought without a Hertel being present.[33]

Governor Frontenac rewarded members of the family for their service as best he could. He granted Joseph-François and several of his sons commissions in the *troupes de la marine*. Beginning in 1689, Frontenac sought letters of nobility for Joseph-François Hertel. He was promised the honor in 1691, but the letters did not arrive. In 1694, the governor renewed his request. It was favorably considered but eventually refused when a question arose concerning Hertel's ability to pay for the required stamp for the letters. The king's minister informed the Canadian governor that "if this Man does not have the estate to pay the stamp of letters of nobility which he was to be given he would have still less to sustain the position. His Majesty would not have given it before being informed of his poverty." Despite this refusal, the Hertels carried themselves as nobles, married into families of the nobility, and used the title *ecuyer* (esquire). Still, the lack of royal ennoblement must have rankled.[34]

By 1704, the Hertel family's hopes for noble status had come to rest on Joseph-François Hertel's third son, Jean-Baptiste Hertel de Rouville. By his exploits, De Rouville had already begun to outshine his brothers and to assume his aging father's position as one of the colony's preeminent military officers. As with his father and his older brothers, De Rouville's knowledge of Native languages and customs gave him advantages that officers born in France or raised in Quebec did not have. In 1696 he was promoted to *lieutenant réformé* only a year after his oldest brother, Zacharie-François, and long before his older brother Jacques. Two years later he married Jeanne Dubois, the daughter of a merchant, and made his home in Trois-Rivières. As a serving officer, he spent almost no time in his seigneury of De Rouville, not much more in Trois-Rivières, and probably even less time there after the death of his wife, Jeanne, in 1700. More than his other brothers, De Rouville appeared to carry the burden of securing his family's position among New France's nobility.[35]

War was the most obvious route of continued advancement for men such as Lieutenant Hertel de Rouville and Ensign René Boucher de la Perrière and their families. Support for a more militantly expansive imperial policy generally had the backing of the colony's merchants and nobles, three-quarters of the latter being themselves military officers or their offspring. The Canadian historian Guy Frégault has argued that "if it had been self-supporting, a small agricultural Canada, restricted to the middle St. Lawrence, could have existed beside the English colonies." However, in Frégualt's opinion, two "compelling factors" undermined the ideal of the compact colony, forcing it to expand and collide with England's expansion: the fur trade and "her governing class, unable to live on the produce of the seigneuries." While this assessment ignores the strategic goals of Louis XIV and his ministers as well as the threat of English conquest, it does highlight the stake that the colony's nobles and its merchants had in supporting a more assertive imperial policy. It also explains the eagerness with which they stepped forward to participate in raids on New England.[36]

T HE rank and file of the French contingent that gathered at Chambly was drawn from enlisted men in the *troupes de la marine* and the militia, a civilian self-defense force established in 1669. The particular character of the contributions made by these two military organizations to raids against New England is not always clear in contemporary records. Because of this lack of clarity, historians have tended to slight the role of the *troupes*. At the same time they have misunderstood, and to a degree, exaggerated that of Canadian militiamen, all of whom are assumed to have shown "no hesitation in participating in long distance raids." Both military institutions, however, made essential contributions to the hybrid forces that carried out long-distance raids such as the one about to be launched from Chambly (figure 1).[37]

The *troupes de la marine* or *troupes de la colonie* or simply the *troupes* were created in the 1680s to serve as the colony's regular military establishment. Like the colony itself, these soldiers fell under the jurisdiction of the Department of the Marine, not the Ministry of War, which oversaw the line regiments of the *troupes de la terre* that constituted France's continental army. Like other colonial institutions the *troupes de la marine* embodied Colbert's efforts at reform. Unlike the *troupes de la terre,* which were organized in regiments owned by their colonels, the *troupes de la marine* were organized in independent companies. By eliminating colonels, officials sought to remove sources of venality and corruption. And in fact, commissions in the *troupes de la marine* were not sold. Organizing troops in small independent companies instead of large regiments trained to fight in formal European battle lines was also innovative tactically. During the 1680s the French had used independent companies as irregular troops for skirmishing and raiding along France's northern frontiers. This war of small parties came to be known as partisan warfare or *la petite guerre,* small war. Units organized as independent companies were therefore better suited to the partisan warfare and garrison duties required of soldiers in Canada.[38]

In reality, the *troupes* failed to satisfy the colony's military needs. The companies were filled with enlisted men recruited from the working classes of metropolitan France. Most recruits were in their late teens and early twenties. About half of them came from urban backgrounds. Officials in New France had a rather low opinion of the quality of these recruits. In particular, they claimed that the enlisted men in the *troupes* did not have the physical stamina and the survival skills necessary to undertake offensive operations in North America. Many agreed with the assessment of Intendant Jean Bochart de Champigny that the *troupes* were "very wretched soldiers and that the habitants are worth incomparably more in the war, for voyages and for other duties." He believed that fewer than three hundred or two hundred of the fourteen hundred to seventeen hundred *troupes* sent to Canada were fit for campaigns in the bush. Because of this, companies of *troupes* stationed in New France were usually employed defensively as garrison units. The bulk of them were located in the Montreal region.[39]

Still, enlisted men drawn from the *troupes* participated in most offensive operations. For Governor Denonville's 1687 invasion of western Iroquoia 800 soldiers

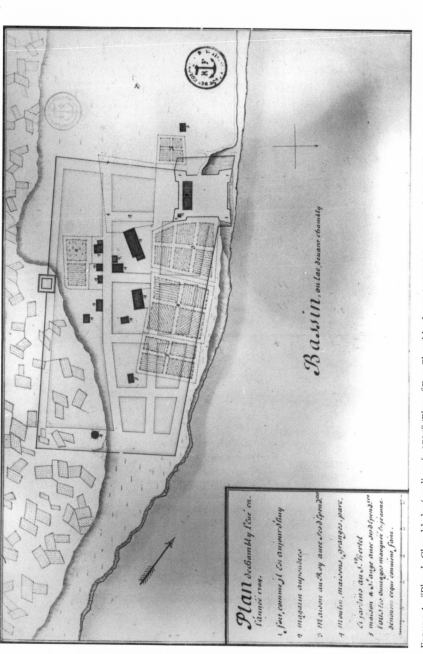

from the *troupes* joined with 900 militiamen and 300 to 400 Native allies. In 1693, 100 soldiers from the *troupes* accompanied 200 Native allies and 325 militiamen on a January raid against Mohawk villages. Several hundred regulars also took part in Governor Frontenac's 1696 attack on Onondaga and Oneida villages of the Iroquois League. Smaller numbers took part as volunteers in Iberville's 1686 overland expedition to Hudson's Bay and the 1690 winter raid on Schenectady. These were particularly grueling expeditions. It is, therefore, very likely that some enlisted men from the *troupes* joined De Rouville's force at Chambly.[40]

The bulk of the French contingent in De Rouville's expedition would have been native-born Canadians drawn from the militia. Though their names are unknown today, it is possible to make some informed conjectures about their residences, ages, and experiences. While all males in Canada between the ages of 16 and 60 were members of the militia and assigned to companies organized geographically by parish, those on the Deerfield raid would not have been a cross-section of New France's militia, which included men who were inadequately armed or unfit for service in the field. The men who undertook raids against New England with Native allies were in fact as exceptional as the raids themselves. Canadian militiamen participated in only three or four of the attacks on the New England frontier during the Nine Years' War and in approximately half a dozen during the decade-long War of the Spanish Succession. There were at any given time perhaps only 300 to 400 inhabitants capable of carrying out winter raids (figure 2). In 1696 Callière had declared to then-governor Frontenac that he could not "find men enough to march in snow-shoes, carry and draw ammunition and stores so far, and storm a town in the very heart of the enemy's country." Even among the regular officers of the *troupes* taking part in these joint raids one tends to see the same names expedition after expedition: Boucher, Hertel, Legardeur, and Le Moyne.[41]

The unusual demands of a winter expedition required highly motivated and skilled individuals, not a unit of impressed militiamen or poorly trained *troupes*. Ability to use snowshoes and winter survival skills were essential. For the large expeditions against the Iroquois League or when faced with invasion, the governor-general personally established the number of militiamen to be drafted from each company. The procedure for smaller expeditions appears to have been more informal, possibly employing personal and family ties and suggests a certain proximity between officers and men. For his 1690 raid on Salmon Falls, New Hampshire, Joseph François Hertel recruited three of his sons, two nephews, several other relatives by marriage, and neighbors from Trois-Rivières. Since the officers leading the Deerfield raiders came from Boucherville, Chambly, Montreal, Varennes, and Trois-Rivières, it is likely that most of the Canadians on the Deerfield raid came from these locales. This assumption is reinforced by the fact that

FIGURE 2. "Canadiens en Raquette allant en guerre sur la nege" (Canadians going to war on snow-shoes). Engraving, circa 1700. From Baqueville de la Potherie, *Histoire de l'Amérique*, 4 vols. (Paris, 1722). This is the only known illustration of a Canadian militiaman on a campaign during colonial wars. The treatment of the snowshoes is rather fanciful, but they played an important role in the winter expeditions against targets such as Deerfield. The hatchet, beaded pouches, coat, and possibly the hat are close approximations of Canadian raiders' dress and equipment. Photograph courtesy of the National Archives of Canada C1854.

some of the captives taken on the raid ended up in Boucherville, Chambly, Montreal, Varennes, and according to tradition, Trois-Rivières. Montrealers had a reputation for being particularly enthusiastic volunteers; Trois-Rivières had a reputation for producing "the best soldiers in the country." The Hertels, Ensign Boucher, and Ensign Margane would have known which of their neighbors and kinsmen from these communities could meet the demands of a winter expedition. For their service, the men received fairly modest recompense: food, powder and shot, a blanket, and clothing consisting of a capot, leggings, and two shirts.[42]

These men would have been relatively young, probably in their early twenties. Among the young men of Boucherville, Montreal, Trois-Rivières, and Varennes were several likely to have to have had experience with the fur trade. Approximately one-half of the men in Trois-Rivières, one-quarter of those in the city of Montreal, and up to one-third of those in the surrounding parishes, such as Boucherville, participated in the fur trade during this period. Throughout New France fewer than one man in five was involved in the fur trade at some point during the late 1600s and early 1700s. But this minority of men skilled in woodcraft—the knowledge needed to live and survive in the woods—was more likely to be called up for militia duty more often than others. They were also the kind of men likely to participate in a winter raid against New England.[43]

Devising military solutions to the crisis facing France's expansive North American empire lay behind Governor Vaudreuil's decision to attack New England's frontiers. Here, as in other instances, the collapse of the beaver trade and the colony's economic problems influenced diplomacy and military strategy. Among the noble military officers, the professional *troupes,* and the unemployed fur traders, Vaudreuil had a dynamic group of Frenchmen willing and able to go on long-distance raids. But their attacks on New England were not designed to defeat Massachusetts militarily or to push back its borders permanently. If the raids prevented the English from invading Acadia or launching another sea-borne assault on Quebec, that was a strategic gain, but again it was not 'the primary purpose of the Deerfield raid. Retaining the support of New France's Native allies in a time of economic crisis and diplomatic uncertainty was. It was for this reason that Hertel de Rouville's raiding party contained warriors drawn from so many Native communities.[44]

CHAPTER 3

NATIVES AND MISSIONS

T HE two hundred Natives who joined the army at Chambly came from
five different villages. Like Deerfield, these communities had been
settled in the 1660s and 1670s by people seeking security and better futures. From the west came Hurons and Algonkins; from the south, Iroquois and
Sokokis; from the east and south, Abenakis and others seeking shelter from the
militantly expanding settlements of New England. Their lives combined traditions from their homelands with practices developed in their new homes, the
villages of Lorette, La Montagne, Sault-au-Récollet, Kahnawake, and Odanak.
The French referred to these Natives as *sauvages domiciliés* because they had permanently settled in villages along the Saint Lawrence. The English called them
French Indians or French Mohawks, depending on their ethnicity. None of these
terms accurately reflected the identity of these peoples, or their ambiguous relationship to the French and their religion.

All of these Native villages were the sites of Christian missions maintained by
French priests. The role of Christianity in these communities was complicated
and contested. It was intertwined with problems arising from social and economic contacts with French colonists. By 1704 Catholicism had become a part of
life in all of these villages but not always to the degree desired by the missionaries.
Natives drew upon Christian beliefs and Native traditions as they struggled to
preserve their communities and cultures. Their on-going encounter with the
Catholic faith influenced their relations with the French and would profoundly
affect the experiences of English captives brought into these villages.

Despite their residence in New France and their acceptance of missionaries,
these Natives were allies of the French, not subordinates or mercenaries. The
suspicious English believed that they willingly did the bidding of their priests
and were in "subjection and vassalage" unto the governor of New France. But
the English were wrong. The Native villages were largely self-governing and relatively autonomous. The missionaries usually had less influence with the men,
who controlled relations with European governments, than with the communities' women, who controlled domestic affairs. French officials had to work
hard to persuade Native warriors to raid the English. To secure cooperation,
they used economic leverage, reminded Natives of particular grievances, and

appealed to shared religious sentiments. For their part, Natives could not easily ignore French demands, because their alliances with the French had become crucial elements of survival strategies. But even when they did go on raids with the French, cooperation lasted only as long as the Natives wanted it to, which was not necessarily as long as the French needed it.[1]

INDIANS in the Saint Lawrence Valley were constantly negotiating the pressures of colonialism and empire. Native villagers handled the demands of French missionaries as they did those of French soldiers, traders, and diplomats. They embraced tenets of Christianity at their convenience, not that of the missionaries. The French liked to call the villages missions or *reductions,* reflecting their idea that the villages were places to convert Native Americans to a Catholic way of life by "reducing" them to civility from their traditional ways, which often seemed to be a state of uncivilized license to these Counter-Reformation Catholics. Native responses to the missionaries suggest that they saw things differently. They assimilated Christianity into traditional communal values in a conscious effort to survive as distinctive peoples in a changing world. In the process they did embrace aspects of the Catholic faith and became new peoples: Christian Hurons, Christian Iroquois, and Christian Abenakis.

Most of the Natives had been moved to establish new communities near the French by the same forces that had caused the Pocumtucks to seek refuge in Canada: the disruptions created by wars and diseases and the hope of a much-needed alliance with a strong new power. Sillery, the first such village, drew its initial inhabitants from Montagnais seeking refuge from Iroquois war parties in the 1630s. Algonkins soon joined them. Both were fur-trading partners as well as allies of the French. Like virtually all the later villages founded by Natives relocating to the Saint Lawrence valley, Sillery was established at a site already in use by Natives, in this instance for eel fishing. French missionaries usually went to where the Natives were; rarely did the Natives come to them. A second mission, La Conception, was soon established at Trois-Rivières, another Native rendezvous point, but because of its greater vulnerability to Iroquois raiding parties, the Native village at this location did not develop. Jesuits also sent missionaries to Huron villages north of Lake Ontario.[2]

Skilled missionaries learned to translate Native concerns into a Christian idiom and Christian doctrine into Native idioms. French priests became virtual shamans using fear, persuasion, and healing to demonstrate their spiritual power. They conjured up images of hell as a form of suffering lonelier and more painful than anything their enemies—generally at this point the Iroquois League—could ever inflict. The power of hell, something unknown in Native systems of belief, had more force than the promise of a Christian heaven, which fell short in comparisons with Native images of paradise and threatened to separate Natives from their non-Christian ancestors. Missionaries strove to convince Natives that Christianity was greater than traditional sources of power. This approach worked well when sick people whom they baptized recovered. It did not when they died. The devastating impact of new diseases, the disruptions of warfare, and the lure of preferential treatment in trade both aided and undermined the missionaries' efforts.[3]

Only after a great deal of turmoil did Christianity become a source of strength and stability for Native communities. French missionaries believed they were bringing salvation to Native Americans, but in the process they brought a lot of trouble. Their introduction of Christianity attacked the old ways, brought new ideas and rituals, and forced people to choose between the two. Dissension and conflict were inevitable. Sillery experienced these divisions in its early years, as did the Huron villages in the Upper Country that were visited by Jesuit missionaries. Some Natives embraced the new religion, and Jesuits wrote enthusiastically about the men and women who supported them and led exemplary lives of devotion. Other natives disagreed and criticized Christianity, blaming the French and their religion for the disasters they were suffering. Many Natives appear to have chosen a course somewhere between rejecting Christianity completely and embracing it uncritically. Indeed, there was never as clear cut a division between believers and nonbelievers as the missionaries desired. Those Indians who adopted Christianity generally did so for traditional reasons, seeing the new religion as a way to gain access to desirable forms of spiritual power. And those who resisted it could do so in Christian terms, as did a group of Hurons who employed the power of hell to dissuade converts, claiming a soul had returned from the dead and informed them that the Jesuits had it all backwards. In reality, heaven was for traditionalist Hurons; hell was for the Christians.[4]

Unfortunately for the Hurons living in the Upper Country, the struggle over Christianity divided their villages in a time of desperate warfare with the Iroquois League. The Hurons had been at war with the Iroquois League when they first met the French. They had been drawn to the French as trading partners and military allies. This alliance had given the Jesuits their initial opening into Huron villages. But the struggles between Christians and non-Christians weakened the Hurons, who could not stop the vicious campaign the Iroquois launched against them in the 1640s. Once strong enough to rival the Iroquois League, the Hurons lost village after village. Thousands of Hurons died or were brought back as captives to Iroquois villages. Thousands more fled for safety. Most went west to the upper Great Lakes, where they eventually became known as the Wyandots. Several hundred moved east to settle with the French.[5]

The Huron Confederacy was the first and most notable victim of a series of wars called the Beaver Wars by those who claim the struggle was essentially over control of the fur trade. But as anthropologists and historians have pointed out, another element was involved: a cultural pattern known as the mourning war. Mourning wars were wars waged primarily for captives, not land or trade goods. In Iroquoian cultures, which included the Hurons, when someone in a clan died and the established rites that channeled the grief of mourners failed to assuage the pain of the loss, clan matrons could demand a raid to obtain a captive or scalp. A captive man, woman, or child or a scalp taken in war against an enemy helped ease the pain and replaced the deceased relative in person or spirit. Captives could be adopted as a family member, literally taking the name and social position of the deceased. They could also serve as slaves. Or, as was more often the fate of men, they could be subjected to ritual torture. Traditionally, a woman, usually the matron of the household or clan, decided a captive's fate. If she did not want to keep the captive alive, she turned the person over to the community to be tortured to death. Sorrow at the loss of fellow villagers was then transformed into cruelty against their enemies, restoring the emotional and spiritual life of a community.[6]

A mourning war could be pursued by a relatively small raiding party or result in a full-scale war. The warriors the grieving woman inspired to fight came from her close relatives, who would have been the nephews, uncles, and cousins of the deceased. These were the relatives who counted most in matrilineal Iroquoian cultures, which, again, included the Hurons. The enemies attacked may or may not have been responsible for the particular death that inspired the mourning war. In fact, the death need not have had anything to do with war; it merely had to be sudden and untimely and the family inconsolable. In their search for captives, raiders avoided pitched battles that would produce casualties, creating a need for more replacements and more raids. But the practice could spin out of control as it appears to have during the so-called Beaver Wars. Devastating losses from disease and battle kept members of the Iroquois League at war throughout most of the seventeenth century as they sought to maintain their rapidly declining populations.[7]

Because of this cycle of loss and war, the conflict between the Iroquois League and the survivors of the Huron Confederacy continued into the 1650s and 1660s. Thanks to the fur trade and their alliance with the French, what began as an Iroquois-Huron war grew into the First Iroquois-French War. The French had stayed out of the war until the collapse of the Huron Confederacy and the resulting threat to their trade routes to the West compelled them to intervene. But they were still too few to hold off the Iroquois League. When the few hundred Huron refugees arrived at Quebec in 1650, the French were weak and demoralized and could do little to protect them. The Jesuits bought some cleared farmland on the Île d'Orléans for the Hurons to settle on but this put them at a distance from the French fort at Quebec. Iroquois warriors continued to attack the Hurons. At one point, ambassadors from the Iroquois League persuaded a number of desperate Hurons to join their captive relatives now living with the Iroquois. On the way to Iroquoia, the Iroquois killed most of the men and turned the rest into captives. The French did nothing. By 1663 the refugee Hurons had lost so many people that those who remained had moved into Quebec for safety. Peace came only after the French launched large-scale invasions of Iroquoia in the mid-1660s.[8]

With the establishment of peace, Natives set up new villages near French settlements, creating the communities from which the Natives came who attacked Deerfield in 1704 (map 4). In 1669 the surviving Hurons moved out of Quebec and settled briefly at Sillery, before relocating in 1673 to a new site called Lorette. Thereafter, they came to be known as the Hurons of Lorette or the Lorettans. In the late 1660s a Jesuit missionary persuaded a handful of Iroquois, some of them Huron captives of the Iroquois League, to move north to Canada. They settled next to the new French village of La Prairie, across from Montreal on the south bank of the Saint Lawrence. By the early 1670s some of these Natives had crossed over to Montreal Island and settled near Mount Royal, and the French came to call the village La Montagne (the Mountain). The Iroquois who remained south of the river set up a separate village, Kahnawake, in 1676, named after the Mohawk village from which many of its people had immigrated. Because of its location just upstream from La Prairie along a set of rapids known to the French as Sault Saint-Louis, the Jesuits called their mission in the village Saint François Xavier du Sault and its people, the Iroquois of the Sault. Finally, in 1683, Jesuits relocated their Algonkin converts and more recent Eastern Abenaki refugees living at Sillery to their new mission of Saint-François-de-Sales, located on the Chaudière River opposite Quebec.[9]

A PARTY of perhaps twenty Hurons from Lorette constituted the smallest Native contingent in the force that gathered at Chambly. The French leaders considered them to be "the most loyal Indians that we have." When the English became active allies of the Iroquois League in 1688, they became the enemies of the Hurons. Still, the actions of the Hurons make clear the complexity of individual Natives' behaviors even among these close allies of the French. A desire to obtain captives for adoption or torture remained an important part of warfare for these Hurons, who were Iroquoian in language and culture. Ties of alliance with other Natives were also important motivations.[10]

The establishment of Lorette in the 1670s coincided with a reinvigorated

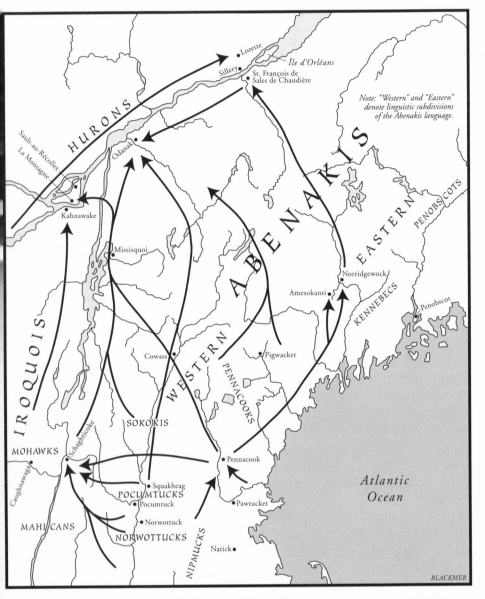

Note: "Western" and "Eastern"
denote linguistic subdivisions
of the Abenakis language.

HURONS

Sault-au-Récollet
La Montagne

Lorette
Sillery
Île d'Orléans
St. François de
Sales de Chaudière

Odanak

Kahnawake

Missisquoi

IROQUOIS

ABENAKIS

EASTERN

PENOBSCOTS

Norridgewock
Amesokanti
Penobscot

WESTERN

Cowass
Pigwacket

KENNEBECS

PENNACOOKS

Schaghticoke
SOKOKIS

MOHAWKS

Caughnawaga

Pennacook

Atlantic
Ocean

Squakheag
POCUMTUCKS
Pocumtuck
Pawtucket

MAHICANS
Norwottuck

NORWOTTUCKS

NIPMUCKS

Natick

BLACKMER

MAP 4. Map of the Northeast showing tribal homelands, Native villages, and movements, circa 1675–1704.

French sense of religious purpose that assigned the village a special place in the sacred landscape of New France. The mission church at Lorette was designed as a replica of the Holy House (Santa Casa) that had flown, according to belief, out of the Holy Land and landed in the Italian village of Loretto. The Santa Casa was the original home of the holy family, where Mary had been visited by an angel and Jesus had grown up. The Jesuits designed their mission at the new Huron village to evoke the experience of visiting the Italian Loretto. The idea of recreating the Holy House, and thereby evoking the patriarchal model of the Holy Family, was popular among missionaries working with matrilineal Iroquoians. The mission at Lorette became a site of religious pilgrimage as soon as its chapel was completed in 1674. Its choirs of women and children drew special praise from French visitors for the beauty and spiritual purity of their singing.[11]

From the French perspective Lorette became famous for the Hurons' attachment to Christianity. Because the Huron village was only a few miles outside of Quebec, the capital of New France and the town most visited by Frenchmen from Europe, it became a sort of model village of the potential of Native Christianity. The Jesuit who oversaw the mission at the turn of the century praised the devotions and "excessive scrupulosity" of the Huron village, where religion appeared to play a central role in binding the community together. Each morning everyone attended "the sacrifice of the mass, which is celebrated in behalf of the whole village." Many others attended a second and even a third mass if it was available. At sunset they again gathered in the chapel, "where prayers are offered up in common for the whole village." Families and individuals prayed regularly on their own. The village priest kept the children busy with religious exercises and games to teach them correct doctrine. The intensity of this indoctrination and the relatively limited contact with non-Christian Indian communities ensured that by the eighteenth century Lorette was outwardly a very Christian town.[12]

Christianity thrived at Lorette because it performed many of the functions that traditional religion had in previous Huron communities. It united the community of the living in peace and charity and kept its members connected with their ancestors. When men went out to trap beavers in the fall, they made a point of returning to the village in time for the Feast of All Saints. There they would "attend the divine mysteries, and relieve by pious prayers the souls of the dead, a duty which they perform with remarkable piety and attention." Parallels can be drawn between the strength of devotion these Hurons dedicated to the Feast of All Saints and their devotion to the Feast of the Dead in their pre-Christian days, both festivals of communal unity with the ancestors. The community's religion was now publicly Christian, but memories would persist into the nineteenth century of powerful snake-beings, witches, and other traditional manifestations of spiritual power. In the end, these Hurons decided that preserving the community mattered more than preserving particular traditions. The result was a strong and cohesive Huron community and a group of exemplary Christians.[13]

Father Louis D'Avaugour, a Jesuit serving at the Huron village during the War of the Spanish Succession, sought to impress on his French readers that the Hurons' vigorous religious life had strategic importance for New France. Like many missionaries, he believed a "loss of religion" in the Native villages could have catastrophic consequences. Such a loss meant no less than "the total overthrow of the French Colony. For nothing else than religion retains the savages in their fidelity to the French." Without it, "they will flock to the neighboring heretics," that is, New England, "from whom they make a much greater profit than from the French, and much more easily dispose of their goods." "The motive of eternal salvation," D'Avaugour concluded, "is the only one to prevent them dealing with those with whom, they know, there is no hope in that direction." Given the economic crisis of the early 1700s and the state of the Canadian fur trade, this was a reassuring observation to the French.[14]

One of Lorette's model Christians, Thaovenhosen, was with the army at Chambly that waited to attack the English heretics. Though young, Thaovenhosen was already a man whose reputation as a warrior and a Christian allegedly extended throughout "the whole country." "To the French as well as to the savages, he is an incentive to live well and to fight well." The sight of him, people said, "kindles their piety, and revives the extinct or slumbering ardor of their charity." At Lorette, he worked closely with the French priest, who "confidently" relied on him to take care of "whatever he considers useful for all." His Jesuit confessor believed "he possesses a special gift for prayer, and that he has God always before his eyes; the most holy name of Jesus is ever on his lips." So great was the fame of his virtue that none hesitated "to commend themselves to his prayers, and they acknowledge that through these they have obtained many favors from God." Thaovenhosen was a man of "remarkable kindness and gentleness." He was also full of the "bravery of the warrior" and "the boldness of the Huron." "As soon as the news of the war was heard, he was the first to take up arms, the last to lay them aside."[15]

Thaovenhosen was one of those exemplary individuals that Jesuit missionaries liked to single out as proof of their success. However, he was not the religious or military leader of the community. When he heeded the call to attack the heretic English, Thaovenhosen went under the command of their "great chief." According to Father D'Avaugour, the great piety of Lorettans such as Thaovenhosen did not "diminish the warlike spirit which these savages commonly possess." Rather "it merely imposes moderation and certain limits upon their

Martial ardor." This too was reassuring. French captains, the Jesuit pastor noted, "enlist no soldiers more willingly than those from the village of Lorette. 'For,' they admit 'we know with certainty that in the fray they will never desert the standard or yield before the enemy's attack.'"[16]

The strong role of Catholicism in the Huron community was due in part to the Hurons' close integration into the society and economy of New France. The community was small, only about 150 individuals. It could not insulate itself from French influence, despite a move in 1697 to a new location, Jeune Lorette (young Lorette) ten miles away. Here the Hurons tried to live as their ancestors had. Women remained the primary cultivators of corn, beans, and squash. Men continued to hunt, fish, and trap furs. Still, their lives were changing. After the turn of the century, they began to construct French-style houses. Women now gathered maidenhair ferns (l'herbe capillaire) to sell to the French for export to Europe. The residents added orchards to their horticultural regime, and some men participated in cultivating the crops. Others devoted themselves to the profits they could make by selling meat, furs, fish, and other products.[17]

Loyalty to the French and their religion undoubtedly inspired some of Lorette's saintly warriors to join the army at Chambly. It appears to have been sufficient motivation for Thaovenhosen. Father D'Avaugour claimed that Thaovenhosen "highly esteems the King of France, on the ground that he had heard that he was an excellent defender of the catholic and ancestral religion." But here as in their village Hurons also responded to other, older allegiances. For some Hurons, alliance with the Abenakis may have motivated them to join the army at Chambly. Such a call for assistance from Native allies had come from Eastern Abenakis in the summer of 1703. Another such call may have accompanied an appeal by Abenakis to the French governor in the fall of 1703. And as Thaovenhausen would learn to his chagrin on the retreat from Deerfield, the mourning war with its ritual torture of prisoners still influenced how and why many Lorettans fought beside the French.[18]

THE pressure to conform to Catholicism and French culture was if anything even stronger in the village of La Montagne on Montreal Island than in the Huron village. Instead of just one or two Jesuits, the Natives living at La Montagne confronted priests and nuns from two very active religious orders, the Sulpicians and the Congregation de Notre Dame. Montreal's distinctively evangelical origins also made it a hotbed of religious proselytizing. Though it was on its way to becoming the center of the North American fur trade by the 1670s, Montreal had begun in 1642 as Ville-Marie, a religious settlement designed to convert Natives. In 1663, the Congregation de Saint-Sulpice, an order established by elite Parisians in 1645 to promote Catholicism in France, inherited this mission when its members became the seigneurs of Montreal Island. As seigneurs of the island, the Sulpicians oversaw Ville-Marie's transition into the fur-trading town of Montreal, actively ministering to the Natives and Europeans who lived both in the town and in several villages scattered across the island.[19]

The piety of these Natives grew out of circumstances similar to those found at Lorette: a relatively small, vulnerable collection of individuals in need of French protection and communal stability. With roughly two hundred inhabitants, La Montagne was only marginally larger than the Huron village. Natives had taken the initiative to found this village and create the resulting Sulpician mission when they began moving across the Saint Lawrence in the early 1670s. Huron captives of the Mohawks at La Prairie, some of them Christians since the days of the Jesuit mission to the Huron Confederacy, had moved to Montreal Island to liberate themselves and secure material advantages, such as more direct assistance in time of famine and during the hunting season. The Sulpicians created a mission for their village located near Mount Royal in 1671. A diverse group of Algonquian peoples including Algonkins, Mahicans, Ottawas, Sokokis, and possibly some Pocumtucks, such as Grey Lock, joined the Hurons and Iroquois at La Montagne. Gradually, an Iroquoian, especially a Mohawk, identity took hold, and the French came to call these people the Iroquois of the Mountain, even though the community remained ethnically diverse during the late 1600s and early 1700s. Its people depended on the French to protect their autonomy from the much more numerous Mohawks at Kahnawake. It was not always enough. In 1689 Kahnawake Mohawks forced thirty-one people at La Montagne to come back to them.[20]

Christianity for the Iroquois of the Mountain was intimately bound up with the community's fundamental concerns for economic security and social independence. The community's alliance with Sulpician priests, who had a reputation for being "more fussy in matters of dogma and morals" than their Jesuit colleagues, meant that life would be significantly different on Montreal Island than in the Jesuit missions elsewhere in the colony. Sulpicians were more committed to the French government's official policy of assimilation than the Jesuits, who had concluded it was best to make Christians first, Frenchmen second. One leading Sulpician, Father François Vachon de Belmont, proclaimed, "We believe that they profit by living among us, and not in their own land; that they must be taught our language, that their women must wear skirts and their men hats and pants; that they must adopt French housing; learn animal husbandry, and how to sow wheat and root vegetables; and that they must be able to read and hear mass and be taught the holy rites." Unwilling to collaborate with Native culture, Belmont taught the boys to speak, read, and write French and to sing Latin canticles in church. In the end they appear to have learned more about Christianity than about French culture, since few became speakers of French, but many did embrace the Catholic faith.[21]

La Montagne also was the only Native community that received religious instruction from women as well as men. Women played a leading role in creating a Christian community at La Montagne. Nuns of the Congregation de Notre Dame aided the Sulpicians with all the zeal of a new movement. Among the Iroquois of the Mountain their influence was evident in the prominent role of Native women in creating and leading the new Christian community. The Congregation, as it was frequently called, began with the arrival in Montreal of an extraordinary woman, Marguerite Bourgeoys. Bourgeoys had belonged to the so-called external congregation of the Congregation de Notre Dame in her hometown of Troyes in France. Though intensely involved with this community, she had not taken her final vows as a nun and was not cloistered. She was therefore able to move about freely. Her personal experience provided the model for the order of uncloistered nuns she established in Montreal in 1653. The ability to move about from settlement to settlement, overseeing schools, farms and, after 1695, a chapel in Montreal was the key to the group's success in this frontier environment. They oversaw the education and religious instruction of La Montagne's girls. And their efforts, together with those of the Sulpicians, proved effective. By 1694 almost the entire village had been baptized.[22]

Though the evidence of daily piety at La Montagne for this period is scarce, the Cult of the Virgin seems to have held a central place. The presence of the Congregation de Notre Dame and the influence of converted Native women undoubtedly played an important role in securing the local prominence of the Virgin Mary. And some of the Natives' Iroquoian traditions would also have predisposed them to appreciate a strong female religious figure. It is also clear that Mary inspired the warriors of La Montagne as well as its women. Sulpician tradition recorded a revealing incident from the Second Iroquois-French War, when the Iroquois of the Mountain joined the French on expeditions against the villages of the Iroquois League. At a difficult point in one battle, their priest reminded the warriors of the power of the Virgin Mary: "Do you not realize that you have at your head the Holy Virgin who you have taken as your protector? That we have received from her so many signs of her assistance, and that she is our shield? What are you afraid of? We are dealing with infidels who only look like real men." He then asked, "Do you not remember that you are subjects of the King of France, whose name causes all Europe to tremble? Do you want to tarnish the glory of your monarch with a laxity unworthy of the French name?" The warriors, probably more moved by the protection of the Virgin than the glory of the king, rallied and the battle was won.[23]

As in the Huron village of Lorette, economic ties to the nearby French town played an important role along with Christianity in transforming the community. The Iroquois of the Mountain had no more reason or ability to resist such ties than the Hurons did. In fact, they took advantage of their community's close proximity to the town of Montreal. When they had first moved to the island, they offered to make canoes, snowshoes, and moccasins for the French. In addition to growing traditional crops, such as corn, beans, and pumpkins, they grew wheat, a marketable crop. They also began to raise chickens, pigs, and, in some instances, cows. Women produced maple sugar and gathered maidenhair ferns to sell in Montreal. The men hunted, fished, and trapped furs, trading much of their catch with the nearby French. The changes could be seen in the French-style log houses some of the Iroquois of the Mountain began to erect soon after settling on Montreal Island.[24]

After a quarter century of ministering to the Iroquois of the Mountain, the Sulpicians faced the same dilemma that had confronted the Jesuits at Lorette and nearby Kahnawake. How much contact with common Frenchmen was too much? By 1689 Father Belmont was clearly having second thoughts about promoting assimilation. He secured lands at Sault-au-Récollet, a site on the north side of Montreal Island, intending to build a new mission far from the bad influence of French traders and tavern keepers as well as harassment by the Kahnawake Mohawks. In 1694 Belmont stepped up his campaign to move the Iroquois of the Mountain by erecting at the new location a stone fort, houses, and a chapel after a drunken villager burned down the mission at La Montagne. Despite this investment, the people of La Montagne resisted the Sulpicians' efforts to move them to a site that was distant, undeveloped, and unappealing. The Sulpicians in turn persisted, organizing great festivals and giving presents to influential members of the community. The first group moved in 1696, and a second followed in 1699. Still, at the time of the Deerfield raid, some of the Iroquois of the Mountain still lived at La Montagne. To force these remaining people to move, Father Belmont rented out to French farmers all the lands near La Montagne that the Natives had cleared but were letting lie fallow. Increasingly hemmed in by the French, the remainder of the people at La Montagne joined their companions at Sault-au-Récollet in 1705.[25]

The Sulpicians' had several motives for wanting the Iroquois of the Mountain to move away from Montreal, not all of them pious. As seigneurs of Montreal Island, the Sulpicians stood to benefit financially from the move. Once the Iroquois left La Montagne, the Sulpicians could lease all of the fields cleared by the Indians to French habitants. When the Natives settled onto the new lands at Sault-au-Récollet, they would begin again the process of clearing more land. This land at some point in the future could and, as it turned out, would be passed on to French farmers as well—just as the old site of Lorette was turned over to French colonists as soon as the Hurons moved to Jeune Lorette. Father Belmont, who wanted the Iroquois of the Mountain to become patriarchal and French, may also have wanted to modify the strength of the Cult of the Virgin at La Montagne. This desire might help explain why he designed the chapel at the new mission to be yet another evocation of the Santa Casa of Lorette, again holding up the patriarchal model of the Holy Family to matrilineal Iroquoians. But the name Lorette did not stick here. Instead, the mission came to be known as the Sault-au-Récollet and, for all their adoption of French economic and religious culture, its residents remained Algonquian and Iroquoian peoples, and among the latter, women continued to decide matters of importance, including the fate of captives.[26]

Despite the often shabby treatment by their Sulpician landlords and missionaries, the Iroquois of the Mountain fought beside the French during the War of the Spanish Succession. Like the Mohawks from Kahnawake, they had a reputation for being good fighters, and the French considered them to be more reliable. Their support, however, was not automatic and had to be negotiated. As with the Lorettans, ties of a shared religious faith helped secure and maintain this support. Father Robert-Michel Gay, the man who had called on the power of the Virgin and the king of France to inspire the warriors from La Montange during the Nine Years' War, had gone to war with such zeal and bravery that his superiors rebuked him for recklessly endangering his life. But there is no evidence that Gay, who ministered to the Iroquois of the Mountain from 1688 until 1725, or any other priest went with the army to Deerfield. Even without his presence, the Catholic militancy Gay had inspired during the battles of the 1690s probably accompanied some of the mission's warriors on the expedition against Protestant Deerfield. The Iroquois of the Mountain were fewer in number than the warriors from Kahnawake, perhaps thirty or forty.[27]

T HE biggest contingent in the army gathering at Chambly would have come from Kahnawake, the largest Native village in New France. At Kahnawake, people did not have to rely on the religion and economy of the French as they did at Lorette and La Montagne. The village's numbers, location, and governance made for a virtually independent community on the outskirts of Montreal. In colonial terms it was actually a very large town. As the historian John Demos notes, it "was larger . . . than the great majority of colonial settlements, French and English." It was in fact almost as large as Montreal itself. With about eight hundred to one thousand people in 1704 it was easily the largest Native American community in New France. It had more warriors—approximately two hundred—than Lorette had people.[28]

Kahnawake was a force to be reckoned with by any terms. Its men had a reputation for being "extremely fierce" fighters. They also had a reputation for being rather independent. The village's location on the south shore of the Saint Lawrence astride the route to Albany had great military and commercial significance. Continued contact with their kin who lived along the Mohawk River and with merchants in Albany gave the people of Kahnawake considerable leeway in their dealings with the French. Residents of the village differed over how they should use their leverage. Some favored a close relationship with the French, others preferred to remain neutral, while yet others espoused pro-English sentiments. The emphasis in Iroquoian culture on individual autonomy and its abhorrence of using coercion made it difficult to achieve a unified stance on policy. This lack of unity, however, was often a source of strength for a community doing business with two competing empires. A frustrated Governor Philippe de Rigaud de Vaudreuil complained that Native "leaders do not have absolute authority. They just state what should be done and afterwards the others do so if they want. Since there is no punishment among them, one cannot subordinate them." French officials and clergy were unable to impose a course of action on the Kahnawake Mohawks. The French had to negotiate to secure the participation of every community's warriors, but they had a particularly hard time at Kahnawake. These Mohawks would fight only who they wanted to, when they wanted to.[29]

Unlike at Lorette or La Montagne, at Kahnawake the economic exchange between French and Natives was between equals. One contemporary claimed that the French traded as much with the Native villages around Montreal as with the Indians from the Upper Country around the Great Lakes. Though its horticulture remained limited largely to the traditional Iroquoian triad of corn, beans, and squash, women sold surplus crops, maidenhair ferns, and maple sugar to residents of Montreal. The men hunted, fished, and, most important, participated in a flourishing fur trade. Almost immediately after Mohawks began settling near Montreal in the 1670s they had started trading with their kin near Albany. The trade grew and prospered. Even the warfare of the 1690s could not put an end to it. The Montreal-Albany fur trade thus became a highly profitable, though illegal, enterprise involving Albany merchants, Mohawks, Canadian coureurs de bois, and Montreal merchants. Because of their location, the Kahnawake Mohawks were well situated to play a central role in this trade, though the people at La Montagne and the Sault-au-Récollet participated as well. They ferried merchandise back and forth along Lake Champlain and carried out the details of a business that the French and English merchants had to keep secret. Such goods were highly prized by the people of Kahnawake, who later stated flatly "that they would rather be dead than deprived of English goods."[30]

Kahnawake's autonomy was also evident in the strength of traditional culture at what the Jesuits had hoped would be another model mission. These Mohawks continued to live in longhouses until well into the eighteenth century. The Jesuits could not force the Mohawks to learn French, as the Sulpicians tried to at La Montagne. They obtained a special dispensation to say the mass in Mohawk. They allowed every new priest to be adopted into a clan and receive a Mohawk name. Every Christian Kahnawake had two names, one Mohawk and one Christian. Some French critics claimed that the Jesuits could not obtain real conversions because Natives were not compelled to renounce their traditional beliefs. Eight decades after the founding of Kahnawake, an English captive observed that some "Caughnewags profess to be Roman Catholics; but even these retain many of the notions of their ancestors." Still, Catholicism was not denied or opposed at Kahnawake. Its people made some compromises in an effort to cooperate with the Jesuits. They proudly identified themselves as the *ongwe honwe tehatiisontha* (real men who make the Sign of the Cross) and most were "a kind of half Roman Catholics," as one of their leaders characterized them.[31]

Catholicism had played a formative role in creating the community at Kahnawake (figure 3). It had drawn League Iroquois to La Prairie in the 1660s. It drew more to Kahnawake in the late 1670s and the 1680s, distinguishing them from their kinsmen who continued to live in Iroquoia. According to the Jesuits, there was a saying among the League Iroquois in the 1680s: "I am off to La Prairie," which meant "I give up drink and polygamy." At Kahnawake, as at La Montagne, women took a leading role in creating the Catholic community. They organized sodalities to promote religious devotion among themselves. The Jesuits supported this intense new female religiosity, which occasionally involved terrific acts of self-mortification. French priests held up as a saint one woman who died from her trials in the 1680s, Kateri Tekakwitha. They used her example to inspire actual and potential Catholics among Natives and colonists alike. For the first twenty years of its existence, the mission of Sault Saint-Louis presented a model of temperance and Christian behavior.[32]

The Second Iroquois-French War that broke out in the 1680s disrupted Kahnawake's Christian unity. Now its people had to choose between cooperating with the French, which meant waging war against their non-Catholic kin, and maintaining peaceful relations with the Iroquois League, which meant risking French displeasure. To keep up their alliance with the French, a number of Kahnawake warriors joined French expeditions, but every raid on Iroquoia presented a conflict of deep and complex political and cultural significance. To men accustomed to the culture of mourning war, the prospect of fighting and possibly killing kinsmen was horrifying. The Iroquois League had begun as an effort to curb the effects of a disastrous cycle of mourning wars by extending the circle of kin outward to include five nations: Mohawks, Oneidas, Onondagas, Cayugas, and

Senecas. People from all of these nations had taken up residence at Kahnawake. Though they had embraced Catholicism, they had not rejected their origins. As a result, they were not the stalwart allies that the French wished them to be.[33]

The people of Kahnawake responded to the challenge of the Second Iroquois-French War by developing the practices that would help sustain the Iroquois's neutrality during the imperial conflicts of the eighteenth century. Initially, they

FIGURE 3. "Les six premiers sauvages de la Prairie viennent d'Onneiout sur les nèges et les glaces" (The first six Natives coming to La Prairie from Oneida over the snow and ice). Drawing, late seventeenth century, père Claude Chauchetère. This illustration by a Jesuit missionary depicts the arrival of the first Iroquois refugees who, in 1667, established the Native community that developed into the village of Kahnawake. © Archives départementales de la Gironde, bibliothèque Bordeaux, France.

had desired to remain neutral. Eventually, French diplomatic pressure compelled warriors from the village to accompany French troops and other Native allies—who had no compunction against killing the Iroquois who were killing them—on raids, starting with a massive expedition against the Senecas in 1687. Fortunately the Senecas fled before the Kahnawake Mohawks, who thus avoided having to decide how they would fight them. Throughout the war, Kahnawake Mohawks seem to have been policing the behavior of the French and other Native allies as much as assisting them. This practice made for a curious sort of parallel war, in which Iroquois from Kahnawake tried to prevent League Iroquois from being killed or captured. During the 1690 attack on Schenectady they spared the lives of thirty of their Five Nations' kinsmen who were found in the village. When a French expedition tried to destroy the League Mohawks in 1693, Mohawks from Kahnawake saved them. They could not stop the French from burning crops and villages, but they refused to kill the many captives the expedition took and then set most of them free. The few times when Mohawks did kill Mohawks caused a crisis at both ends of Lake Champlain as Iroquois diplomats sought to prevent the deaths from igniting a mourning war between kin.[34]

These actions' strained the relationship between the people at Kahnawake and their French neighbors. Continued contacts with the Iroquois League, who until 1701 were allies of the English, made the French suspicious. They took note of the fact that when the French village of La Chine on Montreal Island was attacked and destroyed by members of the League in 1689, Kahnawake, situated directly across the river, was left untouched. And somehow the fifteen hundred Iroquois warriors who carried out this assault had approached La Chine undetected and retreated unharmed. The French governor reacted to this raid by moving the residents of Kahnawake into Montreal, ostensibly to "protect" them but also to separate them from the League Iroquois. In Montreal, according to the Jesuits, some Kahnawake Mohawks took to drinking with a vengeance. For Natives, drinking had become an act loaded with political and cultural significance. It cemented bonds with fur traders, soldiers, and other Natives. It also could lead to deadly fights as Natives dropped their normally circumspect demeanors and gave vent to suppressed hostilities. Drunkenness could be a form of protest or a mask for it, as a Jesuit priest acknowledged when he observed how "[s]ome drunkards, or Indians who appear to be drunk, come and hurl stones at them when the missionaries notify the villages of prayers." The Mohawks in Montreal became so disorderly that the French governor agreed to let them return to their village. However, he added a French fort and garrison to "defend" Kahnawake and, obviously, keep an eye on its residents.[35]

The dilemma in French-Kahnawake relations was resolved by the development of a parallel war against the English. Unfortunately for the people of

Deerfield, it was more convenient for both the French and the Kahnawake Mohawks to attack them than to attack locations along the New York border, which risked conflict with the Iroquois League. The coming of the Nine Years' War to America in 1689 thus provided Kahnawake Mohawks the chance to maintain their alliance with the French and answer the demands of mourning war without attacking their kin. They were probably on the raiding parties that attacked Deerfield in 1693 and again in 1695. It was definitely a party of Kahnawake Mohawks that attacked Deerfield in July 1696 and carried off four captives.[36]

Attacking the English in New England was also better for business. By the end of the Nine Years' War, the burgeoning fur trade had supplanted war as the primary concern of the Iroquois at both ends of Lake Champlain. Once peace between the Iroquois League and the French was concluded in 1701, preserving it and the Albany trade became an overriding consideration for both the Iroquois and the French. When the War of the Spanish Succession began, French officials and the Iroquois took care to prevent it from disrupting the trade. Although technically the English in New York were as much his enemy as the English in New England, Governor Vaudreuil realized the importance of making an exception. Breaking off the Albany trade would not only endanger his relations with the people of Kahnawake and Iroquoia; it would also ruin Montreal merchants who were already suffering from the collapse of the Canadian fur trade. To avoid angering the Five Nations, he resolved against "carrying on any war which might make them unfriendly." New England, however, was "not the same situation." Warriors from Kahnawake and La Montange did not object to another war with New England. The French governor hoped that in addition to captives, such raids would provide a source of plunder that would be an alternative to English goods obtained by trading with New Yorkers. It also might make up for the current inability of French merchants to supply Natives with trade goods.[37]

From the French perspective, the economic and political rationale for attacking New England seemed most significant, but the people of Kahnawake also looked at such raids from another perspective. They still adhered to the customs of the mourning war, according to a local family tradition regarding the Deerfield raid, and this practice played an important role in bringing out warriors. In 1701, a smallpox epidemic ravaged the Saint Lawrence valley, including Kahnawake. The family story claims that at least some of the Mohawks went to Deerfield with the specific goal of obtaining captives to replace family members who had died, probably during the epidemic. The story illustrates the preservation of mourning war culture even in an ostensibly Christian village. Appropriately enough, the story begins with a woman. Her daughter died suddenly, leaving her "inconsolable." She was "so much borne down with [her grief], that some of her relations predicted that she would not survive long." "It was visible in her countenance that she was on the decline, she had lost the vivacity which was a peculiar trait in her character before she was bereft of her child." It would take a new child, seized by the woman's male relatives, to restore her happiness. She called on them to go. They went. And if the family tradition recounted above is accurate, one of these warriors was a young man named Paul, a relative of the bereaved woman.[38]

The exact number of Kahnawake Mohawks in the army at Chambly remains unknown. Most existing accounts of the raid probably exaggerate their presence and role. English accounts that refer to "Maquas" inflate their numbers by lumping together the Kahnawake Mohawks with the Iroquois of the Mountain and the Hurons of Lorette. Subsequent complaints by the spokesmen from Kahnawake indicate that they had gone out in relatively small raiding parties in 1703 and 1704, suggesting a contribution to the Deerfield raid of fewer than one hundred warriors, probably somewhere in the range of sixty to eighty.[39]

T HE sixty to eighty Abenakis who joined the raiding party had plenty of their own reasons for wanting to attack the English besides their alliance with the French. Only some of them were Christians. Most came from a village once known as Arsikantegouk but eventually called Odanak. It began three decades before the Jesuits set up a mission in the village. This mission's name, Saint Francis, eventually became notorious in New England, where the people of Odanak were known as the Saint Francis Indians. Most of the Natives at Odanak were already enemies of the English when they came to Canada. Thus, a shared enmity—directed first at the Iroquois League, then at the English—more than trade or religion formed the basis of these Abenakis' alliance with the French and moved them to join the raid on Deerfield.[40]

Abenaki is a broad term for peoples from many different villages who speak very similar, but still distinctive, languages and have a certain political affinity. The name is derived from the word *Wabanaki,* meaning people of the Dawnland: those who first greet the rising sun as it makes its way across North America. They lived in small bands in what is now northern New England, from Maine to Vermont, and migrated seasonally to hunt and fish. Linguistically, they were divided into two broad groups, eastern and western. The Eastern Abenakis lived in what is now Maine and spoke a different dialect from their western relatives, who occupied the rest of what is now northern New England. Members of the two groups tended to pursue their own independent policies. For example, many Western Abenakis—including the Sokokis—had been allied with the Iroquois League in the early seventeenth century. The Eastern Abenakis never were. The Abenakis did not form a confederacy as the Huron and Iroquois nations had, but by the mid-seventeenth they were regularly joining together against their mutual enemies, the Iroquois League and the English.[41]

The community at Odanak began in the 1660s as a Western Abenaki refuge from attacks by members of the Iroquois League. Sokokis arrived first, after the 1663 attack on their village that had sent some to seek refuge with the Pocumtucks. As the war with the Mohawks heated up, other Western Abenakis, such as the Pennacooks and non-Abenaki peoples such as the Pocumtucks, joined the Sokokis. Eventually members of twenty different groups settled at Odanak. However, speakers of Western Abenaki remained the core of Odanak's population. As at Kahnawake where Mohawk became the dominant language and ethnic identity of an ethnically diverse village, Western Abenaki became the dominant language and prevailing identity at Odanak.[42]

In the wake of King Philip's War Odanak became a refuge from English aggression. Hundreds of Connecticut valley Natives made their way north in 1676–1677, setting up villages outside of the French forts at Chambly and Sorel. After several years some returned south, to Cowass, Pennacook, and Schaghticoke. Others moved over to the village at Odanak. Though they lived in New France, the people of Odanak maintained contact with their relatives living at Schaghticoke and in northern New England. Odanak's population fluctuated again over the next century in response to political conditions along the New England frontier. When war began, Natives from across northern New England would take refuge in the village. With the restoration of peace, they would return to their homelands. Each time they returned, they found the English had claimed more of their lands.[43]

The move to Odanak was by no means a renunciation of their homelands in New England, or their ties to the English. For example, groups of former refugees from the Connecticut valley returned to the Deerfield area repeatedly in peace and war in the decades after King Philips War. The clearest sign of their connection to the English was the ability of many of these Abenakis to speak English in 1704. One of these English-speaking residents at Odanak was a woman named Ruth. At one point in her life, she had been a servant to the Reverend Gershom Bulkeley in Wethersfield, Connecticut. The Reverend John Williams had seen her when he visited Bulkeley's home and she had visited Williams's home in Deerfield. Like Ruth, a fair number of the people at Odanak had undoubtedly lived among the English as neighbors or, involuntarily, as servants. They knew the English, their religion, and their language and had reason to resent them. Several of the Abenakis from Odanak who joined the raid on Deerfield spoke English as well as Ruth did. For them, the raid on Deerfield was just one more battle in a contest with New Englanders that had started in 1675.[44]

Odanak's connection to the Deerfield raid was direct and personal. Just across the river from Trois-Rivières, home of Bouchers and Hertels, Odanak was settled on land granted to the Sokokis by Jean Crevier, the brother-in-law of both Pierre Boucher and Joseph-François Hertel. Boucher had originally sold some of the land involved to Crevier. Thus, members of the Crevier and Hertel families became seigneurs of the Abenakis. When the imperial wars against the English began in 1689, the Hertels helped the people of Odanak take revenge on the New Englanders who had driven them from their homes. Beginning with the 1690 attack on Salmon Falls, New Hampshire, residents of Odanak regularly participated in the Hertels' expeditions against New England. By the time the expedition against Deerfield was gathering in 1703, the warriors of Odanak and Hertel de Rouville's family had fought together for many years. The closeness of this relationship was captured in the Reverend Cotton Mather's unsympathetic but suggestive characterization of the party that attacked Salmon Falls as "being half one half the other, half Indianized French and half Frenchified Indians."[45]

Religion did not enter the close relationship between the Abenakis at Odanak and the Hertel family until the eve of the raid on Deerfield. In 1701, the Jesuits decided to relocate their mission of Saint-François-de-Sales from its site on the Chaudière River (figure 4). With the return of peace in 1701 many of the Eastern Abenakis who had frequented the mission during the 1680s and 1690s returned to their homes in Acadia or Maine. The Jesuits, therefore, took the few remaining, dedicated Christians and moved them to Odanak, a thriving village of several hundred non-Christian Western Abenakis. At the urging of the governor and the intendant, Marguerite Hertel and her son Joseph Crevier provided lands for a new mission and a fort at Odanak. According to the deed of gift, French officials judged "it fit for the service of the king and the benefit of the colony to establish the Abenaki and Socoki Indians with Jesuit missionaries on the lands and seigneury of Saint François to anchor religion among the said Indians, of which the majority are Christians." In return for this gift, the Creviers received a monopoly on trade with the Abenakis at the mission. Most Western Abenakis at Odanak did eventually embrace Catholicism. It strengthened their ties to the French and provided a new ideological dimension to the Abenakis' animosity toward the English, who some Odanak Abenakis now referred to as "hereticks." But the English noticed that the Abenakis were not as zealous as the Mohawks were.[46]

The outbreak of the War of the Spanish Succession made Odanak the Abenakis' main refuge in New France. Western and Eastern Abenakis joined their kin in the village. By 1709 there were hundreds of Abenakis in the neighborhood, too many to be easily incorporated into the community at Odanak. In 1705 a group of Eastern Abenakis from Ameskosanti built a second, smaller village several miles to the east on the seigneury of Becancourt. Here too a fort was

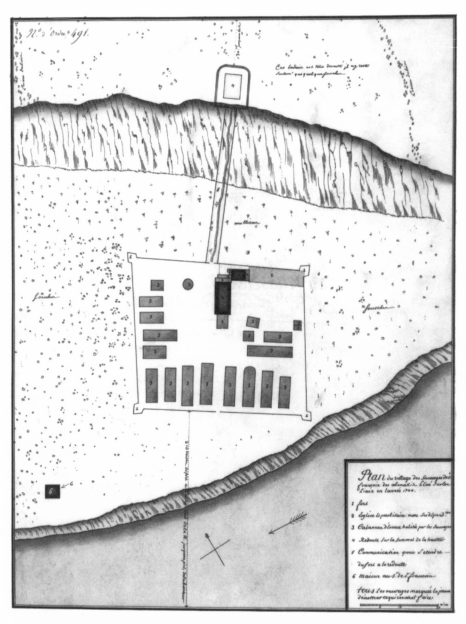

FIGURE 4. "Plan du village des Abénakis levé en l'année 1704" (Plan of the Abenakis' village, drawn in 1704), Levasseur de Néré. This plan shows the palisaded fort that surrounded the Abenaki village at Odanak. Its shape replicated that of European-style forts with bastions at its four corners. The plan shows (2) the Jesuit mission and (6) the home of Joseph Hertel de Saint François, the brother of Hertel de Rouville. The plan underscores the role played by Native villages in the defense of New France and the close ties between the Hertels and the Abenakis. The Reverend John Williams stopped at the home of Joseph Hertel when he was a prisoner. C.A.O.M. Aix-en-Provence (France) Amérique septentrionale 491 (p.f. 5b). Photograph courtesy of the National Archives of Canada, NMC000-4901.

built. The Jesuit priests at Saint Francis included them within their congregation. The two villages contained 250 warriors in 1709. In 1703 far fewer were at hand, but still enough to send 60 or 80 to join Jean-Baptiste Hertel de Rouville at Chambly.[47]

D uring the War of the Spanish Succession, the Native villages of New France formed an essential part of the colony's defenses. All, save Lorette, were located along the exposed southern flank of the colony. All, save Lorette, were fortified at the beginning of the war, making them "strongholds surrounded by stones." In every case except Kahnawake, the inhabitants had come to New France seeking sanctuary from enemies. New France embraced them as a bulwark against their common enemies, the Iroquois League and the English. During the 1680s and 1690s, these Natives had waged overlapping or parallel wars with the French against the Iroquois League and the English. The War of the Spanish Succession was a much simpler matter than the Nine Years' War had been. Now the only enemies were the English of New England. For the Abenakis, the conflict offered an opportunity to resume their on-going, overlapping war against the English. For the other Natives, raids against New England offered the prospect of captives and plunder. Raids on New England also provided a powerful affirmation of the mutual ties of alliance that bound the Native villagers to the French and each other. As the year 1703 drew to a close, around two hundred of them huddled around fires at Chambly and prepared to march south.[48]

CHAPTER 4

BETWEEN EMPIRES

N OT ALL of the Abenakis who attacked Deerfield came from Canada. Some came directly from Wôbanakik, which lay outside of the effective control of either European empire. This country stretched north from the mid-Connecticut valley to the river's headwaters, west to the Hudson River and east through Maine to the shores of the Atlantic. Within this region, Abenaki peoples waged a difficult struggle to preserve their independence in the years after King Philip's War. Unwilling to side entirely with either the French or the English, they had to negotiate their way among competing choices and various threats, reaching out and seizing opportunities when they saw them and withdrawing when threatened.

Among these Abenakis struggling to remain independent were members of the Pennacook nation. The name came from *penakok* (at the falling bank), a description of the site of their main village near what is today Concord, New Hampshire. As with other Abenakis, the name Pennacook did not refer to a unified tribe but to a collection of semi-autonomous bands that lived in and moved among several villages, most notably Pennacook, Pigwacket, and Cowass. Though they maintained these villages where they grew corn, they also ranged widely to various sites to hunt and fish. The English often referred to them as "Eastern Indians" and lumped them together with the Eastern Abenakis of Maine, but the Pennacooks (who spoke Western Abenaki) also had close ties with Native peoples in southern and western New England, such as the Sokokis and Pocumtucks.[1]

Their dwindling numbers and close proximity to the English limited the Pennacooks' ability to maneuver between the competing demands of the English and French empires. Every choice involving trade, religion, and diplomacy could be viewed as either pro-French or pro-English by community members, the two empires, and other Natives. Some leaders, such as Wanalancet, tried to remain friends with the English despite the increasing pressures of New England expansion. But English trading policies and their encroachment on Native lands turned other leaders, notably Kancamagus, into militant opponents of the English. For their part, the French usually exploited the tensions between the English and the Pennacooks to further their own interests. Despite the difficulties, there were leaders, such as Wattanummon, who worked in the later 1600s and early 1700s to preserve Wanalancet's policy of friendship with the English. In the end, his efforts failed, and this failure led him and other Pennacooks to join the raid on Deerfield.[2]

THE Pennacooks' location on the upper reaches of the Merrimack River proved originally to be a source of strength and protection from the ravages of English colonization. Wattanummon was probably not a Pennacook by birth but was drawn to them as a place of refuge. Evidence suggests that he was born at the mouth of the Merrimack, near what is today Newbury, Massachusetts, in the heart of the Pawtucket homeland. The seventeenth-century New England official and historian Daniel Gookin claimed the Pawtuckets originally stood at the head of several tribes, including the Pennacooks. But the terrible 1616–1617 epidemic that destroyed Native settlements along the Massachusetts coast greatly weakened the Pawtuckets. The inland Pennacooks, who do not seem to have been as severely affected, grew in power and influence as a result and soon overshadowed the Pawtuckets. By the 1630s, when English colonists started negotiating with Native peoples along the Merrimack River, they treated with Passaconaway of the Pennacooks. Passaconaway, and after him his son Wanalancet, pursued a policy of peace, trade, and friendship with the English. Wanalancet even went so far as to embrace, at least nominally, Protestant Christianity. Their leaders' policy gave the Pennacooks and those who joined them a measure of security during the 1640s and 1650s.[3]

The Pennacooks undoubtedly wanted peace and a trading alliance with the English because they, like so many other peoples of the Northeast, were then at war with the Five Nations of the Iroquois League. Hostilities between the Pennacooks and the Iroquois League began in the 1630s and escalated into several bloody campaigns during the 1660s, when Iroquois attacks forced various Native peoples in southern New England, among them the Sokokis and Pocumtucks, to abandon their villages and seek refuge elsewhere. Some found it along the Merrimack River with their Pennacook allies. Presumably Wattanummon was born during these difficult years, when his people, greatly diminished by disease, were fighting a protracted war against the Iroquois League and losing land to the English who were beginning to settle in the Merrimack River valley.[4]

The Pennacooks were far enough away from the English that they were able to stay out of the fighting when King Philip's War broke out in 1675. Rather than trust solely in diplomacy, Wanalancet, who had taken over leadership from his father, took his people north to Cowass (today Newbury, Vermont), well out of reach of the English. He knew the English distrusted the Pennacooks because many of King Philip's supporters had been allies of the Pennacooks in their recent war with the Iroquois League. While Wanalancet was away, the English, rather than resorting to diplomacy, sent a military expedition to secure the Pennacooks' submission. Finding no one to subdue, the English went away frustrated. The English became increasingly hostile after Wanalancet returned in 1676 and began accepting hundreds of refugees from the war.[5]

The Pennacooks, by giving shelter to their old allies, appeared to confirm English fears that the Pennacooks were scheming against them. War was still raging in nearby Maine and the English feared it might spread still farther. Desperate, they made a dishonorable pre-emptive strike that would damage their reputation among Pennacooks for decades to come. In September 1676, Major Richard Waldron called Natives to a meeting at Dover, New Hampshire, claiming that he wanted to enlist them in the English war against the Eastern Abenakis. Some 350 to 400 Pennacooks and their neighbors responded. In reality, Waldron had orders to seize all these Natives. Realizing that he could not seize several hundred Indians by force, Waldron had resorted to trickery. He surrounded the unsuspecting Natives and disarmed them. He separated out all of the Nipmuck and other "strange Indians" that he suspected of having fought in King Philip's War and sent them to Boston under guard. These captives were sold into slavery in New England or the West Indies. The remaining Pennacooks, including Wanalancet, were allowed to return to their homes, seething with anger and shame. Memories of the Dover incident were still festering as late as 1704 and would be recalled by some to justify the attack on Deerfield.[6]

More immediately, the Dover incident inaugurated a period of great instability and change for the Pennacooks. Feeling unsafe in their country, many dispersed to a series of villages, new and old, across Wôbanakik and beyond. The population of the Pennacook homeland fell from around twelve hundred at the outbreak of King Philip's War in 1675 to about five hundred by the later 1680s. During the 1670s and 1680s the Pennacooks traveled back and forth in search of comfort and security so frequently that one French observer categorized them as an "erratic Nation." Some went to the refugee village at Schaghticoke, New York. Others resettled along the Androscoggin River in Maine. Some headed north to Cowass or Canada. Pigwacket in southern Maine emerged in this period as a prominent village as some of the Pennacooks moved east. Others moved further east to Amesokanti, where a diverse band of refugees, exiles, and others formed a new, multiethnic community.[7]

Wanalancet found it increasingly difficult to maintain his alliance with the English. In 1677 a raiding party of dissident Pennacooks forced Wanalancet and his followers to move north to Canada for a few years. Because of Wattanummon's close ties to Wanalancet, it is likely that he went on this involuntary journey to Canada. When peace returned to the region in the 1680s, Pennacooks began returning to their homeland. Wattanummon was again living near what is today Newbury, Massachusetts, where he began to take the stage as an important supporter of Wanalancet. But their policy was an increasingly beleaguered one. More English moved into the Pennacooks' homeland along the Merrimack River. A very large percentage of their traditional land base passed into the hands of colonists between 1675 and 1690. Meanwhile, operating from their missions in Canada and Acadia, French Jesuits began to win converts to the Catholic faith. The English made little effort to encourage the nominal Protestantism of Wanalancet and his followers. Losing land, people, and religion, the elderly Wanalancet found himself "wronged by the whites; distrusted by the Indians."[8]

D URING the 1680s, Wanalancet's leadership was challenged by a group of younger men at Pigwacket led by his nephew, Kancamagus. A noted war captain, Kancamagus began to question Wanalancet's policy of friendship toward the English and developed a policy of militant resistance. His more aggressive stance attracted followers by feeding off of the instability and fluidity of Native society in northern New England at the time. Pigwacket became a haven for discontented Pennacooks and Native refugees from southern New England. Still confronting the threat of raids by Mohawks of the Iroquois League, Kancamagus had no time for the niceties of Wanalancet's peace policy. In negotiating with the English he did not hesitate to use threats, knowing he could always withdraw his people to safety in the interior. English authorities, accustomed to dealing with the more accommodating Wanalancet, who usually remained within their reach, became concerned. In 1685 they signed a new treaty of "lasting peace, friendship and kindness" with the Pennacooks that promised them protection from the Mohawks and established procedures for settling disputes. Still, the mutual suspicions of both parties made their way into the treaty, which also provided that "in case the said Indians shall remove with their wives and children, without such fair and timely notice given to the English, that then it shall be taken, *pro confesso,* that the Indians do intend and design war with the English, and do hereby declare that the peace is broke." Kancamagus commanded respect, but he also heightened English fears.[9]

This treaty of peace lasted only three years, until the Second Anglo-Abenaki War broke out in 1688. The English ignored the treaty's provisions for mediating disputes, interfered with fish runs on the Saco River, and damaged Native crops with their cattle. When they ignored Abenaki efforts to obtain redress, Abenakis responded by killing English cattle. The English took Native hostages, and Pennacooks responded by taking English prisoners. Native efforts to negotiate were rebuffed by the English, who had concluded that the Indians "[i]ntend a warr with us." This assessment became a self-fulfilling prophecy. The Second

Anglo-Abenaki War soon overlapped with and merged into the Nine Years' War, but it is important to note that the war between the English and the Abenakis began a year before the French entered the conflict.[10]

The Pennacooks, because of their still autonomous position just beyond the frontier of English settlement, provided the social glue and political leadership for those Natives bent on resistance and revenge. The composition of the first raiding party to attack the English in July 1688 makes clear their role and underscores the connections between conflicts along the eastern and western frontiers of New England. Eleven Natives came down from Canada and killed several English colonists and "friend Indians" who lived in the Connecticut valley of Massachusetts. On the way they met a Schaghticoke, who refused to join them and instead identified these "North Indians" to the English. The leader was Wampolack, a Pennacook. Five of the warriors were Pennacooks, including Walamaqueet who had "lived formerly in the Halfe Moon," a Schaghticoke village just north of Albany. One was a "Nimeneat from Penacook." Two were originally from Quaboag, which was in "Nipmuck Country." One was a "Nassawach." Another was from "Pakantecooke," meaning Pocumtuck. The remaining Native was a Wappinger, whose original home would have been along the lower Hudson River. Though the attack had come from Canada, the attackers' motivations had their origins in confrontations along the frontiers of Maine and western Massachusetts. All of these individuals appear to have had dealings with the English in the Connecticut valley and elsewhere, for an English resident recognized several of them. And most probably hated the English for driving them from their homelands.[11]

Along the eastern frontier, fighting began later in the summer of 1688 with skirmishes along the Saco River. Here the Second Anglo-Abenaki War offered Pennacooks and other Abenakis an opportunity to settle old scores. In June 1689, Pennacooks and Eastern Abenakis met and planned an attack on Dover, New Hampshire. Their primary target was not the town but its leading resident, Richard Waldron. They wanted revenge on the man who had betrayed them in 1676 and then cheated them in trade for years after. They were joined by some of the Natives Waldron had kidnapped but who had subsequently managed to escape from servitude. On June 27, Pennacooks and Eastern Abenakis attacked Dover, killed twenty-three colonists, captured twenty-nine, and destroyed half a dozen houses. Among the dead was Waldron, tortured to death by Natives taking revenge for his earlier treachery and abusive trade practices. Some of the Dover captives were carried to Canada, the second batch of New England captives to make that trip after the 1677 Deerfield captives.[12]

At first Wattanummon did not join the war against the English but instead attempted to insert himself into the colonists' internal politics. In April 1689, after hearing rumors of the successful invasion of England by William of Orange and his replacement of James II as king, residents of Massachusetts had deposed their royal governor, Sir Edmund Andros, dismantled the Dominion of New England set up by James II, and re-established their original colonial government. Technically this was an act of rebellion. To justify their actions, the new leaders of Massachusetts developed a lengthy indictment of Andros. Among the charges lodged against him was the claim that he encouraged Indians to make war on the English, and Wattanummon was among the Natives who stepped forward to help the colonists make their case. "Watanum & David (Two Indians)" swore that Andros "gave the Mohocks two bushells of wompum Peague, and three cart loads of goods to Ingage them to fight against the English." In further testimony, "Waterman and David" emphasized that the Mohawks knew that "the English were their good Friends, and never wronged them, but the Macquas took the pay on the account of the Macquas helping the English to fight their Enemies the last war," which was King Philip's War.[13]

For Wattanummon, his testimony provided an opportunity to carry on the Pennacooks' parallel war against the Mohawks of the Iroquois League who were allied with the English of New York. By leveling charges against Andros and the Mohawks, Wattanummon blackened the reputation of the former New York governor who had encouraged the Mohawks to attack New England Natives during King Philip's War. These raids had continued into the 1680s because English authorities in New England proved unable or unwilling to stop them. It is also possible that the accusation was designed to divert English suspicions from the Pennacooks and other Abenakis who some colonists believed had entered into an anti-Protestant coalition with the French and Governor Andros, servant of the Catholic King James II. In making these charges, which were false, Wattanummon ran the risk of inciting renewed raids by the Mohawks and angering those Pennacooks who had concluded that an alliance with the French offered the best defense against attacks by the Iroquois League and English aggression.

In the short run, Wattanummon's testimony only bred suspicion and did little to further Wanalancet's peace policy and the security of their followers. The first to react negatively were Natives allied with the French. Sometime in 1689 or 1690, Wattanummon and Wanalancet were, once again, taken to Canada by force, and they resided for a while near Montreal. Wattanummon claimed that he had been held prisoner, first by Eastern Indians and then by French Indians. By March 1692, Wanalancet and Wattanummon had returned to meet with English officials in Dunstable, who wondered about the reasons for their stay in Canada. Wanalancet and Wattanummon, who was now referred to as one of Wanalancet's "chief captains," proclaimed their continuing friendship with the English colonists and promised to secure "any of the Enemy Indians that would come among them." Despite these protestations, the English imprisoned Wanalancet in Cambridge, then questioned him in Boston. Finally, in recognition of Wanalancet's many years of friendship, the English released the aging man, now in his eighties, and allowed him to live out the remainder of his life in Dunstable, where he died in 1697 under the care and supervision of Jonathan Tyng, a local trader, militia officer, and frontier diplomat.[14]

Despite French pressure to fight on, the negotiations Wattanummon and Wanalancet had begun continued with various groups of Eastern Abenakis and Pennacooks. Their resistance to the English did not lead them to embrace the French empire, no matter what the English feared. The nature of their attacks indicates that the Pennacooks' overlapping war with the English was often limited to certain people in certain places, though as at Dover, other colonists did die in such raids. As far as most Pennacooks were concerned, once justice had been restored, there was no need to prolong the war. Throughout the Nine Years' War, Pennacooks kept trying to make peace with the English when the French wanted them to fight. Kancamagus signed a treaty at Sagadahoc in the year after the Dover raid and other Pennacooks and Eastern Abenakis signed a treaty at Fort Pemaquid in August 1693. Still, local fears and conflicts, inflamed by the on-going imperial war, broke out into open hostilities again in spring 1694. In July Eastern Abenakis and Pennacooks with French support attacked Oyster River, New Hampshire, killing and capturing eighty to ninety English colonists. During the next year, however, diseases ravaged the Abenakis and the intensity of the fighting gradually diminished. By the end of 1695 a de facto truce prevailed.[15]

Unfortunately, the English had a hard time separating their overlapping wars against the French and the Abenakis, and this inability undermined the efforts of men like Wattanummon to keep the peace. A Massachusetts officer, Pascoe Chubb of Andover, violated the de facto truce so horribly that even Wattanummon entered the war. When some Eastern Abenaki leaders arrived at Pemaquid, Maine, under a flag of truce in February 1696, Chubb, the commander at Pemaquid, fell upon the Abenakis with his soldiers, killing two sachems and taking others prisoner. His deed brought many Abenakis back into the war. Joining with the French, they captured the fort at Pemaquid. Though the Abenakis were eager to get at the English, the French intervened and let the English prisoners return home. It was the Abenakis' frustrated desire for revenge on Chubb that brought Wattanummon into the war. He knew Chubb's hometown of Andover because he was friends with Colonel Dudley Bradstreet, who lived there. Wattanummon engaged in a little parallel war of his own when he guided a war party to Chubb's home in February 1698. The attackers killed Chubb, his wife, and three other colonists. But Wattanummon went out of his way to save Bradstreet and his family. Local tradition claims that Wattanummon "undertook to conduct the Indians to [Bradstreet's] house upon these conditions, that they should neither kill nor captivate any of this family." The house was plundered but the family was spared.[16]

The Second Anglo-Abenaki War officially ended early in 1699, more than a year after the signing of the Treaty of Ryswick, which had ended the Nine Years' War. Ravaged by disease, suffering from famine, and abandoned by the French, the Eastern Abenakis and those Pennacooks who had fought beside them waited more than a year to make their own peace with the English. Neither treaty really settled the issues that had led to ten years of war. In fact, some provisions of the two treaties actually provided new sources of conflict. The European treaty failed to establish a boundary between the competing claims of the French colony of Acadia and the English province of Maine. At Pemaquid, the Eastern Abenakis ostensibly acknowledged themselves to be under English sovereignty and thus subjects of the English crown. Their so-called submission characterized their actions during the war as an internal rebellion attributable to "the ill counsel and instigation of the French": a misleading explanation of the conflict's causes that reflected English suspicions and misapprehensions. There was no recognition of the role that English violations of Abenaki rights had played in starting the war. Abenaki grievances concerning land rights and trade remained, and, despite their "submission," they continued to consider themselves independent peoples free to deal with the English or the French as they saw fit.

J UST as peace had periodically interrupted the last war, war now threatened to put an end to the new peace. The years between the end of the Second Anglo-Abenaki War and the start of the War of the Spanish Succession involved the Pennacooks and other Abenakis in a constant series of negotiations with the English and French as each empire increasingly tried to bend these people to its will. On the ground, English colonists remained apprehensive and distrustful of Abenaki actions. Local tensions and conflicts added to imperial pressures to make life very difficult for men like Wattanummon, who wanted to keep the peace.

The Pennacooks tried to strengthen their position on the English borderlands by joining in the great peace then being made between the French, their Native allies, and the Iroquois League. During the winter of 1699–1700, a large number of people gathered at Lake Winnipesaukee in the Pennacook homeland. Natives from southern New England traveled north to meet with Mohawks and other Natives from New France. One Pennacook boasted to the English "that he had the longest bow ever was in New England: it reached from Penobscot to the Mohawks' Country, meaning that all the Indians were engaged in the design." A defensive alliance was being made. If any of the parties to this agreement were attacked, all would join together in attacking the common enemy. These talks must have been a part of the negotiations leading to the Montreal Treaty or the Great Peace of 1701. The English saw things differently. They worried that an anti-English conspiracy hatched by Natives and promoted by the French was brewing along the frontier. To reassure the English, Captain Tom, an Eastern Abenaki leader from Norridgewock, assured them that the Eastern Abenakis would not join with the Pennacooks who "were but a few and could do nothing [and] were (as he expressed himself) no more than all one a Papoos or Child."[17]

Ideally, most Abenakis wanted peace with all parties, a difficult task involving the maintenance of religious ties with the French, trade with the English, harmony with the Iroquois League, and contacts with kin living all across the borderlands. Knowing the English were concerned by the gathering at Winnipesaukee, Wattanummon and another Pennacook leader informed the English that they had no involvement in it and intended to remain friends of the English. As part of this friendship the two men requested freedom to travel, trade, and lodge among the colonists, agreeing to obey the laws of Massachusetts in their business with the colonists. Massachusetts authorities received their petition but ignored their request to reform trade practices. Instead, when they met on June 3, 1701, with other Abenaki representatives they attempted to set up an exclusive trade agreement to provide the Abenakis with "powder, lead, Armes and other things you may need at such prices as the French (who cheat you) cannot do." They also offered the services of an armorer who would repair Abenaki guns for free. In return, they asked the Abenakis to block the trails to Canada. The Abenakis refused, claiming that by doing so "many of our Brethren would be hindered from coming over to us." They pointed out that "many amongst us are not to be deprived of the liberty of going whither they please." In something of a departure, the English then offered to provide Protestant missionaries to replace the French Jesuits. Unlike the French, the English had done very little to promote missionary activity among the Abenakis. Taken aback, the Eastern Abenaki spokesmen responded that "being instructed by the French we have promised to be true to God in our Religion, and it is this we profess to stand by." Though they accomplished little more than reaffirming their peaceful intentions, the two parties raised two pillars of stones, called the Two Brothers, to remember the conference.[18]

The outbreak of war between the English and the French in the spring of 1702 brought a serious new challenge to the peace. Abenakis entered into negotiations on all their frontiers in a desperate effort to sit out the war that was about to encompass them. Shortly after arriving in New England with the news of the war, Massachusetts governor Joseph Dudley hurried to Sagadahoc in July to meet with representatives of the Eastern Abenakis. They proclaimed their intention to remain neutral in the conflict between the French and the English, affirming, "We will only stand still, and see and will be friends." About a month after this meeting, Eastern Abenakis set out for Canada. There they met with the French governor and reassured him of their loyalty to the French. The French governor encouraged them to attack the English and gave them some muskets and ammunition. But the Abenaki delegation made it clear that they did not intend to begin a war to defend French interests. At roughly the same time, two Pennacooks were meeting with New York officials and agreed to consider a move to Schaghticoke, where as allies of the Iroquois League they would be protected by the League's treaty of neutrality with the French. Earlier the governor of New France had urged the Pennacooks to move to Canada or settle among the Eastern Abenakis in Maine, making it clear that they "must not by any means" remain at Pennacook. Some Pennacooks did move to Schaghticoke and effectively removed themselves from the front line of the impending war between the English and the French.[19]

The English of New England wanted the assistance of Pennacooks in preventing future raids, but they did not want a proper alliance. They offered the Pennacooks no protection while calling upon them to perform actions that were sure to anger the French and their Native allies, not to mention many of their own people. In mid-June 1702 Governor Dudley and his council invited Wattanummon and his cousin George Tohanto to meet with them. When the two sachems met with the English in October 1702, the English attempted to establish a line beyond which Pennacooks would not pass while hunting. They tried to do it again in March 1703. Such a boundary was allegedly a precaution to prevent Pennacooks from being killed by colonists. The implication was that any Abenaki beyond the line might be regarded as hostile and shot on sight. Dudley was aware that the English "can't distinguish you from French Indians now there is a war" and feared the consequences of mistakes arising from the misidentification of Natives inclined to be friendly or at least remain neutral. At the same time, Governor Dudley asked Wattanummon to warn the English of any French and Indians heading toward the New England frontier.[20]

The Pennacooks' options were narrowing. It was unlikely that any of the combatants in the coming war, English, French, or Native, would allow them to remain neutral. Most spent the months of 1702–1703 in a vain quest for a safe place to wait out the coming war. Denied refuge among the English, Pennacooks retreated northward, beginning a series of seemingly erratic movements as they reverted to their time-tested strategy of staying away from trouble. George Tohanto was not at the second meeting with Massachusetts officials in March 1703, having already moved north to Canada to be with the French, who did not threaten to kill him as the English did. The next month Wattanummon and his people also moved north to a place near Quebec called Paquasset, where they resided with Native allies of the French. It is quite possible that Wattanummon did not find the situation in Canada to his liking. By May he was back at Pennacook, much to the relief of the English, who regarded such sudden departures as preludes to hostilities. In June he may have moved on to Pigwacket, where his sister lived.[21]

Local incidents of violence on the Maine frontier pushed the region closer to war in the spring of 1703. In May a group of Natives and French killed an Englishman cutting spars along the coast. In early June some Englishmen killed a Penobscot relative of Jean-Vincent d'Abbadie, Baron de Saint-Castin, a French nobleman and officer who had married a Penobscot. The Penobscots responded by invoking their new alliance with the Native communities in Canada. They sent a messenger to Canada to inform the "Macquas [the Iroquois and Hurons] and Indians [Algonquians and Abenakis living in Canada] that the English had begun a war." They also sought support from the Pennacooks.[22]

Governor Dudley knew that the killing of Saint-Castin's relative was a serious matter and tried to resolve it immediately. For decades Saint-Castin had been a pivotal figure in securing cooperation between the French and Eastern Abenakis. Dudley rightly feared that the killing could mean war. He invited representatives of the Abenakis to meet with him at Casco, Maine. On June 20, a gathering of 250 Penobscots, Androscoggins, Kennebecs, and Pennacooks met with Dudley and other English representatives. Wattanummon attended as a sachem from Pigwacket, though he was late in arriving and may have been a reluctant participant. On the surface, the meeting appeared to go well. The Abenakis claimed that they "aimed at nothing more than Peace." Dudley may have wanted their active assistance against the French but had to settle for promises that they would remain "Neuters" in a war between the English and the French. The Natives gave Dudley a belt of wampum. Plans were also concluded to establish several trading houses with stated prices for commodities, and, once again, there was the promise of an armorer to be supplied and paid for by Massachusetts. Participants added new stones to the Two Brothers.[23]

Despite their reassuring words, English and Abenakis remained deeply suspicious of one another. As the Casco meeting concluded, both sides fired ceremonial volleys. The English fired first at the urging of the Abenakis, who then discharged muskets that appeared to be loaded with bullets. The English saw this as perfidy; those Natives who remembered Waldron's treachery at Dover undoubtedly regarded their actions as prudent. The eighteenth-century New England historian Samuel Penhallow, who was at the conference, accused "Watanummon (the Pigwacket sachem)" of delaying the negotiations in the hope of detaining the English at Casco until a force of French and Indians then on its way arrived. The reinforced Abenakis would have been able to "seize the Governour, Council and Gentlemen and then . . . sacrifice the Inhabitants at pleasure." This would have been a powerful coup, but the English supposedly left just a few days too soon. If such had indeed been the plan, it would have paralleled Waldron's deceitful actions in 1676, repaying his treachery in kind. It is doubtful that such a plan ever existed and Wattanummon would have been an unlikely mastermind for such a scheme. None of the contemporary English reports of the meeting refers to this plot. Nevertheless, the suspicions on both sides were real and deep-seated.[24]

The evidence strongly suggests that the Pennacooks and the Eastern Abenakis wanted peace in the spring of 1703. Many Abenakis still suffered from the effects of the Second Anglo-Abenaki War. They had no desire to initiate another round of fighting. They also remained dependent on the English for critical trade goods, such as blankets, cloth, kettles, hatchets, shot, powder, and even corn. This dependence on trade with the English went deeper than a desire for European trade goods. To a degree this relationship was rooted in a precolonial trade with southern New England Natives who had supplied the Abenakis with corn. The English fell heir to this corn trade, and it along with cheaper prices gave them an undeniable edge in competition with the French.[25]

To assuage English fears about their loyalty, Abenakis kept them informed of French actions. Not long after the meeting at Casco, Captain Bomaseen, an Eastern Abenaki war leader who had close ties to the Pennacooks, warned English officials of the presence of French priests who, the Natives claimed, were working to undermine the peace between the English and the Abenakis. In early July, Bomaseen and an Abenaki sachem, informed the English of the presence of a large French vessel at Mount Desert Island. Later in July, Wattanummon's sister warned the English of the French and Indian army at Chambly and its intention to send raiding parties against settlements in Maine, the Merrimack valley, and the Connecticut valley. Early in August others warned English officials of an approaching force of over two hundred Natives and thirty French that had set out from Quebec. Clearly, in the weeks after the Casco conference, there were many Pennacooks and Eastern Abenakis who wanted to maintain peaceful relations with the English.[26]

T HE French had to work hard and treacherously to bring the Eastern Abenakis and Pennacooks into the War of the Spanish Succession on their side. They knew the Abenakis had little incentive to join their cause. Economically, there were the problems created by the economic crisis in New France and the Abenakis' dependence on English trade. The collapse of the beaver trade in Canada had deprived Eastern Abenakis of a market for their furs and led them to approach the English. Even if the French had been willing to accept the Abenakis' furs, they had little to give the Abenakis in return because English attacks on French shipping had reduced the available supply of trade goods. Given this situation, the governor of Acadia, Jacques-François Monbeton de Brouillan, feared that the Abenakis were not disposed "to make war on the English and they seem to intend remaining neutral because the French cannot supply them with their needs and no longer seek their peltries which are their sole resources."[27]

Religion also provided the French with only limited leverage. A shared Catholic faith did bind some of the Eastern Abenakis and Pennacooks to the French to a certain degree. Because of ingrained fears of "popish conspiracies," the English believed that the Jesuit missionaries living among the Eastern Indians were French agents bent on inciting war with the New England colonists. But such fears appear to have been exaggerated. The Jesuits recognized the Natives' dependence on trade with the English and apparently did relatively little during 1702 and 1703 to push them into the war. Some French officials believed that the Jesuits actually encouraged Eastern Abenakis to remain neutral, an assessment that was probably correct. At the same time, the degree to which Pennacooks and Eastern Abenakis had embraced Catholicism should not be exaggerated. A youthful English colonist who spent time with the Pennacooks concluded that the "Eastern Indians were not [as] zealous as the Maquas [the Mohawks] were." And there were still many who, like Wattanummon, would have nothing to do with the priests and their missions.[28]

French officials ultimately had to resort to intrigue and the threat of force to pull the Eastern Abenakis and Pennacooks into the war. Governor de Brouillan of Acadia first tried intrigue. He sent two Frenchmen disguised as Natives to the Casco conference on a mission to assassinate Governor Dudley. De Brouillan calculated that killing the Massachusetts governor at a peace conference would inevitably lead to war between the English and the Eastern Indians, but his agents failed to carry out their mission, possibly because they lost heart or possibly because they feared for their own safety. Subsequently, the English captured one of the would-be assassins, who informed the Massachusetts governor of the plot and begged forgiveness. De Brouillan then tried forgery. He produced and had translated into English a letter purportedly from Queen Anne, wherein the English queen endorsed Dudley's "designs to ensnare and deceitfully seize on the Indians." Specifically, the letter instructed the Massachusetts governor to give the assembled Abenakis "Wine and Licquors to make them all Drunk and then Cut their throats." He entrusted the letter to an Acadian fur trader, who conveyed it to the Penobscots. Though a forgery, the letter did play upon real fears based on past experiences with Waldron in 1676 and Chubb in 1696. As Kenneth Morrison has concluded, "reminding the Abenaki of English transgressions . . .

could move them as presents could not." Some Abenakis apparently doubted the letter's authenticity, but others were enraged by it. To succeed, the forgery had only to draw some Pennacooks and Eastern Abenakis into the war. Once the killing started, English reprisals could be counted on to expand the conflict and involve the rest.[29]

In the end the less subtle Governor Vaudreuil in Quebec successfully used the threat of force to strong-arm the Abenakis into war. He seized upon the Penobscots' appeal to their Canadian allies to help avenge the killing of Saint-Castin's relative as a chance to activate the defensive alliance. Twenty Candians, most if not all of them officers or cadets in the *troupes,* accompanied two hundred Natives to Maine. The force included Jean-Baptiste Hertel de Rouville and several Mohawks from the villages around Montreal, as well as Odanak Abenakis—virtually the same combination of men that would soon attack Deerfield. Vaudreuil hoped that this expedition would draw the "Abenakis" into the war with the English to ensure that they remained "irreconcilable enemies." Like other French officials, he assumed that if the Abenakis were not enemies of the English they would be their friends and therefore a threat to the French. Like the English, he did not really believe neutrality was possible. When the allied army arrived, "several of the Eastern Indians told them of the peace made with the English [at Casco]" and of "the satisfaction given them from the English for that murder." The Mohawks from Canada replied that "it was now too late." They had been "sent for and were now come, and would fall on them [the Eastern Abenakis] if without their consent they made a peace with the English." As a French priest later reported, the Natives "being enraged by [de Brouillan's forged] letter, and being forced, as it were . . . began the present war."[30]

French pressure thus played on the suspicions and anxieties of the Eastern Abenakis and Pennacooks to create a third Anglo-Abenaki war within the imperial War of the Spanish Succession. For many, this awkward moment may have seemed a welcome opportunity to rid their country of troublesome English settlers. At least two-thirds of them joined with their allies from Canada. A combined force of over 500 men divided into several raiding parties. One was led by Captain Tom, who had earlier proclaimed his friendship for the English and disparaged the Pennacooks as children. Another was led by Nescambiouit, a Pennacook who had fought beside the French, for his own reasons, during much of the Second Anglo-Abenaki War. The whereabouts at this time of less militant leaders, such as Wattanummon, are not known. It is likely that they, along with other Pennacooks and Eastern Abenakis, hesitated to involve themselves in a war between the French and the English. But only some of their kinsmen had to start a fight that would inevitably draw the others in. On August 10, 1703, raiding parties simultaneously attacked settlements at Wells, Cape Porpoise, Winter

Harbor, Spurwink, Scarborough, Purpooduck, and Casco. The attackers killed or captured somewhere between 130 and 170 English colonists. Ambushes and skirmishes, some involving over 100 Natives, continued into October.[31]

The English counterattacked Eastern Abenaki and Pennacook villages almost immediately. On August 18 Governor Dudley declared all of the Pennacooks and Eastern Abenakis to be in a state of rebellion. He called them rebels because the English regarded these Natives as subjects of Queen Anne who had made "soleme promises and stipulations from time to time repeated & renewed, of a steady adherence to her Majesties interests." The governor commanded all her "Majesties good Subjects . . . to do and execute all Acts of Hostility upon them." To encourage local militiamen to go out on punitive expeditions, the Massachusetts legislature passed a law in early September offering a bounty of £20 for every Indian scalp taken. This was one of the first scalp bounties offered by an English colony. The colonies of New Hampshire and Massachusetts (which included Maine) were put on a war footing. By September, 1,100 militiamen had been mobilized. In late September Colonel John March led a force of 360 men to Pigwacket, which the English regarded as "one of their principal Head-quarters." These raiders returned without discovering any Natives. March returned with a second expedition in late October and killed and scalped 6 and took 5 prisoner.[32]

T HE "barbarous" and "cruel" raids by the English in early fall 1703 pulled Wattanummon and the remaining Pennacooks into the war. Among those killed by Colonel March's second expedition—virtually all women and children—were people Wattanummon must have known and was probably related to. Duty called on him to take revenge. In the aftermath of these raids, a group of "Abenakis de Koessek" approached Governor Vaudreuil and asked for French assistance to attack the English. These "Abenakis de Koessek" were Pennacooks and quite likely included Wattanummon, who was living at Cowassuck or Cowass during the winter of 1703–1704. For Pennacooks living at Cowass, Deerfield was the closest English settlement and thus a target of opportunity. Once again, as he had at Andover in February 1698, Wattanummon found himself fighting with the French against the English. His effort to live in peace in his homeland between the two empires had failed.[33]

PART II

THE RAID

CHAPTER 5

WARNINGS

NEws of military preparations in New France and in Native communities started reaching New England in the late spring of 1703. English officials took the reports seriously, as did the residents of Deerfield. Given its exposed location, Deerfield was an obvious target. It had been attacked seven times in the last war. The Reverend John Williams became convinced "that the Town would in a little time be destroyed." But instead of raiders, Deerfield received only warnings and peaceful visitors throughout the summer and fall of 1703. For months reports continued to arrive, while French and Indian raiders did not. Soon the very frequency of reports and alarms lulled residents of the village into a fatal complacency and the warnings of an attack lost currency. Many soon "made light of the intelligence."[1]

The people of Deerfield had reasons not to worry. They knew that not everyone across the frontier was hostile to them. The warnings usually came from Natives who wanted to maintain the peace with the English. Even during wartime the frontier did not present an impenetrable barrier to individuals who wanted to cross it, and the continuing arrival of warnings underscored its porous nature. League Mohawks, who feared that their trade would be disrupted and perhaps their people forced to fight their kinsmen living near Montreal, carried some reports. Other warnings came from Pennacooks, such as Wattanummon and his sister, who until late in 1703 had worked to avoid a conflict. Three Frenchmen and at least one "Indian" seeking to establish peaceful trading relations arrived in Deerfield and stayed. On the eve of the attack, two of them even married Deerfield women. As 1704 approached, the war seemed far away on the frontiers of Maine and New Hampshire.

An initial warning had been relayed in late May 1703 by Edward Hyde, Viscount Cornbury, the governor of New York. A former army officer and a staunch imperialist, Lord Cornbury had arrived the year before and immediately took steps to shore up his colony's defenses and strengthen its ties with the powerful Five Nations of the Iroquois League. To monitor military activity in New France, he used Mohawks from Kahnawake. During the spring of 1703, spies in Cornbury's employ learned that a party of French and Indians had gathered near Montreal. The spies carried news of the gathering to Albany, where it was forwarded to Governor Cornbury in New York City, who then passed it on to Massachusetts governor Joseph Dudley. The report claimed that a party of one hundred French and Indians "may be expected every day at Derefd [Deerfield] and upon that river." By the time this intelligence reached Boston around May 25, it was probably a month old.[2]

Governor Dudley reacted with a characteristic burst of energy that was unlike anything Deerfield had witnessed during the Nine Years' War. He had been at his post for less than a year but, like Cornbury, had spent much of his time preparing his colony for the new war. Upon learning of the possible threat to Deerfield, he ordered militia officers in western Massachusetts to be "in readiness to scout and range for a discovery." Twenty militiamen from neighboring towns in western Massachusetts were sent to Deerfield as a garrison. Dudley also wrote to the governor of Connecticut to pass along the report. Dudley had a royal commission to take command of military forces in all of the New England colonies in time of war or danger, but he diplomatically treated the leader of the neighboring colony as an equal, not a subordinate. He requested; he did not order. However, he did expect that Connecticut militiamen would help defend the western Massachusetts towns that covered their northern frontier. Governor Dudley then prepared to leave for the critical meeting at Casco, Maine, with the Pennacooks and Eastern Abenakis, whose friendship he hoped to preserve.[3]

Governor Fitz-John Winthrop of Connecticut reacted more cautiously. He was skeptical. Such a raid seemed to be "a bold attempt" at a time he considered to be early in the war. Besides, he thought, Deerfield was "so remote & hazardous" from "Quebeek." This misapprehension that French raiders would have come from Quebec, some 400 miles away, not Montreal, only about 280 miles away, gave some of the English a false sense of security. The English were also unaware that they now faced a new French governor, Philippe de Rigaud de Vaudreuil, who would not hesitate to make "a bold attempt" early in the war. Still, Winthrop did recognize that "tis best to have an eye upon them" and approved Dudley's measures. He promised to keep in readiness a party of fifty mounted militiamen to be sent north at any sign of trouble.[4]

Two months later Pennacooks brought Massachusetts authorities more detailed information. On July 28 two Native men and a woman—Wattanummon's sister—had come to the home of Lieutenant Colonel Jonathan Tyng in Dunstable with an alarming report. They related that two Pennacooks had "come lately from Chamlet [Chambly] near MontReal where they saw 150 Indians armed, gathered together and joined with some few French." This force intended to divide into three companies, "one for the Eastward [i.e., Maine], another for

[the] Merrimack [River] and the third for [the] Connecticut River, to insult the English settlements." Tyng rushed to Boston with the news.[5]

Governor Dudley realized the danger of this new imperial war and did his best to protect his frontiers by ensuring cooperation between military commanders at all levels. He immediately wrote again to Governor Winthrop in Connecticut and to Colonel Samuel Partridge, who had recently assumed command of the militia in western Massachusetts. The fifty-eight-year-old Partridge had fought in King Philip's War and overseen the region's defenses during the Nine Years' War. He lived in Hatfield, twelve miles south of Deerfield. Though experienced, he was not really prepared for the threat that he now faced. In western Massachusetts the Nine Years' War had been what the English colonists called a skulking kind of war: relatively small parties of French allies made raids along the frontier. They killed an unfortunate individual here and there or captured an unwary farmer in his fields but did not destroy whole villages. The targets had been opportunistic. If the English resisted, the raiders usually withdrew. Now Partridge faced the possibility of a lengthy conflict involving determined military operations launched from secure bases in Canada designed to devastate entire villages. Governor Dudley authorized Colonel Partridge to call on the Connecticut governor for assistance. At the same time, he instructed the colonel not to trouble Winthrop unnecessarily, but "to be certain of an enemy" when he asked Connecticut for assistance.[6]

The new report brought fear to Deerfield. Almost simultaneously with the news from Tyng, Partridge received "an Indian post from Albany" that had undoubtedly been sent by Major Peter Schuyler, a New York official with close ties to the Mohawks of the Iroquois League. On August 6 three Mohawks had returned from Canada and reported that a month earlier "300 Indians with some French are come Out from Quebeque in order to come upon New England." Even though this expedition was headed for the Maine frontier, the report alarmed people in western Massachusetts. They were now in "dayly & hourely fear of the Enemys approach Especially at Derefd," which had already been identified in at least one earlier report as a target. Partridge admitted that no one had seen any enemy, "yet there being Usually Litl or no tyme betwixt the discovery of the Enemy & their striking their blow that we . . . have thought it or [sic] duty to lay this matter before you." He requested that Connecticut authorities send at once fifty to sixty men.[7]

At this point, the political divisions among the English colonists began to make themselves felt in ways that undermined imperial defense. After some difficulty obtaining the necessary men, a company of fifty-three militiamen rode north from Hartford, Connecticut, to Hadley, Massachusetts, in early August 1703. They patrolled in the Deerfield area for two days. Suspicious tracks found five miles from Deerfield turned out to be a false alarm. After consulting with local militia officers, Colonel Partridge released the Connecticut militiamen, who returned home, apparently grumbling as they rode south. A Connecticut official confessed that his people were "troubled that we shud be at such charge & paines for uncertainties, & indeed it seems difficult to do them any reall good except by keeping [a] garison among them." Realistically, Connecticut could not provide Deerfield with timely assistance.[8]

Deerfield residents responded to these intercolonial problems associated with imperial defense by taking steps to defend themselves. Two weeks after Governor Dudley had brought news of the war to Massachusetts, the Deerfield town meeting voted that the "fort shall forthwith be Righted up." This stockade, somewhat misleadingly called the "Great Fort," had been built in 1690. It was about ten feet high and enclosed roughly sixteen acres of land in the center of the village, surrounding the meetinghouse and ten houses. To accommodate residents whose houses were outside the palisade, the town provided houses within the stockade at public expense or exempted from taxes those who built temporary habitations within the walls for themselves. By the end of 1703 about ten or eleven of these small houses existed, making a total of twenty or twenty-one houses within the palisaded area. Nineteen or twenty houses stood outside, most of these south of the "Great Fort."[9]

To defend their homes, residents looked primarily to the local militia company. With the outbreak of war, the company would have mustered under its officers: Captain Jonathan Wells, Lieutenant David Hoyt, and Ensign John Sheldon. Every fit man between the ages of sixteen and sixty—about seventy in all—were sentinels or privates in this company. It was the law. However, the legislature of Massachusetts could not transform farmers and country craftsmen into soldiers by passing a law. It was the duty of the three militia officers, amateurs themselves, to instill in their neighbors the rudiments of military training. Four times a year, Deerfield's militiamen, like others across Massachusetts, gathered for training days. Armed with a motley collection of flintlock muskets, they practiced maneuvering and firing like European soldiers. Alas, such formal European tactics were of limited usefulness in repelling French and Indian raiders. Worse, they may have actually inhibited the men's ability and willingness to fight on their own.[10]

The so-called garrison soldiers sent from neighboring towns in Massachusetts and Connecticut to strengthen local defenses were not military professionals either. They were mobilized militiamen with no more training than the militiamen of Deerfield. Invariably, towns sent their youngest, least experienced men to frontier garrisons. The men posted to Deerfield early in 1704 from Hadley, Hatfield, and Northampton were unmarried men in their early twenties who could be spared from their hometowns. Lieutenant John Stoddard, the twenty-three-year-old son of Northampton's influential minister, the Reverend Solomon Stoddard, commanded Deerfield's garrison soldiers. Under fire, their performances would vary dramatically.[11]

Some two hundred eighty miles north at Chambly, not far from Montreal, a very different military force had gathered. From its strategic location, this small army of French and Native allies threatened the western frontier of New England while simultaneously protecting Montreal from any assaults by members of the Iroquois League. This was the party of French and Indians Lord Cornbury's spies had reported in May. It was also the group of "150 Indians" with some Frenchmen that Wattanummon's sister had brought word of in late July. The various reports reaching English authorities had, in fact, been quite accurate. But their very accuracy confused the English. The raid against the Connecticut valley had been delayed. This delay nurtured an unwarranted complacency among the English. However, the French and their Native allies were still there, and they still intended to launch an attack.[12]

Unforeseen developments had upset French plans and created, from the English perspective, a confusion of contradictory actions and apparent inactivity. Just as the French and Natives were preparing to move south in late May 1703, many of these French and Natives were called to Quebec to meet a perceived threat from English ships spotted near the mouth of the Saint Lawrence River. It proved to be a false alarm, but the distraction disrupted French preparations. Another distraction came in July when Eastern Abenakis in Maine had requested assistance from Governor Vaudreuil and Native allies. Approximately twenty Frenchmen and about two hundred Natives had gone to the eastern frontier. There they had united with Eastern Abenakis and some Pennacooks before attacking the Maine hamlets of Casco, Blackpoint, Saco, and Wells. This was the party of "300 Indians with some French . . . come Out from Quebeque in order to come upon New England" that Colonel Partridge had learned of in early August. The French and Natives struck their blows to the east during the second week of August, just as reports had set off false alarms in the Connecticut valley. This group of French and Native allies contained some of the men, such as Jean-Baptiste Hertel de Rouville, who had initially gathered at Chambly. This party also included Kahnawake Mohawks and Iroquois of the Mountain from Canada. They stayed in Maine until some time in the fall.[13]

Uncertainty about the intentions of the Five Nations of the Iroquois League also contributed to the delay in launching the attack on Deerfield. Maintaining the treaty of peace negotiated with the Iroquois in 1701 was a cornerstone of French policy. Because officials believed that this agreement gave New France "a certain, indisputable superiority in Canada over all New England," they wanted it preserved at all costs. At the 1701 treaty conference, the spokesmen for the league told the French governor, "We would be angry if you were at war with the English, because you are our friends and they are too. However, if that occurred, we would leave you, smoking peacefully on [our] mats, as you ask." Despite this pledge the French wanted reassurance in 1703 when they did fight the English and remained uneasy until they received it. Because of this uneasiness, their governor had informed members of the league of his decision to aid the Eastern Abenakis in August 1703 and justified his decision to fight the English along the Maine frontier. But it was not until a critical mid-October 1703 meeting in Quebec between Governor Vaudreuil and representatives of the league that the Iroquois made clear their continued adherence to the 1701 treaty. Without the aid of the Iroquois League, the English in New York would not, because they could not, attack Montreal. After receiving assurances from the Iroquois, Vaudreuil could safely commit the force at Chambly to offensive operations against New England.[14]

Further developments during the fall of 1703 reinforced Vaudreuil's resolve to attack New England. At some point, the governor received a letter written on June 20, 1703, by his immediate superior, the Comte de Pontchartrain, minister of the marine. In his letter, Pontchartrain made clear that "if occasions to make some successful expeditions against the English were presented, the Governor would not let them pass." A suitable occasion presented itself in the fall of 1703 when the Pennacooks from Cowass had asked the French to join them in a raid of retribution on New England and Vaudreuil had agreed. He later wrote to Pontchartrain explaining that French participation in the winter expedition demonstrated to these Abenakis that they could "count on us." This consideration was not Vaudreuil's sole reason for launching the Deerfield raid, because the evidence makes clear that such an attack had been a possibility since the spring of 1703. Still, the Pennacooks' request provided an opportunity to recruit more raiders from among the Abenakis' allies at Odanak and Lorette.[15]

The force at Chambly that now began making preparations for a winter raid was relatively large. It included Mohawks from Kahnawake and Iroquois of the Mountain from La Montagne and Sault-au-Récollet, Abenakis from Odanak, and Hurons from Lorette, a body of Canadians from Montreal and the neighboring parishes and Canadian-born officers and cadets of the *troupes de la marine*, along with some French-born enlisted men. In all, approximately 250 warriors—French and Indian—prepared to march south under the command of Jean-Baptiste Hertel de Rouville, whose family's seat just happened to be located at Chambly. De Rouville's raiding party was almost five times larger than the raid that his father had led against Salmon Falls, New Hampshire, in winter

1690, and it was more than twice the size of the force of French and Indians that had been sent from Quebec to attack Casco, Maine, in spring 1690. It was larger than the force that had attacked Schenectady in February 1690, though it was easier to move large bodies of men against targets along the New York frontier than against New England. In the 1680s and 1690s, the French had on occasion sent larger expeditions than these against the Iroquois League. Mounting expeditions of this size against New England was something new.[16]

The diversity of the Native contingent was even more noteworthy. Again, such diversity had been found in larger expeditions directed against the Iroquois League during the 1680s and 1690s, but not against English targets. In the earlier expeditions against Casco, Salmon Falls, and Schenectady, Native contingents had been much smaller and more homogeneous. In the raiding parties sent out from Canada in the winter of 1690, Natives and Frenchmen had been present in roughly equal numbers. In De Rouville's army, in contrast, Natives outnumbered the French by four to one. Five villages and at least three different nations contributed men to the force at Chambly. This diversity resulted from diplomatic considerations, not purely from military necessity. French officials wanted to involve as many Native communities as possible in the war against New England. The expedition gave Native communities an opportunity to affirm their alliances with the French and each other. The army at Chambly literally embodied the pursuit of diplomatic goals by military means.[17]

A mixture of motives brought this diverse group of men together and directed their conduct. For the French officials who promoted the expedition, the overriding goal was to secure the support of Native allies in a time of economic and diplomatic uncertainty by embroiling as many Native communities as possible in the imperial conflict with England. Governor Vaudreuil also undoubtedly hoped that spreading terror along the New England frontier would divert the English from offensive operations against New France. Canadian officers on the raid fought for king and country as well as personal honor and glory and the possibility of promotion. It is hard to determine whether the enlisted men from the *troupes* and the men drawn from the Canadian militia shared the aspirations of their officers and the goals of Governor Vaudreuil. They were, however, subject to military discipline and ultimately the coercive powers of the state. In the final analysis, they did not have much choice, though some may have been motivated by hope for plunder, while others may have sought adventure or been drawn by the opportunity to strike a blow against the English heretics.[18]

Natives participated for various reasons of their own, some of which were very different from those of the French. To encourage Native participation, the French offered payments in kind to compensate for time lost from hunting and to provide for relatives left behind. Beyond such material inducements, community traditions and individual motivations played critical roles. For the Abenakis and the Pennacooks, exacting retribution for wrongs suffered at the hands of the English was important. The expedition against Deerfield was another battle in a conflict that had been going on for a quarter century. This overlapping war was afterall the Third Anglo-Abenaki War. For the Hurons of Lorette, the Iroquois of the Mountain, and the Mohawks of Kahnawkae, the raid was part of more personalized wars that paralleled the imperial conflict. Their motivations owed more to the traditions of the mourning war and the prospect of prisoners than any particular grievance against New England. Later in the century, a group of Kahnawake Mohawks and Iroquois of the Mountain explained that such a war was primarily "an opportunity of distinguishing ourselves, and of getting some prisoners and scalps to show our people that we had been at war." "Taking prisoners and breaking heads" also offered them an opportunity for "fulfilling promises they had given to His Majesty." Alliance with the French and other Natives probably helped bring Hurons to Chambly as well. Whatever their reasons, Native numbers were critical to the success of such an undertaking.[19]

The way in which these French and Indian raiders fought was indebted to both Indian tactics and emerging European concepts of partisan warfare. Stealth, surprise, and quick withdrawal had become the essence of Indian warfare by the later 1600s. As a war leader from Kahnawake later explained it to an English captive: "the art of war consists in ambushing and surprising our enemies and in preventing them from ambushing and surprising us." Over the course of the seventeenth century, the "Indians of Sault Saint Louis [the Kahnawake Mohawks], and of the [Iroquois of the] Mountain, the Hurons of Lorette and the Abenakis of Sault de la Chaudiére had taught the soldiers and habitants of Canada to make war the Iroquois way." The French also had learned by being targets of raids by members of the Iroquois League. At the same time, partisan warfare appealed to the French, who emphasized offensive tactics and allowed their soldiers more initiative than the English, who tended to follow the more rigid Dutch and German military traditions. On the Continent, the French had begun experimenting with partisan warfare in the later 1600s by using independent companies as irregular troops. So the French embrace of irregular troops and partisan warfare in North America should not be seen as solely a product of conditions in a new world.[20]

Despite this embrace of partisan warfare and joint operations, different motivations and approaches to warfare created friction among the allies. On one hand, Natives had little desire to assault fortified positions and suffer needless casualties, regardless of the strategic goals being pursued by the French. This reluctance could frustrate their French allies. On the other hand, Native goals of obtaining captives, including women and children or scalps, ran counter to the evolving European codes of war, which sought to spare noncombatants, such as women and children, and male combatants who surrendered. Native actions could offend French sensibilities. But as a rule, officials in France and civilians in New France appear to have been more upset by these violations of European codes of conduct than were the French and Canadians who fought alongside of their Native allies. And these joint raids, like English raids on Native villages during the seventeenth and eighteenth centuries, sought to spread terror by inflicting indiscriminate death and destruction. Again, this violence probably owed more to expediency than to New World conditions, and several historians have pointed out that the supposedly "limited warfare" in early modern Europe produced civilian casualties. Still, the Natives' scramble for captives could disrupt or even prematurely end an engagement or an expedition.[21]

French participation in the Deerfield raid played an important role in shaping the character of the expedition, making it significantly different from the sort of raid Natives carried out on their own. The usual Indian raiding party of ten to twenty-five warriors would capture a few prisoners, take a few scalps, and return home. The goal of capturing and destroying an entire English village had more in common with European warfare than the low-intensity, low-casualty warfare found in America before the arrival of Europeans. Taking a fortified village required hundreds of men, logistical arrangements to support them, and a willingness to suffer casualties. Only French diplomacy could put together a large army (by colonial American standards) such as the one that gathered at Chambly. The French also supplied needed logistical support. Canadian militiamen and enlisted men from the *troupes de la marine* under the command of regular officers provided added numbers and a cohesive core for joint expeditions. Because of their size and greater persistence in the face of resistance, these larger raiding parties usually killed more people and destroyed more property. They also took more prisoners (see appendix E).[22]

The French also appear to have played a central role in promoting winter raids. Logistical arrangements for long-distance raids, for any military undertaking, were the most critical component. These joint expeditions by Candians and Natives did not conform to the stereotype of Indian raiders as "swift and silent in approach and elusive in retreat." Approach marches were complicated undertakings, lasting anywhere from one to four months. Moving and supplying large bodies of men over the wooded interior of the continent challenged Natives as well as Europeans. Campaigning in winter dramatically increased the difficulties of both movement and provisioning. Winter conditions could also limit the number of captives taken, a critical consideration for Natives. As a rule, Indians suspended warlike activities in the winter months to devote themselves to the hunting necessary for their survival.[23]

During the 1600s, Europeans at home and abroad had undertaken military operations in the winter months with increasing frequency. Campaigning and sieges continued almost year-round during the English Civil War of the 1640s and 1650s. English colonists had launched their largest military operation of King Philip's War in December 1675. The year before, Marshall Turenne of France had surprised the Austrians and their allies by launching an unexpected winter invasion of Alsace. A decade before this, French soldiers of the Regiment Carnigan-Salières had undertaken a winter invasion of the Iroquois homeland. But what worked so well in Europe initially turned into a disaster in North America. Many soldiers starved and froze to death without ever firing a shot. With time and practice, however, the French acquired the ability to move hundreds of militiamen, *troupes,* and Native allies and supplies deep into the territory of the Iroquois League, even during winter. They drew on these experiences to send raiders against New England targets in the winter of 1690 and again in 1704.[24]

Experience was important and adequate preparation could be critical, but in the end the raiders relied heavily on stamina, endurance, and luck. It usually proved to be impossible to carry or cache along the way an adequate supply of provisions to feed French raiders, their Native allies, and their captives. An anonymous author of the time reported that some Canadians "returning from these missions prefer to die at the foot of a tree rather than suffer the agonies of hunger any longer. They would perish there if one did not force them to walk and follow the others." Those who made it back from such expeditions were "unrecognizable" and took a long time to recover. The Native allies of the French also suffered, surviving on even more meager rations. When these gave out and "much reduced by hunger [they] would gird up their loins with a string" and push on.[25]

The men with De Rouville would have been a mixture of youths and veterans of the protracted war with the Iroquois League and the bloody border raids of the Nine Years' War. His officers, all native-born Canadians, had, on average, been in the *troupes* for close to twenty years. De Rouville had served in a French army that had invaded the Senecas' homeland in 1687 and in 1690 had been with his father when he led the attack on Salmon Falls. Now, three or four of De Rouville's younger brothers joined him for this expedition—his first independent command. As a nineteen-year-old, Ensign René Boucher de la Perrière had also been on the expedition against the Senecas. His two nephews, Jacques-René and

Pierre Gaultier de Varennes joined their uncle at Chambly. For the nineteen-year-old Pierre, who later became one of New France's most famous explorers, it was his first expedition. The bulk of the French contingent consisted of young men drawn from the militia of the Montreal region who were reputed to be "the best and the most insubordinate." Approximately one-quarter of the men in the town of Montreal, and up to one-third of those in the surrounding parishes, had participated in the fur trade and knew how to snowshoe, shoot, and survive in the woods.[26]

The Native contingents undoubtedly contained a similar combination of veterans and youths seeking to prove their mettle. Some Indians first went to war in their early teens, but most were around twenty when they started and around fifty when they stopped. Natives from Kahnawake, La Montagne, and Lorette had contributed men to the expeditions against nations of the Iroquois League during the 1680s and 1690s and raids against New York and New England in the 1690s. A "great chief" led the Hurons. He would have been a man in his thirties or forties, who had assumed his position only after demonstrating his skill as a warrior. With him were younger men, such as Thaovenhosen, who may have been embarking on their first raid. Still, even these younger men would have been experienced hunters able to snowshoe, shoot, and survive in the woods.[27]

Though most of the men in De Rouville's expedition knew their business and knew the risks, most of them, in theory, should not have known their specific target. Fearing a disclosure that could warn the English, French commanders preferred to keep secret their particular destination until after they had set off into the woods. In some instances several potential targets, or a general area, would be designated, with the final choice to be determined only as the expedition drew closer to the English settlements. But the size of these expeditions, the distances to be traveled, and the length of time involved made it very difficult to keep such raiding parties and their destinations secret. The French never knew when a Native ally with English sympathies, or with ties to Natives allied with the English, might slip away and give warning. Kahnawake Mohawks who maintained close contact with their kin still living in the Mohawk valley were a frequent source of such intelligence for the English. Pennacooks, such as Wattanummon and his sister, who had ties to both the English and the French, provided another conduit of information. Like furs and trade goods, intelligence could be a currency of diplomacy.[28]

The preparations for De Rouville's raid were a very poorly kept secret. Natives in Canada, New York, and northern New England were all aware of the force at Chambly and of its most likely target. Even English captives in New France learned of the raiding party gathered at Chambly and of its intention to raid the western frontier of New England. They gave some member of the party a bag of mail to be delivered by the attackers.[29]

LONG before the raiders gathered at Chambly headed south, three Frenchmen arrived in Deerfield. The suspicious descendants of Deerfield's colonial inhabitants along with later historians have often regarded these Frenchmen as possible spies. But unlike two Frenchmen who had shown up in Deerfield late in 1702, the three new arrivals were not clapped in chains and taken to Boston. Jacques de Noyon and his unnamed companions were in fact *coureurs de bois,* renegade fur traders, who had previously been in contact with authorities in New York. If captured by the French, these men stood in greater danger of dying than any of the town's English residents. These men had fled to the English in search of economic opportunities denied to them because of the languishing condition of the Canadian fur trade. Their flight was symptomatic of the economic and diplomatic crisis in Canada, and actions such as theirs concerned French officials who feared the loss of trade and possibly Native allies. For their part, the inhabitants of Deerfield appear to have welcomed them into their community.[30]

Jacques de Noyon had much in common with Hertel de Rouville and René Boucher de la Perrière. However, since he was not a nobleman, his connection to the French empire was quite different from theirs. Like the officers, De Noyon had been born in Trois-Rivières, that "cradle of explorers." In 1669 his father, a gunsmith, had moved the family to Boucherville, where Jacques grew up as a tenant of the Bouchers. But unlike his father, a craftsman and farmer, he embraced the more adventuresome life of a fur trader. In 1688, he journeyed to the western shore of Lake Superior, where the French trader Daniel Greysolon Dulhut had erected a trading post. This point marked the farthest west that the French had traveled in the Great Lakes basin. Sometime in fall 1688 De Noyon paddled up the Kaministiquia River and spent the winter at Rainy Lake with a party of Assiniboines. In the spring he may have ventured even farther west before returning to Montreal. At some point De Noyon composed an account of his travels. Other traders and Canadian officials came to know of his exploits.[31]

Unlike most traders, De Noyon did not marry and settle down when he reached his late twenties (figure 5). A man with a longing for adventure, not farming, he continued to travel to the Upper Country to trade for furs during the Nine Years' War, financed by a succession of Montreal merchants. Boucherville was merely his home between trips west. So attached was he to his trade that he continued to travel to the Upper Country even after French authorities officially prohibited travel into the region in 1698. By the summer of 1700, De Noyon and a group of French traders who operated illegally in the West were "in a sort of rebellion." They informed English officials of their willingness to "come and trade with the English." Using an English captive living with the Ottawas as an intermediary, they approached the governor of New York, indicating that they wanted to settle in New York colony somewhere near the Iroquois. They hoped to bring with them some of the Ottawas who claimed that they too longed to trade with the English because "the French in Canada are not able to furnish [them] with goods."[32]

More loyal to the fur trade than the French, Jacques de Noyon was committing treason by proposing a plan that threatened to sever New France's lifeline to the fur trade of the Great Lakes. In October 1700 De Noyon and Louis Gosselin, another renegade fur trader, traveled to New York and made a formal proposal to settle there. In return for "the same rights and privileges as others enjoy" in the town of Albany they pledged to "submit ourselves with promise of fidelity to the laws of the Government" and promised to return next year with

FIGURE 5. "Habillemens des Coureurs de bois Canadiens" (Dress of Canadian coureurs de bois). Wash drawing, eighteenth century, artist unknown. In the winter of 1704, Jacques de Noyon and his two companions, as well as the Canadian raiders who attacked Deerfield, undoubtedly dressed in a manner similar to the individual pictured on the left. The combination of capot—hooded coat—made from heavy European cloth and leggings and footwear made of skins closely resembled the clothing likely to have been worn by Native raiders. The two bare-legged individuals in smocks show fur traders' summer dress. Photograph courtesy of the Yale Collection of Western Americana, Beinecke Rare Book and Manuscript Library, New Haven, Connecticut.

other French fur traders "all laden with peltry" and ten or twelve of the principal sachems of the Ottawa nation. For French authorities such plans embodied
their worst fears, because it came at a time when the Ottawas were, in fact, upset with the price that the French offered them for their furs. Because of Native
understandings of the relationship between trade and alliance, diversion of furs
to the English carried with it the possible loss of France's western allies. Just at-
tempting to bring the Ottawas closer to Albany made De Noyon a dangerous
man, even though there is no evidence that he delivered on his pledge.[33]

De Noyon's whereabouts for the next three years remains uncertain. By early
1704 he and two companions had been living in Deerfield "for some time," indicating that the town had links to New France that are not always well documented. Presumably he returned to the Ottawas and spent 1701 gathering furs.
Sometime in 1702 or 1703 he left the Upper Country and arrived in Deerfield
with two other Frenchmen. The French already knew Deerfield as a way station
for Iroquois captives being carried south, as a destination for deserters from the
troupes, and as a place to trade. For these renegade fur traders it may have provided a less conspicuous base of operations than did Albany, which was frequented by Frenchmen and Natives from Canada involved in the illegal trade
with the English. The ostensibly Catholic De Noyon gained enough acceptance
in the New England town to marry seventeen-year-old Abigail Stebbins. The
thirty-six-year-old French spinner of tales won the girl with stories of his wealth
and position in New France.[34]

Around the same time of this wedding another unusual arrival, "Andrew
Stevens, the Indian," married Elizabeth Price. The origin of Andrew Stevens,
"the Indian," remains a mystery. It appears that he was an "Indian" by adoption
and acculturation, not birth, and the characterization of him as "the Indian"
suggests the degree to which some English still looked at Natives from the perspective of culture, not race. If he had been born a Native, his marriage to an
Englishwomen by a New England minister would have been an unprecedented
occurrence. If he was an Indian, he could have come from almost anywhere
in the Northeast. Natives from all over New England, eastern New York, and
Canada visited Deerfield. That he was able to communicate with, and win the
affections of, Elizabeth Price suggest a degree of fluency in English and a certain
familiarity with English customs. A number of New England Natives possessed
such knowledge. But his very English last name, combined with what would
have been a very unusual proper name for a New Englander, may provide a clue
to his origin. The combination of an English surname with a French-sounding
proper name—Andrew or André—is a pattern often found among English captives rebaptized or merely renamed in Canada where French priests usually replaced the Old Testament names of English captives with those of Christian

saints. In the years after the Nine Years' War, some English captured as children but now in their late teens or early twenties began to return after having lived in Native and French communities for several years. Stevens could have come to Deerfield with De Noyon, who had previously employed an English captive, Samuel York, as an intermediary with New York authorities.[35]

It is quite possible that Andrew Stevens was an English boy-captive who had been raised by Natives, probably Abenakis. He may have begun life as Samuel Stevens, who was captured along with his sister Katharine and brother John on August 5, 1689 at Pemaquid, Maine. Katharine's subsequent life can be glimpsed in French records that mention the Natives who adopted her, Nestyus and Marie Meray, record her marriage in August 1697 at Quebec to Jacques Pacquet, and document the birth of some of her children. In Canada, she was rechristened Marie Françoise. If Samuel made it to Canada, he did not leave such obvious tracks in French records. He may be the "André age fifteen, taken by the savages," who was baptized near Quebec at Île aux Grues on January 12, 1699. This André would have been close to twenty in December 1703. He or someone with a fairly similar experience of captivity, life with Indians, and contact with the French was probably "Andrew Stevens, the Indian" who found a wife in Deerfield.[36]

These stories of Andrew Stevens and Jacques de Noyon are more than romantic footnotes. They highlight the fact that even in times of war people moved between communities situated in antagonistic empires and different cultures. Such movements could be peaceful and unthreatening to the parties immediately involved. But other Frenchmen and Englishmen, and other Natives, could see them as threatening. And for Andrew Stevens his relocation to Deerfield would prove fatal. Though not a direct cause of the Deerfield raid, the migration of De Noyon and his companions was a symptom of the causes and calculations that were launching the expedition against the town.

R ENEWED warnings reached Deerfield in the fall of 1703 and winter of 1704. Even though the summer had passed without any raids on the Connecticut valley, Governor Cornbury of New York remained convinced that the Indians were "ready to attempt something upon our Frontiers this Winter." A late September report from Albany warned that hundreds of Indians had been prepared to march toward the valley but were sent by the Canadian governor to the Quebec area. Local military leaders had concluded hopefully that the French "designe for this year may be disappointed." But two weeks later, on October 8, Natives ambushed two Deerfield men, Zebediah Williams and John Nims, as they watched over animals pastured outside the stockade. Both were captured and carried to Canada. Sixteen additional garrison soldiers were posted from Connecticut to Deerfield.[37]

Deerfield began to resemble a village under siege. The returning soldiers brought added protection but also added mouths to feed and increased overcrowding. Residents' houses were "so crowded, sometimes with souldiers, that men and women can doe little businesse within doors, & their spirits are so taken up about their Dangers, that they have little heart to undertake what is needful for advancing their estates." Working outside in the fields was even less inviting. The Reverend Solomon Stoddard of Northampton reported that "sometimes they dare not goe into the fields & when they doe goe, they are fain to wait till they have a guard." John Williams also admitted that several of his neighbors "would freely leave all they have & go away were it not that it would be disobedient to authority & a discouraging their bretheren." So they stayed and worried.[38]

They became increasingly concerned about the condition of their existing palisade after the October ambush. The town appointed a committee to meet with Colonel Partridge to "consult agree & determin" the best course of action regarding the stockade. After assessing the condition of the palisade, they concluded "it is in vain to mend & must make it all new." Colonel Partridge, the Reverend Williams, and the Reverend Stoddard all wrote to Governor Dudley asking that the impoverished town's taxes be abated and the money put to paying the cost of replacing the village's decayed fortifications. Moved by the residents' plight, the legislature granted their request and "considering the extraordinary impoverishing circumstances the Town of Deerfield is under by Reason of the present War" gave the town £20 toward the Reverend Williams's salary. No other town received an abatement of taxes from the colony's tight-fisted legislature.[39]

In early December, the small garrison of soldiers from Connecticut and Massachusetts stationed in Deerfield was actually withdrawn. The remainder of October and all of November had passed without incident. As leaves fell from the trees, their bare branches exposed to view the movements of any raiding party, and as a rule the final months of the year were quiet during wartime. The only fighting along the frontier this fall resulted from English expeditions sent to harass the Pennacooks living just beyond the frontiers of New Hampshire and Maine. After the departure of the garrison soldiers, the town was left to rely on the courage of its own militiamen, the strength of its rebuilt palisade, and the depth of the snow.[40]

Late in January urgent warnings began arriving once again. At Hatfield, Colonel Partridge received letters from Peter Schuyler with news that "stirrs us up." Apparently Schuyler had received yet another report of a threat against the valley. Though this report appears not to have been precise with regard to timing or location, Partridge believed an attack during the winter was a possibility. He sent the letters on to Governor Dudley and alerted Connecticut's Governor

Winthrop that he might require his colony's assistance. Inexplicably, no additional men were dispatched to garrison Deerfield at this time. Partridge clearly hoped for a "respitt till the rivers break up & the great body of snow yet with us & up the river [be] drawn down."[41]

Another letter containing warnings was written by the Massachusetts governor in mid-February. Governor Cornbury had written to Dudley telling him that "some of our Indians have met with some french Indians upon the Lake, who have told them that the french have a design either upon our northern frontiers or upon some place to the Eastward, but they were not sure which." Dudley warned his frontier commanders that three hundred Indians might be on the march. Meanwhile, Pennacooks, responding to the English attacks earlier in the fall, had raided Berwick, Maine, then Exeter, New Hampshire, and most recently Haverhill, Massachusetts. Partridge feared that they might move west and "come over into our parts" as they sought to elude some two hundred to three hundred English pursuers. The possibility that the Pennacooks might be moving westward towards the Connecticut valley of their own volition, and according to a pre-existing plan, did not occur to him. However, he did recognize the potential threat they represented and finally sent soldiers to garrison Deerfield. The last ones arrived on February 25.[42]

Approximately 110 miles north of Deerfield at Cowass, Pennacooks prepared to join De Rouville's raiding party as it moved south. Twice in 1690, raiding parties of French and Native allies had set out from Canada planning to meet up by arrangement with groups of Abenakis. They had done so again in August 1703 along the coast of Maine. For the Pennacooks the raid was part of the overlapping war begun that summer along the coast of Maine and a demonstration of French support. Possibly as many as thirty or forty Pennacooks joined the French and Native expedition as it moved against Deerfield. Among them was Wattanummon. The addition of the Pennacooks may have brought the strength of the raiding party to close to three hundred men by the time it reached Deerfield.

I T is easy to imagine that over the course of nine months the warnings had lost some of their impact. They had circulated for so long that their value had inevitably depreciated. It was also a hard winter. Snow lay thick upon the ground throughout the Connecticut valley. As winter deepened, so did Deerfield's false sense of security. The most recent alarms do not appear to have called forth an adequate level of increased vigilance. Residents had apparently grown complacent. A frustrated Governor Cornbury of New York later condemned "the negligence of the people, who did not keep guard soe carefully as they should have done, though I had sent them notice a considerable time before, that the enemy was preparing to attack them."[43]

CHAPTER 6

ASSAULT

J UST before dawn on February 29, 1704, the French and Indian army emerged
from the fog of rumors and warnings and fell upon a sleeping Deerfield. The
raiders had arrived in the area on the preceding day. They then spent a fire-
less night camped on Petty Plain just across the Deerfield River about two
miles north of town. They would have been cold, hungry, and tired, but probably not on the verge of surrender, as some authors have wistfully suggested.[1]

Well before dawn the raiders crossed the Deerfield River and took up a position in the meadows north of the village. Scouts were dispatched to spy out the
village. They returned and reported that a watch patrolled the stockade. The
raiders waited. After a while, a second scouting party set forth. This party returned to report that all was now still and quiet. The watch apparently had fallen
asleep. As they made their final preparations, Lieutenant Jean-Baptiste Hertel de
Rouville probably called the *troupes* and militiamen together and, as he did on
another occasion, exhorted "all who had any quarrels with each other to be
reconciled sincerely, and embrace." They undoubtedly prayed. Native leaders
likely delivered their own words of encouragement, and Christian Natives probably prayed as well. Then they set off toward the stockade. It was about two
hours before dawn.[2]

According to local Deerfield tradition, De Rouville had his men move forward in rushes to mimic gusts of wind. They would run forward, pause to lis-
ten, and run forward again. But moving rapidly on snowshoes across the snow
that lay three-feet deep on the open meadows would have been exhausting if not
utterly impossible. They probably moved slowly and carefully, passing by a half-
dozen abandoned houses that stood north of the stockade, until they reached
the ten-foot palisade that ringed the score of dwellings houses in the center of
the village. The thick blanket of snow that had pulled at their feet and slowed
their progress now aided their enterprise. Prevailing winds from the northwest
had banked snow in drifts against the outside of the wall, eliminating its effectiveness as a barrier. Volunteers climbed the snowbanks, clambered over the top
of the wall, and dropped down into the stockade, the deep snow breaking the
fall. Once inside, they opened the north gate.[3]

Ideally, separate parties would have targeted individual houses inside the palisade and waited. Once everyone was in place, they would have struck simultaneously, forcing open the doors of the houses and bursting in upon still sleeping occupants. In the last war such well-coordinated assaults had overwhelmed the sleeping residents of several English villages. At Schenectady raiders had divided into small groups and moved silently throughout the entire stockade to take up positions outside of each dwelling in the village. They then attacked almost every one of the houses simultaneously. Escape had been impossible. Sixty residents died and twenty-seven were captured. Casualties among the attackers had been only two killed and a couple wounded. At Salmon Falls, Hertel's father had successfully targeted and overwhelmed the hamlet's three fortified, garrison houses with coordinated assaults. In the process, his raiders killed thirty-four English and captured fifty-four. Only one Frenchman had been mortally wounded during these assaults.[4]

At Deerfield something went wrong. Soon after entering the stockade the raiders lost the element of surprise and failed to position themselves as the raiders had at Schenectady and Salmon Falls. The Reverend John Williams later wrote that the watch had been unfaithful, allowing the French and Indians to enter the village undetected. Another report, however, claimed that "the watch shot off a gun and cried Arm" and thus gave a warning that very few residents actually heard. Another possibility is that a surprised occupant might have fired the initial shot in response to a premature assault on one of the houses. It is unlikely that the raiders themselves fired such a shot. Their preferred weapons at this stage of an assault were axes, hatchets, clubs, and swords. For whatever reason, the raiders were not in place at each of the houses when the fighting began, nor had they succeeded in reaching the south gate to cut off one obvious avenue of escape.[5]

The great size and diversity of the raiding party was probably to blame. The variety of interests involved worked against the maintenance of the cohesion and discipline needed for a series of precisely coordinated assaults on the village's houses. One senses that there was a loss of control even before a single gun had been discharged. The torrent of attackers divided into three streams as it passed through the gate (map 5). Some turned left and headed toward the houses lying east of the common. Others moved straight ahead and scattered among the small houses that had been erected on the common. Those moving the fastest proceeded to the houses on the west side of the common.

Competition rather than coordination characterized the assaults on individual dwellings as Native attackers raced toward likely houses to grab captives. A mixed party of over twenty Abenakis, Kahnawake Mohawks, and Pennacooks (including Wattanummon) attacked the home of the Reverend John Williams during the initial onset. "Violent endeavors to break open doors and windows

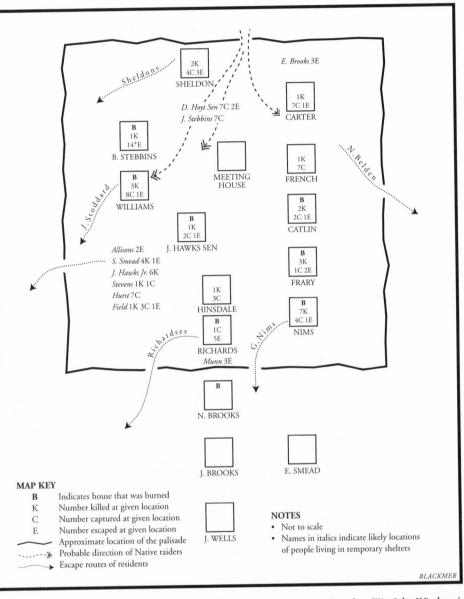

MAP 5. The Deerfield stockade during the assault, February 29, 1704. Sources: Based on "Fitz John Winthrop's Table of Losses," in Sheldon, *History of Deerfield*, 1:304–305; John Williams to Stephen Williams, Deerfield, March 11, 1728/29, Gratz Collection, Historical Society of Pennsylvania; and McGowan and Miller, *Family and Landscape*.

with axes and hatchets" announced their arrival and awakened Williams. He called to two soldiers who slept upstairs and reached for his pistol. Cocking the pistol he pointed it at the first Native who entered his room. Fortunately for Williams, it misfired; otherwise he would have been killed on the spot. Three Abenakis immediately seized Williams and disarmed him. The Native raiders—Williams makes no mention of Frenchmen—moved through his house, ransacking it while rounding up his family. Wattanummon seized ten-year-old Stephen Williams. Mohawks took seven-year-old Eunice and four-year-old Warham. Their older sister, Esther, probably became an Abenaki captive. Two of the young children, six-year-old John and six-week-old Jerusha, were killed as was Williams's female slave, Parthena. One of the soldiers, Lieutenant John Stoddard of Northampton, the commander of the garrison soldiers, escaped by jumping out an upstairs window. He ran to Hatfield to spread the alarm. The other soldier, probably Joseph Eastman of Hadley, was captured. So was Frank, the family's other slave. The captives were allowed to dress while they remained confined to their house. Residents of other homes suffered a similar fate.[6]

Where complete surprise was achieved, as at some of the houses just inside the north gate, whole families were taken with only the very young, those too small and weak to make the journey back to Canada, being killed. On the east side of the common, Kahnawake Mohawks and Iroquois of the Mountain overwhelmed occupants of the Carter and French houses without meeting serious resistance (see map 5). Fourteen members of these families were captured and two young children were killed outright. Only Samuel Carter managed to escape in the ensuing confusion. Nearby Native raiders also captured five of the seven members of the Kellogg family. Hurons and Abenakis captured almost intact the families of David Hoyt Sr., John Stebbins, and Simon Beamon. These families, whose homes lay outside of the palisade, were probably living near the north end of the stockade in small shelters that offered little protection against the raiders. All four members of the Warner family were also taken during the initial stages of the attack somewhere in the northern part of the stockade.[7]

These first, largely unopposed assaults had also bagged the trio of renegade Canadian fur traders. Most likely they were staying with the family of John Stebbins, Jacques de Noyon's father-in-law. De Noyon would have been immediately recognized by his former neighbor Ensign René Boucher and undoubtedly other French raiders, some of whom had been fur traders themselves. It must have been an awkward reunion that ended de Noyon's search for opportunity along the frontiers of New France and New England. He and his two compatriots were now prisoners facing a long march back to Canada and an uncertain fate.

Battle cries, terrified screams, and the occasional gunshot had aroused the rest of the village. Now the English began to fight back and adults were killed.

Farther along the east side of the common, Hurons and Iroquois of the Mountain, probably accompanied by some Abenakis, met with resistance at the homes of the Catlin, Frary, Nims, and Mattoon families (see map 5). The male heads of three of the households were killed: John Catlin Sr., Samson Frary, and Philip Mattoon. Only Godfrey Nims managed to escape. These families had had enough time to rouse and defend themselves, but not enough time to flee. Overall more members of these families were killed outright—twelve—than captured—seven. Resistance had probably provoked their assailants.[8]

These groups of Huron, Iroquois, and Abenaki raiders then crossed to the west side of the common (see map 5). Here, in the southwestern corner of the stockade, residents had the most time to react. Some fled. Some tried to hide. Most of the teacher John Richards's family got away by running through a nearby gate. John Allison and his wife "escaped out the great gate meadowward [the west gate] and ran to Hatfield; she was frozen in her feet very much." Allison's brother Thomas and their eighty-four-year-old widowed mother somehow managed to avoid capture as well. John Field, John Hawks Sr., Robert Price, and Samuel Smead also eluded the raiders, even though the remaining members of their families were taken prisoner or killed. It is possible that the women and children tried to hide while the men ran for help or to muster and fight in a body with the town's other militiamen. If this was their plan, it failed, tragically so for Samuel Smead's wife, mother, and two children, who died in hiding when their house was burned. Nearby, the entire family of John Hawks Jr., along with Martin Smith, who lived with them, perished, either suffocated or incinerated, when their house was burned above them.[9]

Given the confusion and the attackers' likely unfamiliarity with Deerfield, hiding could work. For over three hours, Ebenezer Brooks's family hid in the cellar of a temporary dwelling not far from the stockade's north gate. Sarah Kellogg initially hid under a washtub in the cellar of her house and then escaped the burning house almost naked. Near the south gate, Benjamin Munn and his family remained in a cellar that stood next to the home of his father-in-law, John Richards. The deep snow obscured this low structure, a temporary subterranean dwelling with a roof, and saved the Munn family. But elsewhere in the southern part of the village hiding was less successful. Most members of the Field, Hawks, Hurst, and Price families became prisoners. Relatively few, only four, were killed outright in the southwestern part of the village, underscoring the fact that most of the attackers wanted prisoners and suggesting that those residents who did not flee did not put up much of a fight.[10]

Those who had been captives before did everything they could to avoid being captured again. Former captives such as Benoni Stebbins and Nathaniel Belding resisted or ran to avoid being taken prisoner again. Andrew Stevens, "the Indian," was killed in the southwestern corner of the stockade. He may have died resisting capture, or he may have been recognized by former compatriots who responded violently to his new identity. Whatever his place of origin, he died in an English village. Crossing cultural boundaries or resisting crossing could have terrible consequences. His English wife became an Indian captive and eventually married a Frenchman.

The attackers met their strongest resistance in the northwest corner of the stockade. Here stood the houses of Ensign John Sheldon and Sergeant Benoni Stebbins. They had not been overwhelmed in the initial assaults. At the Sheldon house a barred front door proved to be a temporary deterrent. The Stebbins house, for some reason, had simply escaped the first wave of uncoordinated attacks. A belated attempt to enter the house was beaten back by its fully awakened defenders. Both houses were substantial frame structures with walls filled with nogging—loose, unfired bricks that served as insulation and added to the walls' ability to stop bullets.[11]

The door at the Sheldon house put up more of a fight than its occupants (figure 6). John Sheldon Jr., and his new wife, Hannah, attempted to escape by jumping out a second-story window. Hannah sprained her ankle when she landed and was unable to continue but encouraged John to flee to Hatfield to obtain help. He did, running all the way on feet barely covered with strips of cloth hastily torn from a blanket. Another Hannah, the wife of John Sheldon Sr., was killed by a well-placed shot. At some point, her husband and a garrison soldier ran to the safety of Captain Jonathan Wells's garrison house, a fortified home that stood undisturbed several hundred yards south of the stockade (see map 5). While all this was happening, the front door stoutly resisted the axes of its assailants. Eventually, Kahnawake Mohawks gained access by a less heroic back door. They brained two-year-old Mercy Sheldon just outside the now open front door and made prisoners of the three remaining Sheldon children. This house, along with the meetinghouse, became a holding area for those taken captive elsewhere.[12]

Next door, a larger contingent in the Stebbins house defiantly held out. Up until this point, the French and Indians had met very little resistance, taking prisoners at will and killing those who resisted. Now an opportunity for heroism called forth a competitive, at times reckless, quest for distinction, especially among the leaders. Parties of Hurons, Abenakis, and Frenchmen assaulted the house. The Hurons' great chief, an Abenaki captain—one of John Williams's three captors—and Ensign François-Marie Margane de Batilly received mortal wounds leading charges. Even De Rouville received a wound, though it is not certain exactly when and where he was shot. Several of their men perished in an unsuccessful effort to fire the house. Frustrated, the attackers tried negotiating

FIGURE 6. John Sheldon House, built circa 1698. Photograph by John L. Lovell from a mid-nineteenth-century daguerreotype by William C. North. This house, which survived the 1704 attack and stood until 1848, came to be known as the "Old Indian House." Such a large, two-story house with a framed overhang or jetty was not a typical dwelling and reflected Sheldon's status as one of the town's most prominent and wealthy residents. The door and the hole chopped in it by Native attackers has been preserved in the Memorial Hall Museum in Deerfield. Photograph courtesy of the Pocumtuck Valley Memorial Association, Memorial Hall Museum, Deerfield, Massachusetts.

with the defenders, offering them quarter if they laid down their arms. They refused. Benoni Stebbins did not want to be a captive again. After these fruitless efforts to carry the house by force, fire, and persuasion, the raiders retired to more protected positions. Safe inside the neighboring Sheldon house and the meetinghouse, they fired at the Stebbins house. At one point it appeared as though the entire French and Native force ringed the house and poured in shots.[13]

With a seemingly unlimited supply of powder and shot, the house's occupants kept up a steady fire that held their assailants at bay for over two-and-a-half hours. Seven men, including Benoni Stebbins, David Hoyt Jr., Joseph Catlin, Benjamin Church, a twenty-four-year-old garrison soldier from Hadley, and three others, four or five women, and an uncertain number of children managed to beat back scores of attackers. Quite likely some of them were using fowling pieces or large bore muskets charged with small shot that effectively turned their weapons into shotguns. One did not have to be a marksman: the scatter from a single discharge of a gun with small shot could have hit a half-dozen men.

Some fired forty rounds. Frenchmen and Natives fired back, eventually killing Benoni Stebbins and wounding Mary Hoyt and one of the garrison soldiers, probably Church.[14]

Elsewhere in the village, Frenchmen and Natives set about the work of despoiling Deerfield. They rounded up prisoners and ransacked houses. The captives they herded together in the meetinghouse and the Sheldon House. At some point they started burning houses, beginning with those toward the south end of the stockade and gradually working their way north. They also killed all the cattle, hogs, and sheep they could find, "sacking and wasting all that came before them." All this was part of a spoiling raid designed to terrify and materially damage the enemy. Some Abenakis and the Mohawks began moving their prisoners out the north gate. They headed toward the previous night's camp on Petty Plain. Along the way they looted the six houses that lay north of the stockade and burned four of them.[15]

Now was the most dangerous time for the attackers. Raiding parties were at their most vulnerable as they withdrew. Tired and drained by battle, slowed and distracted by captives, and loaded down with plunder, they could blunder into an ambush or be run down by determined pursuers. Most of the deaths on the Schenectady and Salmon Falls raids and a later Haverhill raid occurred while the raiders were withdrawing or trekking back to Canada. Lacking cohesion and discipline since they had first entered the north gate, the Deerfield raiding party was especially vulnerable. During the ensuing three to three-and-a-half hours, they had been badly shot up.[16]

Some time after the withdrawal had begun, a relief party of English militiamen entered the stockade's south gate. The glow of fires had alerted residents of towns to the south. Thirty to forty men had ridden from Hatfield and Hadley to Deerfield. Still on horseback, they entered the palisade through the south gate. Most of the raiders had probably left, but some remained, looting and shooting at the Stebbins House. Preoccupied with plunder and arson, the raiders still inside the stockade were probably slow to react to this unexpected challenge. Some Natives were apparently more concerned with making a getaway with their captives. According to a French source, "the French, with the Lorettans and Abnaquis Alone Sustained and repelled the onset, the other savages having been shamefully put to flight." It must have been a wild and confused battle.[17]

The English militiamen persisted, gaining strength as the men of Deerfield joined them. At some point men from Captain Jonathan Wells's garrison house entered the fray. This strong point lying south of the palisade had provided refuge for some of those fortunate enough to have escaped death or capture within the stockade. It also contained part of the village's contingent of garrison soldiers. The reinforced militiamen eventually drove out the remaining raiders. As the English militiamen pushed forward, the raiders fled, dropping their plunder as they ran. The rescuers raised the siege of the Stebbins house and forestalled the burning of the stockade's northernmost houses. This timely action spared Ebenezer Brooks and his family, who were hiding in a temporary shelter located somewhere near the northern end of the stockade.[18]

Encouraged by their success and undoubtedly enraged by the death and destruction all around them, the militiamen pushed on. Two defenders of the Stebbins house, David Hoyt Jr., and Joseph Catlin, joined the party. As the relief party passed through the north gate and headed down the street for the meadows, it numbered close to sixty men. Running headlong and undisciplined, the mostly youthful militiamen pursued the retiring raiders. They threw off hats, coats, jackets, and accoutrements in an effort to close the gap between themselves and the last of the fleeing attackers. One of the pursuers, a Deerfield resident named John Smead, killed one Native, who was promptly scalped. He then wounded another. As a contemporary author admitted, such marksmanship was "a rare thing amongst us." But without snowshoes, the English floundered in the deep snow, became separated, and stood exposed in the open meadows.[19]

De Rouville now faced a pitched battle. Given the experiences of previous raiding parties, he may very well have anticipated this contingency. Certainly, the shots fired by the English relief party as it charged into the village and then on to the north meadows would have alerted him to the danger he now faced. Just as his father had at Salmon Falls, he rallied his Canadians and laid an ambush. A mile or a mile and a half from the village, he posted thirty of his men along "a River Bank" (figure 7).[20]

Heedless of their danger the English rushed forward. They ran across the meadows, "imprudently" advancing "too far" in the opinion of a contemporary observer. Sensing danger, Captain Jonathan Wells called a retreat. His men ignored him. On command, Hertel's men "rose up" and fired a volley into the English. The shock caused the English "to give back." The relatively rested Canadians joined by some of the Natives moved forward. The pursuers became the pursued. Much later, English survivors of the Meadows Fight would claim that they fell back cautiously, maintaining their composure, while "facing [about] and firing, so that those that who first failed might be defended." But in the immediate aftermath, participants admitted, "we were over powered & necessitated to run to the fort & in our flight, nine of the company were slain & some others wounded." The number of dead and wounded suggests a breakdown of discipline and flight.[21]

The raiders do not appear to have pressed their advantage. With their superior numbers and greater mobility (because of snowshoes), they could have run down and cut off most of the retreating English. But neither the Natives nor the Frenchmen needlessly exposed themselves. Much safer, less exhausting, and only slightly less effective was their tactic of advancing cautiously and maintaining their distance. Among the nine Englishmen they killed were Catlin and Hoyt. They wounded several others and captured John Marsh, a militiaman from Hatfield. But they had their losses too, five killed and others wounded. The English counterattack had practically doubled the raiders' losses. Fighting ended when the English militiamen regained the protection of the stockade.[22]

Reinforcements from the Massachusetts towns below Deerfield continued to come in during the day. As the alarm traveled south, militiamen from Northampton and the Springfield area mounted and rode north. By midnight almost eighty men had gathered in Deerfield. There were those who favored launching an immediate rescue operation. In the past pursuits had, on occasion, freed captives. Others objected that without snowshoes, they would be forced to follow directly in the retreating raiders' path and thus be open to ambush and flank attacks by

FIGURE 7. View of the Deerfield North Meadows, looking north, 2003. The raiders and their prisoners would have moved in a northwesterly direction—right to left across the snow—as they retreated from Deerfield. Their destination was Petty Plain, on the other side of the Deerfield River and visible as the elevated patch of white in the center middle ground of the photograph just below the clouds. The raiders had camped on the plain the night before the attack and paused there again on their march north. The English militiamen who pursued the raiders across the Meadows were ambushed either just beyond the location pictured in the foreground or at the tree line in the middle ground that runs along the Deerfield River. Photograph by Kevin Sweeney.

the more mobile enemy. The beating that the English had received in the Meadows Fight undoubtedly cooled the ardor of some. The raiders still had a decided advantage in numbers. Finally, some "were much concerned for the Captives, Mr. Williams' family Especially, whome the Enemy would kill, if we come on."[23]

By two o'clock the next day, March 1, militiamen started arriving from the Connecticut towns around Hartford. As night fell again there were about 250 men in Deerfield, a number almost equal to that of the raiders. They debated their course of action. The objections raised the day before were repeated: the lack of snowshoes, the risk to the captives, and the danger to the would-be rescuers. The weather now raised another objection: it grew warmer and began to rain. The deep snow turned into a slushy quagmire that even snowshoes could have traversed only with difficulty. Pursuit on horses would have been difficult as well and would have increased the likelihood of rushing headlong into an ambush. After assigning some of their number to form a garrison to protect what remained of the devastated village, the bulk of the militiamen headed for home.[24]

THOSE men who stayed assisted grief-stricken residents in the grim task of counting and burying the dead. The destruction from fire made identifying and in some cases even finding bodies difficult. Colonel Samuel Partridge composed a detailed tally of losses and sent it on to Governor Fitz-John Winthrop of Connecticut. Allowing for later adjustments, Partridge's accounting revealed that forty-one had died in town: thirty-eight residents and three garrison soldiers. Only two are definitely known to have died of gunshot wounds in the village; at least fifteen had been consumed by fire. Edge weapons or clubs probably killed most of the remainder. Another nine had been killed in the Meadows Fight: seven from the towns below and two Deerfield residents. Others, it is not clear how many, had been wounded.[25]

The overall pattern of casualties reflects primarily choices made by adult males—Native, French, and English—in the heat of battle. A high proportion of those slain were very young children, who had little value as captives and would not have been strong enough anyway to make the grueling trek back to Canada. Though adult men and women had died in about equal numbers, more men than women had escaped capture. At least two garrison soldiers and eight other men had fled and thus avoided the captivity or death that befell a majority of their family members. Some had run for help; some had apparently just run. One hundred and eleven had been captured and removed from the village by the raiders. A majority of the captives were women and older children, who were probably viewed as possible adoptees into Native communities (see appendix E). One of the garrison soldiers, John Bridgman, escaped during the Meadows Fight, but another militiaman, John Marsh, had been captured during the fight.[26]

In addition to taking captives and lives, the raiders had sought to devastate the village and make it unlivable. Burning the houses and killing livestock had been purposeful, not just wanton destruction. Twelve houses inside and five outside of the stockade had been destroyed. Barns had also been torched and in them were lost livestock, tools, and provisions. Only nine houses remained standing within the stockade; to the north of the stockade two houses belonging to the Hoyts had apparently escaped destruction; another thirteen still stood intact and undisturbed along the street south of the stockade. Partridge's Table of Losses makes clear that the thirteen families living in these houses had escaped unmolested by the attackers. They undoubtedly had the resistance at the Stebbins house and the break down of discipline and direction among the raiders to thank for their remarkable delivery.[27]

Casualties among the raiders had also been heavier than one would expect for a battle later characterized as a massacre. The French especially had been hurt. Twenty-two had been wounded, among them De Rouville, one of his brothers, Boucher, Legardeur, and Margane, who was mortally wounded. Two other Frenchmen, 5 "Maquas" [i.e., Mohawks, Hurons and Iroquois of the Mountain] and 3 "Indians" [i.e., Abenakis and Pennacooks] had been killed. It is also apparent that some of the wounded subsequently died during the return march. After the battle the English appear to have stripped about 8 corpses. Other English sources claimed that 30 to 50 of the raiders had died, and John Williams later insisted that "the French always endeavor to conceal the number of their slain." But the English claims are too high to be credible. The English militiamen were not good enough shots to have killed that many French and Indians outright. The admiration for John Smead's marksmanship in the Meadows Fight is evidence of its rarity. Four years later during a fiercely contested attack on Haverhill, Massachusetts, 160 French and Indian raiders faced a force that included 30 garrison soldiers and then retreated into an ambush laid by a relief party of another 60 English militiamen, but only 7 Frenchmen and 3 Indians were killed, 18 wounded, and 1 captured. Still, compared with the relatively light losses incurred in other raids against New England, the Deerfield raid was the costliest for the French and their Native allies.[28]

The French exaggerated their success at Deerfield. In reports and memorials to officials in France, Governor Vaudreuil and the Hertels sought to enhance the stature of their achievement. The size of the raiding party shrank to 200 while the stockaded village of Deerfield became "fort guerifil where there were a hundred and twenty-seven armed men." Additionally, De Rouville and 30 men had to fight off a relief party of "more than one hundred men." The number of English dead almost tripled to 150 and the number of captives inflated to 170. Claude de Ramezay, the governor of Montreal and Philippe de Vaudreuil's rival and critic, appears to have precisely reported the numbers involved and down-played the achievement. He dismissively characterized Deerfield as "a small vil-lage of about forty homesteads." Later, Charles Legardeur would also correctly characterize Deerfield as a "small village."[29]

D ESPITE the high proportion of casualties, the assault was a clear-cut tacti-cal victory that furthered the strategic goals of Governor Vaudreuil. By deploying fewer than fifty Frenchmen, the governor had rallied Native support and spread fear throughout New England. The commitment of these men demonstrated French willingness and ability to stand by their Native allies and helped ensure that these allies would carry the war to the English. After such a bloody raid, it became harder for Natives to make peace with the English. In ad-dition, Native allies gained valuable captives to adopt, or ransom, alleviating some of the economic problems caused by the collapse of the beaver trade. Even before the Deerfield raiders had returned, Vaudreuil had resolved to "send forth another campaign."[30]

In response, the New England colonies had to mobilize and commit hun-dreds of militiamen to frontier defense and expend thousands of pounds to pro-tect and reassure the fearful residents of exposed towns. In the Connecticut val-ley, Samuel Partridge found that "our people are so tranceported with the late stroak at Derefd that I can hardly pacifie them without men to garrison our towns." By summer 1704 Massachusetts had nineteen hundred men under arms. Most of these men were kept in garrisons along a two-hundred-mile fron-tier that stretched from Deerfield in the west to Wells, Maine, in the east. Dis-persal and employment of so many men in passive and expensive frontier de-fenses rather than offensive operations indirectly protected Native and French communities and created political problems for the governments of the English colonies. The alternative of abandoning towns and drawing in the English col-onies' frontiers would have entailed costs as well and created its own problems. The assault on Deerfield gave the strategic initiative in the war to the French.[31]

CHAPTER 7

RETREAT

THE sack of Deerfield had been a tremendous victory for the French and Indian raiders, but the march north threatened to deny the allies of the fruits of their victory. Jean-Baptiste Hertel de Rouville, the nominal leader of the expedition, calculated victory in terms of property destroyed and enemy killed. Now his main goal was to get back quickly and safely. But for most of the 200-plus Native warriors without whom that victory would have been impossible, the fruits of victory were marching alongside them: 109 English captives. Preserving these fruits of victory involved a series of challenging negotiations on the march back to Canada and then in New France. Warriors had to cope with the difficult winter weather, the weak and fearful, yet stubborn, English captives, and the occasionally contradictory demands of their mourning-war traditions and new Christian values. The march back to Canada exposed the complexity of the Natives' relationship to the English, the French, and Christianity.

Most of the warriors had joined the expedition to take captives, and the Deerfield raid had been something of a bonanza in this respect. The size of the expedition and the achievement of surprise had allowed the warriors to gather as many captives as they could get their hands on. There was roughly one captive for every three raiders—an unusually high proportion for raiding parties. So many warriors had captives, or a share in a captive, that those who did not began to grumble. But capturing English colonists was one thing. Getting them back alive was another. As the party moved north, a brutal weeding out process took place. At most, only eighty-nine of the Deerfield captives eventually reached Canada. Most of those who died on the march were adult women—many of whom were weakened by childbirth and pregnancy—and very young children. Few adult males died, and under very different circumstances from the rest. In other words, the retreat was something of a disappointment for those men motivated by the customs of the mourning war. The captives they killed were exactly the sort they preferred to adopt into their communities.

THE English pursuit into the meadows had thrown the raiders into a state of confusion in which they lost control of some of their captives. One of the captured garrison soldiers, John Bridgmen, had escaped during the fighting.

Another captive, three-year-old Marah Carter, had been killed, probably because she slowed down her fleeing master. During the night, as the army camped on the northern shore of the Deerfield River, twenty-three-year-old Joseph Alexander escaped, suggesting disorder among the attackers.[1]

The killing of John Williams's slave Frank is further evidence of a breakdown in discipline and hints at the sometimes tense relations between African Americans and Native Americans in the Northeast. On the evening of February 29, some of the raiders consumed liquor that they had plundered in Deerfield, and "in their drunken fit" killed Frank. He was the only adult male killed outright on the march to Canada. Earlier in the day during the attack on Williams's house, Native raiders had killed Frank's wife, Parthena, an otherwise likely captive. These uncharacteristically arbitrary killings are difficult to explain. It is doubtful that Natives did not believe African Americans could survive the journey. Five slaves—all men—had been taken prisoner during the 1690 Schenectady raid. It is possible that the raiders may not have been aware at this point of the monetary value of slaves. But other evidence indicates that raiders during the War of the Spanish Succession did recognize the value of ransoming slaves to their English masters or selling them to the French in Canada, who were beginning to acquire black slaves in the early 1700s.[2]

What little evidence there is suggests that Natives and African Americans did not always get along well. Jeremy Belknap, the eighteenth-century New Hampshire historian, asserted that Indians "had a strong aversion to Negroes, and generally killed them when they fell into their hands." At Schenectady in 1690, five slaves had been taken prisoner, but eleven others were killed outright. Two of these captives subsequently escaped from their Native captors, preferring a return to slavery in New York to an uncertain fate in Canada. Among the men who fought back at Deerfield in 1704 was "Primus, negro," who participated in the Meadows Fight. Even during times of peace, African Americans and Natives got into drunken brawls in Albany that had turned lethal at least once. In 1702, Maquon, a Mahican and Schaghticoke leader, had been mortally wounded by a party of black slaves. Pennacooks and Abenakis on the Deerfield raid had close ties to Schaghticoke, and it is possible that some may have sought revenge by killing Frank. Whatever their reasons for killing him, the drunken binge and wanton killing were strong evidence that discipline among the raiders was lax.[3]

The next morning, De Rouville tried to restore a degree of order and discipline. A rear guard was detailed to protect the column during the coming day's march. He ordered John Williams "to tell the English that, if any more made their escape, they would burn the rest of the captives." It was a real threat. Only a few years before, Abenakis in Maine had recaptured two English captives who had tried to escape and tortured them to death as an example to the others. As the brother of one of the victims later recalled, their "noses and ears were cut off and they [were] made to eat them, after which they were burned to death at the stake. The Indians at the same time declar[ed] that they would serve all deserters in the same manner." Kahnawake Mohawks and Iroquois of the Mountain also tortured and burned escapees they recaptured. With this fate in mind, no more Deerfield captives tried to escape during the march north.[4]

De Rouville reined in his raiders by setting a rapid pace when the march began on the second day. Keeping his party moving would dissuade those inclined to drink or straggle. To keep up they had to focus all of their energy on moving themselves and their prisoners forward. Wounded French and Natives as well as the younger captives had to be carried on the backs of the unwounded raiders. A rapid march also put distance between De Rouville's army and any English pursuers. After the 1690 Schenectady raid pursuers had followed the retreating French and Natives all the way back to Canada in winter and captured fifteen stragglers "almost in sight of Montreal." At Deerfield, De Rouville had already fought two rearguard actions against on-coming English militiamen. He probably expected them to attack again.[5]

As the English militiamen huddled in the village realized, an attempted rescue represented a serious threat to the captives' lives. Stephen Williams later recalled that the raiders told the captives that "if the English pursued them they would kill us, but if otherwise they would not." French and Native raiders preferred to kill their captives rather than lose them to rescuers. Only four months later, in May 1704, a party of about twenty French and fifty Pennacooks successfully attacked Pascommuck, an outlying hamlet of Northampton. They captured thirty-seven people but were hotly pursued by a company of horsemen from Northampton. As the English troopers drew near, the French and Pennacooks knocked "all the Captives in the head Save 5 or 6." Then, less encumbered by captives, they fought off their pursuers and escaped with three of the captives. Twenty prisoners, mostly adult men and young children, died. The decision not to pursue the Deerfield captives probably averted a real massacre.[6]

N ATIVE warriors had much more to gain by bringing the captives back alive. Apart from Frank, they did not kill any captives unless they felt compelled to by the rigors of the trek north over snow and ice. By the 1690s, English prisoners had acquired a special place in the practices of the mourning war. A Schaghticoke had explained this to four Deerfield captives taken in 1696. On the return trip to Canada, their Kahnawake Mohawk captors had encountered and seized the Schaghticoke along with a "young Albany Mohawk." Fearful of what lay in store, one of the English asked the Schaghticoke "what he thought the enemy would do with them." The man replied "that they would not kill the English prisoners, but give some of them to the French & keep some of them themselves; but he expected to be burnt himself," in accordance with the traditional treatment meted out to enemy warriors. A few nights later the Schaghticoke escaped. The Mohawks kept the "young Albany Mohawk" alive and undoubtedly adopted him, "being of their own nation." On arriving at Kahnawake, the English captives "found what the Scatacook Indian had said to be true, for the Indians kept Mr. B[elding] himself & his daughter with them, & gave" the other two—Nathaniel Belding and John Gillett—"to the French." They all spent the remainder of the war working as servants for the Kahnawake Mohawks and the French.[7]

Warriors' actions during the assault on Deerfield appear to have been influenced by a belief that English colonists were worth more alive than dead. As a rule, only a few children obviously too young to survive the journey and men who fought back had been intentionally killed in the fighting. And there is no record that any scalps were taken. On the march to Canada, "an Indian captain to the Eastward," that is, a Pennacook war leader, did speak to one of John Williams's captors "about killing me and taking off my scalp," but nothing came of the threat, which may have been intended only to terrify or humiliate him. If so, it worked. Williams stood by and lifted up his "heart to God to implore his Grace and mercy in such a time of need." He was outraged at the idea of being killed after he had surrendered—that went against the European codes of war. But here Native customs prevailed. John Williams told his captor that "if he intended to kill me I desired that he would let me know of it, assuring him that my death after a promise of quarter would bring the guilt of blood upon him." The Abenaki said he would not kill him. Over the course of the journey north, this one of Williams's masters displayed a command of English that betrayed likely New England origins. But he put aside any animosity he may have felt and treated Williams well. In William's case, as in most others, warriors wanted to bring the captives back alive. This desire is evident in their treatment of captives, though English accounts of the march emphasized killings. They did, however, begrudgingly acknowledge instances of kindness and assistance, though they explained them away as acts of divine intervention.[8]

For some captives, the physical demands of the journey did prove to be too much, and they were killed by their captors (map 6). During the first three days of the retreat the army moved overland through twenty miles of wooded, hilly terrain, covered with several feet of waterlogged snow. Few if any of the captives had snowshoes at this stage of the march. The journey was exhausting and their enemy's "manner was if any loitered to kill them," usually with a swift blow to the head. As the eighteenth-century Massachusetts historian Thomas Hutchinson acknowledged, "If they left their grown captives in the woods, they would discover them to the pursuers. To leave young children to die would be

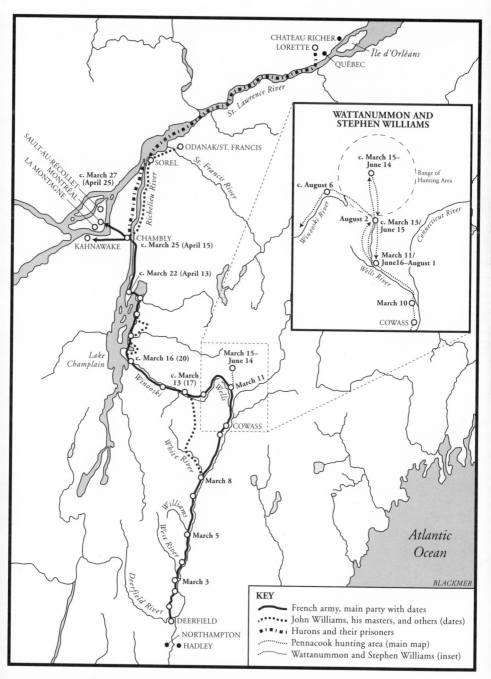

MAP 6. Routes of the captives, 1704. Sources: John Williams, "Redeemed Captive"; Stephen Williams, *Narrative of the Captivity of Stephen Williams;* and Carter, "Route of the Captives," 1:126–151.

more cruel than to kill them outright." It was also a fearsome lesson to the rest of the captives. A bitter Stephen Williams called his captors "liars," feeling betrayed because they had promised not to kill anybody if the English did not pursue them. He worried that his feet "were very sore so that I was afraid they would kill me also." Somehow he kept moving. Others could not. In addition to Marah Carter, two other children, Marah's seven-month-old sister Hannah and ten-year-old Jemima Richards, perished during the first two days of the march.[9]

The most vulnerable captives were adult women, especially those who were pregnant or had just given birth. Ten women unable to keep up were killed during the course of the march (see appendix F). Among the first to die on the second day of the march was John Williams's wife, Eunice, the "desire of [his] eyes and companion in many mercies and afflictions." For all Eunice's piety and learning, her fate, like that of most other New England wives, was profoundly influenced by the demands of childbearing. She had delivered seven children so far. The last birth, that of the slain Jerusha, had been just six weeks before the attack. Eunice was all too aware of her weakened condition and took advantage of the first opportunity on the second day to talk with her husband. He tried to "help her on her journey," but Eunice knew it was not enough. She told him that "her strength of body began to fail and that [he] must expect to part with her, saying she hoped God would preserve my life and the lives of some, if not all of our children with us, and commended [him], under God, the care of them." Eventually, one of John's Abenaki masters forced the two to separate. Soon after they separated, the army crossed the Green River and went up a hill. An exhausted John Williams entreated one of his masters "to let me go down and help my wife, but he refused and would not let me stir from him." As he desperately "asked each of the prisoners as they passed by me after her," he learned that she had fallen down in the stream. Weak and soaking with freezing water, she traveled only a short distance farther. At the foot of the mountain, her master "slew her with his hatchet at one stroke" (figure 8).[10]

On the next day, the third day of the retreat, distribution and disposition of captives became a source of concern among the Native leaders. There were so many captives, taken in such a haphazard fashion that Native leaders realized that conflicts over the possession of the captives were imminent. As Stephen Williams noted, some were "disturbed, for some had five or six captives and others had none." To forestall trouble, the leaders of the Abenakis, Hurons, Pennacooks, Kahnawake Mohawks, and Iroquois of the Mountain met in council. They gathered together the captives "to make a more Equal Distribution" of them among their warriors. At this point, the captives came as close to being slaves as they would ever be. The warriors plundered the captives of whatever valuables they had left before bringing them to the gathering. John Williams's "best clothing" was taken. His son Stephen lost the "silver buttons and buckles" that he had on his shirt. Their masters sold some of the items to "French soldiers of the army," who took advantage of the chance to trade in their old outfits for fresh English clothing. As a result, John Williams had to wear some "lousy old clothes of soldiers" for the rest of his journey. Stripped of their possessions, the captives waited while Native leaders debated. Finally, "several of the captives

FIGURE 8. Eunice Williams's gravestone, sandstone, circa 1729, probable carver Thomas Johnson. Photograph from stereocard, circa 1860–1870, by Benjamin F. Popkins. Deerfield residents retrieved Williams's body and buried it in the town's graveyard. This gravestone was erected in 1729 when a similar marker was erected over the grave of her husband, John. Williams's children, whose sentiments appear in the inscription, commissioned and paid for this marker, which was produced in Middletown, Connecticut, and transported to Deerfield. Courtesy of Pocumtuck Valley Memorial Association, Memorial Hall Museum, Deerfield, Massachusetts.

were taken from their former masters and put into the hands of others." It is unclear how much reshuffling occurred, or whether prisoners moved from one nation to another. Both John and Stephen remained with their original masters.[11]

For Indians, the disposition of captives was a delicate matter that had to take
into consideration the claims of the warrior, the community, and the community's allies. Natives were acutely conscious of a master's control over his captive. Generally, whoever grabbed a captive first in the heat of battle became the
person's master. After a captive was seized, all other warriors respected the captor's rights and did not interfere with his management of his prize. However,
when several warriors had seized a captive at the same moment, matters could
become complicated, forcing the captors to strike some kind of bargain among
them. John Williams, for example, had been "seized by three Indians." One had
been killed attacking the Stebbins House, leaving Williams in the custody of
two men all the way back to Odanak. He was fortunate: one of his masters was
very strict, while the other was rather indulgent. But multiple masters could
also be a curse. When warriors could not agree over the ownership of a captive,
they sometimes resolved the dispute by killing the captive, a fate another New
England captive, John Gyles, had almost experienced a few years earlier in
Maine. When one of his two Abenaki masters died, the widow and the surviving master "disputed whose slave [he] should be, and some malicious person ad-
vised them to end the quarrel by putting a period to [his] life." Fortunately for
Gyles, the local French priest "told them it would be a heinous crime and ad-
vised them to sell me to the French," which they did.[12]

As a rule, French officers familiar with the culture of their Native allies
avoided interjecting themselves into such disputes and let Natives dispose of
captives as they deemed fit. Experienced Canadian officers, such as Hertel de
Rouville, knew that their superiors wanted English towns destroyed and depopulated. To achieve this goal on the New England frontier they needed the
help of Native allies in Canada, who now largely fought parallel wars to capture
people rather than towns. Especially on campaigns where most of the raiders
were Indians, not French, officers had no way of enforcing European customs
regarding the treatment of prisoners. When French officers tried to give English
prisoners the sort of treatment Europeans expected, as Pierre Le Moyne de
Iberville had at Pemaquid in 1696, and as the Marquis de Montcalm would during the Seven Years' War, they risked alienating their Native allies. The Hertels
did not because they usually let their Native allies control the captives taken in
their joint raids. At Deerfield De Rouville had made something of an exception,
because of the presence of the three Frenchmen. The French raiders clearly retained control of Jacques de Noyon, his wife, and the two other *coureurs de bois*.
Some members of the Stebbins family, De Noyon's in-laws, and at least two

members of the Burt family also apparently stayed in French custody the entire way back to Canada. In all at least ten captives turned up in the home villages of French raiders—Boucherville, Chambly, and Varennes—sometime in mid-April without any sign of having passed through the hands of Native captors.[13]

For some of the warriors, the question was not only who would have a captive but whether or not they would exact revenge for their battle losses by torturing some of the English men. The fight at Deerfield had been bloody for the Natives. They normally did all they could to avoid battle losses, which brought on sorrow and the need for vengeance. John Williams "observed after this fight no great insulting mirth and saw many wounded persons, and for several days together they buried [several] of their party." Male captives offered opportunities for vengeance that women and children did not, and the humiliation and mutilation of enemy men had long been a vital part of their culture. At Deerfield, as on most other raids, such acts started even before the retreat began. John Bridgmen, a garrison soldier who escaped during the confusion of the Meadows Fight, had had his index finger severed almost as soon as he was captured. Removing this finger humiliated a male captive by destroying his ability to draw a bowstring or fire a musket, critical functions for a warrior. Such mutilation, standard treatment among Native captives, could also be a visible mark of servitude in a Native community. For New England captives, however, it was rare. Perhaps some of the other captured militiamen also had their fingers severed, but there is no indication that the other Deerfield men did.[14]

One captive—most likely Jonathan Hoyt—did come close to facing death by ritual torture. While the English prisoners waited for the deliberating chiefs to make a more equal distribution, some of the captives informed their minister that "they thought the enemies were going to burn some of us for they had peeled off the bark from several trees and acted very strangely." John Williams assured them that "they could act nothing against us but as they were permitted by God, and [he] was persuaded He would prevent such severities." At that very moment, unbeknownst to Williams, a godly "Huron warrior" was in fact acting to prevent "such severities."[15]

The nephew of the "great chief" of the Hurons demanded that a prisoner be turned over to him. The "great chief," mortally wounded in the futile assault on the Stebbins house, had died and been buried on the second day of the march. In a later description of the scene, Father Louis D'Avaugour reported it was the "custom among the Canadians [i.e., Indians] to seek, as it were, expiation and consolation for the death of Their chiefs by the slaughter of some captive." A relative of the "dead man presents himself, and demands the prisoner." Once he is "handed over, his owner destines him to the flames, and prepares to satisfy his barbarous cruelty by torturing the wretched man. Thus custom of the nation regulates." The chief's nephew was his most direct male relative according to Iroquoian matrilineal calculations. His request caused a stir in the council. Many began to murmur. The struggle between Christian norms and mourning-war culture seemed to have a generational element—with the younger generation appealing to pre-Christian values. According to D'Avaugour, the elders reluctantly kept silent. The "young men clamor[ed] for this right of arms, this reward of victory, this sole consolation for the chief and afflicted family." Outside, as some of the young warriors peeled the bark off of a tree and began to make a stake to tie the victim to, the Deerfield captives feared the worst.[16]

Inside, Thaovenhosen rose to speak. For years the missionary priests of New France had been trying to persuade Christian converts to stop torturing their war captives and treat them as Europeans did. Though the French wanted their allies to behave like Christians, they also needed them to be warriors. Ideal Christian warriors were few, but Thaovenhosen appears to have been one. He was speaking out of turn, for he was "not yet honored with the dignity or the title of chief." Before any council member could protest his audacity, he began to "boldly plead for the life of the Captive." Turning to his fellow Hurons, he reminded them "that they are Christians and citizens of the village of Lorette." He told them "that dire cruelty is unbecoming to the Christian name." He warned them "that this injury cannot be branded upon the reputation of the Lorettans without the greatest disgrace." The zealous young Catholic feared that his people were about to compromise their religion by doing something Hurons had done for a long time, but which their Jesuit mentors opposed.[17]

Few of his fellow Lorettans agreed with him. Traditions of the mourning war still had a strong hold over Thaovenhosen's people. The nephew insisted on his rights, and his relatives urged his claim. They reminded Thaovenhosen of their people's traditions. They warned him that "clemency shown toward a single head will bring ruin to all." If they let the captive live and their chief's death go unpunished, their enemies would "grow more ferocious, and more audacious to harm them," because they would not have to fear a terrifying death by torture if they were captured. These Lorettans saw nothing unchristian in the painful death of an enemy.[18]

In response, Thaovenhosen shifted his argument from Christian logic to traditional Huron values. "'I also,' said he, raising his voice, 'am related to that Chief whose fall in battle we mourn, and whose death you would avenge by an unworthy cruelty. To me also is the captive due; I claim him as my own, and I contend that such is my right.'" Already speaking out of turn, Thaovenhosen now challenged the nephew's right to avenge their chief and relative. He was violating generations of Huron tradition. He knew this was dangerous. "If any one lay hands on him against my will," he continued, "let him look to me for chastisement." Shocked, the assembly was mute. No one "dared to decide upon any greater severity toward the captive." Thaovenhosen's bold action ensured that the nasty side of the mourning war was suppressed, at least for the moment. Christian behavior had won out, but only through the medium of a traditional Huron claim stressing the rights of relatives, and the threat of fratricidal violence.[19]

The council determined that men would not be tortured and killed—but women too weak to travel continued to die. On the fourth day, while still traveling overland to reach the Connecticut River, Waitstill Warner, twenty-four-years-old and pregnant, became weary and was killed. When the expedition reached the river, the army paused to pick up their sleds and to recover and eat provisions that had been cached at this site. After the break, the army began traveling over the jagged ice and waterlogged snow covering the frozen Connecticut River. The pace accelerated. As Stephen Williams later remembered it, "they traveled (we thought) as if they Designed to kill us all for they traveled 35 or 40 miles a day," though in fact they covered only about a dozen miles on the fourth day. His father doubted he could survive the hard marching in water up to his ankles. John had sprained his ankle before setting out and was becoming lame. He told Stephen that "he thought he should be killed." The next day, the fourth of March and the fifth day of the trek, the army covered eighteen miles. The raiders "traveled with such speed that four women were tired and slain by them who led them captive." All of these women were older married women: fifty-four-year-old Hepzibah Belding, sixty-four-year-old Mary Frary, thirty-six-year-old Mehitable Nims, and twenty-nine-year-old Hannah Carter, who had already seen two of her daughters die on the march.[20]

After adult women, the youngest captives were in greatest danger of being killed. Their survival depended on the warriors' ability to bring them through the rigors of the march and their age. Most warriors went out of their way to bring young captives—prime candidates for adoption—back to their villages, and most of the children between the ages of three and twelve survived the march (see appendix F). Only one of the five children aged two or less did. Warriors killed several children during these days of rapid movement on the Connecticut River. Though John Williams makes no mention of their deaths, Stephen, a child at the time, remembered that "they killed near a dozen women and children" along this stretch of the journey. Most of the children who perished here— Mary Alexander, Abigail Hoyt, and Benjamin Hurst—were very young, all around two years of age. They were particularly vulnerable to the harsh weather and least able to chew and digest a diet relying heavily on dried corn or meat.[21]

Captors made greater efforts to preserve the lives of older children. Native and French raiders carried "children, incapable of traveling, upon their shoulders and in their arms." John Williams's four-year-old son, Warham, had been spared even though "they that carried him or drawed him on sleighs were tired on their journeys" and "in their pity he was spared and others would take care of him; so that four times on the journey he was spared and others would take care of him." Warham, who remained with a larger party of Kahnawake Mohawks, was carried in this manner all the way to Montreal. Thirteen-year-old Esther and fifteen-year-old Samuel Williams were also spared and "pitied so as to be drawn on sleighs when unable to travel." Eight-year-old Ebenezer Hoyt was not so fortunate. He was killed as the raiders traveled up the Connecticut River. But as a rule, the older children who remained in large parties containing enough men willing to share the burden of transporting them made it to Canada.[22]

What would have been the sixth day of the march was a Sunday and thus it became a day of rest. John Williams "was permitted to pray and preach to the captives," choosing for his sermon a passage from Lamentations 1:18 proclaiming, "The Lord is righteous, for I have rebelled against his commandment. Hear, I pray you, all people, and behold my sorrow. My virgins and my young men have gone into captivity." Williams later remembered that, "When the Maquas and Indians were chief in power, we had this revival in our bondage to join together in the worship of God and encourage one another to a patient bearing of the indignation of the Lord till He should plead our cause." By interpreting all that happened to them as a just God's punishment for their sins, the English symbolically denied the power of their Catholic captors and affirmed their Protestant faith. The Natives saw it differently. Those who were not Christians had little fear of the Englishman's God and those who were Christian saw the English worship service as an opportunity for sectarian competition. After Williams's sermon, some of the Christian Indians called on the English to "Sing one of Zion's songs." When the English sang a psalm, some of the Christian Natives scoffed at them "because [the English] singing was not so loud as theirs."[23]

The day's stop had been a calculated risk, for even at this stage the army did not know for certain that it was not being pursued. When the march began again on the seventh day, the raiders appeared to be particularly tense, worrying perhaps that their day's rest had allowed English pursuers to draw closer. At one point, some of the men at the rear of the column "fired at some Geese that flew over." Once again, discipline in the ranks was lax. The rest of the army, hearing the guns but not seeing the geese, was given a "considerable fright, for they thought the English were come up with them." They immediately began "to bind the prisoners and to prepare themselves for battle." But, once they understood "what the matter was they shot a volley for joy, boasting that the English could not overtake." Still, they remained wary. Stephen Williams estimated that on this day they traveled "a great way farther than we had at any time before," covering probably twenty-four miles. Two more women, possibly Elizabeth Corse and Esther Pomroy could not keep up with the punishing pace and were killed. The next day another woman, Mary Brooks, was killed.[24]

After a fourteen-mile march on the eighth day, the expedition reached the junction of the White River with the Connecticut and prepared to split up. Since each of the smaller groups would be more vulnerable to pursuers, the decision to split up suggests that the army had concluded that they were not being pursued and felt secure enough to take the risk. They also probably had no choice. Provisions had run low; in some instances they had been exhausted. The raiders had to hunt and could do so successfully only in small groups. During the next two days Stephen Williams had only a few kernels of corn to eat. John Williams's masters kept him well-enough fed, but his other children and many neighbors "were greatly wounded . . . with the arrows of famine and pinching want, having for many days nothing but roots to live upon and not much of them either."[25]

The army divided into its component groups on March 8 (see map 6). The Natives from Canada headed up the White River to the headwaters of the Winooski River, breaking up into small parties to follow the rivers' separate branches as they wound through the Green Mountains, hunting along the way. The bulk of the Deerfield captives—John Williams among them—probably went with groups passing along one of these routes. But the handful of captives taken by Pennacooks, including his son Stephen, continued north along the Connecticut River to the meadows at Cowass. The French and their prisoners followed the Pennacooks at a much slower pace. Eventually the French left the Connecticut and struck off to the northwest following the Wells River into the Green Mountains, where they also reached the headwaters of the Winooski River, which flowed into Lake Champlain.[26]

The dependence of English captives on their particular captors increased as they split up into smaller groups and moved away from the Connecticut River. The going got rough. The parties now waded through deep, encrusted snow as they climbed alongside of the streams heading up into the Green Mountains. Hunger and starvation threatened captors and captives alike, making it harder for some to keep up. Deep in the mountainous woods, John Williams watched as a Mohawk struggled through the deep snow with six-year-old Elizabeth Hawks on his shoulders. Finally he stopped and killed her, for "he could not carry the child and his pack too." This man, who was now largely on his own, had no one with whom to share his burden. The same day forty-year-old Mary French, who was traveling with another small party, also was killed along the White River.[27]

John Williams's captors made more of an effort to ensure that their valuable prisoner survived the crossing of the Green Mountains. Williams was lucky enough to be with fortunate hunters. After what were undoubtedly several lean days, his masters killed five moose. It was the thirteenth day of the march. The party spent three days roasting and drying the meat. Williams's English-speaking master made him a pair of snowshoes from the sinews, telling him "'you cannot possibly travel without, the snow being knee-deep.'" Williams would recall that, as they went from the White River over to the Winooski, "my master was very kind to me, would give me the best he had to eat, and by the goodness of God, I never wanted a meal's meat during my captivity." He also bound up and treated Williams's cut feet and gave him a piece of a Bible to read and respected the minister's private devotions.[28]

It was a hard journey for the English captives. Even with spiritual support and enough food, the trek took its toll on the Deerfield minister. Sometime around the twentieth day of the journey, he felt that he could go no farther. His "feet were so tender, swollen, bruised, and full of pain that [he] could scarce stand upon them without holding on the wigwam." His master said "'we must go a great way today'" and that Williams would have to run. He replied he could not run. "Pointing to his hatchet," his master responded "'then I must dash out your brains and take off your scalp.'" Weary and despairing, Williams answered, "'I suppose then you will do so, for I am not able to travel with speed.'" But somehow he found the strength, walking in that one day "two of their day's journey as they came down." They covered about thirty miles. Upon reaching the mouth of the Winooski River, they turned north on frozen Lake Champlain, then, after a day or so, they turned back east and headed inland, where the Abenakis rejoined their families near Missisquoi. Here they spent additional time hunting and gathering meat for their village. About a month and a half after the assault, on April 15, they reached Chambly. At the fort, Williams learned that "the greatest part of the captives were come in and that two of my children [Samuel and Warham] were at Mont-Royal, and that many of the captives had been in three weeks before my arrival."[29]

Not all of the captives were destined for New France. Those taken by the Pennacooks settled into the area around Cowass, where their families awaited them in their mountainous hunting territories (see map 6). Proceeding up the Connecticut River, the Pennacooks split off from each other to seek out their respective families. Lieutenant David Hoyt, the fifty-two-year-old patriarch of one of Deerfield's prominent families, was taken directly to Cowass, along with Jacob Hickson, a young garrison soldier. Wattanummon took Stephen Williams past Cowass, part way up the Wells River, and into the mountains. There they found two wigwams inhabited by a single Pennacook boy because everyone else was out hunting. Wattanummon was home.[30]

Wattanummon left Stephen alone with the Pennacook boy and immediately "took his gun and went out hunting" as well (figure 9). The two boys "made a fire, but had not vituals to dress, only a moose's paunch which the hunting Indians had left." They boiled the paunch, drank the broth it made, and went to sleep. The next morning, "an Indian girl" brought the two boys "some moose's meat dried." Stephen thought it "was the best victuals ever I eat." Wattanummon's hunt had gone well. The girl took the boys several miles away, to a place where

FIGURE 9. "Sauvage allant a la Chasse" (A Native going hunting). Detail from "Village des Sauvages de Canada." Engraving from Louis Armon de Lom d'Arce de Lahontan, *Nouveaux voyages de M. le baron de Lahontan dans l'Amerique,* 2 vols. (The Hague, 1703). This contemporary image may offer a close approximation of the appearance of the Native raiders who attacked Deerfield. They most likely were clothed in heavy outer garments fashioned from European blankets. Their leggings and footwear were fashioned from skins. Photograph courtesy of the Department of Rare Books and Special Collections, Princeton University Library.

his relatives "had killed some moose." There they built wigwams. As Stephen noted, "their manner was when they killed any moose to move to them and lie by them till they had eaten them up." Soon other Pennacooks arrived. With them came two other Deerfield captives, Deacon Hoyt and Jacob Hickson.[31]

Captives of the Pennacooks found themselves living among people in straitened circumstances. The winter hunting season was the most difficult time of the year for these semi-sedentary people. Anticipating these conditions, the Pennacooks apparently did not take any female captives at Deerfield, at least none survived the trip to Cowass. The eventual fate of the captives that did make it to Cowass was determined largely by their age and condition. Deacon Hoyt and Jacob Hickson were adults. They had fought against the Pennacooks and stood little chance of fitting into Pennacook society. They were treated as slaves. Their masters were not as fortunate in the hunt as Wattanummon, giving them all the less reason to be generous to their captive enemies. They worked the Englishmen hard, and the two men had to survive mostly on whatever they could scrounge for themselves, which was not very much. Both eventually starved to death.[32]

Ten-year-old Stephen Williams, who was a prime candidate for adoption, was treated very differently, much like any other Pennacook boy and survived the winter in good health. While Steven waited with his two fellow captives, Wattanummon "went out to look for his family" and found them a day's travel away. A messenger came for Stephen. He found it hard to leave behind the other English prisoners and "go away alone," but he had no choice. After a rough journey he arrived at the camp where Wattanummon gave Stephen to his kinsman, George Tohanto. They "took care of [his] toe that was frozen" on the march up, "would not suffer [him] to do any work, gave [him] a dear skin to lie on and a bear's skin to cover [himself with]" until he recovered." Then Stephen joined them in hunting moose, bears, and beavers. They forced him to "carry such a pack when I traveled that I could not rise up without some help." Though Stephen complained, the move away from the other captives spared him much anguish. Lieutenant Hoyt died soon after Stephen left. Hickson grew thin from starvation. As the spring planting season approached, Hickson's masters took the weakened man down to Cowass to make him plant corn—women's work.[33]

The Pennacooks intended to stay in this area, what is today northern Vermont, despite appeals from the French to move to one of the Native villages in Canada. In early June, some of the Pennacooks traveled to Montreal to meet with Governor Philippe de Rigaud de Vaudreuil. They thanked him for sending the raiders against Deerfield at their request. The French governor was pleased that the expedition had "accomplished everything that was expected of it" and asked them to settle in Canada. The "Abenaki de Koessek [Cowassuck or

Cowass]" did not accept the governor's offer. They intended to continue living and planting on their own land near Cowass. Wattanummon and his companions still sought to live in Wôbanakik as an autonomous people, dependent on neither the French nor the English.[34]

English and Mohegan raiders, however, forced the Pennacooks to leave their country and take refuge with the French. Wattanummon and his family had every intention of settling in at Cowass with the coming of spring. But on their way down, they met people fleeing the village, who reported that a wigwam just south of Cowass had been attacked by a raiding party of Mohegan allies of the English. Seven members of the family living in the wigwam had been killed. The assault had taken place at almost exactly the same time as the Pennacook delegates met with Vaudrueil. The Pennacooks planting corn at Cowass fled, and no one planned to return anytime soon. They had brought with them their captives, including Hickson, who "looked like a ghost, was nothing but skin and bones."[35]

Wattanummon, the refugees from Cowass, and their prisoners remained in the mountains for somewhere between a month and six weeks. They suffered much for the want of provisions. Unable to plant and apparently having little success hunting, they finally decided to accept Vaudreuil's offer of hospitality in Canada. They had so much to transport that they "were forced to carry a pack a mile or two and, then go back and fetch another, which was tedious." In all, it was "an exceedingly tedious march" with little to eat along the way. At one point they had only "skins &c." to eat. Hickson died at the first portage on the Winooski River. When they reached Lake Champlain they found plenty of fish and fowl and continued their journey by canoe. Stephen Williams arrived in Chambly in late August, approximately six months after he had been taken. There the French told him "that my father and brothers and sisters were got to Canada, which I was glad to hear of, for I was afraid my youngest brother was killed."[36]

M OST of the captives survived the difficult winter journey. In Canada they faced new dangers, though the challenges were now primarily spiritual and mental rather than physical. On the march the destinies of captives had depended almost entirely on their age, sex, or race. The one African American was not even given the chance to survive; he had been killed the night he was captured. Eighteen women and children had been killed on the march. The two English men who died had starved to death as slaves of the Pennacooks. Almost half of the adult women—ten of twenty-three—had perished, as did four of the five captives aged two years or younger. Most of the children aged from three to twelve survived, thirty-one of thirty-six. All twenty-four of the captives aged thirteen to twenty lived. Nineteen of the twenty-four men taken from Deerfield made it safely to New France; two had already escaped; two had starved to death; and one, Frank, had been killed. In Canada their fates would be more affected by social and cultural factors, though biology would still play a critical role. As for the Indians and the French, the struggle over what to do with the eighty-nine remaining captives would strain an alliance that was proving to be much more fragile than the English imagined.

PART III

NEGOTIATING EMPIRES

CHAPTER 8

ADOPTING CAPTIVES

I N CANADA the religious struggle between Catholic and Protestant that had been rather muted on the march became paramount. The captives—and especially their minister—feared for the loss of their souls. For a devout circle of prominent French clergy and laity in Montreal, the overriding concern was the transformation of Protestant Englishmen into good Catholics. Some Christian Natives supported them in this concern. Others, especially the Kahnawake Mohawks, wanted to turn their captives into Natives first and Christians second. The struggles to possess the persons and souls of Deerfield's hapless colonists pitted French against Indians and English captives against one another.

The contest for souls was not the entire story, however, though it would figure prominently in English accounts of captivity experiences. Economic calculations, cultural pride, family ties, and human frailty were important too in determining the fate of individuals. Depending on the community—even the family—in which captives found themselves, they could be used as slaves or servants, adopted as family members, bartered for money and ransomed, retained as hostages, or even tortured to death. What happened to individual captives was also influenced by who they were. The Reverend John Williams—the first New England minister to be captured by a French and Indian war party—experienced a far different reception in Canada from that of nine-year-old Mary Harris, who had no relatives to help her. Chance and whim played roles as well. Nonetheless, certain patterns can be discerned in the fates of the Deerfield captives who reached New France in spring 1704.

A S MOSTLY prisoners of Native warriors, the Deerfield captives observed New France, the home of their political and religious enemy, and the relationship between their Indian captors and the French from a unique perspective. They quickly realized that the relationship was full of tension and mistrust. The great concern French colonists showed for the welfare of the English captives sometimes made their Native allies wonder whom the French really valued, them or the people they warred against.

John Williams's first impression of New France was that the "French were very kind to me." But French hospitality, so welcome to the captives, was viewed by Native masters as a challenge to their authority over their prisoners. At Chambly, "a gentleman," who was most likely De Rouville's father, Joseph François Hertel, "took me into his house and to his table and lodged me at night on a good feather bed. The inhabitants and officers were very obliging to me the little time I stayed with them and promised to write a letter to the governor-in-chief to inform him of my passing down the river." Wherever John went after this, "the French were very courteous." When his party "came down to the first inhabited house at Sorel, a Frenchwoman came to the riverside and desired us to go into her house." Once they were inside, "she compassioned our state and told us she had in the last war been a captive among the Indians and therefore was not a little sensible of our difficulties." The woman then gave the Abenakis "something to eat in the chimney-corner and spread a cloth on the table for us with napkins, which gave such offense to the Indians that they hasted away and would not call in at the fort" of Sorel. Soon thereafter, just before they arrived at Saint Francis, they stopped at "a French officer's house." The officer, probably Jean-Baptiste Hertel de Rouville's brother, Joseph Hertel de Saint-François, took the Reverend Williams "into a private room out of sight of the Indians, and treated us very courteously."[1]

Stephen Williams had a similar experience, encountering friendly French who insulted their Native allies. The cultural differences in the alliance came into conflict over food and lodging. On the march to Canada, Natives had had exclusive control over their captives' access to food. This power had allowed the Natives to begin the process of acculturation and underscored their prisoners' dependence. Now the French in Canada challenged this control by offering the captives familiar food in inviting environments. When Stephen arrived in Chambly, he recorded, "the French were kind to me," as they had been to his father. They told him the rest of his family had arrived safely and gave him "bread which I had not eaten in a great while." A Frenchman "came & desired the Indians to let me go with him, which they did." Stephen "went with the Frenchman who gave me some vituals, & made me ly down in his couach."[2]

Stephen Williams's master, Wattanummon, who did not even pretend to be a good Catholic, had less reason to trust the French than did his Christian kinsmen. When his son told him that he saw Stephen relaxing on a French couch, Wattanummon hurried over and "fetcht me away and would not let me go to the fort any more for which I suffered." Wattanummon thought the Frenchman had taken the boy in "to hide me & did desighn to steal me." The French soon intervened again, dressing Stephen's injured feet "at which the Indians seemed to be vext." When his party headed down to Sorel, they camped "a day or two near" a Frenchman's house. Stephen remembered that he "was kind to me & would have lodged me in his house but the Indians would not allow it mistrusting he would convey me away in the night privately." Once in Sorel a Frenchwoman came across the river "on purpose to bring me some vituals." Quite possibly she was the same woman who had hosted his father several months earlier, for she "seemed to pity me." The Pennacooks camped for "a day or two" outside Sorel, and Wattanummon let Stephen "go to the fort a visiting." A Frenchman persuaded Stephen to stay over "all night & till next day about noon, when my master came for me." Wattanummon "was very angry with" him "& after that would never suffer [Stephen] to go to a French house alone."[3]

Unlike partisan leaders such as De Rouville, these French colonists did not understand or chose to ignore the importance of captives to their Native allies. Many French colonists could not abide what they felt was the barbarous treatment Natives often meted out to their prisoners. Like most other Europeans, the French, as a matter of principle, detested the torturing of war captives. Prisoners of war could be ransomed, paroled, held in prison for an eventual prisoner exchange, or even conscripted into the army that had captured them, but killing them was usually considered an atrocity. Many educated Frenchmen were uncomfortable with the idea that they were fighting alongside Indians. John Williams was "persuaded that the priest of the parish where I was kept [Chateau Richer] abhorred their sending down the heathen to commit outrages against the English, saying it was more like committing murders than managing a war." This was personal as much as cultural. Several, such as the French woman who cared for John and probably for Stephen Williams, had themselves been held captive by Natives, undoubtedly members of the Iroquois League.[4]

Because most of the French sympathized more with the plight of the English captives than their Native allies, some of the Deerfield captives never set foot in a Native village. The two captives who greeted John Williams at Chambly had been ransomed as soon as they entered New France. John's son Warham was also ransomed before he arrived at Kahnawake. Others probably had similar experiences or spent only brief periods of time in Native communities. John Williams spent only about a week at Odanak; the Deerfield father and daughter who were ransomed with Williams (probably Nathaniel Brooks and Mary Brooks) may have been there for a month. Within a year's time, a majority of the Deerfield captives were in the hands of the French.

Many Native masters often appear to have willingly parted with their captives after a bit of hard bargaining. Like furs and scalps, captives had become commercialized commodities by 1704, and Montreal was the center of this trade. The degree to which individual masters entered into this commerce depended on the captives in question, the strength of traditional values, economic calculations, and the persistence of the French.

The Abenakis from Odanak and the Pennacooks mostly preferred to sell their captives. They had joined the Deerfield raid to protect their homeland by sending the English a message; captive taking was a by-product of their overlapping war for retribution, not its main goal. They also did not have the tradition of adoption associated with the Iroquoian practice of fighting wars specifically to obtain captives. Thus, Abenakis tended to take adult and male prisoners who would be more likely to survive the journey to Canada and were more likely to appeal to potential buyers once in Canada.

Adoption presented the small, relatively mobile Abenaki bands with more of a challenge and less of an opportunity. Their villages were relatively small and seasonal. Their economy was more mobile than that of Iroquoian nations, their kin groups less extensive. The seasonal nature of the Abenaki economy, which did not have as strong an agricultural base as Iroquoian villages, meant that most families would be off on their own for the fall and winter, hunting and gathering maple sugar. As a result, responsibility for the integration of a captive fell to the immediate family, not an extended lineage or village community. And many of the families at Odanak in 1704 were only temporary residents, awaiting an opportunity to return to their homes once hostilities ended. Not surprisingly, virtually all of the English captives taken by the Abenakis and Pennacooks from Deerfield and elsewhere made their way into French society and eventually back to New England.[5]

Stephen Williams's account of his captivity provides some idea of the difficulties facing the Abenakis who attempted to assimilate English captives. Originally a captive of the Pennacook Wattanummon, he arrived at Odanak with his master's family as a refugee. Because Wattanummon, "could not comply" with the Catholic "rites & customs" at the mission of Saint Francis, he left for Schaghticoke and gave Stephen "to his kinsman Sachamore George." By this time Stephen had already given ample evidence of his ignorance of woodcraft and hunting. There was no chance he would make a good Abenaki. His status seems to have shifted down to that of unwilling servant or slave. George and his wife put Stephen to work in and about the village. Here too he proved to be an unsatisfactory worker. When his new masters needed support in disciplining him, they turned to their Jesuit priest, not to any Native authority in the village, suggesting the tenuousness of their connection to the rest of the village.[6]

In the winter, George took his family and Stephen to hunt for beaver along the streams and brooks around Chambly. When De Rouville's father found out that Stephen was nearby, he "came to buy me." Stephen could not hide his willingness "to go with him" and, thus, insulted his Pennacook masters once again. They "were much disturbed & would not let me go because I showed a forwardness to go, & did likewise threaten to kill me." After returning to Odanak,

George complained to the Jesuit "who came & said to me, what no love Indian they have saved your life, etc." Stephen was clearly an inept and insolent member of the community and more trouble than he was worth. His master eventually signaled his willingness to sell him to the French.[7]

Despite great pressure from the highest officials in the colony and his master's willingness, it still took several months to ransom Stephen. At John Williams's urging, Governor Philippe de Rigaud de Vaudreuil of New France made repeated entreaties to the Abenakis, offering to redeem Stephen for "30 crowns." His master held out for 40. Wearied by Vaudreuil's insistence, he had Stephen write a letter saying that Vaudreuil could purchase him for 40 crowns by springtime, otherwise "they would not sell" him. When the first English negotiators for a prisoner exchange appeared in Canada, Stephen's mistress took him "up in ye woods about half a mile" away from the Saint Lawrence River, "lest the French should then take me away for nothing." Eventually, in spring 1705, Vaudreuil bought Stephen for 40 crowns "after a long parley."[8]

Unlike the Abenakis, Iroquoian peoples—the Mohawks from Kahnawake, the Iroquois of the Mountain, and the Hurons from Lorette—fought mourning wars specifically to obtain captives. Over the course of the seventeenth century under the impact of almost constant warfare and pressure from French missionaries, Iroquoian practices evolved. Because of losses from disease and battle, Iroquoian communities were more likely to incorporate captives into their communities rather than killing them. They would adopt prisoners outright, keep them as slaves for a period of testing or perhaps permanently, or trade them to other Natives or the French. Traditional attitudes and practices still persisted as Thaovenhosen discovered on the march north. A prisoner could be tortured to death, especially if he attempted to escape, but the practice of incorporating souls by torture gradually became less common.[9]

Nevertheless, a ritual death by torture and burning remained a possibility, and Thomas Baker, one of the Deerfield captives, was almost a victim. A twenty-one-year-old soldier, Baker was determined not to accept his fate as the will of God punishing him for his sins. Soon after he arrived at the Sault-au-Récollet, he learned of a major expedition being organized to go against the frontiers of New England. Wanting to warn the English before the army struck, he escaped and headed south. He was soon caught. His captors decided to burn him as an example to dissuade any other captives who might be contemplating flight. Before they could tie him to the stake, Baker escaped again. Closely pursued, he ran to the house of a nearby Frenchman. The colonist stood up to the warriors and ransomed Baker for £5, which Baker promised to pay back. French authorities then put him in irons for several months before releasing him.[10]

The small communities of La Montagne, Sault-au-Récollet and Lorette, had little more capacity to absorb English captives than did the Abenakis. Almost all of their captives were sold to the French. The practice had begun earlier in the 1600s by Jesuit missionaries who offered gifts as ransom in order to have access to their allies' Indian captives, whom they hoped to convert. Soon the French were purchasing the captives outright, though the ransoming process always retained its roots in the Native gift economy. Whether or not a captive was ransomed, and at what price, remained matters for negotiation. Now, however, there was an accepted way for warriors to turn captives over to the French for a profit.[11]

By the second half of the seventeenth century, these alterations in mourning-war culture were evolving into a petty slave trade involving English, Native, and eventually African victims. While minuscule and inconsequential when compared with the contemporary African slave trade, it nevertheless involved selling captives to the French, who made the holding of Native as well as African slaves legal in New France in 1709. This change occurred at a time when the war had cut off the flow of immigrants from France and colonists were complaining about a shortage of farm workers and servants. Native slaves came from out West, beyond the Great Lakes, and were known as "panis," because many of them were in fact Pawnees. The French trade in Native captives paralleled the more extensive and vicious raids along the southern English frontier, where Carolinians and their Native allies obtained hundreds of Indian slaves over the course of the War of the Spanish Succession. The number of Indian slaves in New France proved to be rather modest in comparison, totaling approximately eighty-eight during the decade from 1702 to 1712.[12]

Captive New Englanders, however, arrived in much greater numbers during the same period. Even though Europeans could not be enslaved in New France, they could be sold into servitude. By the 1690s warriors were regularly selling their English captives, especially adults, to the French. The willingness of the French to pay good money for captives led some warriors to go straight for the profit and sell their captives off without necessarily consulting their communities. At the same time, some Natives retained their adult captives as slaves in order to benefit from their labor. They, too, sometimes did so without consulting the community. And one observer claimed even after a community had made a disposition of a captive, "the warriors in some nations never divest themselves entirely of their prisoners, and those to whom the council has distributed them, are obliged to make redistribution to them if demanded." English captives were particularly appreciated because the men did not mind doing the farm labor that Native men regarded as women's work.[13]

The commodification of captivity was most evident in Montreal. As the established center of the fur trade, this town was well situated to take advantage of the market in captives. For Abenakis returning to Odanak by way of the

Richelieu River, a stop in Montreal involved only a minor detour. Kahnawake Mohawks either stopped there on their way home or ferried over the captives they did not want to keep soon after returning to their village. The Iroquois of the Mountain, in contrast, usually had to travel through Montreal on their way back to their villages at La Montagne and Sault-au-Récollet. Unlike the others, who could choose whether or not to bring a captive to Montreal for sale, they had to pass through town with all of their captives, including any children they desired to keep. In a sense the Iroquois of the Mountain with captives had to run through a "gauntlet" of French men and women offering money for their prisoners.[14]

As the warriors moved through Montreal, wealthy and devout French colonists accosted them. Agathe de Saint-Père, a noblewoman, redeemed four-year-old Warham Williams "in the city as the Indians passed by." Six weeks later, the merchant Jacques Le Ber, rich enough to buy himself a title of nobility in 1696, "obtained" Samuel Williams, who "was taken to live with him." These children, ripe for adoption and conversion, were as valuable to the French as they were to their Native allies. Redeeming them was a complicated transaction. Jacques Le Ber had to take "a great deal of pains to persuade the savages to part with" Samuel. Those who sold Warham so suddenly—probably Kahnawake Mohawks—had second thoughts after they "had been at their fort and discoursed with the priests." They went back to Agathe de Saint-Père and offered her "a man for the child alleging that the child could not be profitable to her, but the man would, for he was a weaver and his service would much advance the design she had of making cloth." But, as John Williams reports, "God overruled so far that this temptation to the woman prevailed not for an exchange, for had the child gone to the Indian fort in an ordinary way, it had abode there still, as the rest of the children carried there do."[15]

The change of masters from Native to French often happened quite quickly. Governor Vaudreuil ransomed John and Esther Williams within days or weeks of their arrival in New France. Later he had ransomed Stephen. While the Williamses benefited from their father's status, others from more humble families—Brookses, Hursts, and Kelloggs—along with Elizabeth Stevens, the widow of "the Indian" Andrew Stevens, all passed rather quickly into the hands of the French. The rapidity of the turnover makes the process seem very straightforward, though everyone experienced a unique passage from Native master to French master. And at least seven Deerfield captives never did make the passage.

THOSE captives who were taken to Native villages and spent some time in these communities soon found themselves pressured to embrace a new way of life and in some instances to convert to Catholicism. As one Canadian historian has observed, "Amerindians worked hard to evangelize Europeans

and in the process became some of North America's most successful missionaries." Whether or not Natives attempted to convert the English, they did put
them to work, regardless of age or sex.[16]

At first, captives generally found themselves in a state of virtual slavery. They
had no real kin to protect them, and thus, their status hinged on their ability to
be accepted as kin by their masters. This was easiest for young children, who
could simply be adopted into new families and raised as one of their own. Older
men and women had to prove themselves as warriors and workers. Some could
gain great respect in their adoptive communities, but it was harder for adults to
forget their original identities. Most lived in a state of perpetual servitude and
uncertainty. Fundamentally, this was not a process in which the captives exercised much choice. If they were lucky, and their peoples made peace, they might
be adopted or returned in a captive exchange. If not, they could be killed if they
offended their masters.[17]

The marginal status of English captives even within Iroquoian communities
is strikingly recorded in some of the names that were initially assigned to those
individuals who were adopted. Abigail Nims was referred to as Kanawkwa, a
French rendering of *kenaskwa,* meaning captive or slave. In Mohawk this word's
root, *enaskwa,* came to signify domestic animal as well as captive or slave, which
is indicative of the position of such individuals. Josiah Rising was Shonatakakwani, "he who has been taken away from his village." At Kahnawake, Eunice
Williams was Waongote, "they took her and place her as a member of their
tribe." The last two names underscore the fact that renaming captives cut them
off from their original community and potentially incorporated them into a
new one. However, these captives faced a time of testing before they would be
placed securely as members of their masters' tribe.[18]

Age seems to have been the first category by which the raiders sorted out their
captives. Soon after they returned, they isolated the children from English adults
and each other, undoubtedly to speed up their acculturation by making them dependent on Native adults and immersing them in a new language. John Williams,
who lost one daughter to the process, was particularly sensitive to what was going on. When he arrived at Odanak, he saw there "several poor children who had
been taken from the Eastward the summer before, a sight very affecting, they
being in habit much like Indians and in manner very much symbolizing with
them." He believed that "the Jesuits counseled the Macquas to sell all the grown
persons from the fort [Kahnawake]—a stratagem to seduce poor children."[19]

Two insiders' glimpses of this process largely confirm Williams's observations. Here, what to the father and the minister seemed like a dangerous pro-
clivity of young children to abandon their native language and culture is revealed
to be the product of coercive social pressure and, to a degree, dissembling.

Stephen Williams later remembered how some of the English children at Odanak "would scofe at me when before the indians whorse than the indian children, but when alone they would talk familiarly with me in English about their own country, etc., whereas when before the indians they would pretend they could not speak english." In his opinion it was "no wonder that children that are small will not speak to their friends when they come to see them, but they will scofe and deride them, because the indians have taught them so, will be angry if they do otherwise." At the Sault-au-Récollet, Joseph Kellogg also experienced the mixture of coercion and persuasion used to isolate English children from their elders. First, "By the priests' means all the grown persons were put away." Then, he and the other children were constantly told "that unless I really hated my father and mother I could not be saved." Meanwhile, as at Odanak, "the Indians prohibited the children speaking together in the English tongue, if we did speak it must be in the Macqua language."[20]

To promote their integration into community life and to evaluate their worth and adaptability masters put their captives to work. In Iroquoian communities where corn cultivation was the basis of subsistence even young girls worked, grinding corn, a nearly endless process requiring the daily equivalent of an hour's work from each member of the community. When necessary, coercion was used, as Stephen Williams learned. On a "tempestuous day" he disobeyed his mistress's order to gather wood, judging that they "had half a cart load of wood at the door (which is a great deal for indians to have)." This made her "very angry," and she had the Jesuit—most likely Jacques Bigot, a veteran of the mission to the Eastern Abenakis—whip him. Later, when left in charge of a barrel full of boiling maple sap, he forgot to stir the mixture and so ruined a large batch of maple sugar. Again his Abenaki masters "were very angry & would not give me any vituals." As the negotiations for his redemption wound down, his mistress told him "your time is short you have to live with me." Stephen could only think "truly I hoped it was." Unlike some other English boys who were freed from captivity, Stephen did not miss life among the Indians for a minute.[21]

The names of captives are suggestive of the kind of work they performed for their masters. At some point in her life, Eunice Williams, initially named for her captive status, came to be known as Kanenstenhawi, "she brings in corn." Abigail Nims at the Sault-au-Récollet eventually went by the name Elizabeth Twatogwach, "Elizabeth who goes and gets water." According to later New England sources, Mary Field was called "Walahowey," a possible corruption of the Mohawk name Waienhawi, "she is carrying fruit." A later eighteenth-century captive of Kahnawake Mohawks, James Smith, claimed that he was called by an "Indian name, which was Scoouwa." Most likely the name Smith remembered was a mishearing of *skoha,* a Mohawk word that literally means, "Go get it."

Unlike Stephen Williams, these probationary captives must have proven themselves to their masters, for they were adopted into Native communities.[22]

The role religion played in the process of integration appears to have varied according to captives' age and sex. John Williams, for example, throughout his stay at Odanak, was under pressure to convert, both from the Jesuit priests of the Saint Francis mission and from one of his Abenaki masters. "One day" in the spring of 1704, according to his later narrative, while he sat outside of his masters' house "a certain savagess taken prisoner in [King] Philip's war, who had lived at Mr. Buckley's at Weathersfield [Connecticut], called Ruth, who could speak English very well and who had been often at my house, being now proselyted to the Romish faith, came into the wigwam." On this day Ruth joined the effort to convert the determined Protestant minister, quoting scripture to persuade him to obey his master's commands to cross himself and kiss a crucifix. Eventually, Williams's master gave up in frustration exclaiming, "No good minister, no love God, as bad as the Devil."[23]

More persistent and more successful efforts were made to convert young girls as part of a broader effort to integrate them into Native communities. The only account of a girl's experience of captivity comes, appropriately enough, from Kahnawake. It was apparently passed down orally in the Mohawk family of Eunice Williams for two or three generations before it was written down in the mid-nineteenth century. According to this story, Eunice was taken to replace a child lost to a Mohawk woman only a few years before. Once Eunice arrived in Kahnawake, "the relations of her adopted mother took much notice of her, and the children were instructed to treat her as one of the family." Other young captives taken at Deerfield may have fulfilled similar needs in other Mohawk families. With such an enthusiastic and accepting welcome, it is not surprising that after several years captive children, like Eunice, might prefer to stay at Kahnawake with a family that they knew and loved rather than return to a virtually forgotten life back in New England. Such was the power of the adoptive impulse within the mourning-war culture.[24]

Christian religion complemented traditional Mohawk social techniques to spur the assimilation of English captives into Kahnawake. The locally venerated Kateri Tekakwitha "was held up to [Eunice's] view" as a model of devout behavior. According to the family tradition, Eunice was greatly affected. Perhaps she was impressed that at Kahnawake a woman could have the most prestigious spiritual reputation both within the community and outside of it. She converted and soon acquired a reputation for "great piety and strictness."[25]

Mohawk family tradition remembers Eunice's conversion as a rather straightforward spiritual awakening encouraged by a loving and devout family. From the little we know from Eunice, however, it was probably a much more harrowing struggle. With the direct intervention of Governor Vaudreuil, her father finally managed to see her for an hour. He later wrote of how the seven-year-old girl "was very desirous to be redeemed out of the hands of the Macquas and bemoaned her state among them." With relief, John Williams noted that "she could read very well and had not forgotten her catechism." But she was clearly ill at ease in her new surroundings. This minister's daughter knew her Protestantism well enough to be suspicious of the Catholic mass. She told her father that the Mohawks "profaned God's Sabbaths and said she thought that a few days before they had been mocking the devil, and that one of the Jesuits stood and looked on them."[26]

Eunice's predicament reveals how vulnerable Protestant children were to proselytizing in New France. John Williams, determined to keep his daughter Protestant, told her to "pray to God for His grace every day. She said she did as she was able and God helped her. But," she added, "They force me to say some prayers in Latin, but I don't understand one word of them; I hope it won't do me any harm." All her father could do was tell her "she must be careful she did not forget her catechism and the Scriptures she had learned by heart." After he left she passed on his words to the other captives "and said she was much afraid she should forget her catechism, having none to instruct her." Williams saw her only once more for a few minutes in Montreal and "improved to give her the best advice I could."[27]

Young boys appear to have been better able to resist integration into Native communities, perhaps in part because the efforts to convert them to Catholicism were more perfunctory. Stephen Williams's experience was undoubtedly tempered by the fact that he belonged to a family of Pennacooks whose zeal was not as strong as that of the permanent Abenaki residents of Odanak. Religion did not even become a topic for him until he arrived at Saint Francis. There, as he recalled, "the indians did say something to me about religion but not much, being eastern indians were not zealous as the macquas are." But Stephen's experience is somewhat confirmed by Joseph Kellogg, who spent a good deal of time with the Iroquois of the Mountain at Sault-au-Récollet. As Joseph recalled, "the Indians indulge english boys abundantly, let them have the liberty they will, while they outwardly conform to them, and so an easy way of life and libertinism is more prevailing with them than any affection they have to religion." Both boys would eventually return to New England, though not before spending time with the French.[28]

T HE French actually outdid Natives in Canada in their desire and success in converting and adopting English captives. The zeal with which French men and women sought to ransom English captives from their Native allies was more than religious. It also went beyond humanitarian considerations. Adults could provide much-needed labor in the underpopulated colony. Children could be taught to forget their origins and adopt a new community as their own. New Englanders, who were already culturally European, were much easier to integrate into French society than Natives were. In a small colony, where the sex ratio did not even out until about 1710, new subjects, especially female subjects, were always welcome.[29]

A well-established market for indentured servants or *engagés* provided a social and economic framework for incorporating the captives into a Canadian society. New England captives lived and worked for households lay and religious. These households provided the context for keeping them in Canada. Only Thomas Baker suffered actual imprisonment for a time, and his experience was exceptional. The rest of the captives, who did not get caught trying to escape, experienced a surprising degree of freedom of movement. Some even had access to guns.

Among the French, the Deerfield captives worked as house servants, farmers, and laborers. In this they resembled many French immigrants. Benjamin and Sarah Burt probably worked as servants at the Sulpician seminary and in the convent of the Congregation de Notre Dame. Samuel Hastings worked as a servant in the seminary in Quebec. The work of the rest can only be surmised from where they lived, either on the rural seigneuries near Montreal or in the homes of artisans, merchants, and officers or in one of the religious houses under the care of priests or nuns. New England captives differed from most of the servants and soldiers who came over from France in that many of them possessed skills New France desperately needed. French immigrants were mostly from towns and cities and few had the skills needed to develop the rural economy of New France. New England colonists, however, knew how to farm, to build and operate sawmills, and to weave textiles.[30]

In an effort to start a colonial textile industry, Agathe de Saint-Père, the woman who had ransomed Warham Williams, assembled nine New England captives by the end of 1704. Apart from Warham, aged four, she had two Deerfield captives, twenty-six-year-old Judah Wright and twelve-year-old Ebenezer Sheldon. The rest of the captives had been taken on the Maine frontier in 1703. Though a noblewoman, Saint-Père had an entrepreneurial streak. She needed it. She had a large family, her estate was small, and her husband, an officer in the colonial troops, was fairly lazy. If any money was to be made, she had to make it.

Saint-Père had already raised ten half-siblings on the family farm at Pointe-Saint-Charles outside of Montreal. An experienced household manager when she married Pierre Legardeur de Repentigny, she extended her activities into the business world of money-lending, fur-trading, and real estate dealing to support their growing family. Sometime in 1703, after the war had cut off the flow of textiles from France, she had the idea of manufacturing cloth in the colony it-self. The home government, which did not want to encourage the growth of co-lonial industry at the expense of textile manufacturers in France, agreed to it only when she promised to use exclusively local materials to produce cheap, rough textiles for poor colonists. She put captives to work in her household and succeeded in producing a number of textiles, though her fledgling industry did not survive the return of peace and French imports. It is doubtful that she really wanted to do more than support her family during the war by supplying much-needed cloth. By the end of the war all of her captives had returned and her op-eration shut down.[31]

Depending on the pace of negotiations to exchange prisoners, the terms of service for English captives could be relatively short, from one to two years. In the end, they were more valuable as prisoners to be exchanged for French cap-tives than as servant labor. Even so, the French managed to get almost as much work out of them as they got out of the average French *engagé*. In the English colonies, seven years was the usual term of service. But in the French colonies it was three years, or thirty-six months. Like the Deerfield captives, many of the so-called *trente-six mois* did not stay in the colony very long, preferring to return to France as soon as their time of service was up. Those who did stay were gen-erally men who found a wife and started a family of their own in New France. Among the Deerfield captives, those who stayed had arrived at a much younger age than most of the *trente-six mois,* many of them were female, and those who did stay settled down and started families.

DEERFIELD captives who remained permanently in New France were held by bonds of religion and family, not servitude. As with the Indians, chil-dren were most susceptible to conversion and integration into French society. However, unlike the situation in Native villages where conversion was part of a broader effort to integrate English captives into their communities, it was the primary means of persuasion among the French. Religious argument—in which the English, because of their upbringing, would engage—often gave the French the opening they needed.

Those French colonists who took an interest in converting captives saw themselves as part of a wave of Catholic expansion that had been pushing back the gains of Protestantism since the Thirty Years' War. Only twenty years be-fore, their homeland had suppressed Protestantism within its borders with the 1685 revocation of the Edict of Nantes. French Protestants had been forced to convert or flee as a wave of militant Catholic activism swept across France. Young Joseph Kellogg was told that "it was but a little while & all of the English [would become] good Catholicks, and not the name of a protestant among them." How could pious French men and women resist the opportunity to re-store to the Catholic cause souls that were culturally European and undoubt-edly Christian, though deluded? This was especially appealing to devout French colonists in the waning years of Louis XIV's reign, when the Sun King turned pi-ous and went from disliking Jesuits to supporting them.[32]

The task of converting English Protestants preoccupied a core group of elite Montrealers and churchmen. Heading the campaign to convert English captives was Henri-Antoine Meriel de Meulan, a Sulpician priest who had arrived in Montreal in 1690, at the age of twenty-nine. He knew English and had a re-spectable family fortune to support his evangelizing efforts. In his first years he had some doubts about his pastoral abilities, particularly when it came to hear-ing confession. But the arrival of English captives during the Nine Years' War gave him the sense of mission he needed. For almost twenty years, until he went back to Paris to die in 1713, he devotedly presided over the vast majority of bap-tisms, conversions, and marriages of English captives in and around Montreal. At least thirteen of the Deerfield captives converted to Catholicism under his su-pervision (figure 10).[33]

Father Meriel served as the director and confessor of pupils at the Congrega-tion de Notre Dame and ministered to the patients at the Hôtel-Dieu. This brought him into contact with the many captives, particularly the young, who were often placed in the Hôtel-Dieu and with the Congregation by their French masters. He also roamed the countryside and often visited the Sulpician mission at Sault-au-Récollet. By 1704 he was assisted by one of his protégés, Mary Say-ward, an English captive taken in Maine during the Nine Years' War who became one of the nuns of the Congregation, and Robert Potier Dubuisson, a Frenchman born and raised on Staten Island who had moved to Montreal in 1699. There he worked in the Church of Notre Dame, where his father was the organist.[34]

Members of the noble Le Ber and Le Moyne families aided the efforts of the Congregation. Jacques Le Ber, his wife Jeanne Le Moyne, sister of Charles Le Moyne de Longueuil et de Chateauguay, their son Pierre, and Jeanne's nephews Charles Le Moyne de Longueuil, Baron de Longueuil, and Paul Le Moyne de Maricourt, as well as other members of the Le Moyne family ransomed cap-tives, stood in as godparents at captives' baptisms, and witnessed their wed-dings. The Le Moynes took particular care of captives at Sault-au-Récollet. The Baron de Longueuil was New France's ambassador to the Iroquois at this time and therefore remained in close touch with the Kahnawake Mohawks and the Iroquois of the Mountain. Maricourt was also an officer who knew Indian lan-guages and had served on many expeditions. These families brought together all the elements—involvement in the fur trade, the military, and the church—that characterized Montreal's elite.[35]

FIGURE 10. "Vue de la Ville du Montréal" (View of Montreal). Watercolor, circa 1720, artist unknown. Montreal in the early 1700s was a medium-sized town surrounded by a palisade. Among the sites indicated in this view are (A) the general hospital, (C) the Seminary of the Sulpicians, and (D) the Church of Notre Dame. Photograph courtesy of Edward E. Ayer Collection. The Newberry Library, Chicago.

The Le Moyne and Le Ber families, together with Meriel, the nuns of the Congregation of Notre Dame, and the Hôtel-Dieu formed a powerful network for incorporating English captives. The list of Deerfield captives who benefited from their attentions is long: young Mary Brooks, John and Sarah Burt, whose son Christopher was born in Canada and baptized by Meriel, young Elizabeth Corse, Freedom French, Martha French, Sarah Hurst, Elizabeth Hurst, Thomas Hurst, Ebenezer Hurst, Abigail Nims, Elizabeth Stevens, and Samuel Williams. There were probably more, such as Joseph Kellogg, but there are gaps in the records.

The two adult captives from Deerfield who converted to Catholicism were widows. The recently widowed Elizabeth Stevens converted not long after her arrival in New France and remarried in a Catholic ceremony. Her godfather was Pierre Le Ber; her godmother was Damoiselle Elizabeth Le Moyne, daughter of Baron Charles Le Moyne; and Father Meriel officiated. Meriel also performed her marriage ceremony in 1706. Another Deerfield widow, Sarah Hurst, was married to William Perkins by Meriel in 1710. John Williams also heard stories of at least two widows from other New England towns, Abigail Turbet and Hannah Batison Stilson, who converted while he was in New France. Hannah Stilson actually worked to convert other English captives to Catholicism, and even though Williams discounted her efforts, he is probably not a reliable source in this instance.[36]

These conversions may have been related to the desire or need to obtain church approval for remarriage. Some English women in French and Native communities do appear to have been tempted or pressured to marry or to enter into sexual liaisons. While it is true that Natives in the Northeast rarely if ever molested or raped women captives, there is evidence of pregnancies outside of marriage. Joanna Ordway, a captive taken in August 1703, had a child with an Abenaki man, and John Williams's daughter Esther heard that fourteen-year-old Esther Wheelwright "is with child by an Indian." Neither woman remained in a Native community. Pregnancy could precede marriage in French communities as well. Williams learned that nineteen-year-old Rachael Storer of Wells, Maine, was "debauched and then in twenty-four hours of time published, taken into communion and married." According to Williams she subsequently "had time since to lament her sin and folly with a bitter cry." Elizabeth Corse, a fifteen-year-old Deerfield captive, also had a child out of wedlock. There is evidence of pressure from Native masters and French priests to marry. Williams heard of "great essays to get others married among them." Taking a spouse could protect one from what may have been unwanted suitors. Conversion could have been a necessary first step to a church-sanctioned marriage and the protection of a spouse. The fact that both Hannah Batison Stilson and Sarah Hurst Perkins returned to New England after they had converted, remarried, and become

naturalized French subjects makes one question the role of purely religious motivations in their conversions.[37]

Children were subjected to even more intensive evangelization. Only twelve
years old at the time he arrived, Joseph Kellogg was exposed to the full range of
pressure and persuasion to convert that French priests could muster. Coercion
headed the list of proselytizing techniques. Joseph recounted how he "was
forced by my master to go to church. He forced me to cross myself when I was
unwilling, he threatened to beat me, & would by force take my hand, & make
it for me, would deny me victuals unless I would conform to them." Alternatively, Joseph was showered with kindness and attention if he acceded to the demands of his captors. He remembered how the "priest always humoured me,
giving me any thing if I complied with them."[38]

For all the use, or threatened use, of force, the conversion campaign relied
primarily on a steady and intensive education in the lies of Protestantism and
the blessings of the Catholic religion. Ironically, the priests' arguments were
predicated on Joseph Kellogg's Protestant up-bringing and familiarity with the
Bible. French clergy "used all their art to make us in love with their religion,"
Joseph recalled, and "were often crying against our religion." The priests told
the English children that "our bibles were defective and did not contain all,"
pointing out that the English had taken out the Apocrypha from their scriptures.
They exploited the young boy's own knowledge of Christianity and the Bible to
persuade him to convert.[39]

More was involved than logic and arguments and much was made of the
power of miracles. One Jesuit priest emphasized that "miracles were one great
mark of the true church, and though there were none in our country, yet I
should see one there." He then took Joseph to watch a religious procession bless
some fields plagued with worms that "were eating their grain." As Joseph
watched "they went in procession saying of their prayers, & sprinkling holy water." Then he saw how, "within a little time all the worms were gone away."
Other priests confronted Joseph with a series of miracle stories involving European saints, French colonists, and the "great miracles wrought by 'Saint Katherine' . . . a Macqua squaw, that was dead & sainted." Protestantism, they claimed,
was proved all the more wrong for its failure to produce miracles.[40]

In the end, disease and the miraculous power of Catholic relics accomplished
Joseph's conversion. Joseph fell sick with smallpox during his first year of captivity. At the height of his illness, when the thirteen-year-old boy's sores were
"white and just ready to run, a Jesuit came to me, and told me my case was very
hazardous, and that he had used all ordinary means but without success." Then
he held out the hope of extraordinary help. By chance, when the priest "was looking over his medicines some of the relick" of the sainted Katherine Tekakwitha

"came into his hand, but though he knew the great virtue in them, he dare not give them to me, because I was not a Roman Catholic in heart, and told me I was near dying, and that if I would now promise, that I would confess, & be Roman Catholick, if upon taking some of these relicks I should have help, he would give them to me." Desperately ill, Joseph accepted this divine deal. The Jesuit gave him "something under the name of the relicks of the rotten wood of the coffin, after which I slept better, & grew better." And when Joseph awoke, he made good his part of the bargain promising "God and the Church to live and die in their religion and land."[41]

Samuel Williams, John's son, was subjected to similar pressures. The French "threatened to put him to the Indians again if he would not turn, telling him he was never bought out of their hands but only sojourned with them, but, if he would turn, he should never be put into their hands anymore." Other captives were similarly threatened with return to the Indians. Samuel was forced to make the sign of the cross, dragged to mass, and subjected to constant arguments emphasizing the virtues of the Catholic faith. Dramatic stories of other captives who died allegedly embracing Catholicism were recounted to inspire him. Samuel eventually caved in to the pressure and converted. Within a year and after several passionate and polemical letters from his father, Samuel regretted and reconsidered his decision. "I am sorry for the sin I have committed in changing of religion, for which I am greatly to blame," he wrote in the spring of 1706. Not long after he was back in Massachusetts and again a Protestant.[42]

We have no direct account of what young female captives experienced among the French. We can, however, infer a pattern from a few facts about the French family. After Mary French, a "captive damsel, about sixteen or seventeen years of age," returned to New England in a captive exchange, she published a poem she had written as she was leaving Canada. She was "afraid that her younger sister, at a distance from her would be led away by the popish delusions."

> Dear Sister, Jesus does you call
> To walk on in His ways.
> I pray, make no delay at all,
> Now in your youthful days.
> Oh turn to Him, who has you made,
> While in your tender years:
> For as the withering grass we fade,
> Which never more appears.

Mary's valiant effort to keep her sister on the side of the Protestant Jesus and away from the Catholic Mary came to naught. Her sisters Freedom and Martha later wrote to their father that "they would come hum if it was not for the sake of ther soules."[43]

A WELL-EDUCATED, mature adult, John Williams fought back, biblical verse for verse when challenged by French priests. To a degree he appears to have enjoyed the contest. He did, however, realize that the contest was harder for the rest of his flock, particularly the youngest. The dilemma drove him to compose: "these following sorrowful, mournful considerations":

> Oh Lord! Mine eyes on Thee shall waiting be
> Till Thou again turn our captivity.
> Their Romish plots Thou canst confound, and save
> This little flock, this mercy I do crave.
> Save us from all our sins and yet again
> Deliver us from them who truth disdain.[44]

He had reason to fear. By the time these lines were published at least thirteen of his former parishioners (among them two adults and four teenagers) had been baptized into the Catholic Church. And other Deerfield captives appeared ready to succumb to "Romish plots." Among the latter was his youngest daughter, Eunice. For the French and Natives who won them over, these conversions represented a small but ideologically tremendous victory in the cultural and demographic struggle with the "heretics" of New England. For English colonists in Massachusetts it was a bitter loss that would have political repercussions.

CHAPTER 9

DIPLOMACY AND SCANDAL

S ERIOUS efforts to secure the return of the Deerfield captives began late in 1704 and continued in earnest for three years. These efforts were the result and a cause of greater imperial influence over the lives of common colonists. For many colonists, like those of Deerfield, this was a welcome change from the last war, when they had been largely on their own. For others, however, especially those around Boston, the closer contacts between New England and New France and between New England and old England brought fears of corruption and conspiracy as each side used the negotiations to exchange prisoners as opportunities to spy on the other and, if possible, make some quick money.

As the negotiations for the release of the Deerfield captives and the scandals they caused reveal, imperial power grew at the initiative of both local communities and the colony's central government. As family man, local official, and government agent, the Deerfield resident John Sheldon shuttled back and forth to Canada three times to redeem New England captives in New France. The years from 1705 to 1707 also saw an intense flurry of activity between higher-level emissaries on both sides. But negotiations over the captives' release got hung up over the fate of a captured French privateer named Pierre Maisonnat. Further complications arose from consideration of a treaty of neutrality that proposed to end all hostilities between New France and New England. Much was at stake for both parties, and the frustrating pace of the negotiations produced charges of bad faith, illicit trading, and spying. The strains of the slow-moving process heightened internal political divisions in Massachusetts as some individuals resisted the growth of imperial influence. By 1707 the Deerfield captives, with John Williams at their head, found themselves at the center of a political controversy that ultimately vindicated Governor Joseph Dudley and the new imperial politics and secured Deerfield's place in history.

E XCHANGING prisoners of war was more complicated in the colonies than in Europe. Both sides took prisoners, but of a very different sort. French and Native raiding parties took men, women, and children, soldiers and civilians. The English took mostly soldiers, privateers, warriors, and war leaders caught along the Acadian frontier or on the high seas. As a rule, the populous English colonies had little incentive to exchange captured French soldiers for English civilians while fighting continued and Natives were often retained as hostages. They sent only one emissary to Canada to negotiate a captive exchange during the Nine Years' War. At the end of the war, over sixty captives remained in New France and almost all of them had refused to return, having lived in the French colony long enough to marry, settle down, and otherwise become assimilated. Most of these captives had been from the frontiers of Maine and New Hampshire and lacked the resources and influence needed to engage the government's assistance.[1]

No single English prisoner in the Nine Years' War had the importance of John Williams, an ordained minister. Thanks partly to his prominence and the shocking number of captives taken with him from Deerfield, the Massachusetts government made a sustained effort during the War of the Spanish Succession to secure the return of captives, in marked contrast to the government's lack of effort during the previous war. Williams's capture ensured the involvement of his clerical colleagues and relatives, the Reverends Increase and Cotton Mather, and of Governor Dudley, who, like Williams, was a native of Roxbury, where the two had been neighbors. Several merchants with connections in Canada formed another active, if self-interested, lobby for sending emissaries to Canada. Residents of Deerfield who had escaped capture also stepped forward to undertake missions to New France.

The first, halting steps to secure the Deerfield captives' return began in the spring of 1704. Governor Dudley wrote to Governor Philippe de Rigaud de Vaudreuil in April criticizing the cruelty of the war waged by the French and Indians and insisting that the French governor recover all of the captives and send them back. In August, Dudley wrote again proposing a mutual exchange of prisoners. Neither letter reached its intended destination. To insure delivery of his next letter, the governor proposed sending an English messenger overland guided by two Frenchmen. But nothing came of this initiative. One frustrated captive, Samuel Storer, who had been taken at Wells, Maine, in August 1703, complained that "if the Governor of Massachusetts had only sent one man for me, I and all my family would have been restored."[2]

Two Deerfield residents made the first diplomatic contact with New France. In December 1704, John Sheldon and John Wells approached authorities in Boston, asking permission to go to Canada. Ensign Sheldon wanted to recover his three children and a daughter-in-law who had been taken in the raid. Wells, a man in his mid-to-late twenties, sought to redeem his mother who, unbeknownst to him, had died on the captives' march to Canada. The Massachusetts Council approved the request and recruited two French prisoners to guide them overland to Quebec. It was a difficult route, especially demanding in winter.[3]

Governor Dudley favored an alternative approach that also offered an opportunity to develop crucial ties to New York that would make it much easier to get in touch with New France (figure 11). The governor met with Captain John Livingston, an Albany merchant with contacts in New France. Livingston volunteered to lead Sheldon and Wells to Canada by an easier route that ran from

FIGURE 11. Joseph Dudley (1647–1720). Oil portrait, circa 1682–1686, artist unknown. Born in Roxbury, Massachusetts, Dudley attended Harvard College. During the 1680s he served as an official of the hated Dominion of New England and left Massachusetts in disgrace in 1690. He returned as royal governor of the colony in 1702 and served until 1715. Though his long list of political enemies included the Reverends Increase Mather and Cotton Mather, the Reverend John Williams was a supporter of the governor. Photograph courtesy of the Massachusetts Historical Society, Boston.

Albany to the Saint Lawrence River. This proposal won the approval of the Massachusetts Council. In January, the two Deerfield men accompanied Livingston to Albany. From Albany, the party headed north along the well-traveled route marked by the Hudson River, Lake Champlain, and the Richelieu River. Once they reached the mouth of the Richelieu, they followed the Saint Lawrence northeast to Quebec, arriving in February 1705.[4]

The Deerfield emissaries carried with them letters from Governor Dudley laying out the framework for diplomatic talks with Governor Vaudreuil. Dudley informed Vaudrueil that Massachusetts held about 150 French prisoners and stated his desire to trade them for the English captives in Canada. The French governor accepted Dudley's proposal in its broad outline but stipulated a couple of conditions. He wanted assurances that 16 French prisoners who had been sent to the West Indies and England would be returned, and he demanded the release of the French privateer Pierre Maisonnat, known as Captain Baptiste or Battis to the English. Baptiste had captured an English ship that had been fishing or trading without permission in French territorial waters before the outbreak of the war, an action that the English saw as piracy. Vaudrueil rejected this charge, claiming Baptiste was merely defending French territorial waters, and insisted that the captain be included in any prisoner exchange. If Dudley agreed to these two conditions, all of the prisoners would be sent back with Livingston, Sheldon, and Wells.[5]

Sheldon and Wells took advantage of their time in Canada to establish contact with their captive Deerfield neighbors. They were not able to meet with many captives. But as John Williams later reported, their presence became known and "it gave revival to many and raised expectations of a return." The envoys did meet with John Williams, and Wells learned then, if not before, that his mother was dead. Sheldon received a letter from his daughter-in-law Hannah, who was in Montreal, living with the French. He heard from another source that his three children were alive and two of them were still with their Indian captors. With the aid of Canadian officials, he secured the release of Hannah, his son Ebenezer, Esther Williams, and two other captives. None of these captives appear to have spent much time with their Indian captors.[6]

At this point intrigue and commerce began to enter the diplomatic negotiations. The three English envoys and the released captives left Canada in early May before Vaudreuil received Dudley's response to his letter of mid-March. Why they left prematurely remains a mystery, but the French governor appears to have encouraged them to return by providing an escort of six soldiers. He also sent with them a personal envoy, Captain Augustin Legardeur de Tilly, Sieur de Courtemanche, whose brother, Charles Legardeur de Croisille, had been on the Deerfield raid. Officially, Courtemanche was directed to facilitate the prisoner exchange; unofficially, he was to gather intelligence.[7]

For some Deerfield captives the failure of the English emissaries to obtain their release was a crushing disappointment. Four men decided to take matters into their own hands and escape. Thirty-two-year-old Joseph Petty, who was living with a French family at Pointe-aux-Trembles, organized the attempt. He was joined by twenty-six-year-old John Nims, who had been captured in 1703, twenty-two-year-old Thomas Baker, who had already tried to escape once, and eighteen-year-old Martin Kellogg, who appears to have been a prisoner of the Iroquois of the Mountain. On May 10, which was the Feast of the Holy Sacrament and a "great procession day," they had "Liberty to go in & about the city of Mont Real, & there . . . happened all to meet together." At this meeting Nims and Petty informed the other two of their plan to escape. The men "agreed that the other three were to come down to where [Petty] lived, which was about 9 miles from the city." Three days later, Petty made ready, having gathered provisions, obtained guns, and set up a sign by the river to guide his companions. They arrived at "about break of day" on Monday, May 14. Then they paddled across the Saint Lawrence in a canoe "by sun rising." Two days later the escapees reached the Richelieu River nine miles below Fort Chambly, crossed over it on a raft, and proceeded south along the east bank.[8]

After walking for a week, the four Deerfield men came to Lake Champlain and found two abandoned canoes. Taking one of the canoes, they paddled up the lake following its eastern shoreline. After being forced by strong winds to abandon the canoe, the party traveled by foot to the Winooski River. They ascended this river to its headwaters and crossed the Green Mountains to reach the White River. At this point their provisions gave out, and they were forced to spend time and energy hunting and fishing. Their catch consisted mainly of fish and reptiles. Moving on they reached the confluence of the White with the Connecticut River. Here they built a raft and floated down the river. "Weak and faint," the four men finally reached Deerfield on June 8. Their remarkable journey to freedom had taken twenty-six days.[9]

The four men were doubly fortunate in undertaking their bold escape, for the negotiations to return the English captives had bogged down. Boston's maritime community was determined to prevent the release of Baptiste. A group of "merchants, traders and sailors" petitioned the General Court to block this exchange, fearing "the Dangerous Consequences which will unavoidably attend his release." For his part, Dudley was willing to exchange the French privateer, but he wanted guarantees to insure the return of all English prisoners held by France's Native allies. To obtain such guarantees and to establish procedures that would regulate the exchange of prisoners in the future, Dudley proposed a formal treaty. Though Vaudreuil's envoy, Courtemanche, accepted the treaty's proposed terms, he was not empowered to sign such a document. At this critical point he fell ill, effectively ending the Boston negotiations. To advance the process, negotiators now had to secure Vaudreuil's consent and signature, which necessitated a move back to Quebec. This move forced a delay in the proceedings.[10]

This delay made the French suspicious. Officials in Canada later concluded that Dudley's main interest at this point was in delaying a prisoner exchange and in moving the negotiations in Quebec. It is apparent from his subsequent actions that Dudley did want to extend the truce, which had suspended fighting during the negotiations. Such a truce provided a very effective and inexpensive defense for the frontiers of Massachusetts. He may have hoped to use the negotiations to transform the temporary truce into a formal treaty of neutrality that would remove New England and New France from the War of the Spanish Succession. Failing this, he intended to play for time. The governor also planned to use the opportunity of returning the negotiations to Canada to gather intelligence.[11]

The shift in negotiations provided new chances for illicit contacts between French and English that many on both sides feared would lead to espionage and corruption. For reasons never made clear, Courtemanche agreed to return to New France by ship under a flag of truce. Such a voyage represented a serious security breach. It offered the English a valuable opportunity to learn more about navigating difficult points on the Saint Lawrence River, "depriving New France of what constituted its principal strength." The captain of the ship was Samuel Vetch, a thirty-seven-year-old Scots merchant and adventurer who had or would very soon develop a proposal for invading Canada. Like his brother-in-law, John Livingston, who had led Ensign Sheldon to Canada a year earlier, Vetch was fluent in French and had commercial contacts in New France. He had volunteered to sail his ship to Quebec at no charge, asking only for permission to return with enough French beaver pelts to cover debts owed to him by merchants in Canada. Dudley's eighteen-year-old son William accompanied the captain as the governor's personal emissary. Once in New France, both men would engage in obvious efforts to gather intelligence about the river approaches to Quebec and the city's defenses.[12]

The arrival of Vetch and Dudley revived the captives' morale. Soon after the two men reached Quebec on September 6, 1705, they began to meet with captives and work to secure their return. Governor Vaudreuil allowed the English emissaries to visit some of the Deerfield captives and arranged for John Williams (figure 12) and his son Stephen to meet with the two men. William Dudley also happened upon Jonathan Hoyt and his Huron master, presumably Thaovenhosen, selling vegetables in Quebec. For twenty silver dollars the Huron sold Jonathan to Dudley. Regretting his bargain, the Huron soon attempted to return the money and get Hoyt back. But by then Hoyt had been taken aboard Vetch's ship. The Reverend Williams sensed that the French priests "were ready to think their time was short for gaining proselytes and doubled their diligence and wiles to gain over persons to their persuasion." But it turned out that he was being overly optimistic. After three weeks, he was sent back to Chateau Richer, several miles from Quebec. In all Dudley and Vetch secured the release of only eleven English prisoners.[13]

Diplomatically, it began to look as if the colonial French and English might work out a treaty of neutrality that would allow them to sit out the imperial

FIGURE 12. Philippe de Rigaud de Vaudreuil (1650–1725). Oil portrait, copied from the original by Henri Beau, 1923. A younger son of an old noble family of the province of Languedoc, Vaudreuil moved to New France in 1687 as an officer in the *troupes de la marine*. He married a Canadian woman and spent the remainder of his career in the colony, serving as governor from 1703 to 1725. Photograph courtesy of the National Archives of Canada, C010614.

war. Governor Vaudreuil had quickly rejected the formal treaty regulating prisoner exchanges. To revive the stalled negotiations, Vetch and Dudley raised the possibility of an even broader treaty of neutrality. It would end hostilities between New England and New France and return all prisoners held by both sides. In making this proposal, the envoys probably went beyond their formal instructions, though they may have had Governor Dudley's verbal authorization. Both French and English officials had considered such a treaty, which took for its model agreements between European colonies in the West Indies. In fact, just before the English negotiators arrived in Quebec, Vaudreuil had received dispatches from France authorizing such a treaty. The draft treaty by Vetch and Dudley called for a cessation of hostilities on land and sea, provided for the issuing of passports to facilitate trade and hunting, and mandated a general exchange of prisoners. No unauthorized actions by Native allies would invalidate the treaty. Natives committing hostile acts would be handed over to the aggrieved party for punishment. The treaty's last article pledged the parties to refrain from hostilities until Governor Dudley formally accepted the proposal.[14]

The treaty negotiations involved a series of conflicting political calculations that made it very difficult to find mutually agreeable terms. The French initially responded favorably to the idea of a treaty of neutrality. If nothing else, Vaudreuil intended to sow discord among the English by leading them "to understand that, if war continued between both Colonies, it was solely the fault of the Council in Boston so as to be able in this way to create division between the people and the Council." He was also under pressure from authorities in France who had become concerned about the cost of his policy of defending New France by launching large expeditions against New England. Still, he offered alternatives that made English acceptance unlikely. Most important, he wanted explicit guarantees that the treaty's provisions included not just Canada but also Acadia and restrained New York and other English colonies from attacking or indirectly supporting assaults on these French possessions. These were guarantees the Massachusetts governor could not make. For his part, Dudley was playing for time.[15]

Back in Boston and Paris, the slow progress of the negotiations led some important people to suspect that something else was going on. On October 12, Vetch, Dudley, and their redeemed captives sailed for Boston, arriving on November 21. Even though they carried with them Vaudreuil's revised version of the treaty of neutrality, they appeared to have little to show for their efforts. Reports soon began to circulate that Vetch had successfully pursued another mission: illegal trade with the French. Dudley's political enemies charged that only "the Meanest" prisoners had been returned, "leaving the Principal of the Captives behind" so that they "might have a Pretense to go again" to carry on "their

Treacherous Design of Trading." Officials in France shared these suspicions. The story of Courtemanche's supposed illness only deepened French suspicions. Stories from Vaudreuil's enemies, especially Governor Ramezay of Montreal and Antoine Laumet de Lamothe Cadillac, the founder of Detroit, fed their concerns.[16]

There was good reason to be suspicious. The evidence clearly indicates that Vetch did use the flag of truce to engage in trade that both sides regarded as illegal. Before leaving Boston, he had filled his ship with trade goods desperately needed in New France. For his part, Vaudreuil appears to have turned a blind eye to this trafficking. Though illegal, it did supply the colony with some needed provisions. The governor's political enemies asserted that he was delaying the prisoner exchange so that he could trade personally with Dudley. How much Dudley knew of Vetch's activities is harder to determine. The governor's political foes assumed the worst. It is clear that Dudley's son did use the negotiations to gather intelligence. Many in Quebec were scandalized by the freedom Vaudreuil had given young Dudley to move about and inspect the city's defenses.[17]

The Massachusetts governor continued to push for a prisoner exchange even as he backed away from the proposed treaty of neutrality. In December 1705, "as an exemplary act of generosity" the governor sent Captain William Rouse, a merchant and privateer, to Port Royal in Nova Scotia with forty-seven French prisoners in an effort to force Vaudreuil's hand. However, Baptiste was not among this group of prisoners. Rouse returned with just seventeen English captives. On a second trip Rouse secured the release of only eight additional captives. None of these English prisoners was a captive taken on the Deerfield raid. Not long after he had dispatched Rouse to Port Royal, Dudley sent Ensign Sheldon on a second overland mission to Quebec. John Wells of Deerfield, Joseph Bradley, the husband of a woman taken prisoner at Haverhill in early February 1704, and two French prisoners accompanied Sheldon. They left for Canada in late January, carrying with them Dudley's evasive response to Vaudreuil's proposed treaty of neutrality. The party followed the same route that Sheldon and Wells had taken a year earlier. By March, the envoys reached Canada.[18]

Vaudreuil saw through Dudley's maneuvers. He correctly concluded that the English did not want the treaty of neutrality and informed officials in France that the Massachusetts governor was now merely "seeking to gain time." He unilaterally ended the temporary truce by once again sending raiding parties against the frontiers of New England. The prisoner exchange negotiations also stalled again. The failure to release Baptiste remained an impediment to a mutual exchange of prisoners. New France's intendant, Antoin-Denis Raudot, threatened to put John Williams "into prison and lay [him] in irons" if Baptiste remained in prison any longer.[19]

Despite these setbacks, Ensign Sheldon persisted and made some progress.

He met with Williams and made two trips to visit the captives at Kahnawake. He eventually persuaded Vaudreuil to release some of the captives. On May 30, 1706, Sheldon embarked for Port Royal in Acadia with forty-four captives. His son Remembrance and his daughter Mary accompanied him, as did Joseph Bradley's wife, Hannah, Thomas French Sr., John Burt, Benjamin Burt, and Benjamin's wife, Sarah, and their son, Christopher, born on the march to Canada in April 1704. Another child was born on the voyage home and named Seaborn Burt. On the same voyage Mary Hinsdale would also give birth to a son, named Ebenezer. The names of the other members of Sheldon's party, which undoubtedly included other Deerfield captives, remain unknown. When the vessel reached Port Royal it stayed there for several weeks, awaiting the return of "all French prisoners without distinction." The failure to release Baptiste remained a sticking point.[20]

In Boston, the stalled prisoner exchange and the seemingly fruitless voyages by Vetch and Rouse fueled the suspicions of those who believed the negotiations were merely a cover for illegal trade. Suspicions also grew in some quarters that Dudley himself was involved. In June 1706, the General Court moved against Vetch, Rouse, and their associates. A 1705 parliamentary act had declared any correspondence with France to be a treasonable offense, making the merchants vulnerable to prosecution even if the charges of illegal trade could not be substantiated. After securing passage of a resolution absolving him of any direct participation in any illegal trading, Dudley worked to protect his erstwhile emissaries. He encouraged the legislature to try the merchants in the assembly on a charge of high misdemeanors rather than holding a treason trial in the Superior Court. It was a questionable procedure, but Dudley persuaded the Council that a clause in the 1691 Charter allowing the legislature to impose fines and imprisonment provided the necessary authorization. In August the lower house of the legislature indicted the merchants. The legislature found them guilty as charged, levied fines, and imposed prison sentences, ranging from three months to one year. The trial was later disallowed by authorities in London—as Dudley probably knew it would be. The merchants were his friends and allies. He did not want to see them ruined, but he had to deflect the legislature's wrath.[21]

To diffuse the growing political controversy, Dudley made yet another effort to obtain the release of the remaining Deerfield captives. On August 2, Sheldon and the forty-four prisoners delayed at Port Royal finally sailed into Boston to much rejoicing. But concern regarding the fate of those, such as John Williams, who had not returned was only heightened. Dudley responded by moving to return all remaining French prisoners including Captain Baptiste. He sent two men overland to Canada to inform Vaudreuil of his intentions and asked the

French governor to gather the English prisoners. By late August all of the French prisoners had been collected and sailed for Quebec, which they reached on October 1. Captain Rouse, who had just been tried for illegal trade with the French, commanded the brigantine *Hope* that carried the repatriated Frenchmen to Quebec. Samuel Appleton, a member of the Massachusetts Council, served as Dudley's envoy to oversee the prisoner exchange. With the returning French prisoners came a letter from Dudley to Vaudreuil requesting that the remaining Deerfield captives be sent to Port Royal, where they could be exchanged for any remaining French prisoners.[22]

Delighted with the return of Baptiste and his fellows, officials in Canada attempted to obtain the release of the remaining English captives. But, as Governor Vaudreuil reminded the English, his ability to redeem the captives held by Natives was limited. The English were skeptical, because they did not understand that the Natives were allies, not subjects of the French. Even in a matter as diplomatically important to the French as the prisoner exchange, they had to negotiate for Native cooperation. They could not compel the Natives to do anything without endangering their alliances. And at this critical juncture, New France's economic crisis reduced the government's ability to ransom English prisoners from their Native captors. English interdiction of ships carrying trade goods from France only aggravated the situation. Vaudreuil was in a better position to enlist the participation of the colony's clergy in this project. Still, the priests' influence varied from mission to mission: probably greater at Lorette and Sault-au-Récollet; much less at Odanak and Kahnawake. Only three of the prisoners still in the hands of Natives at this time appear to have been ransomed. Despite their limited success, persistent French efforts to free the English captives held at Kahnawake angered and alienated the Mohawks. For them, returning adopted captives was the equivalent of giving up family members.[23]

French officials had more power to repatriate captives living with French families or in the care of religious orders. But here too there was active resistance. John Williams later claimed that "the clergy and others labored to stop many of the prisoners; to some liberty, to some money and yearly pensions were offered if they would stay." Though the English tended to credit the Jesuits with all such nefarious designs, it was the Sulpicians and parish priests who apparently worked the hardest to retain those captives who were on their way to becoming good French Catholics. They made a final effort to hold on to Samuel Williams by promising him "an honorable pension from the king every year" and claimed "that his master [Jacques Le Ber], who was an old man and the richest in Canada, would give him a great deal." Most, however, chose to return to New England. The ship left Quebec on October 25 with—finally—John Williams, his sons Samuel

and Warham and fifty-four other English captives. They arrived in Boston on
November 21, 1706.[24]

O NCE they returned to New England, the former prisoners soon learned
that captives and captivity had become political weapons in a struggle to
oust Dudley from the governorship. The return of John Williams and the bulk
of his flock did not end the matter for Dudley's critics. For the Reverend Cotton
Mather the charges of illegal trade confirmed his belief that Massachusetts was
being ruled and endangered by a corrupt governor and his cronies. He delivered
a sermon devoted to the controversy over illegal trade with the French. Embarrassing the government by reminding people of the fate of captives taken to
Canada appears to have been one of the aims of the stories of captivity included
in *Good Fetched Out of Evil,* which Mather published in August 1706. The publication, containing a "Pastoral Letter" from John Williams, some "edifying Poems"
written by captives, and stories of "Astonishing Deliverances," sold a thousand
copies "in a week's time." Later a defender of Dudley would charge that such
stories of captivity were "heaped together to endeavor to Incense the People
against their Governor."[25]

Dudley's struggle with Cotton Mather grew out of long-standing differences
and recent slights. Mather had initially supported Dudley's campaign to be appointed governor because he regarded him as the least objectionable of the possible candidates. He made this pragmatic decision despite Dudley's service as an
official of the hated Dominion of New England in the late 1680s and his reputation as one who "perfidiously undermined the welfare of his Native country."
Having left Massachusetts in 1690 a prisoner charged with committing 119 illegal acts while an official of the Dominion of New England, Dudley had returned
in 1702 as a newly appointed governor. But his troubles continued. Not long after his return, he had angered Cotton Mather by revealing a confidential con-
versation, upset the Reverend Increase Mather with his political appointments,
and further antagonized them both by refusing to seek a royal charter for Harvard College, something for which the Mathers had been lobbying for over a
decade. The legislature was also soon at loggerheads with the governor when
he sought to carry out his instructions from London to obtain a permanent
salary and to rebuild the fort at Pemaquid in Maine. Dudley responded to the
House's opposition by vetoing elections to the Council and vetoing the House's
election of its speaker. By 1703 Cotton Mather and others had begun working
behind the scenes to secure the governor's removal.[26]

The campaign against Dudley reached a critical point just a month before
John Williams and his fellows returned from Canada. In October 1706 Cotton

Mather had joined other opponents of Dudley in petitioning Queen Anne to remove the governor. He wrote an anonymous letter, gathered supporting testimonials from like-minded individuals, added selections from *Good Fetched Out of Evil,* and sent the material off to England. There it was published in July 1707 as *A Memorial of the Present Deplorable State of New-England . . . by the Male-Administration of their Present Governor.* While some historians have questioned Mather's authorship of the *Memorial,* no one in Boston doubted it. When a delegation from the Council confronted him and asked him whether he had written the *Memorial's* anonymous letter attacking Dudley, Cotton Mather would neither confirm nor deny his authorship.[27]

Dudley's opponents turned his efforts at diplomacy against him. The title page of the *Memorial* charged that Dudley engaged not only in "Mercenary and Illegal Proceedings" but also in "private and Treacherous Correspondence with Her Majesty's Enemies the <u>French</u> and <u>Indians</u>." The text began by reiterating presumed misdeeds from his tenure during the Dominion of New England. In recounting Dudley's more recent failings as governor, the *Memorial* accepted as fact the charges of illegal trading with the French, added illegal trade with the Indians for good measure, and claimed that Dudley corresponded with a "<u>Fryer</u> or <u>Jesuit</u>, or one so called, a Frenchman that Lives among the Indians, and hath great influence over them." The *Memorial* made much of the war's human cost, highlighting the lengthy captivity of John Williams and suggesting that it was all Dudley's fault. At the same time, the *Memorial,* somewhat illogically, criticized Dudley for the costs of military operations to defend the colony's frontiers and attacked him for releasing Baptiste, which had been necessary to secure Williams's return. A characteristic expression of the period's "politics of scurrility," it aimed primarily at influencing imperial officials in England who were in a position to remove Dudley from office. It also undoubtedly embodied suspicions and fears circulating in parts of Massachusetts about the colony's growing involvement in the English empire.[28]

For his Boston audience, Cotton Mather spoke more guardedly in the language of the jeremiad to criticize the governor's conduct of the war. He also criticized the conduct of frontier residents, suggesting that their sins had brought on the French and Native raids. Early in 1707, lamenting the "Sad condition of our Frontiers . . . [and the] Irreligion and Profaneness and Disorder in many of them," Mather resolved to "write a little Book, agreeable to the Condition of our exposed Plantations." In this book, *The Frontiers Well Defended,* Mather interpreted Indian raids that "have befallen some of our <u>churches</u> in the <u>War</u> upon us [as] Loud <u>Sermons</u> and warnings." He identified "sin" as the real enemy, and only true reformation fought this enemy. In a curiously worded passage, seemingly designed to promote internal divisions, Mather labeled as "Traitors" "The Vices which get in among you" and urged his readers to "Revenge yourselves upon these Traitors; by doing which, you will, as by a <u>Sacred</u> <u>Magic</u>, even wound and Slay the Absent Enemy." In a more straightforward manner, he called upon frontier residents to maintain well-ordered families and to suppress "Profane Swearing," "Sabbath-Breaking," "Unchastity," "Dishonesty," and "Drunkenness . . . that worse than Brutish Vice." In closing he warned frontier residents and their pastors of the papist threat, lamenting: "God forbid, that a <u>Popish</u> <u>Priest</u> should out do a Protestant Minister in his Industry."[29]

T HUS, when Deerfield's Protestant minister returned to New England in November 1706, he found himself at the center of a major political crisis. Though copies of the *Memorial* had not arrived in Boston, echoes of the charges it contained could be heard in the city. Against this backdrop Cotton Mather sat down with John Williams "and united Counsils with him, how the Lord might have Revenues of Glory from his Experiences." Mather, who had already used the fate of the captives in general and Williams in particular to attack Governor Dudley, probably hoped to use the sufferings of Williams and his flock to add more fuel to the fire. He "particularly employ'd [Williams], to preach my Lecture, unto a great Auditory (the General Assembly then also sitting) and, directed him, to show how great Things God had done unto him." This meeting produced Williams's 1706 sermon "Reports of Divine Kindness." It also inspired the writing and publication of the book that would make him, and the 1704 Deerfield raid, forever famous in early American history *The Redeemed Captive Returning to Zion* (see figure 13).[30]

Written early in 1707 with Cotton Mather's support and published in March, *The Redeemed Captive* recounted the sufferings of Williams, his family, and his flock during the raid, the march to Canada, and the subsequent captivity. Like Mather and other ministers, Williams placed his captivity within a framework of providential history. He began by acknowledging his "lively and awful sense of divine rebukes which the most holy God has seen meet in spotless sovereignty to dispense to me, my family and people in delivering us into the hands of those that hated us." He saw the hand of Providence in the captives' physical trials and spiritual afflictions at the hands of the French and Natives. He abundantly documented how, when they were stripped of all that had meaning in life, the captives were brought to depend solely on faith in God and God's mercy. However, God had brought them lower only to exalt them in the very face of their papist foes. The narrative thus illustrated the workings of Providence while providing inspiration for personal redemption and conversion.[31]

For many years, historians and other readers have supposed that Williams allied himself unreservedly with Cotton Mather. And on the surface there is no reason to doubt this supposition. For one thing, they were related by marriage and worked together to preach God's Word as clergymen. Williams shared Mather's concerns about contemporary sinfulness. He observed on more than one occasion that "it was a dangerous thing to be set in the front of New England's sins."

FIGURE 13. The Reverend John Williams (1664–1729). Oil portrait (detail), circa 1707, artist unknown. It is believed that this portrait was painted around the time of Williams's return from New France. The painting of this portrait is another indication of the celebrity Williams experienced after his return from captivity. Photograph courtesy of Historic Deerfield, Inc. Photography by Amanda Merullo.

At the outset of his narrative, Williams warned that "the history I am going to write proves, that days of fasting and prayer, without reformation, will not avail to turn away the anger of God from a professing people." But there were certain subtle differences in the men's approaches to the problem of sin and suffering during the war. Unlike Mather, Williams did not devote any space to enumerating the sins that led to his capture. He was more interested in the spiritual benefits of affliction and evidence of God's blessings and mercies. In the body of his narrative, and in the public sermons he gave in Boston before its publication, Williams echoed Mather's concerns but spoke in vague terms of the need for repentance and reformation.[32]

Williams was more explicit in his defense of Mather's foe, Governor Dudley, whose diplomatic efforts had led to his release. *The Redeemed Captive* must have shocked and dismayed Cotton Mather when he finally read it. Unlike every other captivity narrative published in Boston since 1682, *The Redeemed Captive* did not contain a preface written by a Mather. Instead, Williams's narrative was preceded by the imprimatur of Governor Joseph Dudley. After the imprimatur came a remarkably effusive dedication to the governor "since heaven has honored you as the prime instrument in returning our captivity." Dudley had sent "his own son" to facilitate their redemption. Claiming that "all your [Dudley's] people are cherished under your wings," Williams asserted that "those who are immediately exposed to the outrages of the enemy have peculiarly felt refreshment from the benign influences of your wise and tender conduct." According to John Williams, Dudley had acted as an instrument of God's Providence.[33]

John Williams turned Cotton Mather's use of captivity on its head. The Deerfield minister devoted an entire paragraph of the dedication to lauding Dudley's conduct of the contested negotiations that had secured the captives' release. He thanked Dudley for his "uncommon sagacity and prudence in contriving to loose the bonds of your captivated children" and for his "unwearied vigor and application in pursuing them to work our deliverance." At two points in the body of his narrative, Williams affirmed that his exchange was dependent on the release of the privateer Baptiste—exactly the thing that Mather and his allies had opposed. Most important, he made clear his hope that for Dudley "God, whom herein you have served, will remember and gloriously reward you, and may heaven long preserve you at our helm, a blessing so necessary for the tranquility of this province, in this dark and tempestuous season." Given the political context, this was not merely a "standard" or "formulaic" opening, as some scholars have claimed. On the contrary, the dedication was an important public endorsement of an embattled governor and a refutation of everything Cotton Mather had been saying for the past year.[34]

The Deerfield minister transformed the trope of captivity from a criticism of the sins of frontier folk to a celebration of their heroism in the war against the Catholic enemy. He used stories of his parishioners' spiritual trials to vindicate the virtue of common New Englanders. He laid the blame for Deerfield's capture not on their sins but on the unfaithfulness of their watch, probably a garrison soldier from a less exposed town. According to Williams, Deerfield residents had bravely resisted their captors' efforts to convert them to Catholicism. "Some," he wrote, "were flattered with large promises, others threatened and beaten because they would not turn." One Deerfield woman was beaten by nuns who threatened to "give her away to the Indians" if she continued in her refusal to cross herself. Zebediah Williams, "a very hopeful and pious young man" (and no relation) "carried himself so in his captivity as to edify several of the English and recover one fallen to popery taken the last war." The strength of their adherence to Protestantism even won grudging praise from one of the Jesuits who "came to the [French] governor and told the company there that he never saw such persons as were taken from Deerfield."[35]

Williams took advantage of his newfound celebrity to rally New Englanders against what he saw as the real enemy: not Dudley and corruption but the Catholic French empire. He devoted most of his narrative to his stay with the French, not with his Native captors. He recounted his pastoral industry in Canada, where he had protected his parishioners and himself from the wiles of Catholic priests. He rehearsed impromptu debates with Jesuits in which he confounded them with arguments drawn from their own books. In a lengthy defense of Protestantism written to his forcibly converted son Samuel, he refuted Catholic beliefs and practices. He was certain that if Samuel would "make the Scriptures a perfect rule of faith, as you ought to do, you can't believe as the Romish Church believes." His arguments provided an answer to those New Englanders who found it "a stumbling block . . . that such a Religious Family Should meet with so much Adversity." Clearly, John Williams believed that he had been sent to Canada to confound New England's Catholic foes, to refute their errors, and to support his flock as a faithful shepherd in a time of great trial.[36]

For Williams, the real sinners were those who resisted the expanding power of the English empire as it rose to combat the Catholic foe. Delivering a sermon before the governor, legislature, and presumably Boston's ministers, Williams explored in more depth the character and causes of the "dark and tempestuous season." His March 1707 sermon, *God in the Camp* was, on its surface, a more traditional jeremiad, though as the historian John Demos has observed it "does not fit the type at every point." Williams's sociology of wartime sin differed significantly in emphasis from that of Cotton Mather. Specifically, those who stayed at home and "murmured against Rulers" or those who complained "against the

Commanders of the Forces employed" had much to answer for. Rhetorically he asked, "you who are censuring others for their cowardice, and imputing the want of success in our War, to those that are employed in sending Forces abroad, or to those that are sent forth, whither you hant [have] reason to be turning some courses to make God angry with the Land." Williams was clearly suggesting to the province's leaders that it was the critics of Dudley and not the governor, the frontiersmen, or the army who needed reforming.[37]

DUDLEY needed John Williams's support, for he was in deep trouble in 1707. Political opposition to him became public once Cotton Mather's *Memorial* arrived in Boston in late October 1707—several months after Williams had delivered his sermon. The war was also going badly. Massachusetts forces had suffered two humiliating repulses in attempts to capture Port Royal. The appearance of the *Memorial* brought to a head the struggle between the governor and his political foes that the historian Michael Hall has termed "the Crisis of 1707." Revived charges of illicit trading with the French were, in another historian's opinion, "the most serious accusation against any Massachusetts governor between 1692 and 1760." The Council quickly supported the governor. Its members declared, "the Allegations therein of the Governor's Trading or allowing a Trade wth Her Matys Enemies the French & Indians is a Scandalous and wicked Accusation." But the House moved more slowly. The political situation here was complicated by a simultaneous debate over the choice of Harvard's next president. Dudley had picked John Leverett to be the new president. Cotton Mather lobbied the legislature to block the approval of Leverett as Harvard's president and prevent the vindication of Dudley on charges of corruption.[38]

The frontier rallied to the defense of their governor. On November 11, ministers of towns along the province's western border met and addressed a memorial to Dudley's superiors in England. In their memorial, they declared "that Colonel Dudley so far as we have observed is ready upon all occasions to encourage and strengthen the hands of the ministers, in their works, that he doth by his Authority and Example promote Religion & Virtue in the Province." They went on to emphasize "that under the difficulties of the present war he has with utmost diligence endeavored the safety of the Exposed Towns, and that our preservation from the fury of our enemies is under God to be ascribed to his vigilance and care." Once again, Dudley was portrayed as an instrument of Providence. With due deference, they requested that Dudley be continued as their governor. John Williams signed the petition under the signature of his father-in-law, the Reverend Solomon Stoddard, who had drafted the document. Many others also came to Dudley's defense, but Williams and his six clerical colleagues in western Massachusetts were among the very first.[39]

Back in Boston, Dudley mounted an aggressive defense of his conduct. On November 10, he met with the legislature to argue his case. He also wrote to authorities in London defending his conduct at some length. His eldest son, Paul, wrote an anonymous public defense of his father's administration that was published in London as *A Modest Enquiry into the Grounds and Occasions of the Late Pamphlet Intitled, A Memorial of the Deplorable State of New-England by a disinterested hand*. Deft use of patronage combined with the House's inability to uncover any evidence that the governor had participated in or had countenanced illegal trade convinced the legislature to exonerate Dudley. It voted that "we firmly believe and are of the Opinion The Allegations . . . of the Governours' Trading or Allowing Vetch, Borland & Lawson to Trade with her Majesties Enemies, the French & Indians in their Interest is a scandalous and wicked accusation."[40]

Joseph Dudley's term as governor pulled Massachusetts more closely into the workings of the English empire than ever before. While many in Boston did not like this, others out on the frontier applauded it. There is no question that he "exemplified the assiduous" placeman who strove to satisfy his superiors in England. Ambition was his "ruling passion." His political principles in general were, in the opinion of a later royal governor, Thomas Hutchinson, "too high for the Massachusetts people." At the same time he proved to be an energetic administrator and adept politician, and he succeeded in attracting supporters inside and outside of the legislature. Frontier residents, in particular, appreciated his largely successful efforts to provide them with greater security than Governors William Phips and William Stoughton had during the 1690s. The legislature also endorsed his military leadership by appropriating without restrictions an unprecedented expenditure of funds for frontier defense. There is much truth in the historian William Pencak's conclusion that the "popular party's exaggerated assaults on Dudley's character in 1706 and 1707 arose from the realization that he commanded the respect they lacked." Clearly, he had won the respect and gratitude of John Williams.[41]

E FFORTS to obtain the return of the remaining Deerfield captives had continued while the political crisis had raged in Boston. In January 1707 Dudley told the Council that ninety English prisoners were still in Canada. That same month, Deerfield's Ensign Sheldon agreed to undertake a third mission to New France, even though no close relatives of his remained in captivity. Deerfield's new town clerk, Edward Allen, and Deacon Edmund Rice of Sudbury went with him to make up "a suitable retinue." Nathaniel Brooks, a returned captive, whose daughter Mary and son William remained in Canada, also joined the party. The Englishmen employed an Indian to guide them on their way "when bewildered." Traveling rapidly overland, they reached Quebec in three weeks.[42]

By now, New France had much bigger worries than negotiations with New England. Reports of an impending English invasion of Canada had Quebec in a state of consternation when Sheldon's party arrived. Given the situation, French officials understandably regarded them as spies rather than negotiators and kept them under surveillance. After spending six weeks in Quebec, Sheldon and his companions were sent up the Saint Lawrence to the less exposed town of Montreal. Here they were detained though not imprisoned. While at Montreal, they were allowed to visit the captives still at Kahnawake. Nathaniel Brooks failed to win the return of his children. But Sheldon managed to secure the freedom of Henry Segar of Newton, Massachusetts, a woman from Woodbury, Connecticut, and a mulatto man from Exeter, New Hampshire, who reimbursed Sheldon for ransoming him. The emissaries and their three redeemed captives were escorted to Albany by a detachment of five French soldiers under the command of René Hertel de Chambly.[43]

Now it was the French who used the excuse of prisoner negotiations to spy on their enemies. After arriving in Albany, Sheldon and the six Frenchmen were sent on to New York City to meet with Governor Cornbury. This excursion to the colony's capital facilitated Hertel de Chambly's intelligence gathering. Up until 1707, the colony of New York and the Iroquois League had not engaged in hostilities with the French. But Vaudreuil feared that this situation might change. He instructed Chambly to look for any evidence of alterations in the colony's state of military preparedness. Instead, Chambly learned directly from Governor Cornbury that he "was not having his people take any action, for he knew the importance of letting them live in peace and not mix in European affairs." Cornbury told Chambly that he was surprised that Dudley had not accepted Vaudreuil's treaty of neutrality. The New York governor also informed Chambly that he had not provided Dudley with a single man for the 1707 expedition against Port Royal. Clearly, Cornbury wanted to reassure Vaudreuil that New York intended to maintain its de facto neutrality. So effective was the continued observance of this unwritten truce that officials in both England and France suspected a written agreement did in fact exist.[44]

Meanwhile, Ensign Sheldon and his party traveled along the Connecticut coast to Boston, where he set about gaining a reward for his services. In September he reported to Massachusetts authorities on the meager results of his third trip to Canada. A month later, he submitted his expense account and petitioned the Massachusetts legislature for "a Gratuity by Granting me a tract of some of the country's Land undisposed of, within or Nere the County of West Hampshire, in some conveynient place where I can finde it, to the quantity of five hundred Acrs or thereabouts." In consideration of his "good services," the legislature granted him three hundred acres.[45]

B Y THE end of 1707, fifty-two of the captives taken at Deerfield had returned. Forty-six came back as the result of negotiations. The forty-seventh, Ebenezer Carter, had been brought to Albany in February 1707 and sold by his Native captors. Five had escaped. In all, Ensign John Sheldon's efforts had directly or indirectly secured the return of 113 New England captives. Between 33 and 36 Deerfield residents remained in Canada. Twenty-three captives were in French communities. Two Deerfield captives were with the Hurons at Lorette, 3 were with the Iroquois of the Mountain at Sault-au-Récollet. Between 7 and 9 lived with the Mohawks at Kahnawake. And there they stayed until the end of the war. There were no more large-scale prisoner exchanges while the War of the Spanish Succession recommenced in earnest.[46]

CHAPTER 10

IMPERIAL AND PARALLEL WARS

FROM the perspective of the attackers, the 1704 raid on Deerfield appeared to be a near-perfect raid. But its effects did not last long. Unfortunately for the French and their Native allies, the War of the Spanish Succession continued for nine more years. The alliances that the Deerfield raid had been launched to preserve and that had made the raid so successful broke down almost immediately after the raid. The French and Indians had a hard time carrying out a similarly successful attack.

By the summer of 1704 it was clear that the French and their Indian allies were actually fighting several loosely connected, overlapping, and parallel wars that could only with great difficulty be joined into a united front. The Abenakis' struggle against the English was at times tenuously connected to the War of the Spanish Succession. In 1703–1704 they had briefly overlapped, and even though the Abenakis remained willing to accept help from the French, they showed no interest in risking their lives to defend the French empire when the English came to conquer Acadia. Nor did the Natives from villages of the Saint Lawrence valley. They undertook raids on New England, but their war only paralleled that of the French. They were often willing to hunt for new captives, but few warriors were willing to risk their lives in bloody assaults on English fortifications. These divergent motives and goals help explain the "spasmodic, half-hearted" character of the war that has puzzled historians.[1]

The English took some time to mobilize their war effort, but once they did so, it was overwhelming, as thousands of New England villagers took up arms against their outnumbered enemies. They redoubled their guard all along the frontier and began to send out raids of their own, which they called scouts. These "scouts" took the war to the enemy by ambushing Native camps and flushing out raiding parties. Never again would the French and their Native allies achieve total surprise as they had at Deerfield in 1704. By 1709 it was New France, not New England that waited in fear of an invasion. The Deerfield raid, it turns out, was an exceptional success for the French and Indians that overshadowed their failures and obscured English gains during the War of the Spanish Succession.

STRATEGICALLY, the French attempted to build on their victory at Deerfield. True to his resolve, Governor Philippe de Rigaud de Vaudreuil did his best during the remainder of 1704 "to ravage the English on this side of Boston" and demonstrate his support for the Abenaki cause. In May, shortly after the Deerfield raiders returned, he sent a party of between fifty and seventy French and Natives to attack Pascommuck, near Northampton (map 7). A garrison house was captured and the raiders took thirty-seven captives in what looked like a successful repeat of the Deerfield raid. In fact the allies were outdoing their comrades at Deerfield. They had netted about one captive for every two fighters, compared with the roughly one to three ratio at Deerfield. But their success was short-lived. Mounted English militiamen from Northampton pursued the raiders, and the excessive number of captives proved a dangerous burden. The raiders tried to first kill off most of the hapless captives before turning and fighting off the militiamen. They managed to carry only two women and a boy captive back to Canada. Twenty of the prisoners died. The militiamen managed to recover the other fourteen, half of them wounded but not killed by their captors. In the future, Native raiders would not be so greedy for captives.[2]

In the summer of 1704, Vaudreuil tried to outdo the success of the Deerfield raid with an expedition over twice as large that was intended to destroy Northampton. The idea came from some of his Native allies—probably some of them descendants of Connecticut valley refugees now living in Abenaki villages. Vaudreuil ordered about 100 to 125 French to join with approximately 600 Native allies—about 700 in all—under the command of Captain Jean-Maurice-Josué Bubois Berthelot de Beaucours. Launched with high expectations, this undertaking soon collapsed under its own weight.[3]

Although Vaudreuil was encouraged by some of his Native allies to launch the raid, the variety of political interests involved in such a huge expedition made it almost impossible to carry out. Even before the expedition set out, Vaudreuil and his officers could not agree with their allies on the destination and tactics of the expedition. The French preferred a target in eastern Massachusetts; the Natives favored western Massachusetts. At the same time, the Natives disagreed among themselves. Some wanted to operate in "small detachments." Others, including some influential war leaders among the Kahnawake Mohawks, favored forming one large party "with which they could undertake something considerable." By keeping their warriors together in a large body, the war leaders also maintained a degree of control that would allow them to scuttle an expedition simply by withdrawing en masse at a critical point, a sort of de facto veto on French policy that the Kahnawake Mohawks in particular would exercise with great skill. In fact, it seems that some of them may have joined the raid intending merely to maintain the appearance of alliance and to keep an eye on what the French and Abenakis were up to rather than to attack the English. In the wake of the Deerfield raid, Peter Schuyler of Albany had worked hard to dissuade the Iroquois of the Mountain and the Mohawks at Kahnawake from continuing their active support of the French war effort. At some point a Mohawk brought news of Beaucours' expedition to the English. After crossing the Green Mountains, French officers proposed a change in plans, suspecting that "the enemy might have notice" of their destination.[4]

The French contingent generated its own problems that threatened to sabotage the mission. Though large, the French contingent was of uneven quality. As on the Deerfield raid, the party included Canadian militiamen and an outsized complement of "several of the most active of the young officers." These usual sources of manpower were insufficient, however, to make up a force of over one hundred Frenchmen. Many of the most likely young Candians in the Montreal area had probably headed west early in the spring of 1704 when fur traders began to re-enter the Upper Country. Captain de Beaucours's force therefore included a "sizeable contingent" of enlisted men drawn from the *troupes*. Among them was Peter Newgate, an approximately thirty-year-old, disaffected French Protestant who had spent most of his military service in Canada employed as a civilian baker. One detects here the telltale sounds of scraping the bottom of a barrel. After the party crossed the Connecticut River, Newgate deserted and set off to warn the English.[5]

The desertion of this disgruntled French soldier helped dissolve the Beaucours expedition and prevented it from accomplishing much of anything. All likelihood of surprise was lost and two hundred of the Natives deserted. Even before Newgate's desertion, they had not been committed to the French officers' decision to strike out toward eastern Massachusetts. Some of them appear to have returned to their original plan, attacking targets of opportunity in the Connecticut valley during July in small detachments. These actions clearly constituted a parallel war for captives and plunder that only secondarily furthered French aims. After half-heartedly assaulting about six garrison houses near Lancaster and Groton in eastern Massachusetts, the French and those Natives who remained with them returned to Canada. They had killed four English colonists and captured two more, a sad comparison to the accomplishments of the Deerfield raid. Vaudreuil claimed to be satisfied, since the expedition had forced the English to "remain a great portion of the summer idle not knowing where this party might strike" and thus cost the "enemy considerable sums." Still, the expedition came nowhere near the "great success" that had been anticipated when the raiders left Canada. Many in New France criticized its paltry accomplishments.[6]

Even strategically, then, the Deerfield raid was of little lasting help to the French. Vaudreuil's policy of aggressive defense was turning out to be quite

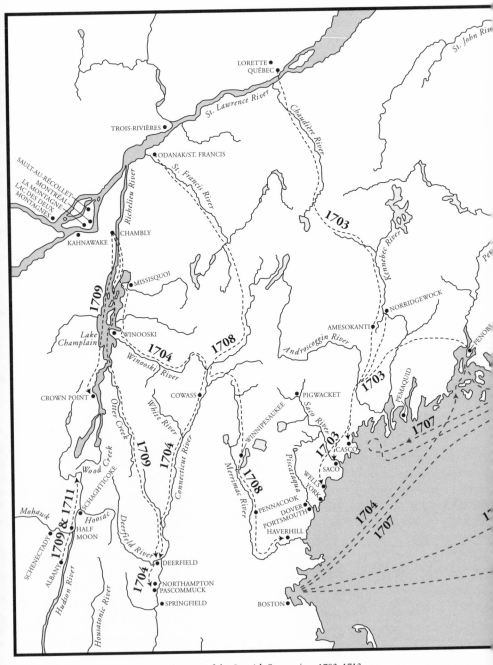

Map 7. Offensive operations during the War of the Spanish Succession, 1702–1713.

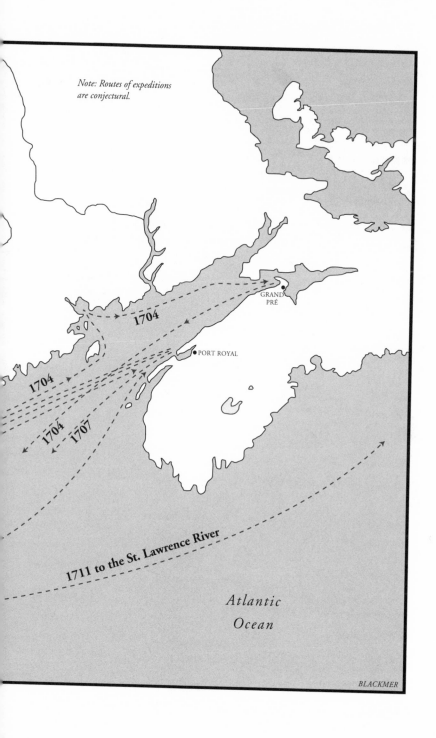

Note: Routes of expeditions
are conjectural.

1704

1704

1704   1707

1711 to the St. Lawrence River

GRAND
PRÉ

PORT ROYAL

Atlantic
Ocean

BLACKMER

impractical. The great disappointment of the Beaucours expedition brought about a temporary halt in large-scale, joint French and Indian raids against the New England frontier only a year after the war began in earnest. Officials in France became concerned about the costs of military operations against New England. They also still worried that the English would use every means "to induce the Iroquois [League] to break off peace with us." Facing improved English defenses, having to respond to the concerns of his superiors, and unable to repeat the success of the Deerfield raid, Vaudreuil had begun to explore with Governor Joseph Dudley of Massachusetts the possibility of a truce along their respective frontiers.[7]

At the same time, New France's Native allies were losing interest in the war. This development seriously limited Governor Vaudreuil's options and made the treaty of neutrality all the more appealing to him—and less urgent for Dudley. Wattanummon's departure for New York, probably in the summer of 1704, signaled disenchantment among some of the Pennacooks. Though a majority of the Pennacooks along with a number of the Eastern Abenakis moved to Odanak and established the new village of Becancourt, bringing them physically closer to the French, the move distanced them from English villages and therefore reduced the military pressure on the frontiers of New England. At the same time, Peter Schuyler continued his efforts to secure the neutrality of the Kahnawake Mohawks and the Iroquois of the Mountain. Claude de Ramezay, the governor of Montreal, managed to prevent them from accepting Schuyler's wampum peace belts, but their commitment to the war was noticeably weakened. Only four men from Kahnawake went on raids as 1704 drew to a close.[8]

N EW England's initial military responses to the Deerfield raid had been to place most of its effort into static defensive measures. By the summer of 1704, Massachusetts had nineteen hundred men under arms—almost one out of every five able-bodied men in the colony—while Connecticut had between five hundred and eight hundred men in pay, two hundred to three hundred of whom were in Massachusetts. Most of the men taken into service and onto the colony's payroll were impressed militiamen. But a fair number of Native men still living in southern New England joined the war effort as well. These soldiers were placed in garrisons along the two-hundred-mile frontier that ran from Deerfield to Wells, Maine. This system did provide a measure of security. According to French sources, the failure of Beaucours's raid in the summer of 1704 had been due in part to the fact that the New England "frontiers [were] well covered with men, that they were as thick as the bushes." The success that the French and Pennacooks had experienced at Pascommuck in early May 1704 had been exceptional. Even there the party had fallen on the small hamlet near Northampton only after failing to discover a more exposed target along the Merrimack River. For most of 1704, raiding parties of Eastern Abenakis, Iroquois of the Mountain, and Mohawks from Kahnawake had inflicted relatively few casualties during some two-dozen ambushes and assaults along the frontier from Deerfield to York, Maine (see appendix E). The contrast with the staggering English losses during the first four years of the Nine Years' War, which saw attacks on Dover, Salmon Falls, Casco, York, and Oyster River as well as innumerable smaller raids, was striking.[9]

Defense was expensive and unsatisfying to many New Englanders, who wanted to strike back and do some plundering of their own. The new defensive measures added between £25,000 and £30,000 to the Massachusetts budget, tripling the colony's annual expenses. Critics charged that it cost the colony approximately £1,000 for every Indian killed or captured. Officials in Connecticut also objected to the cost of providing men to defend the borders of Massachusetts. Better sailors than bush fighters, New Englanders preferred to launch seaborne operations against the French colony of Acadia rather than patrol the frontier. Targeting Acadia can be seen as an overlapping war in which the goals of Massachusetts imperialism coincided with those of the English empire. The economic advantages to be gained by driving the French from Acadia appealed to Boston's merchants as well as its humble fishermen. In 1690 Massachusetts had responded to the Salmon Falls and Casco raids by sending an army under William Phips to capture Acadia's capital, Port Royal. They launched a seaborne assault on Quebec later that same year. But it had failed and instilled in Governor Vaudreuil a misguided contempt for the martial abilities of New England. Still, the pattern had been established: French and Indian raids led to amphibious counterstrokes against Acadia and possibly Quebec itself. In the Nine Years' War New England had been on its own. In the War of the Spanish Succession, the English empire would soon add its martial weight to New England's imperial aspirations to create a force able to conquer and hold French territory.[10]

Strategically, the Deerfield raid came to have precisely the opposite effect from what Vaudreuil had intended. The English were angry, not scared. In the immediate aftermath of the raid, the governors of Connecticut, Massachusetts, and New York had all called for a full-scale invasion and conquest of Canada. They regarded conquest and the expulsion of the French as the only way to end the border raids. Governor Dudley put it succinctly: "the destruction of Quebeck and Port Royal [would] put all the Navall stores into Her Majesty's hands, and forever make an end of an Indian War." But with no realistic expectation of effective assistance from London and the neighboring colonies, the Massachusetts governor had to settle in 1704 for a spoiling expedition against the coasts of Acadia. A force of 550 men "both English and friend Indians" under sixty-five-year-old

Colonel Benjamin Church spent the months of May and June attacking Native and French settlements along the coast from Penobscot to Port Royal. They destroyed four villages and took fifty to one hundred prisoners. In Montreal Governor Claude de Ramezay complained that Church's expedition was the inevitable consequence of Vaudreuil's strategy of border raids.[11]

Scalp bounties and hopes of plunder also inspired land-based raids on Natives, called "scouts" by the English. In May 1704, officials from Albany passed on intelligence that Pennacooks were gathering at Cowass. They must have learned this from a Mohawk who valued his connection to the English more than that with the Pennacooks. In June a raiding party of five Mohegans from Connecticut and one Englishman, Caleb Lyman, killed seven Pennacooks near Cowass and brought back plunder, in the form of guns, furs, and canoes. This was the raid that had driven Wattanummon to seek refuge in New France. The raiders took back only six scalps because the Mohegans had decided to "give <u>one</u> to the Country, since we had each of us one; and so concluded we should all be rich eno'." They received £31 as a reward for their effort. At least one prominent colonist felt they deserved "eight times as much."[12]

By the fall of 1704 there was a lull in the fighting that continued into the spring and summer of 1705 (appendix E). Waging war on such a scale had exhausted both the French and the English colonies. At the same time the Native allies of both empires had grown wary of continued participation in the ongoing imperial conflict. During the lull, Governors Dudley and Vaudreuil had discussed a treaty of neutrality and played for time as hostilities on land almost came to an end.

T HE prospect of a treaty of neutrality was a bleak one for French officers. There were simply too many good officers and not enough opportunities for advancement even during a war. Peace only made things worse. Seniority, family background, and patronage connections always played important roles in determining promotions and the process was usually excruciatingly slow. War provided the chance to distinguish oneself in action and perhaps to die gloriously in battle. Unable to understand the Canadian military system and unwilling to pay for it, superiors in France were again criticizing the employment of the supernumerary, half-pay *officiers réformés,* such as Jean-Baptiste Hertel de Rouville and his brothers, whom Vaudreuil continued to carry without assignment to particular companies of the *troupes.* They wanted him to reduce the number of *officiers réformés,* further limiting the opportunities of the aspiring nobles.[13]

The 1704 Deerfield raid had helped the Bouchers in their quest for status. Within months of the raid, Pierre Boucher had again petitioned for reconfirmation of his original grant of nobility. In his memorial he recounted his services as governor of Trois-Rivierès and his founding of Boucherville, while also highlighting the military services of his five sons—including Deerfield the veteran René Boucher de la Perrière. Governor Vaudreuil supported the petition, citing Boucher's past services and "those by his sons in the *troupes*." This time, the king was favorably disposed. After a delay occasioned by an inability to produce the original letters of nobility, which had been destroyed in a fire, new letters were issued and officially entered in 1707. Finally Pierre Boucher and his sons were legally entitled to be addressed as *écuyer*, though René failed to win promotion and remained a thirty-six-year-old ensign .[14]

Despite their greater contribution to the Deerfield raid, the Hertel family had even less to show for their efforts. Governor Vaudreuil commended Hertel de Rouville's service in several letters to Minister Comte de Pontchartrain, minister of the marine and supported Joseph François Hertel's renewed application for letters of nobility. He did so in recognition of Joseph François's service and that of nine of his sons, including "Sieur de Rouville who was given a mark of valor [i.e., a wound] in the party that he commanded last winter against the English." Nothing came of these efforts.[15]

The lull in the fighting from late 1704 to the summer of 1706 must have been frustrating for De Rouville and René Boucher, who spent the years from 1705 to 1708 in relative inactivity, probably stuck with garrison duty. But peace gave René Boucher the chance to marry in 1705—at the age of thirty-seven, late even for members of the Canadian nobility. His wife, Françoise Malhout, came from a Montreal mercantile family involved in the western fur trade. In 1708 Boucher, though still an ensign, became French commandant at the critical post of Sault Saint-Louis, where it was his job to keep an eye on Kahnawake and its independently minded warriors. Hertel de Rouville, a thirty-nine-year-old widower, remarried in February 1708. Governor Vaudreuil, his wife, the intendants, and other civil and military leaders in Quebec witnessed the signing of the marriage contract with Marie-Anne Baudouin, the eldest daughter of a Quebec doctor, Gervais Baudouin. This marriage brought a welcome infusion of bourgeois money into the impoverished Hertel family and gave the Baudouin family much-cherished links to the aristocracy. The couple settled in Montreal in a house given them by Madame Baudouin as a marriage settlement.[16]

These militant members of the nobility had everything to gain and nothing to lose—except their lives—from a renewal of hostilities. Vaudreuil certainly had them in mind when he gave up on the truce negotiations and encouraged warriors from the Saint Lawrence villages to recommence raiding New England. In future years Vaudreuil would be remembered as one of the most popular governors

New France had ever had. Keeping Canadian officers happily employed in warfare, the sport of nobles, was undoubtedly a significant part of his appeal to the colony's elite.[17]

THE renewal of raids in the summer of 1706 came as a shock to the English. Most of the assaults and ambushes were carried out in July by a large party of Abenakis from Odanak operating in groups of about forty, followed in August by a party of about forty Mohawks and Iroquois from the villages near Montreal. Most of their victims were ambushed on the open road, in a field, or in isolated houses. Vaudreuil concluded that these smaller parties actually did more damage because "big parties which are not always successful do harm to only one place, but a good many little ones destroy the country and ruin the inhabitants." New Englanders agreed. Samuel Penhallow, a New Hampshire official during the war and afterward its foremost chronicler, claimed that "the Enemy dispersing into smaller parties did much more mischief than in larger; which put the country into a far greater confusion." The psychological impact of such raids was undoubtedly greater. But cumulative English losses were not as large as those inflicted by the larger, joint French and Indian expeditions (see appendix E).[18]

Massachusetts authorities responded by once again targeting Acadia. At Governor Dudley's prompting, Massachusetts raised over one thousand men, gathered a fleet, and sent them to capture Port Royal in May 1707. After landing and ranging itself in front of the fort at Port Royal, the New England army began to disintegrate, seemingly justifying Vaudreuil's low estimate of the English colonists' military capacity. It proved to be, according to the nineteenth-century historian Samuel Drake's apt summary, "another wretched exhibition of aggregated incompetence, ignorance, and pulling at cross-purposes." After eleven days of arguments and indecision, the army's leaders finally decided to abandon the effort. The army reembarked and the fleet sailed for the coast of Maine. An angry Governor Dudley sent the army back to Port Royal in August for a second attempt. It met with no better success. Without trained military leadership or sufficient heavy artillery, siege operations were at this point beyond the colonists' capabilities. The English lost a lot of money but not many men on these debacles: only sixteen killed and a like number wounded.[19]

More effective and cheaper were the activities of English scouts. The English were beginning to learn that the tactics that worked against them could work just as well against the French and Natives. A more active, forward defense by scouting parties marked a departure from New England's usual posture of static defense along its frontiers. Some scouts were men drawn from the garrison soldiers already in the pay of the province. Others were volunteers who went on scouts in the hope of taking scalps and collecting the bounty paid by the colonial government. Allied Indians, such as Naticks from eastern Massachusetts and Mohegans from Connecticut, sometimes accompanied the English on these scouts. Their activities had already succeeded in driving the Pennacooks to the Saint Lawrence valley, and they occasionally intercepted French and Indian raiding parties, denying them the element of surprise. In the aftermath of the Deerfield raid, winter parties on snowshoes were particularly effective in ensuring that the French and Indians "never [again] attempted coming at such a season." Winter scouts into the now largely deserted villages of the Pennacooks and Eastern Abenakis became annual occurrences on the eastern frontier of Massachusetts, while on the western frontier parties ranged west to the Berkshires, east to Brookfield and Lancaster, and north into what is today Vermont.[20]

For many participants, scouting expeditions became a parallel war fought for pay, scalps, and revenge. Deerfield residents, veterans of the Meadows Fight, and returned captives often took a prominent role in these expeditions. Former captives Thomas Baker, John Burt, Jonathan Hoyt, Martin Kellogg, John Nims, and Samuel Williams made use of their newly acquired skills in woodcraft, snowshoeing, and languages as they guided scouting parties north. Before the Deerfield raid the English never ranged more than twenty or thirty miles above Deerfield. Now they went as far as Cowass, the shores of Lake Champlain, and even to the banks of the Richelieu River (see map 7). Deerfield became the western base of operations for scouts and ranging companies.

A pattern of sending out a ranging party on snowshoes in winter, followed by a long scout in April, and a final scouting party in August or September eventually established itself. On April 28, 1707, Captain John Stoddard set off with twelve men and headed for the Winooski River, where two weeks later they began trailing a party of Natives. Three members continued the pursuit onto Lake Champlain, where one of them shot a woman, who turned out to be an English captive. During the winter of 1708, Captain Benjamin Wright led a party of English and Native allies as far as Cowass and ranged the woods without sighting any enemy activity. In August of the same year, a party of six men again scouted north from Deerfield to Cowass, where they ran into a party of Iroquois of the Mountain. Martin Kellogg was taken prisoner for a second time, but not before discharging his gun and wounding a Native. One Native and one Englishman also killed each other. The next spring Captain Wright went to the Winooski River with a party of eighteen that included former captives John Burt and Jonathan Hoyt. They tangled with a couple of parties of Iroquois of the Mountain returning to Sault-au-Récollet. The scouts claimed to have killed eight while losing four or five of their own, among the latter, John Burt, who became lost in the woods and presumably died of starvation. It was hard to tell who won these skirmishes in the woods since both sides usually inflicted some casualties, claimed victory, and retreated as quickly as possible.[21]

THE renewal of fighting along the New England frontier in 1706 put additional pressure on New York and the Iroquois League to start fighting the French. Authorities in the colony and in London tried to pull the Iroquois League into the war. The Five Nations of the Iroquois League had managed to remain neutral so far. As a result, the New York frontier had remained quiet, much to the disgust of officials in New England. The New Englanders' anger grew as raids continued in 1706 and 1707. Finally, in May 1708 the Massachusetts legislature appealed directly to Queen Anne with a "Complaint as to the Neutrality of the Five Nations" that asked her to instruct the governor of New York to push the Iroquois into the war.[22]

New York had less to gain and even more to lose from a war with New France than did New England. Seeking to avoid open conflict, New York authorities responded to the New Englanders' pleas and London's instructions by stepping up their efforts to win the neutrality of the Iroquois in Canada. Peace belts of wampum were again sent north, apparently at the urging of a Kahnawake sachem. This time the belts were accepted. The Mohawks of Kahnawake had grown tired of fighting what they saw as a French war. They also resented the fact that the French had forced them to give up so many of their prisoners in the aftermath of the Deerfield raid. Without captives the war had little meaning. Stiataque, a sachem at Kahnawake who had received one of these English belts, informed Governor Vaudreuil that he and his warriors were laying down the hatchet. Five other sachems from Kahnawake went to Albany to negotiate peace in return for inexpensive trade goods and a fair price for their furs. They secretly agreed not to attack New England.[23]

At the same time, peace along the New York frontier was becoming inconvenient to New France. From the beginning of the war, French authorities had consciously avoided doing anything that would initiate hostilities on the New York frontier. For several years, they had watched as Mohawks from Canada and Abenakis from throughout the borderlands attended conferences at Albany to reaffirm their peace, and to continue the trade, with New York. The French governor even turned a blind eye to the illegal trade between Albany and Montreal. By 1706, the illegal fur trade with Albany had cut so deeply into the legal trade that it had begun to worry officials in France. Scores of Kahnawake Mohawks and Iroquois of the Mountain were heading south to trade with Albany rather than raid New England. It has been estimated that between one-sixth and one-half of the furs trapped in New France ended up in Albany rather than Montreal. When edicts issued in 1706 and in 1707 failed to suppress the illegal trade between Natives in Canada and the New Yorkers, Pontchartrain reversed established French policy. In June 1708, he instructed officials in Canada "to excite a vigorous and general war between these Indians and the English."[24]

Vaudreuil worried about the declining militancy of his Mohawk and Iroquois allies and decided to resolve the problem with the same old medicine: a large French and Indian raid on New England. By the time he received Pontchartrain's letter, Vaudreuil had already taken steps to strengthen the French alliance with the Mohawks at Kahnawake and Iroquois of the Mountain at Sault-au-Récollet. He had watched with growing concern the efforts by English authorities in Albany, primarily Peter Schuyler, to secure their neutrality. He had also been goaded by Pontchartrain's criticism that he had failed to maintain enough pressure on New England's borders to prevent the attacks on Port Royal during 1707. This was apparently the case even though the frequency of raids by France's Native allies had remained fairly constant during 1706 and 1707 (see appendix E). The minister urged Vaudreuil to undertake more frequent and larger operations against New England's frontiers and if possible to take command of these expeditions in person. Not being in a position to accompany raiders to New England himself, the sixty-year-old governor turned to men that he could rely on: Hertel de Rouville and René Boucher de la Perrière.[25]

De Rouville shared command of the proposed expedition with Jean-Baptiste Saint Ours Deschaillons, scion of an ancient French noble family. Deschaillons had married a daughter of Agathe Saint-Père and thus linked himself to one of the oldest noble families in New France. Newly promoted to captain on June 9, 1708, Deschaillons set out with Lieutenant De Rouville and about one hundred Frenchmen from Trois-Rivierès on July 26. Deschaillons had the distinguished ancestry and prominent political connections, but less command experience than De Rouville. And even though Captain Deschaillons outranked Lieutenant De Rouville, their command was officially a joint one. In the governor's subsequent reports on the raid and in the account in Father Charlevoix's history, De Rouville clearly emerges as the more prominent leader of the expedition. Had he been a member of a more prominent or better connected family, he probably would have been the captain and would not have had to share authority.[26]

The composition of the expedition's French contingent also differed from that of the 1704 Deerfield raid. This operation was a somewhat less demanding summer raid, which may have been merely the result of timing but more likely it was necessitated by an inability to obtain enough of the right kind of men needed for a large winter raid. For over a decade, officials in New France bemoaned a decline in habitants' use of snowshoes. They attributed this unfortunate development to an increasing availability of horses and the use of sleighs. One concerned intendant had called for placing limits on horse ownership. Madame

Vaudreuil, the governor's wife, had a more drastic remedy: shoot the horses. But the problem went beyond horses and the lack of skilled snowshoe men. Vaudreuil himself admitted that he could no longer count on obtaining enough men from the militia to undertake lengthy, demanding expeditions. This situation necessitated greater use of soldiers from the *troupes,* who, as a rule, did not have the skills or endurance of the Canadians. Use of French soldiers favored summer campaigning.[27]

The size and strategy of this expedition made it a more complicated endeavor than the Deerfield raid. It was projected to be almost double the size, probably over 400 men. And in an effort to mask their intentions and confuse the English, the raiders planned to set out from three different locations and meet up on the march south. Boucher would accompany a party of 220 Kahnawake Mohawks and Iroquois of the Mountain marching from the Montreal area. The main French party, which would leave from Trois-Rivierès, included approximately 50 Canadian militiamen, 50 French soldiers drawn from the *troupes,* and "a great number of volunteers, chiefly officers in [the] troops," among them Deerfield veterans René Hertel de Chambly, and Charles Legardeur de Croisille and nine other ensigns plus an unknown number of cadets. The cadets included two more of De Rouville's brothers. In all, nobles constituted about one-fifth of the French contingent. Nippisings and Abenakis traveled with the French. Additional Abenakis from Becancourt and Hurons from Lorette would leave from near Quebec. The parties planned to rendezvous at Lake Winnipesaukee, where they would be met by Eastern Abenakis and Pennacooks. From there, they planned to attack New Hampshire towns along the Piscataqua River.[28]

Problems plagued the expedition from its inception. Unlike the Iroquois of the Mountain at Sault-au-Récollet, the Mohawks at Kahnawake "seemed very tardy & unwilling to join." The Hurons from Lorette never made it to Trois-Rivierès, turning back after one of them was killed in a hunting accident. The large party from the villages near Montreal eventually turned back also, claiming that some of them were sick. René Boucher could do nothing to stop them. Vaudreuil concluded that it was merely a ploy intended to wreck the entire expedition. Indeed, as the Kahnawake Mohawks later informed English officials in Albany, they had thrown away "all of their Provisions & left the other forces after recollecting their Engagments . . . not to join in war against New England." Their mass desertion—reminiscent of the Beaucours expedition—made clear the leverage that Natives acquired by participation in large bodies. The raid almost ended there. An exasperated Governor Vaudrueil urged Deschaillons and De Rouville to proceed even if the remaining Abenakis and Nippissings deserted them. When the main French party arrived at Lake Winnipesaukee, they found no Eastern Abenakis or Pennacooks waiting to join them. With only 160 men remaining, the raiders had to reconsider their target. They now chose to strike Haverhill, Massachusetts, a frontier village of twenty-five to thirty houses and about 150 residents.[29]

The assault was a disaster. The English were waiting for the raiders. Natives had already informed English authorities that a large raiding party had gathered near Montreal, preparing to strike the New England frontier. Governor Dudley of Massachusetts posted about two thousand men to the frontiers and concentrated them in fairly sizeable garrisons. There were at least thirty garrison soldiers in Haverhill when the French and Indians attacked about half an hour before dawn on August 29. Spotted as they entered the village and before they were in position, the raiders met stiff resistance at several garrison houses. Elsewhere the raiders succeeded in forcing their way into houses. They killed sixteen men, women and children, and captured several others. They plundered the houses and burned several but had to withdraw rather precipitously when they heard the sounds of an approaching relief party. Unbeknownst to the raiders, another party of sixty militiamen had already positioned themselves in a wood that lay in their line of retreat. Upon entering the woods, the French and Indians were greeted by an English volley that froze them in their tracks. Behind the raiders in close pursuit came an even larger party of militiamen. Recovering from the initial volley, the French and Indians charged forward and set upon the militiamen in the woods. They succeeded in breaking through but lost their packs, their medical supplies, their plunder, and most of their captives. Ten of the raiders died, among them De Rouville's brother René, and eighteen were wounded. At least one young cadet was captured. The casualty rate of 18 percent exceeded that of the Deerfield raid. For the survivors, it was a long and hungry journey home.[30]

For all sorts of political reasons, Governor Vaudreuil needed the attack on Haverhill to be a tactical and strategic victory and he misreported it as such to his superiors. He put the English losses at one hundred killed, when in fact the total was thirty-three killed and captured, a number almost equaled by French and Indian casualties. He claimed that France's Native allies were inspired to launch new raids against New England, though there is no evidence of these attacks during the remainder of 1708 in French or English sources. He sought promotions for Cadet Hertel de Moncours to ensign, for Ensign René Boucher de la Perrière (who never made it to Haverhill) to lieutenant and for Lieutenant Hertel de Rouville to captain in recognition of the "prudence, valor, and firmness" with which he conducted the raiding party. In addition, Vaudreuil used the opportunity to support yet another petition by Joseph-François Hertel for letters of nobility. In his endorsement, the governor again emphasized the service in the *troupes* of the elder Hertel's ten sons, especially De Rouville.[31]

The raid turned out to be a political as well as military failure. Instead of being impressed by the Haverhill raid, the French ministry was alarmed. Exaggerated reports passed on by officials in Acadia shocked Minister Pontchartrain. From Port Royal, Acadia's new governor, Daniel d'Auger de Subercase, wrote that the attackers had killed "4 to 500 persons without giving quarter to women or children." Once again, evolving European codes of warfare appeared to clash with the conduct of wars in which the French had to depend on Native allies who fought according to their own rules. Officials in France decided such "cruel actions" should be moderated. In particular, they shared the justified fears of Acadian officials that these attacks would lead to more English reprisals against Acadia. No more was said about the Canadian governor's leading large expeditions against New England. Vaudreuil's requests to promote the Hertels and Boucher were ignored, as was the renewed application to ennoble the elder Hertel.[32]

Thanks to Vaudreuil's favor and their close ties to Native warriors, however, Hertel de Rouville and René Boucher found a new opportunity in 1709 to advance their careers at the expense of the English—and, more particularly, of Deerfield. Natives from Canada continued to make small raids on New England homesteads in search of captives and plunder. Iroquois of the Mountain from Sault-au-Récollet who had tangled with an English scouting party from Deerfield commanded by Captain Benjamin Wright approached the governor. "Feeling piqued" because of their losses, they asked Vaudreuil "to undertake a raid" with some fifty of the most active Frenchmen and allow "De Rouville and de la Perier" (René Boucher) to command. Vaudreuil assented at once. After gathering a force of 40 Canadians and 140 Indians, many of them from Kahnawake, the two officers set out for Deerfield. Spies and at least one Native deserter soon carried detailed reports of their intentions to the English.[33]

Once again, Hertel and Boucher plotted an assault on Deerfield. Given the small size of their force, they apparently concluded that they could not take Deerfield's stockade by storm. Instead, they intended "to post themselves near the fort and then send out a skulking party to draw out the English, thinking by that means to take the place." The plan almost worked, even though residents of Deerfield had received a timely warning of De Rouville's approach. On June 24, 1709, the raiders captured two Deerfield men, Joseph Clesson and John Arms. The next day De Rouville posted twenty-five Natives near the village while preparing an ambush with the remainder. A party of ten Englishmen took the bait, mounted their horses, and sallied forth. Subsequent claims submitted to the Massachusetts legislature for killed and wounded horses and lost weapons confirm that the mounted pursuers, among them former captive Jonathan Hoyt, rode into the ambush. One garrison soldier was killed and three wounded, one mortally. The allies did not suffer any casualties. De Rouville's ruse had worked, but not well enough to enable the raiders to capture the stockade. This expedition was to be De Rouville's last against the frontiers of Massachusetts.[34]

W HILE French and Native cooperation was becoming more uncertain, authorities in London, Boston, and New York began to coordinate their war efforts. In 1709, the main theater of the war shifted away from the New England's western frontier to Acadia and New York as England's imperial strategy began to make itself felt (see appendix E). New York raised an army of about fifteen hundred colonists and six hundred Natives—League Iroquois, Mahicans and Schaghticokes—to attack Montreal with prodding from England and assistance from Connecticut, New Jersey, and the Iroquois League. The Reverend John Williams served as a chaplain to the New England forces. Four or five former captives from Deerfield were also part of the expedition because they "knew the territory." Colonel Francis Nicholson assumed command of this army, which was to act in concert with a seaborne assault on Quebec. During the summer, Nicholson led his army to the Great Carrying Place between the Hudson River and Lake Champlain watersheds. There he made preparations to move north. On its way back to Canada after the June raid on Deerfield, De Rouville's party passed by Wood Creek to scout Nicholson's preparations.[35]

Preparations for the invasion of New France of necessity involved negotiations and intrigue with the Mohawks of Kahnawake. Into this web of imperial intrigue fell Mehuman Hinsdale. Though he was one of the prominent residents of Deerfield—in fact he was the first English child born in the town—he was a most unfortunate frontiersman. His father, grandfather, and two uncles had been killed in the ambush near Deerfield during King Philip's War. His only child had been killed in the 1704 raid and he and his wife, Mary, had been captured. They both returned within a few years. On April 11, 1709, he drove up from Northampton with a team of horses loaded with apple trees. He was alone and unafraid because the "leaves not being put forth" it was earlier than Native warriors usually attacked. But two Mohawks from Kahnawake defied custom, took him captive, and carried him back to their village, treating him "civil & courteous" on the journey north.[36]

In Canada, Mehuman became a pawn of imperial politics. He managed to ransom himself from his Iroquois captors, but this put him in the hands of Governor Vaudreuil. Vaudreuil actually remembered Mehuman from the last time he had been a captive in Canada. He ordered Mehuman to give him as much information as possible about the impending invasions that the English were planning. Mehuman tried to keep what little he knew secret and managed to forestall Vaudreuil until a captive was brought in from eastern Massachusetts who told all that he knew. Vaudreuil then threw Mehuman into prison at Quebec, where he stayed for six weeks until some Kahnawake Mohawks "desired of the Governeur, that they might have Mr. H. to burn, (pretending they should fight the better if they could burn an Englishman) and he was delivered" to them. That the governor granted this request was striking evidence of the extent to which French authorities were willing to disregard European codes of war to satisfy their Native allies. As it turned out, these Kahnawake Mohawks, with the aid of a League Mohawk named Arousent "were plotting to leave ye French & go over to Genll Nicholson & ye Dutch and designed to have made use of Mr. H. to have introdud them." Mehuman was of course "overjoyed with the account (for he thought of nothing but being sacrificed by them) & encouragd it." They made it all the way to Montreal and were getting ready to leave when one of the plotters "fell sick, and in his sickness making confession to a priest, discovered the plot, and so all was dashd." Arousent escaped back to the English army. Hinsdale was put back in prison, eventually shipped to France, and only returned home by way of London and Rhode Island in October 1712.[37]

The Kahnawake Mohawks' plot to defect with Mehuman Hinsdale may have failed, but it was a clear indication that the French could not rely on that village to protect them from the impending English invasion. Factions divided the town: "one half is for the English & the other half for the french." The Mohawks asked Vaudreuil to allow them to remain neutral rather than have to fight the English and their Iroquois kin. The next year, 1710, the people of Kahnawake promised New York officials that they would "no more join in any Excursions upon New Eng[land] & as a Sanction of their Sincerity had sent a Belt of Wampum." And there is no evidence of their participation in raids against New England after the second Deerfield raid in June 1709.[38]

Uncertain of some of his Native allies, Governor Vaudreuil decided to send a French army to make a preemptive strike against the English and Native invaders. Based on the report by Hertel de Rouville and René Boucher de la Perrière, he entrusted Governor De Ramezay of Montreal with fifteen hundred militiamen, troupes, and Natives and sent him up Lake Champlain later that summer to surprise the English. De Rouville was given command of a battalion of one hundred militiamen. His men formed part of the van as the army advanced up the lake. Success "seemed inevitable." But beneath the surface divided counsels among the French and a "lack of subordination in the troops" eroded the army's effectiveness. It had been more than a dozen years since New France had mounted such an ambitious expedition against New York, and it appears that the commander encountered unanticipated organizational problems.[39]

Once again, the French effort to mount a large-scale attack on the English failed miserably. Near Crown Point the French army met and skirmished with English scouts. The element of surprise was lost. Then, after some of the French landed, Ramezay became lost in the woods. Unit cohesion and discipline, always suspect among the Montreal militia, were soon lost as well. Natives and Canadians fired at each other. In their panicked flight some militiamen literally "somersaulted." One ran all the way back to Chambly. Exaggerated reports claiming that nine hundred English had been sighted on the lake added to the confusion and seemed to be confirmed when seven canoes filled with about one hundred English and League Iroquois came into view. Fortunately for the French, the *troupes* retained their order and fired on the English, who beat a hasty retreat. Ramezay eventually reappeared and gradually so did order among the French and Indians. However, the expedition's Native contingent refused to advance any farther because there were "too many English." After a contentious council of war, the army retreated.[40]

Hertel de Rouville actually emerged from this fiasco with his reputation enhanced. Superiors in Canada and in France subjected Ramezay's actions to close and critical scrutiny. In particular, his superiors asked him to explain his decision to place an officer other than De Rouville with the Abenakis. Attention focused on the performance of the expedition's Abenaki scouts because they had begun the battle by blundering into the English ambush and then fired upon the Canadian militia. The officials' unspoken assumption was that De Rouville should have been with Abenakis and undoubtedly would have done a better job of coordinating their actions. The Montreal governor's only defense was to invoke the status hierarchy so important to France: De Rouville was a lieutenant; the man he had chosen was a captain. Thanks to Ramezay's punctilious deference to rank and seniority, Lieutenant De Rouville had been spared deeper involvement in the fiasco and had finally won favorable notice from officials in France.[41]

Fortunately for New France, disease and intercolonial politics put an end to Nicholson's invasion of Canada in 1709. But Nicholson remained determined to strike a blow against the French, and with the help of Samuel Vetch, Governor Dudley, and his political allies in England, he assembled a more successful invasion. This one was less ambitious than that of the year before, which had been designed to conquer all of New France. Now the English aimed at only one part: the vulnerable province of Acadia. The desperate French called on the Abenakis to help them fight off the English, but the Abenakis did not see any reason to die in defense of Port Royal. Isolated and unsupported and faced by a determined enemy, the French surrendered. Ever after, Acadia would be known as Nova Scotia.[42]

While the fortunes of New France waned, Hertel de Rouville's reputation grew. By 1711, he was regarded as one of "the two best partisan officers in all Canada." Early that year Vaudreuil entrusted him and his loyal companion, Simon Dupuys, with a special mission. The governor sent them to Boston to further prisoner exchanges and to carry a letter to Colonel Nicholson, who was then in the Massachusetts capital. A diplomatic mission to Boston was a seemingly odd assignment for a partisan officer. But Vaudreuil saw it as an opportunity to "obtain information through them of the movements of our enemies, and at the same time to make them acquainted with the Country and the most favorable routes to send parties thither." The year before he had sent Dupuys and René Boucher on a similar mission to Albany "pretexting an exchange" to "learn distinctly the condition of things." When De Rouville returned from Boston in April, the exigencies of the war took him back to the frontiers of New York, not Massachusetts.[43]

In 1711, New France faced a coordinated invasion by two English armies. Francis Nicholson once again prepared to lead an army of twenty-three hundred men down Lake Champlain to attack Montreal while an English fleet sailed toward Quebec with an invasion force of sixty-seven hundred men, most of them regular soldiers from England. Vaudreuil responded to the threat by concentrating his forces at Quebec and Montreal. It was a tense summer in New France. Then in mid-October came news that the English fleet had turned back after ten ships had foundered on the rocks at Îles aux Oeufs and sunk. Not long after the English fleet turned back, De Rouville led a scout of two hundred men toward Albany, advancing as far as the Great Carrying Place. Here he met three Frenchmen, including one of his brothers, who had recently been released by the English in Albany. They reported that Nicholson had turned back after learning of the fate of the invasion fleet. New France had been spared by sheer luck or, as many in Canada believed, the intervention of the Virgin Mary.

THE failure of these invasions was disheartening to the English, and, not surprisingly, historians have regarded them as unmitigated disasters. They failed to achieve their objectives, and they were financially very costly. The loss of life in the 1711 seaborne expedition was considerable. The Reverend John Williams, who served as a chaplain during both the 1709 and 1711 campaigns, undoubtedly saw such reverses as the rebukes of a just God. But if he had looked closer to home, he would have seen something else. More precisely, the significance of these expeditions lay in what he would not have seen: French and Indian raiders. The aborted expeditions of 1709, the conquest of Acadia in 1710, and the failed invasions of 1711 had given the English the strategic initiative that they had lost with the Deerfield raid in 1704. For the better part of three years, French forces and the bulk of their Native allies were held in place near Montreal and Quebec, waiting to fight off a coming invasion. From the Connecticut valley to Maine the New England frontier was unusually quiet and safe (see appendix E).[44]

The final year of the war, 1712, saw a small wave of attacks along the frontiers of New England. But now the fighting was mostly between Natives and

English. These raids tended to be small and French participation was rare. Their targets were opportunistic and English casualties were light. Almost all of these attacks took place in Maine and involved Eastern Abenakis occasionally supported by Abenakis from Odanak. The Kahnawake Mohawks had already removed themselves from the war. Beginning in 1709 Eastern Abenakis living in Canada had begun to move back to their eastern homelands in search of subsistence and peace. Tribal elders in particular had grown weary of the war and sought to distance themselves from the French. In 1710, they had refused to help the French defend Port Royal in Acadia. They wanted peace with the English. Samuel Penhallow estimated that "Cold, Hunger, and Sickness" had wasted a third of the Eastern Abenakis and Pennacooks that had once lived along the eastern frontier of Massachusetts. The ambushes of 1712 were small overlapping or parallel wars by those few who remained committed to the fight.[45]

The English war effort became more vigorous as the French and Indian military campaigns dropped off. Frequent and aggressive English scouting parties continued to push the war away from New England's frontiers and into the Abenakis' homeland, providing former captives with the opportunity to get revenge on their former masters, as Wattanummon soon learned to his chagrin. In April 1712 what proved to be one of the last of the long-range scouts left Deerfield. Twenty-eight men set out under the command of Captain Thomas Baker and Lieutenants Samuel Williams and Martin Kellogg, all three of whom had been taken captive at Deerfield in 1704. They initially headed for Cowass "to Destroy a family or two of Indians that they heard was there." Finding no one at Cowass, they headed east, crossing over to the upper reaches of the western branch of the Pemigewasset River, which today is known as Baker's River. Following Indian tracks, they descended the river. The cautious officers then sent ahead a small reconnaissance party that reported seeing several wigwams not far off. After confirming the report, the whole company then moved to within a half mile of the wigwams located along the bank of the river. Dividing into two parties, they began to encircle the Native hamlet when they spied "a straggling Indian Coming directly towards them." Fearing discovery, they shot him. They then raced on to the wigwams, abandoning any effort at encirclement. At the bank of the river, they found "12 Indians Jest entered into their Canoes to Cross the river" and saw "a number of Squas & Poposes on the other Side running into the woods." They fired at the canoes, hitting some occupants and forcing others into the water. They continued firing. When they finally stopped shooting, eight or nine Pennacooks were dead.[46]

One of the confirmed dead was Wattanummon, who here reappears in the historical record after an absence of eight years. Wattanummon seems to have done his best to stay out of the war after the Deerfield raid. Unfortunately, wherever he went, the war caught up with him. He had probably lived at Schaghticoke, New York, in relative safety until 1709. But, as the undeclared truce along the New York–New France frontier broke down in 1708 and 1709, the Schaghticokes had to cope with the pressures of war. They requested a stockade for protection. New York authorities recruited them to join Nicholson's army. Eventually some of them did in 1709, which was just about the time that Wattanummon probably left. As war returned to the Champlain valley, the only place that appeared to be outside of a war zone lay deep in the interior of northern New England. Looking over the deserted wigwams, Samuel Williams and the others "judged that they had lived there two or three years, by the quantity of Furs . . . found there." The settlement was located in an area known to be "choice beaver hunting grounds." From the stockpile it appears that Wattanummon and his companions had been in the area since 1709, when the situation along the New York frontier had turned dangerous. The English scouts took his scalp along with "a small quantity of plunder" and headed back to Massachusetts.[47]

T HE 1704 raid on Deerfield marked the zenith of French and Indian raids directed against New England towns. From the perspective of the attackers, it was a stunning tactical success. But the degree of cooperation among the Natives from the Saint Lawrence valley and New England and their French allies that had ensured the raid's success was never achieved again. The Beaucours expedition could not do it in the summer of 1704, nor could Hertel de Rouville in 1708. His raid on Haverhill marked the last large-scale, joint attack by French and Native forces on a New England town, and it was basically a failure. Because of limited French resources and disagreements with their Native allies, no other large raid would be mounted against New England for the rest of the war. Also, under the energetic leadership of Governor Dudley, Massachusetts got much better at anticipating and repelling raiders. Soon after the 1704 Deerfield raid, the tide turned. The English became the invaders, and the French and Indians were put on the defensive.

The war between the French and the English empires finally ended in 1713 with the Treaty of Utrecht. English victories on the Continent and in North America made it a costly peace for the French. France lost Acadia and Newfoundland and had to recognize England's claims to Hudson Bay and the fur trade its posts controlled. The French also acknowledged an English claim of sovereignty over the Five Nations of the Iroquois League—even though members of the league did not recognize it. The Iroquois League emerged from the war in better shape than the combatants, having avoided a major involvement and heavy casualties while maintaining its independence from both the French and the English.

The "Eastern Indians"—the Pennacooks and the Eastern Abenakis—suffered the most during the war and from the peace that followed. When they signed their peace treaty with representatives of Massachusetts and New Hampshire at Portsmouth in July 1713, they had to acknowledge themselves "The Lawful Subjects of our Sovereign Lady Queen Anne" and promised their "hearty submission and obedience to the Crown of Great Britain." On one hand, they were forced to accept the fact that "the English shall and may quietly and peaceably enter upon, improve and forever enjoy all and singular the Rights of Land and former Settlements, Properties and Possessions within the Eastern parts of said Provinces." On the other hand, they could not cross south of the Saco River to even visit or trade with the English. In addition to land and sovereignty, they lost the counterweight formerly provided by the French presence in Acadia.[48]

The English empire emerged from the War of the Spanish Succession stronger than ever. The English war effort had grown in strength and ambition even as that of the French and their Native allies faltered. They had conquered new territory and slain many of their foes. By all rights, they should have conquered all of New France. Only by luck or, as the French believed, divine intervention, were the French and Native peoples of Canada allowed to continue living independent of English Protestant rule. The French and Natives living in Acadia were not so lucky.[49]

The New Englanders had losses as well. These would have a stronger hold on local memory than the war's successes. Approximately 400 colonists had died as a direct result of French and Indian border raids and on scouts or punitive expeditions. Seventy of the dead were Deerfield residents or garrisoned militiamen who had died defending the village. Around 372 captives had been taken, and not all of them had returned at the end of the war. Some never would. Thirty-six former residents of Deerfield were among those still absent in 1713 (see appendixes E, F, and G.).

PART IV

PRESERVING COMMUNITIES

CHAPTER 11

NATIVE VILLAGES

THE Deerfield raid had only temporarily advanced the interests of the Natives allied with the French. The War of the Spanish Succession did mark the high point of adopting New England captives into Native communities, and the captives taken at Deerfield constituted the single largest cohort of English adoptees. But for those allies of New France for whom adopting captives had been an important aim, the War of the Spanish Succession was, in the final analysis, something of a disappointment. At the same time, the war had done nothing to improve the security of the Abenakis' homeland. It actually made them more vulnerable to English expansion.

For many reasons it was difficult to turn New England Puritans into Native Americans and few permanently made the transition. When the last negotiators left Quebec in 1714 about a score of English-born colonists appear to have remained in Indian communities of Canada. The French did much better, taking in twice as many English, about forty-nine, sixteen of whom were from Deerfield. Not every captive taken from New England during the War of the Spanish Succession can be accounted for, but approximately three-quarters can be. None is known to have become a permanent member of the Huron community at Lorette. Three may have stayed with the Abenakis at Odanak, but none with the Pennacooks. Only one Deerfield captive, Hannah Hurst, is known to have permanently joined the Iroquois of the Mountain, though three youngsters from other New England towns probably did. Even the Mohawks of Kahnawake, who secured by far the largest share of captives, appear to have obtained only ten English captives, seven of them from Deerfield (appendixes F and G).[1]

By the early 1720s English colonists were again pushing into the lands of the Pennacooks and the Eastern Abenakis. And once again, the Abenakis fought back. This time when they called on their allies in Canada for assistance, the Natives heeded, but the French—at peace with England in Europe—held back. Without the support of an overlapping imperial war, the Abenakis had even more difficulty than before in staving off English expansion, now often spearheaded by returning captives.

As the fighting drew to a close in 1712, the Deerfield captives made up a significant proportion, roughly 36, of the approximately 130 to 140 English captives remaining in Canada. Among these about two dozen lived with the French and another dozen lived in Native communities. Most, about 21 or 22, were female, and perhaps as many as 14 were male. As had been true throughout their captivity, their fates continued to be determined in large measure by their age and sex. Already, 9 or 10 of the Deerfield women had married French or Native men. Most of them would have been practicing Catholics by this time; at least 22 had been rebaptized into the Catholic Church. Eighteen had become naturalized French subjects. Natives and French officials no longer regarded these people as captives. Only Eunice Williams appeared on a 1710 "Roll of English Prisoners in the hands of the French & Indians at Canada" provided by Governor Philippe de Rigaud de Vaudreuil. The presence of her name was undoubtedly due to the untiring efforts of her father to ransom her. As relatives in New England soon discovered, most of these individuals, including Eunice, no longer considered themselves to be either captives or English.[2]

Relatives in New England hoped, prayed, and worked for the captives' return. Even before the Peace of Utrecht officially ended the war, the Massachusetts government had dispatched yet another party to Canada in the summer of 1712 to further the exchange of prisoners. Once again, men from Deerfield took the lead in imperial negotiations for largely personal reasons. Lieutenant Samuel Williams led the group because he had "the French tongue." Three other Deerfield men accompanied him: John Nims, Ebenezer Warner, and Jonathan Wells Jr. Samuel's sister Eunice was still at Kahnawake; Warner's daughter Waitstill may have been there as well; and the family of John's brother Ebenezer Nims was at Lorette. The emissaries brought with them a small group of French prisoners being repatriated. Traveling overland, they started north in early July and returned in late September. They brought back with them only nine English captives.[3]

After the peace treaty had been signed and formally proclaimed, another commission was sent to New France to "attend Mons Vaudreuil in Order to [secure] the Return of the English prisoners there." Captain John Stoddard and the Reverend John Williams headed this group. Martin Kellogg served as interpreter. Captain Thomas Baker, another former captive, Ebenezer Warner, who was still searching for his missing daughter, and Jonathan Smith, whose connection to the group is unclear, made up the rest. The party set off in mid-November 1713, heading west to Albany. There they secured the services of Hendrick, a leader of the Iroquois League, to guide them north to Montreal. It was not until January 22, 1714, when the ground and lakes had finally frozen that they set out for Canada, reaching Quebec on February 16.[4]

The commissioners met with Governor Vaudreuil, who informed them that all of the remaining captives had "free liberty to return" and could do so with his blessing. Despite this promise, difficulties soon arose. Stoddard and Williams argued that minors needed more than permission to obtain freedom; intervention by French authorities might be necessary. For his part, the governor informed Williams and Stoddard that "he looked upon" the Natives "as allies, and the king must do so too—for, by force, he could not oblige the Indians to deliver their prisoners." There were also problems with the French. One French nobleman hid an English boy to prevent his return. Clerics apparently went "from house to house to solicit" people to remain in New France. Vaudreuil claimed that he could "as easily alter the course of the waters as prevent the priests' endeavors." He did, however, order the man hiding the boy to produce the lad. At the same time, Vaudreuil erected a new barrier informing the English commissioners that those individuals who had become naturalized French subjects could not return. They were no longer considered prisoners but French men and women. Stoddard and Williams protested and sent Captain Baker back to Massachusetts for additional instructions. Three captives went with him. The negotiations dragged on into spring and summer.[5]

Some of the captives proved quite reluctant to leave their new homes. John Williams managed to visit his daughter Eunice, but the interview only added to his frustration. Eunice, now married to a Mohawk, informed him through an interpreter that "she is yet obstinately resolved to live and dye here." Furthermore, she would "not so much as give [him] one pleasant look." In this instance as in others, Williams had to confess "we are like to be very unsuccessful." He was forced to admit defeat because "the English are so naturalized to the customs and manners of the French and Indians, and [, like Eunice,] have forgotten the English tongue, and are so many of them married, or gotten into nunneries, &c." He concluded "it would be far easier to gain twice the number of French and Indians to go with us than English."[6]

The response of Native leaders to the commissioners' appeals varied in ways that reflected the particular status of captives within each community and the degree of French influence in the community. The Mohawks at Kahnawake negotiated from a position of strength. Their leaders informed Stoddard and Williams that "those taken by them were adopted into families, and not held as prisoners, but as children; and it was not their custom to compel any to return, but should leave them to their own liberty." Free to choose, the captives at Kahnawake chose to stay. However, a woman known as "Madame le Ford" ransomed two boys and Vaudreuil ransomed a girl. The Abenakis at Odanak refused to release their four remaining prisoners, claiming that the English continued to hold Abenakis as hostages. A former Pennacook leader, Nescambiouit, was especially angry, claiming he had been to Boston "to demand his son, but could not obtain him." Only one prisoner was obtained at Odanak, and then only after the payment of a hefty ransom. At Lorette, where French influence was greater, Governor Vaudreuil had more luck in securing the release of the Nims family.[7]

The English commissioners eventually gathered together just over two dozen captives who wished to return to New England. In the end Vaudreuil had relented and allowed naturalized individuals to leave surreptitiously and several did. On September 21 the commissioners and twenty-six captives arrived in Boston by ship. Four Deerfield captives, Sarah Hurst Perkins, Ebenezer Hurst, Ebenezer Nims and his wife, Sarah Hoyt Nims, are known to have been among these returnees as was the Nims' young son, Ebenezer. Joseph Kellogg returned overland with his brother Martin. It is likely that Elizabeth Hurst Beecraft and Samuel Price also returned at this time by one of these routes and Samuel Hastings may have done so as well. Eunice Williams and Waitstill Warner, if she was still alive, remained in Canada along with 23 to 26 former residents of Deerfield.[8]

O N THE boat back to Massachusetts in 1714 were the last of the Huron captives: Ebenezer and Sarah Nims and their son, Ebenezer. It is doubtful that they would have gotten away if Lorette had not been so close to Quebec. Since it was, they were able to learn of the general release of prisoners at the end of the war. They tried to seize this chance to leave. It was not easy. The Hurons and their priest did not want them to go. The couple had to hide their eagerness to return until they finally made it on to the ship at Quebec. The next day, Ebenezer's adoptive mother and "a great number of Indians" came to Quebec and demanded that they be returned. The Hurons assumed that the Nimses had been kidnapped. Two of them went on board to talk with Ebenezer. When he assured them of his determination to return, they demanded that the child Ebenezer be left at Lorette. His parents refused. The Hurons returned home empty-handed.[9]

The Hurons lacked the means to shield and hold onto their captives but not the desire. Ebenezer's Huron mother exercised as much control over him and his offspring as did any other Iroquoian matron. Ebenezer, Sarah, and their son made good their escape because Quebec, the seat of the French government and land fall of the English negotiators' ship, was only half a day's journey away. The only other Deerfield captive known to have been at Lorette, Jonathan Hoyt, had been ransomed in 1706 by William Dudley, who had seen him with his master in the market in nearby Quebec. Hoyt's master, who may have been Thaovenhosen, was so attached to him that in the years after the war ended he frequently visited him, often in the company of his sister. The fate of these Deerfield captives underscored the vulnerability of the smaller Native villages located near French towns where priests, officers, and merchants took an interest in English captives and English emissaries sometimes succeeded in gaining the assistance of sympathetic French men or women.[10]

Marriage could be an important means of integrating English captives into the community, but here too conditions often worked against assimilation into Native villages. Deerfield captives tended to marry other Deerfield captives or nearby French colonists. Sarah Hoyt's experience at Lorette is revealing. Her Huron masters wanted the young woman, who was seventeen when she was taken, to marry a Frenchman. To avoid this fate, she publicly offered to marry one of her fellow captives. There were not many to choose from, so a match was made with her former neighbor Ebenezer Nims. Judging from the birth date of their son Ebenezer, they appear to have married around 1712. Although nineteenth-century descendants may well have seen their marriage as a romantic story, Sarah probably saw things differently at the time.[11]

It is impossible to count the number of English captives adopted into Lorette during the colonial wars, but the number must have been quite small. None of the captives taken during the War of the Spanish Succession appears to have remained. A few captives from the Nine Years' War living around Quebec may have been Huron captives, but none of them is known to have married into the community. The grandson of a seventeenth-century captive, Stephen Otis, did marry a "chief's daughter" and "became one among the Hurons of Lorette." But this reflected more the pattern of Huron intermarriage with the surrounding French community than the absorption of English captives into the Huron community. Several captives were taken to Lorette during the Fourth Anglo-Abenaki War and King George's War. At least one of these captives stayed on in the community, for he showed the Swedish naturalist Peter Kalm around Lorette in 1749.[12]

By the mid-eighteenth century, the appearance of the Hurons at Lorette was gradually transforming from that of "Indians" to that of "French" (figure 14). They spoke French, "built all their houses after the French," and dressed like the French. At some point, the families of these Iroquoian people became patrilineal. By the early nineteenth century the process had gone so far that the government did not want to consider them "Indians" any longer. Speculation abounded among their French neighbors about how this had happened. Clearly the small community had drawn on outsiders from several sources in an effort to continue its existence. Explanations have tended to stress more exotic sources, such as English captives, French orphans, and illegitimate children abandoned by their parents. Doubtless a few recruits came from each of these sources. It is more likely, however, that the largest influx probably came from intermarriage with their French neighbors.[13]

If the Hurons wanted to stay on their lands, they had few options apart from intermarrying with their French neighbors. They had nowhere else to go, unless they wanted to move west to join the Hurons who lived near Detroit. Instead of moving away, they remained and cultivated ties with their French and Native

FIGURE 14. Huron woman and man. Watercolor, eighteenth century, artist unknown. The clothing reflects Huron adoption and adaptation of European fabrics. The woman's skirt and the man's shirt were made of European cloth. The blankets and the man's hat are also European. Leggings and moccasins made of skins, as well as the beadwork and jewelry, would have been fashioned according to Huron traditions. City of Montreal. Records Management and Archives.

neighbors. Among these ties were those of alliance that had brought Huron warriors to Deerfield in 1704. They remained particularly close to the Abenakis. They fought beside them against the English in the 1720s when, once again, a Huron chief from Lorette died attacking Massachusetts with Abenaki allies.[14]

Like the Hurons from Lorette, the Iroquois of the Mountain brought several captives to Canada but retained only a few in their community and like Lorette, their villages at La Montagne and Sault-au-Récollet were close to a large French town, Montreal. But unlike all the other Native villages, it was under the supervision of Sulpician priests, not Jesuits (map 8). Most English captives in these villages were soon ransomed or married to other captives or French colonists. As at Lorette, most of the former captives lived in nearby French communities. Deerfield's Jonathan Carter and Thomas Hurst both got lands near Sault-au-Récollet after the Sulpicians released them from servitude. For the Sulpicians, a gift of land at Rivière-des-Prairies seems to have been part of a bargain designed to keep captives in New France and a means of developing this far corner of their island seigneury.[15]

The Sulpicians were perhaps the most vigorous and successful advocates of converting captive New Englanders in those French parishes and Native communities where they had some influence. These priests held to the old royal policy of cultural and religious assimilation and applied it to Natives and New Englanders alike. According to Joseph Kellogg's account of his life at the Sault-au-Récollet, "several of them that are yet with the Indians are such as by the instigations of the Priests & Jesuits have on their knees promised God and the Virgin marry to live and die with the Indians, and are by them threatened with Eternal damnation if they break their vow." Still, the Sulpicians were clearly more committed to turning English captives into French Catholics rather than let them live as Indians. Like Thomas Hurst and his family, some of the Deerfield captives held by the Iroquois of the Mountain and their offspring received special attention and support from the Sulpicians. As a result of this attention, they eventually developed ties with the French that were much closer than their ties to the Native community.[16]

Persistent Sulpician priests turned Abigail Nims and Josiah Rising into excellent Catholics but in the process transformed them from Iroquois of the Mountain into French habitants. Both of these Deerfield captives were especially vulnerable to the Sulpicians' ministries. They were young when taken. Abigail was three and Josiah was eight. Neither child had much family remaining in New England. Both of Abigail's parents were dead by 1705 and her brother Ebenezer was still at Lorette. Soon after her capture, Abigail was adopted into a leading family of the bear clan and baptized as Elizabeth Twatogwach in June 1704. Josiah was taken directly to Sault-au-Récollet and baptized as Ignace Shonatakakwani.

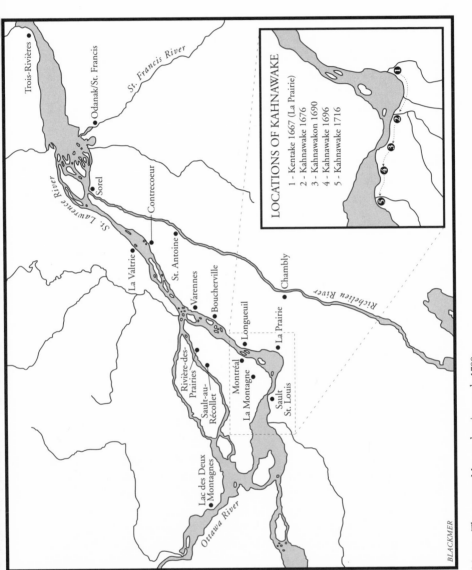

MAP 8. The greater Montreal region, early 1700s.

LOCATIONS OF KAHNAWAKE

1 - Kentake 1667 (La Prairie)
2 - Kahnawake 1676
3 - Kahnawakon 1690
4 - Kahnawake 1696
5 - Kahnawake 1716

Trois-Rivières

Odanak/St. Francis

St. Francis River

St. Lawrence River

Sorel

Contrecoeur

La Valtrie

St. Antoine

Varennes

Boucherville

Longueuil

La Prairie

Chambly

Richelieu River

Rivière-des-Prairies

Sault-au-Récollet

Montréal

La Montagne

Sault St. Louis

Lac des Deux Montagnes

Ottawa River

BLACKMER

He still had relatives in New England but had little reason to be attached to them. He was in Deerfield in 1704 only because his father did not have room for him in his house in Connecticut and decided to place him in the care of his cousin Mehuman Hinsdale, who lived in one of the most dangerous places in New England. When his father, John, died in 1719 he left his "well-be-loved son Josiah, now in Captivity" the modest sum of £5, "provided he return from captivity."[17]

The Sulpicians quickly seized upon these two vulnerable Deerfield captives. As the priests saw it, not long after the two captives arrived at Sault-au-Récollet, the "odor of virtue which they spread throughout the mission" persuaded the Sulpicians to ransom the two captives from their Native masters. In July 1715 the fifteen year-old Abigail married twenty-one-year-old Josiah under their Native Christian names. The Sulpicians had "persuaded the indians to marry the english propounded such & such to them, and though the indians at first unwilling they persuaded them to it, to secure them there." For their part, Abigail and Ignace told their priest, Maurice Quéré de Treguron, that they wished "to remain with the Christian Indians, not only renouncing their nation, but even wishing to live en sauvages." Their names and their witnesses—Jean-Baptiste Haronhiatek, Gabriel Tsirokwas, Pierre Asonthen, Alexis Tarhi—were all Iroquoian. Their first two children, Marie Madeleine, born in 1716, and Simon, born in 1719, both had Iroquois of the Mountain for godparents. At Sault-au-Récollet, the two former Deerfield residents clearly lived as Iroquois and Catholics.[18]

The Rising family became less Iroquoian and more French when the Native village and its Sulpician mission moved to a site on the Lac des Deux Montagnes in 1721 (figure 15). The priests, impressed by the virtue and devotion of the young family, granted them a large piece of land just outside of the Native village. Around the Rising farm the French community of Oka soon developed. Here the Iroquoian names and associates of the Risings drifted away and a French Catholic identity took hold, as evidenced by the lives of their eight children, most of whom lived as devout French Catholics. The oldest daughter, fluent in Mohawk, joined the Congregation de Notre Dame and spent fifty-four years as a schoolteacher at Lac des Deux Montagnes. Her younger brother joined the Sulpicians and spent his life ministering to French parishes in the countryside between Trois-Rivières and Quebec. Her youngest sister joined the Church as well, eventually becoming Superior of the Congregation de Notre Dame. The rest of the Risings' eight children married French colonists. Among the grandchildren of the Risings two became members of the Congregation de Notre Dame, two joined the Hôtel-Dieu, two joined the Grey Nuns, and one became a priest. Few colonial families gave so completely to the French Catholic Church as did that of Josiah Rising and Abigail Nims.[19]

Only one Deerfield captive is known to have married one of the Iroquois of

FIGURE 15. Homestead of Josiah Rising and Abigail Nims at Lake of the Two Mountains. Photograph by Emma Lewis Coleman, circa 1890. According to tradition this house was the dwelling that the Risings built on the land given them by the Sulpicians when the Iroquois of the Mountain relocated to Lac de Deux Montagnes in 1721. While this relatively substantial house probably postdates 1721, its style underscores the fact that subsequent generations of the Risings identified themselves as French habitants, not Natives. Courtesy of Pocumtuck Valley Memorial Association, Memorial Hall Museum, Deerfield, Massachusetts.

the Mountain: Hannah Hurst. Her 1712 wedding to an older man holds much interest. It is the first known marriage of a captive from New England into this Iroquois community. The Sulpician missionary who presided over the wedding, Maurice Quéré de Tréguron, clearly had some qualms about it, suggesting how unusual and possibly novel it was. At the time Hannah was actually a naturalized French subject. Most captives living in Native villages (such as Eunice Williams at Kahnawake) were not. Before eighteen-year-old Hannah married the thirty-year-old widower Michel Anenharison, Father Quéré "proposed to her to leave the Savages." She, however, "declared that she wishes to live with them always." Mary Sayward, originally from York, Maine who was now Soeur des Anges of the Congregation de Notre Dame and an active proselytizer among the English captives, confirmed that she "has often heard her say this." Quéré had already spoken to the Sulpicians' Superior, François Vachon de Belmont. He told Quéré that he "must treat her as if she were an Indian." The missionary priest had also notified "Mr. Meriel about this marriage, as well as Thomas her brother," who lived nearby at Rivière-des-Prairies. Thomas did not attend the wedding, but he was at the mission church two days earlier to hear the publication of the marriage banns. An apparently perplexed Father Quéré, uncomfortable with the idea of Hannah's becoming "an Indian," had consulted all possible authorities that could or would object to Hannah's marriage before proceeding.[20]

The actual marriage itself was a purely Native affair. Their wedding together with the couple's Iroquoian way of life at Sault-au-Récollet indicate the continuing strength of Iroquoian society on Montreal Island. Hannah's witnesses were Louis Tehorontisati, Martin Tiokwanekane, Philippe Tekaraweron, and Father Robert-Michel Gay, Quéré's colleague at the mission, who had just baptized Hannah as Marie Kaiennonni the day before. Only one birth, that of a son named Simon in 1719, is recorded for the couple. Thereafter there is no more record of them. Unlike her siblings and the Risings, Hannah presumably became part of the Native community at Lac des Deux Montagnes.[21]

OTHER Deerfield captives besides Hannah Hurst embraced a Native way of life, though their numbers were few. Like the majority of New England captives who became Natives, they lived at Kahnawake, a specificity that often gets lost in most discussions of captivity. Conditions at this Mohawk village were better suited than in other Native villages to the successful integration of English captives. Unfortunately the lack of records before the mid-eighteenth century makes it difficult to understand in much detail how integration happened. The paucity of information about those who fully integrated themselves into life at Kahnawake reflects just how successful their adoption by the Mohawks was. Not much is known about them because relatively little is known about any individual Kahnawake Mohawks at this time. Waitstill Warner, two-years-old when taken, and Daniel Crowfoot, who was three, possibly lived out their lives as Kahnawake Mohawks as well, but there is no way to prove it. There is only a little bit of information about the others, and that is primarily because they were girls who married and had children.

The story of the Deerfield captive Mary Field reveals much about the concerns of English colonists and their descendants but very little about her or Kahnawake. Mary Field became infamous in nineteenth-century Deerfield because she "became a savage and married one." Little else is known about her except her name "Walahowey," a likely corruption of Waienhawi, meaning, "she brings fruit." According to tradition, she once visited her birth family, then living in Connecticut, with her Mohawk husband. She had a brother, Pedajah Field, who traveled down from Northfield, Massachusetts, to see her. He had been born after the attack on Deerfield and so had never met her. The story claims she told him "that he would some day be carried off, that he, too, might enjoy the savage life and the benefits of the Catholic religion." After he was almost captured near his Northfield home, he believed her.[22]

Ever since the late seventeenth century, New Englanders had been trying to understand why some English captives stayed with their Indian masters and became, for all intents and purposes, Natives. They feared what they saw as the combined seductions of the Native way of life and the Catholic faith, both of which challenged everything they stood for. Deerfield's nineteenth-century local historian George Sheldon believed that a boyish "fascination with <u>camping out</u>" was explanation enough. And this conclusion would appear to find confirmation in the statements of some boy captives who spoke about their experiences. For example, Samuel Jordan, who was a captive at Odanak from 1703 to 1709 and subsequently spent a year with the French, always responded when asked whom he preferred living with: "the Indians."[23]

The problem with Sheldon's theory is that most of those who stayed with Native peoples were girls, such as Mary Field, not boys, and structure, not freedom, appears to have played a critical role in acculturation (see appendix G). The most famous unredeemed Deerfield captive was Eunice, the seven-year-old daughter of John Williams. Apart from her social status, Eunice was typical in terms of age, sex, and experience of the seven captives from Deerfield who are known to have remained for many years at Kahnawake. Mary Harris was nine; Joanna and Rebecca Kellogg were eleven and eight; Mercy Carter was ten; and Abigail French and Mary Field were six when captured. Theirs was not a story of boys hunting in the woods but of women gathering and grinding corn. In these agricultural communities as soon as Native girls learned to walk they had "a little stick put into their hands to train them and teach them early to pound corn, and when they are grown somewhat they also play various little games with their companions and in the course of these small frolics they are trained quietly to perform trifling and petty household duties." Eunice's second Mohawk name was Kanenstenhawi, "she brings in corn." When Eunice and the other Deerfield girls were older they married in the Catholic Church and raised families of Mohawks. In their experiences they followed the established life course of Kahnawake women.[24]

The incorporation of the Deerfield girls fit into an age-old pattern in Native America. Indian societies had usually preferred to incorporate females rather than males, and the situation was no different when English colonists were involved. An intensive study of New England captives has found that the "prime candidate" for incorporation into Native communities "was a girl aged seven through fifteen." Studies of captivity elsewhere in Native America confirm that this was the crucial age-range for captives to be wholly adopted into their captors' society. Deerfield boys who remained with their French or Native captors largely fell within the same age range, but nearly twice as many girls (nine) stayed behind as did boys (five). Indians knew youthful captives were more amenable to adoption and sought them out. Shortly after the Deerfield raid in 1707, Governor Vaudreuil sent an officer to Detroit to obtain a "Pawnee" slave girl no more than twelve or fourteen years old to give to the Abenakis, who refused to take someone older or male.[25]

Intermarriage and religion were the primary ties that bound captives to Native communities. At Kahnawake, captives married Mohawks, not other captives. Abigail French defied the general pattern by neither marrying nor having any children. She did, however, become a devout Catholic, and her grand-nephew, the Bishop of Quebec, would remember seeing her in church. All of the other female captives are known to have married and to have had children, though perhaps not as many children as they would have had in French or English communities. Captive females appear to have been around seventeen or eighteen when they married, if the experiences of Hannah Hurst and Eunice Williams can be taken as typical. Women at Kahnawake did not have children as frequently as did colonial English or French women, who had children, on average, every twenty-two months. Kahnawake women spaced their children out more, by nursing longer, avoiding cohabitation, and using abortifacients. On average, they had a child every three years. The infant death rate also appears to have been higher in Native communities, where most people still remained particularly vulnerable to imported European diseases. Of Eunice Williams's children, only two daughters and possibly a son survived childhood. The combination of low fertility and high mortality tended to produce families that were smaller than their French and English counterparts.[26]

Some evidence suggests that English women living with the Kahnawake Mohawks did have families that on average were larger than those of Native women. When Joanna Kellogg visited her brother Martin, then living near Wethersfield, Connecticut, she came in the company of her seven children. Mary Harris had "several children" and Mercy Carter had several sons and at least one daughter by a Kahnawake man. It is possible that their children may have had more resistance to European diseases. It is also possible that these English girls retained enough of their original cultural heritage to devote themselves more to child-bearing than Native women traditionally did.[27]

The selection of godparents at Kahnawake usually reinforced membership of the women and their children in the Mohawk community. When Eunice Williams stood in as a godmother, she did so only once for an adopted English captive. Another time she stood in for a twenty-seven-year-old Iroquois woman newly arrived from New York. Her other two godchildren were Kahnawake girls. As birth-mother and godmother, Eunice played a vital role in maintaining Kahnawake's strength. Presumably the pattern for the other former residents of Deerfield and their children was similar.[28]

Despite their integration into the Mohawk village of Kahnawake, the women from Deerfield maintained ties with their kin in New England. These connections seem to have been part of the appeal that such captives held for the Kahnawake Mohawks. Unlike Eunice Williams, Mary Harris, Rebecca Kellogg, and possibly Mary Field retained their ability to speak English. Joanna and Rebecca Kellogg, Eunice Williams, and Mary Field all visited their English relatives. In other instances the children of these women visited their relatives in New England. Two of Mary Harris's sons visited Joseph Kellogg in Suffield, Connecticut, in 1744. Kellogg "indeavoured to critically examine them about the affairs of Canada" and found one of them to be "a very inteligable man about thirty years of age." Joseph Harris also traveled back and forth between Kahnawake and Albany as a participant in the illegal fur trade between New France and New York. Two of Mercy Carter's sons passed through Albany and stopped at Fort Massachusetts in July 1751 on their way to visit Carter relatives in Norwalk, Connecticut. The commander of the fort suspected that they were gathering intelligence, another use that could be made of connections with the English. It is not known if any of these offspring understood English.[29]

Kahnawake's regular contact with the English world helped keep the captives' memories of their origins alive even if they never returned to New England. In the mid-eighteenth century Mary Harris lived in an Iroquois village along a creek in the Ohio Country. English traders christened it "White Woman's Creek" in her honor, suggesting an affinity that Mary herself clearly had not abandoned. She still retained her English name, Mary Harris, as well as a knowledge of English, even though she had been probably around nine years old when she was captured. She also spoke of her connection to Deerfield. When Christopher Gist passed by "White Woman's Creek" in 1751, he met Mary and described her as a "White Woman . . . taken away from New England when she was not above ten Years old, by the French and Indians. . . . [S]he she is now upwards of fifty and has an Indian Husband and several Children. Her name is Mary Harris. She still remembers they used to be very religious in N[ew] E[ngland] and wonders how the White men can be so wicked as she has seen them in these woods." Five years later, she made herself known as Mary Harris to a Pennsylvania man captured in the Seven Year's War. She told him, too, that she had been "taken Captive when a Child, from Dearfield, New England." One of her sons, Peter, had by now become an important war leader. It is uncertain when she died, but it seems quite likely she witnessed the British conquest of New France four years later, in 1760.[30]

The experiences of these women represent the most complete examples of Deerfield captives' integration into Native communities. Kahnawake was big enough to provide a virtually self-sufficient environment in which captives could become thoroughly Mohawk, even if they did not forget their English relatives or the English language. Contact with surrounding and neighboring French communities and fellow captives seems to have been more limited, however, than it was at Lorette and Sault-au-Récollet, and Lac des Deux Montagnes. The females from Deerfield living at Kahnawake undoubtedly knew each other, but no special subcommunity of captives appears to have developed. The attitudes of the Jesuit missionaries at Kahnawake also influenced the experiences of English captives in this village. They appear to have been less intrusive than their Sulpician counterparts, and there were no nuns from the Congregation de Notre Dame resident in the village. The Jesuits were satisfied to see the English converts become Native American Catholics, and unlike the Sulpicians saw no need to make them into French Catholics.

In 1716, Kahnawake made its final move to the site where it remains to this day (figure 16). In this new location, the Mohawks maintained their autonomy by reaching out to other communities to counterbalance the influence of the French. Making use of former captives' ties to their families in New England was part of this strategy. More important the residents preserved their connections with the Mohawks of the Iroquois League. Participation in the clandestine fur trade between Montreal and Albany continued to be an important part of this relationship. One of Mary Harris's sons and Eunice Williams's husband, Arosen, were among those who transported Canadian furs to Albany. At the same time, members of the community worked to preserve their alliance with the French and other Native communities, such as the Abenaki village at Odanak. The ties binding them to the Abenakis and other Canadian Indians were personal as well as diplomatic and military. Early in the nineteenth century, Abenakis from Odanak visited Deerfield, announcing they traced their ancestry from a member of their community who had married Eunice Williams.[31]

For the Abenakis and the Pennacooks who joined the attack on Deerfield the taking of captives for adoption, even for ransom, had been a secondary consideration in the greater struggle against the English colonists. No Deerfield residents are known to have permanently merged into the community at Odanak or to have remained with the Pennacooks. Although the destruction of Odanak's early records in 1759 makes it impossible to know with any assurance, it seems that the Abenakis added only a handful of English—possibly three—to their community as a result of the raids during the War of the Spanish of Succession.[32]

After peace was made in 1713, most of the Pennacooks and other Abenakis living at Odanak and Becancour returned to their homes along the New England frontier. The villages in Canada suddenly lost a significant portion of their population as people started moving south to reestablish villages abandoned

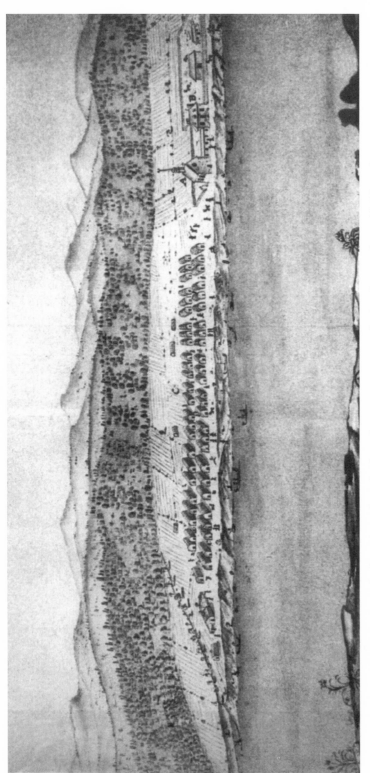

FIGURE 16. View of Kahnawake in the mid-eighteenth century. Drawing with ink and watercolors, mid-eighteenth century, artist unknown. The sketch shows (A) the church, (B) the missionary's house, and (C) the Mohawks' longhouses. Traditional housing remained the norm at Kahnawake well into the eighteenth century. The mission, while prominent, was separated from the village proper. Cliché Bibliothèque nationale de France, Cabinet des Estampes, Paris.

during the war. One Pennacook leader, Atecuando, dreamed of transforming his former home at Pigwacket into a major center of Abenaki life. He asked Governor Vaudreuil for permission to take all of the inhabitants of Odanak and Becancour and their missionary, Father Aubrey, to settle at Pigwacket. He planned to lure the Schaghticokes there from New York as well. If he had succeeded, Pigwacket would have become a melting pot and a new refuge for the displaced Natives of New England. But Vaudreuil would not give his permission. He cherished the two Abenaki villages in New France as vital posts protecting the colony's southern flank. He feared that the new village of Pigwacket would quickly fall under the influence of the nearby English and their trade goods. He gave more thought to Father Aubrey's proposal to merge the small settlement of Becancour into Odanak, but not even that plan was carried out. For their part, the Schaghticokes demonstrated no interest in moving to Pigwacket. In the end, Atecuando had to revive Pigwacket with only twenty-five warriors and their families. Some Pennacooks resettled their village on the banks of the Merrimack River. Father Sebastian Rale, a Jesuit, moved down to minister to the spiritual needs of the Kennebecs at Norridgewock. Priests also maintained missions among the Penobscots, Maliceets, and Mi'Kmac. These priests were evidence that their ties to the French were closer than those of Atecuando and his followers (figure 17).[33]

The failure of the war and the resulting peace treaty to resolve persistent disputes with the English ensured that the 1713 peace treaty would not last for long. The returning Abenakis had welcomed the resumption of trade with the English, which they regarded as a better deal than trade with the French. But the trade was not well regulated and trading posts did not remain trading posts for long. They soon became the centers of English villages as colonists took up lands around them. The English also reoccupied settlements abandoned during the war. Inexorably, English colonists were once again creeping up the coast and river valleys into Abenaki country. If anything, the English were even bolder since the French expulsion from Acadia. They now acted with less restraint than before the war, claiming that the Treaty of Utrecht had ceded the Abenakis' land to them, and that the Abenakis themselves were now subjects of the English crown. The expansion of English settlements, along with their dams, fisheries, and mills, cut off the Abenaki villages situated upstream from their traditional runs of fish. Their hunting territories were reduced and game diminished. Those most affected by these changes lived at Norridgewock, which became a center of militant opposition to English expansion. Their missionary, Father Rale, encouraged them in their resistance and obtained the backing of Governor Vaudreuil.[34]

English intransigence and trickery pushed the growing crisis to the verge of war. Most Abenakis, especially those at Penobscot and elsewhere, farther away from the English settlements, wanted to keep the peace at any cost. They repeatedly sought to prevent hostilities. But English settlers continued to take over Abenaki lands. With Father Rale's help, the Norridgewocks determined to take a stand. Both sides resorted to force in 1722. In January, a party of one hundred English soldiers pillaged Norridgewock's church after failing to seize Father Rale. In revenge for this attack about forty Norridgewocks burned houses

FIGURE 17. Abenaki woman and man. Watercolor, eighteenth century, artist unknown. The clothing indicates the ways in which the Abenaki used European blankets and cloth to fashion distinctive costumes. Their hoods and the woman's blouse were made of European cloth; the leggings and moccasins were made of skins. The conical headgear was associated with both Eastern and Western Abenakis. City of Montreal. Records Management and Archives.

and a mill at the English settlement of Merrymeeting Bay in July. On July 25, 1722, Governor Samuel Shute declared war on the Abenakis, calling them rebels and traitors to the crown.[35]

This action began the Fourth Anglo-Abenaki War, which pitted Massachusetts against an extensive Indian alliance. Neither Connecticut nor New York saw any justice in Massachusetts' cause and refused to provide any direct aid. Even in Massachusetts, the justice of the war was questioned. John Williams confessed to his son Stephen that he was "Greatly concerned because of the war—he is fearful whether it is just on our side." Colonel Samuel Partridge, who still led the militia in western Massachusetts, wrote to the governor urging that a settlement of disputes over land be reached with the Eastern Abenakis instead of "a whole Province and neighboring Provinces put to such vast expenses, yea the loss of many lives."[36]

Despite the treaty of peace between France and England, Governor Vaudreuil did use the Fourth Anglo-Abenaki War to strengthen his alliance with the Abenakis. The French also had diplomatic reasons to support the fighting. The boundaries of their conquered province of Acadia had not yet been determined and the fighting could be seen as a sign that the lands of Maine belonged to the French and their Abenaki allies, not the English. Vaudreuil's barely covert support helped recreate the alliance of 1703–1704. Once again, Hurons from Lorette, various Abenaki peoples from beyond the frontiers of New Hampshire and Maine and the Canadian villages, Mohawks from Kahnawake, and Iroquois of the Mountain joined together in attacks on the frontiers of Massachusetts and New Hampshire. The French governor also supported the Abenaki war effort by providing arms and supplies to the Abenakis and their Native allies.[37]

Deerfield was again subject to attack. In the Connecticut valley, raids began in 1723 under a new Western Abenaki leader, Grey Lock. Descended from Woronocos, who may have been Pocumtuck refugees living along the Westfield River, Grey Lock had probably grown up at Schaghticoke. At some point either before or during the War of the Spanish Succession, he had moved north to Canada, where he had participated in several French and Indian raids against the Connecticut valley towns. Now he led the war effort in the west from his new base at Missisquoi, a traditional Western Abenaki village site on Lake Champlain. Not all of the Western Abenakis supported Grey Lock in his war. In fact, his most militant followers seem to have been Schaghticokes like him. These "Once Numersous, Powerful and faithful Allies" of the New York colony had been driven to fight the English as a result of "Injustice & Encroachments." Their efforts were supported or paralleled by raiders operating from Odanak.[38]

The Fourth Anglo-Abenaki War returned to patterns of conflict that had dominated the final years of the War of the Spanish Succession. Fighting consisted mostly of fairly small-scale raids by Indian warriors against frontier settlements. They acted opportunistically, picking off farmers in the fields who had let down their guard or ambushing travelers who had failed to take precautions. No English towns were destroyed. Few women and children were captured. To retaliate, the English mounted expeditions against Eastern Abenaki villages. Convinced that Father Rale was to blame for the war and inspired by hefty scalp bounties, Massachusetts soldiers prowled the northeastern woods. Eventually, an expedition launched in summer 1724 surprised him and hundreds of Norridgewocks in their village. Rale and several villagers died in the fighting. The rest fled to Canada. Another English party attacked and burned Penobscot. Scouting parties in western Massachusetts ranged far up the Connecticut River and over the mountains to the shores of Lake Champlain. Some considered attacking Odanak, but none made it quite that far.[39]

While there were always some warriors willing to follow Grey Lock's lead and attack the frontiers of Massachusetts, there were also many Abenakis eager to make peace. In the end, the fighting lasted only as long as Governor Vaudreuil was alive. Within months of his death in October 1725, supporters of peace among the Eastern Abenakis treated with a Massachusetts government no longer willing to bear the costs of the war. Peace negotiations continued over the next two years with the Abenakis at Odanak. They finally agreed to end the fighting in 1727. Massachusetts officials desperately tried to contact Grey Lock and secure his acceptance of the peace, but they failed. Nevertheless, the raids stopped.[40]

I RONICALLY, the numbers of English captives who were successfully adopted declined over the course of the eighteenth century as the intensity of the imperial wars increased. A total of 372 English men, women, and children had been taken during the War of the Spanish Succession, and of this group maybe 20 remained in Canada in Native villages and another 49 were in French communities. Of the approximately 55 captives taken during the Fourth Anglo-Abenaki War, only 4 are known to have stayed behind. Three of them—Mary Scammon and Charles William Rollins and his sister—stayed with the French. Only one, Sarah Hanson, is known to have settled in or near a Native community, that of the Iroquois of the Mountain. There she joined the Risings as a Frenchified neighbor of the Native village at Lac des Deux Montagnes and watched her daughter marry the Risings' son. In King George's War some 267 captives made it to Canada, but only 4 or 5 stayed behind. During the final imperial war, the Seven Year's War, of about 536 captives taken, only about 23 remained with their captors. Most of these later captives were soldiers who were viewed as prisoners to be ransomed, not potential adoptees. Despite the rather small numbers of captives that the Deerfield raiders had successfully adopted, they marked the high point of such activity in the Native villages along the Saint Lawrence.[41]

The experiences of the majority of Deerfield captives point out the problems that Natives faced. The size of the Native villages and their proximity to French towns also affected their success. Apart from Kahnawake, which had 800 to 900 residents, Native villages in New France were relatively small and their populations fluctuated. Lorette had about 150 to 200 persons in 1714. Odanak had about 400, but that number would increase and decrease as different groups of Abenakis moved in and out in response to the changing tide of war. The Iroquois of the Mountain had about the same number, but they were spread out among at least two mission sites before the move to Lac des Deux Montagnes and remained ethnically divided. All of these villages were close to sizeable French towns and closely watched by priests, officers, and merchants, who took a keen interest in the welfare of English captives and occasionally intervened to secure their removal from Native villages, depriving Indian captors of the time and leisure to properly incorporate the New Englanders. Increasingly, the Mohawks of Kahnawake turned to Indians from far away who lacked the connections or cultural impediments of New Englanders and therefore made better captives and adoptees. In the years after the War of the Spanish Succession, the captive population at Kahnawake—the only village with a significant number of captives—changed from English to Catawbas, Pawnees, Chickasaws, and Cherokees as the Mohawks began to wage their mourning wars elsewhere.[42]

CHAPTER 12

NOBLES AND HABITANTS

T HE experiences of the Deerfield captives bridged the two worlds of New France that occasionally intersected. The first was the far-flung empire of trading posts, missions, and Native villages, reaching from Newfoundland and Acadia to the banks of the Mississippi River. It was a world of diplomacy, trade, and war requiring frequent contact with Natives and English as allies and enemies. This was the world of the nobles, merchants, and religious orders. The second was the world of seigneuries and farms strung out along the Saint Lawrence River from Quebec to Montreal. This was the world of habitants and parish priests. In many ways it resembled New England with its large families, influential church, and gradual development of agricultural lands. Sometimes these two worlds of New France intersected in the towns of Montreal and Quebec, which were home to nobles, merchants, and religious orders as well as humbler folk who served as craftsmen and laborers. Alternatively, a habitant might travel to the Upper Country to trade furs or participate in a military expedition. But most residents of New France tended to live most of their lives in one world or the other.

Most of the Deerfield captives passed from the first world into the second one as they were brought to New France by Natives and settled into French communities. The first Frenchmen they came in contact with were noble officers, soldiers, and young men who were often veterans of the fur trade. The Deerfield captives quickly passed through this world with its imperial reach and commercial preoccupations and settled in the colony's Saint Lawrence heartland. They became farmers or the wives of farmers living in seigneuries around Montreal or became the wives of craftsmen who lived in Montreal. In this process they sometimes had the assistance of nobles, merchants, and clergy who bridged the two worlds of New France.

The Canadian officers who had led the raid on Deerfield continued to move throughout the broad expanse of New France, much as they had before 1704. Many married women from merchant families, but the core values of these noble officers remained aristocratic, defined by honor and service to the king. And they and their offspring continued to serve until the fall of New France in 1760.

J EAN-BAPTISTE Hertel de Rouville and his brothers, along with René Boucher
and his nephews and Jacques-René and Pierre Gaultier de Varennes maintained some ties with the seigneuries and rural parishes near Montreal, but as
serving officers they spent most of their time in distant military posts. Duty and
opportunity pulled them to the borders of New France, from the Atlantic frontier to the Upper Country, where officers in the *troupes* had regained the right to
engage in the fur trade. Several of them moved their families to Montreal, a re-
flection of increasing intermarriage with the city's bourgeois families and growing involvement in the fur trade.[1]

Hertel de Rouville's actions during the war had advanced his career. He had obtained promotion to captain in the *troupes de la marine* in 1712. The next year he
was sent to Cape Breton Island to oversee work on fortifications at Port-Toulouse.
After the loss of Acadia, this previously ignored French possession had assumed
a new role as a military base for protecting French fisheries, shielding the approaches to the Saint Lawrence River, and keeping an eye on the English colony
of Nova Scotia. In 1715, De Rouville was moved to Port-Dauphin to fortify this
strategic harbor on the island's north shore. His men completed this task so expe-
ditiously that Hertel won praise from the island's governor, who proclaimed him
to be a "phoenix of toil." Overseeing such work was more suited, however, to
an officer of the engineers than a partisan leader, and the governor, Philippe de
Rigaud de Vaudreuil, asked to have De Rouville posted back to Canada. Vaudreuil
claimed that he did not "know anybody better fitted to be sent among these Indian nations . . . both because of the ascendancy that he has over these nations and
furthermore because he is capable of opposing all the ventures that the English
might undertake in this part of the continent." French officials granted the governor's request but soon reversed themselves, fearing an English attack on Cape Breton Island, now named Île Royale. An officer of De Rouville's proven ability was
too valuable to the new colony. He continued in command at Port-Dauphin.[2]

De Rouville's service had finally won the recognition that secured his place
and that of his family in Canadian society (figure 18). In 1716 the king ennobled
his father, Joseph François Hertel. The Hertels were the last Canadian family
to be ennobled. The grant of nobility cited the elder Hertel's service as well
as that of his sons, two of whom "were killed in service and seven others who
presently serve in our *troupes du Canada et de l'Isle Royalle* who gave on many
occasions marks of their bravery and good conduct." The father and his sons,
the grant stated, continued to serve "with the same zeal and the same affection."
The king specifically recognized De Rouville's service in 1721 with the award of
the Cross of Saint-Louis. Six months later, De Rouville died at the age of fifty-
four. His father had died the month before and been buried in Boucherville.[3]

Hertel's surviving brothers continued to serve in the *troupes*. Zacharie-François, who had assumed his father's title of "de La Fresnière," was for many years a lieutenant in *troupes*. He finally obtained promotion to captain in 1731, years after his younger and more active brother De Rouville had attained the rank. That same year, La Fresnière was assigned to the important post of supervising the construction of Fort Saint-Frédéric at Crown Point on Lake Champlain. Pierre Hertel de Moncours, who had probably been with his brother De

FIGURE 18. Jean-Baptiste Hertel de Rouville (1668–1722). Oil painting, prior to 1713, artist unknown. This portrait was probably painted around 1712 when De Rouville was promoted to captain. When he was made a knight of the order of Saint Louis in 1721 the insignia of the order was added to the portrait. Photograph courtesy of the McCord Museum of Canadian History, Montreal, M966.62.1.

Rouville at Deerfield and at Haverhill, commanded the garrison at Crown Point. In 1734 Moncours was sent to command the French post at Baie des Puants, which today is Green Bay, Wisconsin. This appointment carried with it fur-trading privileges that were granted Pierre and Zacharie-François to help restore their finances. Pierre was recalled from this post in 1737 for interfering with other traders and died two years later in Montreal. Other brothers continued to serve in the military until they died. But none of the remaining brothers, including likely veterans of the Deerfield raid René (who was killed at Haverhill in 1708), Lambert, and Michel, advanced beyond the rank of cadet or *ensign en second*.[4]

Like their older brother De Rouville, the younger Hertels tried to secure their economic position through marriage. As the family was rising in Canadian society during the later 1600s, Zacharie-François and Jacques had married into the ennobled Godefroy family of Trois-Rivières. Three others, Claude, Louis, and Pierre married into merchant families and, along with their brother De Rouville, made their homes in Montreal. De Rouville married at age thirty in 1700, Pierre married at thirty-four in 1721, and Claude married at thirty-seven in 1729. Louis did not marry until he was fifty-seven in 1730. René, Lambert, and Michel never married. The failure of three Hertels to marry and the late marriage ages of the others suggest strained economic circumstances compounded by the demands of military service. Celibacy among men of the nobility was twice as common as it was among the habitants and reflected concerns with property retention. On average, during the eighteenth-century, members of the nobility married later and had smaller families than did their parents and grandparents. Demographers speak of the nobles' "pruning of families." Among the Hertel family the pruning appears to have been rather severe.[5]

Unfortunately for the Hertels, marriages into bourgeois families and lengthy military service did little to improve the family's economic position. If anything, the demographic evidence suggests that it may have deteriorated. A military career often had to be subsidized with personal resources. Zacharie-François exchanged his extensive landholdings in Chambly for sixty acres in Boucherville that belonged to his brother-in-law, Jean-Baptiste Boucher de Niverville. Zacharie-François and Pierre lost most of their worldly possessions in the Montreal fire of 1734. Jacques left little when he died. Still they were able to provide dowries for their daughters and positions for their sons. Sons of De Rouville and several of his brothers all served in the *troupes* as officers. Eleven Hertels served as officers during the Seven Years' War (1754–1760); three died in the fighting. Only one other family provided the *troupes* with as many officers during this last imperial war: the Bouchers.[6]

The subsequent career of René Boucher de la Perrière resembled those of his

Hertel comrades in arms. His nearly half-century of military service broke his health and ruined him financially. In 1710 he was finally promoted to lieutenant. Two years later, Governor Vaudreuil sent detachments from the *troupes* west to garrison key posts in the Upper Country, and Boucher appears to have been one of the officers. He spent the remainder of the decade and most of the following at posts in the West. He received a captain's commission in 1726. The following year he erected what was then the colony's westernmost post, Fort Beauharnois, which stood on the west bank of the Missouri River. A thirty-eight-year-old nephew served as second-in-command of the post. René's brother, Jean Boucher de Montbrun, a fur trader, and two of his sons were probably at the post as well. Illness forced De la Perrière to turn over command to his nephew and return to Montreal in the summer of 1728. Appointed commandant at Crown Point in 1732, he once again had to step down because of illness. During these years he sold off most of the lands in Boucherville that he had received from his father, though he continued to make his home there. In 1734 he obtained a seigneury along Lake Champlain but subsequently lost it because he failed to develop it. Given the amount of time he spent in the Upper Country and the poor state of his health, this failure was not surprising. He was apparently able, however, to provide for his two children. In recognition of his years in the military, the king awarded Boucher the Cross of Saint Louis in 1736. He died in Boucherville six years later at the age of seventy-four. His only son, François-Clément, rose to be a captain in the *troupes*.[7]

Two other veterans of the Deerfield raid, René Boucher's nephews, Jacques-René Gaultier de Varennes and Pierre Gaultier de Varennes et de la Vérendrye, had also gone West during the 1720s. Jacques-René had risen to the rank of lieutenant by the end of the War of the Spanish Succession. He had married into the prominent Le Moyne family and settled in Montreal, though he remained seigneur of Varennes. In 1726 the acting governor of New France, his wife's uncle, Charles Le Moyne, Baron de Longueuil, gave him command of the post at Kaministiquia on the western shore of Lake Superior. Here he involved himself and eventually his brother Pierre in the western fur trade. From this lucrative post he returned to the garrison of Montreal, where in 1736 at age sixty he obtained promotion to captain. For his sons he secured places as cadets in the *troupes* and subsequently commissions as officers. Captain Varennes was stripped of his rank in 1743 for refusing to supply civil authorities with soldiers to arrest his brother-in-law. French officials wanted to make an example of Varennes to curb what they saw as widespread insubordination among the officers of the *troupes*. Disgraced and impoverished, Jacques-René died in 1757. He was eighty.[8]

Jacques-René's younger brother, Pierre, who died seven years earlier, had become a legendary figure. Future generations erected monuments to commemorate the deeds of La Vérendrye, the great explorer of the Canadian West. From 1706 to 1709 he served with the French army in Europe. After his return from France in 1712, Pierre had resumed his career in the *troupes de la marine* as an ensign, attempted to work his modest farm in Varennes, and participated in the fur trade. These sources of income proved inadequate. He was forced to sell land and to borrow to support his growing family. During the 1720s he revived his languishing military career by joining his brother at Kaministiquia. In 1730 he embarked on a quest for the western sea. As an explorer he failed to achieve this illusory goal. His supporters in France often believed that his real quest was only for furs, though his trading ventures did not bring riches to him or to his Canadian partners who financed the expeditions. His efforts did advance a French presence in the West as far as present-day Manitoba; he made friends among the region's many Natives; and his posts in the West did challenge the reach of the English trading posts on Hudson's Bay. For his efforts, he earned a promotion to captain in 1744, and a few years later, the king awarded him the Cross of Saint Louis. He also obtained for his sons appointments as cadets and eventually commissions in the *troupes de la marine*. During his later years he made his permanent home in Montreal. When he died at sixty-four in 1749, he was, like most of his fellow officers, "an impecunious gentleman."[9]

The final Deerfield veteran about whom anything is known with certainty, Charles Legardeur de Croisille, found that civilian enterprises produced greater returns than his military career. In 1709, he married Marie-Anne-Geneviève, the daughter of Pierre Robineau de Bécancour and Baron de Portneuf, and became seigneur of part of the barony of Portneuf. His interest in Portneuf led to his involvement in the tensions leading up to the Fourth Anglo-Abenaki War but more significantly pulled him into the fishing industry and seal hunting. His advancement in the *troupes* was painfully slow. He had been commissioned an ensign in 1710 but did not receive promotion to lieutenant until 1728, when he was fifty-one. He considered retiring the next year, hoping to succeed his father-in-law as chief road commissioner of New France. But he failed to obtain this appointment. He remained in the *troupes* and was finally promoted to captain in 1741. The next year he began a five-year posting to Fort Saint Frédéric which ended with his service as commander. In 1748 he too received the coveted Cross of Saint Louis in recognition of his status and lengthy, if not particularly noteworthy, military career. He died the next year in Trois-Rivières at age sixty-three.[10]

These families' growing connections with commerce and bourgeois kin helped consolidate the power of Canadian nobles, whose aristocratic status grew stronger during the eighteenth century. They had survived the crisis of the early 1700s when their large families, diminishing opportunities for service, and the colony's generally poor economic state threatened to undermine their hard-won status. During the 1720s and 1730s, their privileges enabled them to engage in the western fur trade and to benefit from some improvements in seigneurial revenues as population growth led to the development of their habitants' farms. At the same time some families appear to have limited the number of their children to strike a better balance with available resources. Government actions clearly helped: no more families were ennobled after the Hertels; fewer seigneuries were granted to non-nobles; and the officer corps in the *troupes* became a rigid caste that accepted only the sons of the nobility. Throughout the remainder of the colonial period, an aristocratic, military ethos continued to shape the careers and social privilege of family members.[11]

LARGELY unaffected by the world of the nobility, the Deerfield captives settled into the rhythms of life in the Saint Lawrence valley. By 1713 thirty-six remained in Canada. Sixteen of them would live out their lives in New France. Since none of these Deerfield captives possessed any special status, skills, or connections, their lives differed little from those of habitants or, for that matter, the lives of Deerfield's residents. Their predicament, of course, was quite different from that of the average French colonist. As with all other colonists in Canada, ties of family and the favor of elites played important roles in determining the captives' success. Those who remained in 1713 came disproportionately from certain families. If one counts those who entered Native communities as well as French communities, there were five Hursts, five Stebbinses, three Carters, three Frenches, three Kelloggs, two Brookses, two Fields, and two Prices. Some of them had little if anything, be it family or property, to return to in Deerfield.[12]

Like Native villages, French society absorbed women better than men. Ten females would remain with the French but only six males (see appendix F). This difference was probably influenced by the peculiar demography of New France, where the sex ratio did not balance out until about 1710 and male immigrants from France continued to outnumber female immigrants. With the notable exception of Sarah Hurst, who was forty at the time of her capture, all of the captives were twenty or younger, most under sixteen. The two oldest ones, Sarah Hurst and Elizabeth Stevens, who was twenty, were widows with little left to return to. The women married, stayed put, and raised large families—usually in the town of Montreal. Some outlived their first husbands, remarried, and had more children. The men worked in and about the countryside. If they were lucky, they eventually married and settled down on a family farm.[13]

The Deerfield captives who married into French society found spouses among members of the lower social orders. They married the artisans, farmers, and soldiers who worked for the nobles and merchants who had sponsored the captives' entry into French society. Examining dowries fixed before weddings from across New France's social spectrum, the historian Peter Moogk has divided the colony's social hierarchy into five categories reflecting social status and worth as the colonists recognized them in practice, regardless of official social theory: (1) the elite of nobles, officials, and wholesale merchants, (2) good and profitable occupations that included the better-paying crafts, (3) respectable trades that included tailors, joiners, and metalworkers, as well as noncommissioned military officers, (4) modest occupations such as tenant farmers, shoemakers, stonemasons, carpenters, and private soldiers, and (5) base occupations that included journeymen, carters, and day laborers. Most Deerfield captives married into category four, which was largest in terms of population.[14]

Like many immigrant French servants, men from Deerfield wound up initially where their labor was needed: on farms. In the early eighteenth century the Canadian countryside was only beginning to be developed. Seigneuries still needed all the hands they could get to clear land and start up new family farms. Six Deerfield boys lived in rural parishes around Montreal until the war's end. One young man, Samuel Hastings, lived in a rural parish near Quebec. The experience of these captives closely resembled that of the French servants and habitants who worked to transform the countryside. Only a minority was able to settle and marry, and those who did married at a later age than female captives. Those men who did settle had the sponsorship of some part of the colonial elite, either a noble or a religious order.

For most of these male captives, the failure to find a wife or an economic stake in French society discouraged them from living out their lives in New France, even though some of them took almost a decade to return. There was not much room for poor men of little social standing in the marriage economy of New France. Samuel Hastings, Ebenezer Hurst, and Samuel Price all went back to New England in 1713, still single. All had been baptized as Catholics and naturalized as French subjects in 1710. Back in New England, Samuel Price married a Protestant English woman in 1714. Nothing further is known about either Ebenezer Hurst or Samuel Hastings.[15]

More unusual was the experience of Joseph Kellogg, who did acquire valuable skills in New France but was persuaded that they would be of even greater value in New England. After his conversion to Catholicism, he embarked on the career of a young warrior and fur trader. At seventeen he joined Governor Claude de Ramezay's 1709 expedition to Lake Champlain. The next year he was naturalized and headed out West with six other French traders. His voyage took him as far as the Mississippi River, making him one of the first, if not the first, Anglo-Americans to reach it. He continued to roam across the length and breadth of New France, meeting many different peoples and learning several Indian languages. But he never put down roots in the Saint Lawrence valley. In 1714 his brother Martin convinced him that he could turn his language skills to a more profitable career in New England, and Joseph returned to the land of his birth.[16]

Just as the lack of property and economic security in New France discouraged male captives from remaining there, the promise of property and economic opportunity could be a lure back to New England, even for those who had spent years in Canada. Parents often left special bequests in their wills reserving part of their estate for a captive in Canada, to be paid out only on condition of the offspring's return. Samuel Carter of Deerfield tried to secure the return of his children John and Mercy by leaving John £500 "if he would live permanently in New England" and Mercy £100 if she would only live in Norwalk with her Kahnawake family for ten years. Neither accepted the offer.[17]

Another Deerfield father, John Stebbins, had somewhat better luck. He had watched all of his children be carried into captivity among the French. His daughter Abigail's marriage to Jacques de Noyon, which had helped keep them alive and safe in the hands of the French on the march to Canada, had also given them easy entry into Canadian society. Five of John's captive children stayed in Canada after the war; only his son John had returned before the end of the war. The senior Stebbins did succeed in enticing his grandson Aaron de Noyon to stay when he visited Deerfield, but the boy's mother and four siblings remained in Canada. In an effort to lure them back to New England, Stebbins offered them each in 1723 a one-eighth share of his "lands provided they come and live in New England." One of the sons, Samuel, responded. He seems to have lived quietly among his siblings in Chambly or Boucherville until about 1728. By then he was forty. He probably heard of the will's provisions from his sister Abigail, who visited Deerfield in 1726, but he waited two more years—until the Fourth Anglo-Abenaki War had sputtered to an end—before returning to claim his inheritance. By 1731 he was back in New England. He may have been baptized in New France, but there is no evidence that he ever married while living there.[18]

The children of John Stebbins who remained in New France account for many of the captives—and half of the Deerfield males—who entered into French rural life. Unlike most captives, these men were under secular supervision. The Bouchers and Hertels watched over them and set them up on their seigneuries. Ebenezer Stebbins appears to have lived out his life as a farmer in Boucherville. Joseph Stebbins, four when captured, set himself up at Chambly, where the seigneur was initially Zacharie-François Hertel who subsequently sold the land to Jean-Baptiste Boucher de Niverville. Joseph married Marguerite James some time around 1734, when he was in his mid-thirties. Marguerite seems to have been a former captive herself, judging by her surname and nickname of "Langlais." They had eight children, all but two of whom lived to adulthood, just about average for an eighteenth-century habitant family. After Joseph died in 1753, Marguerite remarried.[19]

More dramatic support for Joseph's sister Thankful came from Joseph-François, the Hertel family patriarch. He had taken in Thankful Stebbins as soon as she arrived in Chambly. The Hertels seem to have made sure that she achieved about as much social status as a habitant could. Joseph-François and his wife sponsored her baptism and gave her the name Therese. In 1711, when she was nineteen, she married habitant Charles-Adrien Legrain, called Lavallé. The couple settled in Chambly, where he became a militia captain, the most prominent civil office a habitant could hope to hold. She bore eleven children and died in July 1729, from complications during the birth of her last child. The godparents of her children reveal the network she was able to draw on for support. Claude Hertel de Beaulac and Therese Hertel, wife of Jean-Baptiste Boucher de Niverville, sponsored her first child and relatives of her brother-in-law Jacques de Noyon sponsored the last child.[20]

While Abigail Stebbins de Noyon's French contacts helped her family out enormously, they did not benefit her much. Jacques de Noyon had seduced Abigail in part with tales of the great amount of property he owned in Canada. But much to her dismay, she "found nothing not even a home" in New France and had to "support her family by work of her hands; to lie at the expense of charitable persons, receiving nothing from her husband." Fortunately for Jacques, French authorities rescinded the death penalty for those who had violated the ban against trade to the Upper Country. Thus, he escaped the ultimate punishment for his earlier actions and departed with a brigade of fur traders almost immediately after their arrival in Canada in April 1704. Subsequently, he became a sergeant in the *troupes de la marine* in the company of Alphonse de Tonty and probably spent much of his time serving out West with his captain, who was posted to Fort Frontenac and Detroit.[21]

Left on her own in Boucherville, Abigail petitioned for and received a separation of goods so that she could hold property and transact business under her own name. Under the laws of New France a family's property was regarded as part of a "marital community" owned equally by both spouses and contracts required the signature of both members of this community. Legal protection was therefore available for a wife when a husband's actions threatened to dissipate property that belonged equally to his wife. In New England such protection did not exist because under England's common law a husband legally subsumed his wife in all matters involving the ownership of property. The laws of New France thus gave Abigail and other French women a protection their sisters in New England lacked, though in practice it did little to reduce the patriarchal authority of husbands. The law also made it clear that "the husband is the master of the [marital] community," and, as one historian has observed, the protection accorded women such as Abigail "was the corollary of subjection" to a husband.[22]

This separation of goods involving the De Noyons was not a divorce. Abigail and Jacques continued to have children, and Jacques and his family continued to be involved with the rest of the Canadian Stebbinses. It was a business arrangement, one that allowed Abigail, rebaptized as Marguerite in 1708, to conduct real estate transactions on her own, which she did with some success. The arrangement insulated the family's real estate holdings from the vagaries of Jacques's participation in the fur trade and possibly spend-thrift ways. As long as Abigail lived, the family did well economically, paying off their mortgage, renting out land, and accumulating some wealth. After she died in 1740, Jacques was unable to add to what Abigail had left him. An inventory of his goods, taken after her death and shortly before his in 1745, reveals his estate was worth less than it had been while she was in charge. He was in debt and everything he had was old and used, acquired by Abigail and never replaced.[23]

Most women from Deerfield had to forge their way in New France through a different set of networks less dependent on the patronage of elites. These women moved in two distinct but overlapping social circles, among other English captives and French soldiers and artisans living in Montreal or in the surrounding countryside among habitants and artisans.

Like Canadian-born and immigrant French women, the female captives from Deerfield married at a significantly earlier age than their male counterparts. Most married around the age of twenty, which was on average about two years earlier than the age at which women in Canada and New England married. Most of the men from Deerfield married before the age of twenty-eight, the average age of marriage for men in New France. The females tended to be absorbed into the communities to which they were first brought as captives. This meant that most of them, eight in all, stayed in Montreal. The rest settled into rural life in the surrounding countryside. Mary Brooks, who disappears from the records after her naturalization in 1710, may be the only Deerfield captive living among the French who did not marry. The lives of these former Deerfield residents differed very little in their broad outlines from their former neighbors in Deerfield, who married in their early twenties and tended to have six or seven children spaced about two years apart.[24]

The two widows, Elizabeth Price Stevens and Sarah Hurst, together with Hurst's sixteen-year-old daughter, Elizabeth, took on the important, if unofficial, job Canadian women had of domesticating newcomers to New France. Officials always hoped that French soldiers would eventually marry and settle down in the colony once discharged. For almost one hundred years, from the arrival of the Carignan-Salières Regiment in the 1660s to the arrival of several regiments of *troupes de la terre* in the 1750s, soldiers from France represented the single largest group of immigrants who settled permanently in Canada, about 3,000 settlers out of the 10,825 immigrants who put down roots in New France. Captives made up a much smaller but still significant group of about 500, or about 5 percent of the total. As both were rootless, without established ties or patrons in the colony, and of roughly similar social backgrounds, it is perhaps not surprising to find evidence that French soldiers developed ties to English captives, female and male.[25]

Connections among craftsmen provided immigrants and captives with ready-made networks. Shoemakers, carpenters, and metalworkers appear to have had a stronger sense of community than those in other occupations. Since guilds were forbidden in New France, carpenters and shoemakers formed religious confraternities. These groups existed to support the worship of a particular saint, but they also brought together a certain group of people for social, spiritual, and material support. Carpenters had organized the first confraternity, for Saint Anne, in Quebec in the mid-seventeenth century. Shoemakers in Montreal formed the confraternity of Saint-Crepin at some point in the early eighteenth century. Almost all of the people who attended the weddings of Sarah Hurst, Elizabeth Price Stevens, and Elizabeth Hurst were either shoemakers or carpenters, some of whom were former soldiers.[26]

It is quite possible that a few of the ties between captive women and soldiers may have been forged on the march back to Canada. For example, when, less than a month after her arrival in Varennes, Sarah Burt gave birth to a child, Christopher, the godfather was Pierre Dupuis, an illiterate French-born soldier. One would assume that before the baptism some connection had been established between Benjamin and Sarah Burt and Dupuis and that it was made on the return from the Deerfield raid. Dupuis may have been with the contingent of enlisted men from the *troupes de la marine* that went on the raid. This tie presumably was broken when the Burts moved on to work at the convent of the Congregation de Notre Dame and the Sulpician Seminary and eventually returned to New England in 1707. A more permanent bond between a captive and a French raider may have been made in 1730 when Elizabeth Corse married François Monet of La Prairie, who was the son of François Monet, a former soldier whose descendants believe that he participated in the Deerfield raid.[27]

The marriage of Elizabeth Price Stevens, the first Deerfield captive to marry a Canadian, testified to the importance of links between French soldiers and English captives. Her husband, Jean Fourneau, was an ex-soldier turned shoemaker. He appears to have employed and possibly trained Elizabeth's brother Samuel

Price, a shoemaker who lived with Fourneau. Two witnesses at the couple's February 3, 1706, wedding also had ties to English captives. One, Philippe Robitaille, a master cooper, had married Grizel Warren Otis of Maine in 1693. The other, a carpenter named Jacques La Selle, took in many English captives over the years and even married his daughter to one. On Elizabeth's side, all of the witnesses were New England captives. They included Samuel Williams, the minister's son, who had converted to Catholicism a month and a half earlier; the widow Hannah Wheelwright Parsons from Maine; Esther Sayward, another captive from Maine taken in the Nine Years' War; Margaret Otis; and Hannah Dunkin. Otis and Dunkin both married French carpenters soon after Elizabeth's wedding.[28]

The many names of Elizabeth Price Stevens Forneau bore witness to her penchant for cross-cultural liaisons. She had married the young man, probably a former captive, described by her fellow townsmen as "the Indian." Now she converted to Catholicism in 1706, became a naturalized French subject in 1710, and had seven children with Forneau. She continued to cultivate her ties across cultures for the rest of her life. Philippe Robitaille, husband of another former captive, stood as godfather at Elizabeth's 1706 baptism and for that of her firstborn child. Her second child had Samuel Price for a godfather and another captive, Martha French, for a godmother. Elizabeth died, probably from the complications of childbirth, in November 1716. Her husband married a French woman eighteen months later.[29]

Networks among urban craftsmen also brought together male and female captives from different parts of the English empire. There were in New France an often-overlooked group of Englishmen who had been captured on Newfoundland. Most had shipped to desolate Newfoundland as soldiers, sailors, or fishermen. Some had trades and moved in the same circle of artisans and soldiers as did the Prices, the Hursts, and the Frenches. These were by-and-large poor men with few prospects. New France looked more inviting than a return to Newfoundland or England, and they were much more likely than adult New England males to put down roots in Canada. And even though captive men and women from England were probably fewer in number than captives taken from New England, they provided more converts to Catholicism. Approximately thirty men from Newfoundland were naturalized in 1713 and many of them remained in New France. Among those who left were the men who married New England women and returned with their wives—further testimony to the strength of the New England cultural complex.[30]

One of these men, forty-five-year-old William Perkins, married the widow Sarah Hurst. Originally from Lincolnshire, he came as a captive from Newfoundland in 1710. Too old to assimilate fully into French Canadian society, Sarah took the Englishman as a husband. All of the witnesses at the couple's wedding, both French and English, were shoemakers, including Sarah's fellow Deerfield captive, Samuel Price, here under his Catholic baptismal name of Louis. Despite their entrance into the Catholic Church, the newlyweds, Sarah's son Ebenezer, and Samuel Price all returned to New England when peace came in 1713.[31]

Sarah's daughter Elizabeth, only sixteen when captured, also married an Englishman. Her ultimate destiny is not known with certainty, but the surviving evidence strongly suggests that she returned to New England. Her October 1712 wedding was perhaps the grandest gathering of the English captive community in Canada. Nary a Frenchmen, save the officiating priest, the ubiquitous Father Meriel, was present. Elizabeth's bridegroom was a thirty-three-year-old English weaver, Thomas Beecraft or Buraff (possibly Bancroft), who was probably captured in Newfoundland along with Elizabeth's step-father, William Perkins, and two other attendees, Daniel Joseph Maddox, a carpenter, and John Thomas, a shipwright. Also present were two New England captives, Joseph Bartlett, a shoemaker, and Jacob Gilman, a woodworker and millwright, who eventually purchased his freedom by building a sawmill for the French. In addition, two Deerfield captives, Elizabeth's brother Thomas, a carpenter, and Freedom French also witnessed the marriage. Elizabeth Hurst and Thomas Beecraft had two children in Montreal in 1713 and 1714 before disappearing from the historical record. They probably returned to New England along with Bartlett, Gilman, and the Perkinses, given their apparent preference for English over French culture and comrades.[32]

Mary "Marguerite" Field was another Deerfield captive successfully assimilated by Montreal's soldier-artisan network. Only a toddler when taken, she was a committed Catholic by 1710 and a French bride at the age of twenty-one in 1722. Her husband, Jean Serré, known as Léveillé (Wide-awake), was a soldier in the company of René Robineau de Portneuf. René Robineau had often fought alongside the Abenakis in Maine, and his father, the Baron de Portneuf, had helped establish the Abenaki village of Becancour on his lands. His son René may have had a hand in ransoming Marguerite from Abenakis and introducing her to his men. At their wedding, Léveillé had two comrades from another company in the *troupes,* none from his own, and two artisans as witnesses. After his marriage, Léveillé became a butcher in Montreal. Marguerite bore him twelve children before dying at age forty in 1741.[33]

Another network for absorbing captives centered on Pierre Roy, a prominent habitant of La Prairie. This community's location next to Kahnawake enabled habitants like Roy to develop special ties to the fur trade and the officers who managed it. These connections gave him and his circle an unusual degree of access to English captives. They assimilated three Deerfield women into New French society.[34]

On November 24, 1711, sixteen-year-old Martha French married twenty-two-year-old Jacques Roy, Pierre's son, who was a mason and stone-cutter. In addition to Jacques's father and his brothers, Pierre and François, and "several other relatives and friends," the witnesses included several influential military officers. These men and others counted as the "friends of the bride," suggesting that Martha had powerful patrons looking out for her interests. The connections may have also aided her husband's career as a mason, which took off in the 1720s and 1730s just as Montreal's elite were building more and more buildings in stone and French officials began fortifying the town itself with a stone wall. Martha French Roy bore eleven children, six of whom survived into adulthood. These children became tradesmen like their father. Two of the sons, Jacques and Pierre, became masons and married local girls, as would their brother, the master shoemaker Laurent. The one daughter known to have married chose a habitant for a husband, but none of the children moved outside of Montreal. Martha's husband, Jacques, eventually became a "merchant butcher" sometime before his death around 1732.[35]

Martha French Roy may have moved a bit farther up the social scale when she married a second time in 1733. Jean-Louis Mesnard, a weaver, was able to provide a 600 livre dower that brought Martha into the circle of "respectable trades," which included tailors, notaries, and metalworkers. Mesnard's public service raised him higher in terms of community status. By 1742 he was a militia lieutenant and within ten years he was a militia captain. Martha, who was thirty-seven at the time of their wedding, had three daughters with Jean-Louis, for a total of fourteen children. The eldest married a young carpenter from France. The youngest married a habitant living at Sault-au-Récollet. Marie-Louise, the middle daughter, married Joseph-Amable Plessis, a blacksmith, in 1752. Their son Joseph-Octave, born in 1763, became bishop of Quebec in 1806 and the first archbishop of Quebec in 1819. However, the New England–born Martha died sometime in May 1762 long before her grandson became head of the Canadian Catholic Church.[36]

Martha French's sister Freedom appears to have married into the same circle, though under more auspicious circumstances. In February 1713, the twenty-one-year-old Freedom also married a mason, Jean Daveluy, who was ten years her senior. Louis-Thomas Chabert de Joncaire, a military officer and frontier diplomat, stood as a witness at her wedding, as did Charles Guillimin, a wealthy Quebec merchant. As at Martha's wedding, the bridegroom had a much less distinguished entourage that included his brother Paul and his brother-in-law-to-be, Jacques Roy, and, like Jacques, he could not sign his name though both of their wives could. Freedom and Jean settled in Montreal and had eleven children, only four of whom survived into adulthood. Perhaps because she lived in a town and not in a rural area, Freedom seems to have maintained closer ties with the community of English captives. She served as godmother to Martha's son André in 1720. She witnessed the marriages of Mary Austin in 1710, Elizabeth Hurst in 1712, and John Carter in 1718. Her husband witnessed Thomas Hurst's second marriage in 1718. Freedom died in Montreal in 1757, two years after her husband.[37]

Elizabeth Corse, who lived in Pierre Roy's household, had a more difficult transition to French society. On April 20, 1712, the fifteen-year-old captive gave birth to an illegitimate child. At the time, this was an unusual occurrence in both New France and New England. It could have resulted from the exposed circumstances that female captives without kin or influential patrons could find themselves in. That November she married Jean Dumontet, a fifty-three-year-old Huguenot who had come to New France from New York. Among the marriage witnesses were Pierre Roy and his son Jacques (who had just married Martha French), suggesting that the Roys formed something of a surrogate family. After marriage, Elizabeth lived the life of a typical habitant, bearing seven children before her first husband died in 1728–1729. Soon afterward, on January 19, 1730, she remarried, this time to a man nine years her junior, Pierre Monet. Martha French and her husband again witnessed the event on Elizabeth's behalf. Elizabeth had seven more children, one a year for the next seven years until she was forty-three, for a total of fourteen—just like Martha. She died at La Prairie in 1766.[38]

APART from the exceptional case of the Stebbins boys, the male Deerfield captives who settled into the life of habitants owed their careers to the Sulpicians. This included the Carter brothers, John and Samuel, and Thomas Hurst. Granting land in Rivières-des-Prairies was part of the Sulpicians' efforts to develop this far corner of their seigneury, which covered the Island of Montreal. They evidently ransomed several captives from the Iroquois of the Mountain and offered them parcels of land if they converted, married. and settled down.

Thomas Hurst, who was twelve when captured, spent his life working for the Sulpicians in and around their missions at Sault-au-Récollet and Lac de Deux Montagnes. He may have felt a great debt to his clerical benefactors. After all, the Sulpicians ransomed him from the Iroquois of the Mountain, taught him a trade—carpentry—and loaned him money to buy a house, clothes, and tools that he needed to set himself up as an independent artisan and to marry. He married twice. First he married Marguerite Thibault, age twenty, in April 1716. She was the daughter of one of his neighbors in Rivières-des-Prairies. Her dower was 300 livres, placing Hurst at the bottom of the artisan class of "modest occupations" as outlined by Peter Moogk. Marguerite died in December of the same year. Just over a year after her death, in February 1718, Hurst married again, this time to Françoise Rouleau, also of Rivières-des-Prairies. Thomas and Françoise had six children, four of whom outlived their father, who died around 1741. Avoiding the difficult life of a colonial widow, Françoise remarried the next year.[39]

John Carter, who also benefited from the assistance of the Sulpicians and other powerful Frenchmen, was unusual because he lived in both worlds of New France. Only eight when captured in 1704, he was naturalized at fourteen in 1710 and married to Marie Courtemanche in October 1718, at the relatively young age, for a Canadian man, of twenty-three. After their marriage, the Carters, now known as Jean and Marie Chartier, moved to Rivierès-des-Prairies, where they received a plot of land from the Sulpicians in December 1718. He acquired more land in 1721 and 1722. Over the next nine years, John and Marie had six children.[40]

Like a good New Englander, John Carter spent his life expanding his landholdings to provide for his children, demonstrating that an active and well-connected farmer could thrive in New France as well as in New England. His contacts from captivity actually helped him. Hertel de Rouville's older brother, Zacharie François Hertel de La Fresnière, lured him off Montreal Island and into the Richelieu River valley by granting him some land in 1725. Carter held it for five years and began to sell some of his land at Rivierès-des-Prairies. He then returned La Fresnière's grant and acquired land in the seigneury of Contrecoeur in 1732 and more in 1734. His new seigneur, François-Antoine de Pecaudy de Contrecoeur, was an old comrade-in-arms of Hertel de Rouville and had served with him on the 1708 Haverhill raid. Unlike many seigneurs with military careers, Contrecoeur worked hard to develop his seigneury. He must have offered Carter good terms, for John sold more of his land on Montreal Island and settled into Contrecoeur's parish of Saint-Antoine.[41]

The next twenty years (1730s to 1750s) was a time of economic growth for New France and for John Carter, who did quite well for himself as the Frenchman Jean Chartier. He specialized in developing frontier lands, which he subsequently sold or passed on to his children, then moved on to the next edge of French settlement. He also became involved in fur trading—still an important source of wealth—and then lumbering, a new source of wealth launched in part by New England captives who showed the French how to build sawmills. He developed business contacts with Montreal merchants. In 1742 he signed on briefly as a voyageur for Paul Marin de la Malgue, commander of Fort La Baie in what is now Green Bay, Wisconsin. A skilled diplomat, La Malgue was also a vigorous participant in the fur trade. At the time Carter signed on, La Malgue's convoys of voyageurs were expanding rapidly, increasing from 11 men in 1739 to 190 by 1750. In 1746, Carter formed a partnership with Françoise-Louise de Ramezay, the business-minded daughter of the one-time governor of Montreal Claude de Ramezay. They built a sawmill at a creek on the Richelieu River still know as ruisseau Chartier (Carter creek).[42]

For the next two decades Carter continued to move about and buy and sell land. In the 1750s, his interest in lumbering probably led him to look beyond the Richelieu and into the Champlain valley. By then his children were starting to marry and settle in the Chambly region. He gave lands at Contrecoeur to his children in 1751, sold off more, and moved south. In September 1754 he bought some land in the seigneury of Longueuil, which extended to the shores of Lake Champlain. This property he bought in the name of his sons Joseph and Theodore and his young niece Catherine who lived at Kahnawake. "Jean Chartier" was then listed as living on the Lake Champlain seigneury of La Colle, also known as Beaujeu, after its seigneur, Daniel Hyacinthe-Marie Liénard de Beaujeu. The Seven Years' War ended Carter's push southward. He withdrew to Longueuil, where his wife died in 1760. He was now an old man in his sixties but this did not stop him from acquiring and selling more land. He made land deals at Longueuil in 1763, 1764, and 1765 before returning to the family seat at Saint-Antoine, near Chambly, where he continued to deal in land. When he died in 1772 at the age of seventy-six, he was one of the last survivors of the 1704 raid on Deerfield.[43]

THE imperial ambitions of French authorities and the relentless expansion of the English colonies ultimately brought on a war that the habitant core of New France could not win. The Seven Year's War, which began in 1754, pitted New France against the greater population and vast resources of Britain and its colonies. With little aid coming from France, New France did not stand a chance. The British conquest removed the imperial aspects of New France, leaving behind the small but growing community of *canadiens*. But in the early 1700s New France had seemingly controlled the destiny of the continent and threatened the survival of Deerfield.

CHAPTER 13

NEW ENGLAND IMPERIALISM

THE 1704 attack on Deerfield had momentarily interrupted the engine that drove New England's expansion. In the immediate aftermath of the February 29 raid only 125 people remained in town: 25 men, 25 women and 75 children. Approximately 60 residents had died. About 89 more were prisoners in Canada. Several families had been entirely destroyed; others seriously disrupted. And yet, the town did not die; it was not abandoned as it had been in 1675 and 1677. By the end of the War of the Spanish Succession in 1712 the population had rebounded to around 220. Over the next two decades the town completely replaced its losses as captives returned and the population continued to grow from natural increase. The "intertwined process of family formation and town founding by which the English took the land and displaced its original inhabitants" was not halted by the 1704 raid.[1]

As Deerfield matured, it became more like other New England towns. Most returning captives settled back into earlier rhythms. Drama came less often from war and violence, though both remained not too distant. Politics grew a bit more contentious at times but also more predictable and more closely linked to Boston and the empire. Residents still adhered to their church. If anything, Deerfield's people appeared to be unusually pious. During the religious revivals of the 1730s and 1740s, they were demonstrably so. At its core, Deerfield was still a relatively homogeneous community whose residents' lives were defined by their relationships to the town and its church and to their families and their lands. To an even greater degree than before 1704, one's family and its access to land determined the course of one's life.

Even as settlements were established north and west of the town, Deerfield continued to play an important role in the diplomacy and defense of the English frontier. When the Fourth Anglo-Abenaki War broke out in the 1720s, Deerfield men took up arms and went on scouts to find and kill Natives. When the fighting ended, Deerfield became an important council site. Former captors paid friendly visits to their former captives. Those who spoke Native languages worked as frontier diplomats, translating and negotiating with former foes. But this generation was special. Their skills and experiences distinguished them from their fellows. Their knowledge of Native cultures was not passed on to the next generation, most of whom adhered to the norms of New England society with a special fervor.

O N April 20, 1704, the town of Deerfield had held its annual spring meeting in an effort to carry on as if nothing had happened. In addition to selecting Edward Allen to be town clerk, voters elected selectmen, a constable, and fence viewers for the coming year and authorized repairs to the fence around the common field. The town book contains no mention of the events of February 29. But not everything was as normal as it seemed. The meeting was called about seven weeks later than usual. And several town officials were missing, among them the town clerk, Thomas French. Handwriting in the records changes as Allen picks up where French's entries stopped.[2]

The misleading silence in the town book gives an illusion of normalcy that belies the raid's devastating impact on the community. The families of Samson Frary, John Hawks Jr., Godfrey Nims, Philip Mattoon, and Samuel Smead had been virtually wiped out. Most members of the families of Simon Beamon, John Burt, Nathaniel Brooks, Samuel Carter, Thomas French, Mehuman Hinsdale, Sarah Hurst, Martin Kellogg, Joshua Pomroy, John Sheldon, John Stebbins, Ebenezer Warner, and John Williams had been removed to Canada. The Burts, Carters, Hursts, Kelloggs, and Pomroys would never re-establish themselves in Deerfield. Seventeen houses had been destroyed as well as half a dozen barns. Household possessions and livestock were also lost. An estimate of the total value of the property lost came to £3,015 pounds, the equivalent of over 30,000 days of work, representing for some families the work of a lifetime. For this reason alone the attack would be know for years as the "destruction of Deerfield."[3]

In the months and years after the raid, Deerfield remained a dangerous place to live. On May 11, 1704, raiders killed John Allen at the Bars, just south of Deerfield, and captured and then killed his wife, Elizabeth. Residents claimed that they "were Unanimously Determined to Desert the Town and seek shelter and safety whear we could find it." But Colonel Samuel Partridge had prevented this departure by drafting all of the town's able-bodied men as garrison soldiers. His action restrained adult men from leaving and provided them with income to support their families, who were also expected to stay in Deerfield. Massachusetts sought to retain its "frontier towns" as shields and wanted to protect more secure towns from being overburdened with refugees. The town's men complained that they were "obliged to be in actual Duty as souldiers three fifth part of our time" but their "hope of saving our lives by quitting our Habitations [was] superseded by fear of Incuring the Penalty of Deserting Her Majetys Service." Faced with the punitive power of the empire, the men stayed. And so did their families. Despite the oft-repeated claim that "non-combatants were sent to lower towns," women and children stayed in Deerfield. The town's book of births, marriages, and deaths continued to record couples married and children born in Deerfield from at least 1705 on. The Massachusetts government provided the garrison with a chaplain, Benjamin Choate, who also served the Deerfield church in the absence of the Reverend John Williams.[4]

Some residents did leave despite the government's efforts to restrain them. Among the first to leave were most of the half-dozen men who had left their families during the attack. Samuel Carter moved to Norwalk, Connecticut, in 1705 and had remarried by 1706; John Hawks Sr. moved to Waterbury, Connecticut, in 1705; John Field settled in East Guilford (today Madison), Connecticut in 1707; John Sheldon Sr. relocated permanently to Hartford, Connecticut, by 1708; and some time before 1715 Robert Price left as well. But most of these men had few kin to hold them in Deerfield. All that remained were painful memories and possibly guilt. Only Samuel Smead lived out his life in Deerfield. In April 1707 he married the former captive Mary Alexander, who had been widowed during the attack. Together they started a new family.[5]

Other Deerfield residents also left during these years. Around 1706 Michael and Sarah Mitchell and their four children moved to Wallingford, Connecticut, where twenty-four-year-old John Mattoon joined them. Next year the town's school teacher, John Richards, and his family went to Westfield, Massachusetts. He eventually moved south to Newark, New Jersey. Several returned captives—Benjamin and Sarah Burt, Ebenezer Carter, Abigail Hoyt, Mary Field and her son John, Martin Kellogg Sr., Samuel Price—and members of their families relocated to Connecticut. Another former captive, Joshua Pomroy, settled in Dorchester just outside of Boston. Most of John Williams's children lived with relatives in Northampton or Roxbury. In all, thirty-three captives returned and resettled for a time in Deerfield while at least twenty-four, possibly thirty, lived elsewhere after their return from Canada.[6]

The Reverend John Williams was among those who did return. His example played an important role in shoring up the community. He had come back from captivity in Canada a celebrity, a status undoubtedly enhanced by the publication of *The Redeemed Captive*. Calls to settle had come from churches in the Boston area. At the same time, Deerfield's town meeting had unanimously voted to "treat with thair pastor the reverand mr. jno Williams, in regard to his resetl'g with them againe in ye work of ye ministry." The town secured from the Massachusetts legislature a grant of £40 for Williams on the condition that he settle again in Deerfield and remain a year. As a further enticement, the town voted to build him a house "as big as Ensign Jno Sheldon's [and] a back room as big as may be thought convenient." The people of Hartford, Connecticut, took up a collection to raise funds to refurnish the rebuilt parsonage. Despite the efforts of churches in places where Williams's "worldly Interest might be more promoted," he returned to Deerfield and soon remarried, taking as his second wife Abigail Allyn Bissell, a first cousin of his first wife, Eunice. Together they had five children.[7]

New men moved to Deerfield even as the war continued. Some came as garrison soldiers, but others came to settle. Like previous settlers, these men usually came from the nearby towns of Hadley, Hatfield, and Northampton. Unlike those who settled in town during the 1670s or 1680s, however, these men, with one exception, arrived single. They were also young, usually in their twenties. Also unlike earlier settlers, two-thirds of these men had trades. They were weavers, saddlers, a blacksmith, a shoemaker, and a teacher. One opened a store; another kept a tavern. Their special skills or ready capital undoubtedly facilitated their entry into the community, which had apparently developed to the point where it could support these trades. New arrivals were also no longer guaranteed access to sufficient amounts of land or proprietary rights giving them shares in future land divisions. Most who stayed, and most of them did stay, married into Deerfield families and acquired proprietary rights. Those who failed to acquire wives and land tended to move on. Deerfield was no longer a community of opportunity but a community of families who became increasingly concerned with securing their children's futures.[8]

Families in Deerfield and throughout New England continued to grow, replacing the losses of 1704 and sending forth sons and daughters to found new towns on the expanding frontier. On average, sons and daughters of the original settlers produced six to seven children when they married. This fecundity and migration to the town supported a replacement and expansion of population that kept pace with that of neighboring towns, such as Hatfield and Northampton. The population of each town increased by about 150 percent between 1690 and 1765. In demographic terms the losses of 1704 were more than made up by the late 1720s. Still, the children of Deerfield's settlers married on average two years later than their parents had, and this change reduced the number of children per family from the previous generation's average of seven children per family. Providing for offspring remained an overriding concern for the town's residents, and producing fewer children reduced the strain on critical resources, which in Deerfield remained land. Access to land was a particular concern for those families who had arrived in town between 1688 and 1715; over half of their sons left town. This out-migration reached a peak between 1710 and 1720. Delayed marriage and increased emigration by offspring were both symptoms of land pressure as land values rose quickly after 1712.[9]

The desire for land led several Deerfield residents, including some newcomers, to look beyond the town to the former settlement at Northfield. Originally established in 1673, Northfield had been evacuated during King Philip's War, re-settled in 1685, but abandoned again in 1690 during the Nine Years' War. Early in the spring of 1714, a year after the War of the Spanish Succession had ended, twenty men, eight of them from Deerfield, signed articles engaging to resettle Northfield. Over the next twelve years, thirteen men from Deerfield and their families moved to Northfield. Few came from prominent or wealthy Deerfield families. Some gained prominence and large landholdings in the new community. Among the settlers of this new frontier town were four former captives: Joseph Alexander, Sarah Mattoon Field, and Joseph and Sarah Petty.[10]

In Deerfield, growing pressure on the town's reserves of undivided land led to some of the first recorded disputes and provides evidence of growing economic stratification. The original 1666 grant of land creating the English settlement of Pocumtuck had been to the Dedham proprietors, and rights to this land passed on to those persons who bought out the individual Dedham proprietors and their heirs. But during the 1680s and 1690s, the town meeting, which included both proprietors and nonproprietors, had granted undivided common lands to newcomers. When the town meeting on March 3, 1718, began to divide common lands, some proprietors objected, claiming that they and not the town had exclusive authority to grant such lands. A March 28 proprietary meeting voided the actions of the town meeting, branding it illegal. More than half of the grants made by the town were not regranted at the proprietors' meeting. The proprietors also voted to stop laying out any additional lands until a committee could investigate past records and determine who actually held proprietary shares and were therefore legally entitled to receive land. This committee did not unravel disputed claims until 1723 and new lands were not granted until 1727. By 1727 over a dozen Deerfield residents had moved to Northfield. What had once been a critical governmental function controlled by the town meeting had passed into the hands of individual landowners acting collectively as the proprietors.[11]

Another important function of town government passed into the hands of a narrow group of landowners in the early 1730s, when another body was formed to control the operations of Deerfield's common field. The Proprietors of the Common Field in Deerfield was created to regulate fencing, to levy fines on negligent users, to settle disputes over ownership, and to handle other functions previously performed by the town as a whole through the town meeting. This new body had the power to tax and to enforce its orders. Even though this group usually met in the meeting house, its creation formalized subdivisions within the community. Officers of the group tended to be less representative of the town as whole. Mehuman Hinsdale, who rarely held important positions in town government, regularly served in prominent capacities for the proprietors.[12]

Town governance underwent other changes during the early decades of the eighteenth century as a local elite began to dominate its affairs. Opposition and dissension replaced the consensus of the old days. During the decade from 1715 to 1725 sons of the original settlers, joined by newcomers, were elected to the town's more prominent offices. In 1721 the town elected its first board of selectmen consisting entirely of second-generation residents. Among these leaders were such familiar names as John Catlin Jr., John Catlin 2nd (Joseph Catlin's son), Thomas French Jr., Jonathan Hoyt, Thomas Wells Jr., and, eventually Elijah Williams, the youngest of the Reverend John Williams's sons. Each served at least six terms as a selectman. Joining this group of recognized leaders were Deacon Eleazer Hawks, descended from one of the town's founding families, and Timothy Childs, a newcomer. Most of these men had first participated and served in town government after 1710. They had less contact with the consensus that had characterized the politics of the community's first quarter century. Participation at some level in town government remained very high in Deerfield, though issues were no longer "agreed and voted" but are passed by a "great majority." Important measures such as selecting a successor for John Williams, who died in 1729, led to major disputes. What had once been opportunities for an almost ritualistic affirmation of community cohesion and its values became causes for conflict and dissention.[13]

Still, the changes should not be exaggerated. In a number of ways the mark of an earlier New England persisted in the lives of the eighteenth-century residents of Deerfield (Figure 19). The town remained relatively homogeneous, harmonious, and conservative. After some controversy, the town did succeed in finding and settling a new minister, the Reverend Jonathan Ashley, who served for almost half a century. Membership in the church remained very high by contemporary standards. The town continued to seat its meeting house according to "age, estate and qualifications" until 1824, making it one of the last towns in Massachusetts to maintain this official ratification of a community's perceived hierarchy. Deerfield's proprietors periodically met and granted its remaining undivided common land, apportioning it according to proprietors' shareholdings and thus ensuring that the agrarian basis for the town's hierarchy remained fairly fixed. As late as 1754 Joseph Severance Jr., was condemned to walk the streets of Deerfield wearing a "Capital I two Inches long, and [of] proportinonable Bigness on his upper Garment" as punishment for incest.[14]

I T IS harder to assess the impact of the Deerfield raid on individual captives and members of their families than on the village itself. Only John and Stephen Williams, both of them ministers, and Joseph Kellogg wrote about their experiences. For most of the men and women who returned to New England one has to infer the raid's legacy from the ways in which they, and in some instances their children, lived their lives. Most appear to have fit themselves back

FIGURE 19. "Delineated at Deerfield." Drawing by Dudley Woodbridge, 1728. Woodbridge journeyed to Deerfield in October 1728 and stayed at the home of Mehuman Hinsdale. His drawing shows the town common with its third meeting house built in 1696 and a variety of houses that apparently lined the common. The large house at the bottom right-hand corner is presumably the Ensign John Sheldon House, which survived the 1704 attack. There is no evidence of the stockade, which had probably been taken down or had fallen down before the beginning of the Fourth Anglo-Abenaki War in 1722. Photograph courtesy of the Massachusetts Historical Society, Boston.

into the agricultural, demographic, and religious rhythms of the world that they had left. They re-established farms and families. If married, they added children to their families; if not, they married or remarried and had children, *lots* of children. Most remained close to the frontier, though as noted above a certain percentage clearly turned their backs on the frontier.

For most returned captives, the Deerfield raid and subsequent captivity do not appear to have dramatically altered the course of their lives. Status and success still depended largely on their family connections. Only for a few, such as Mehuman Hinsdale, Thomas Baker, and the Kellogg brothers, did the jarring experiences of 1704 noticeably alter what would otherwise have been quite ordinary New England lives. Most of the young garrison soldiers and the militiamen in the Meadows Fight returned to their homes, married, and lived out their lives much as they probably would have. After petitioning to receive compensation for his losses on February 29, Joseph Eastman, who came from a prominent Hadley family, married and had eleven children. He served nine terms as a Hadley selectman and became a deacon in the church. He died in 1769 at the age of 86. Samuel Hastings, a garrison solider, and John Marsh, a militiaman, both from Hatfield, lived out their lives in relative obscurity. Judah Wright of Northampton married Mary Hoyt and settled in Deerfield. They had six children. A farmer and weaver, he was never prominent in town affairs, serving only one term as a selectman. He died in 1747 (figure 20).[15]

Those who had been prominent before the attack and their sons maintained their prominence in local affairs. Thomas French Sr. again found himself on the board of selectman and eventually resumed his duties as town clerk. His son Thomas, who shared his captivity, also served as a selectman and town clerk. John Catlin Jr., a housewright and ropemaker, served as town clerk and a selectman. He and his wife, Jemima, had eleven children. Jonathan Hoyt served a half dozen terms as a selectman and became a lieutenant in the town's militia company. He and his wife, Mary, had six children. Two of John Williams's sons, Stephen and Warham, followed their brother Eliezer to Harvard and then into the ministry. Eliezer had started before February 1704, and his brothers would very likely have followed the same path even if they had not been taken captive, though Stephen's particular ministry bore some evidence of his time spent with the Pennacooks.[16]

For one of the town's more privileged families the return to Deerfield was difficult and the aftermath of the raid cast a very long shadow. Mehuman Hinsdale had been before the raid and remained after his return one of the wealthiest men in town. He does not appear to have been the happiest. During her return from Canada, his wife, Mary gave birth to a son they named Ebenezer. It is unclear whether Mehuman and Mary returned together. The identity of Ebenezer's father was also unclear. Under the entry for Mehuman's family in

FIGURE 20. Judah Wright's gravestone, slate, circa 1785, probable carver Solomon Ashley. This gravestone is noteworthy because it was carved and erected about forty years after Wright's death, but he is still remembered by those who commissioned the marker as "one of the unfortunate persons who was captured by the Indians Feb. 29th 1703–4." Photograph by Kevin Sweeney.

the Deerfield town records there is the following note: "Query: whether to record the birth of Ebenezer?" No entry was ever made. Late in 1706 not long after their return, Mehuman, Mary, and Ebenezer had moved to Colchester, Connecticut. The next year they moved back to Deerfield, where Mehuman was again captured. Released in 1712, he returned to his wife. They had only two more sons, Samuel and John. When he died in 1736 (figure 21), Mehuman

FIGURE 21. Mehuman Hinsdale's gravestone, slate, circa 1736, probable carver James Foster. The quality and cost of this finely carved gravestone made in Dorchester, Massachusetts, reflects the wealth and status of the deceased. The inscription captures a claim to the land—"first male child born in this place"—and a characterization of Natives as "salvages" undoubtedly shared by Deerfield's residents. Photograph by Kevin Sweeney.

owned fifty-six hundred acres of land and was remembered for having been "twice captivated by the Indian Salvages."[17]

Ebenezer Hinsdale's life never really fulfilled its promise. He went to Harvard and after graduating in 1727 tried his hand at preaching, missionary work, surveying, and trading. He filled a number of elective offices in Deerfield and became a colonel in the militia. He established the town of Hinsdale, New Hampshire, just north of the Massachusetts line. But despite his education, his family's wealth, his marriage to John Williams's daughter Abigail, and the assistance of influential in-laws, his life was dogged by questions about his paternity and plagued by alcoholism. He died in Hinsdale in 1760. The marker over the graves of Ebenezer Hinsdale and his mother, Mary, bears the following inscription: "Her husbands were Lieut. Mehuman Hinsdale and Mr. George Beal. By the first she had two sons, Samuel and John."[18]

The frequent military service of several returned captives—Thomas Baker, John Burt, Joseph and Martin Kellogg, Jonathan Hoyt, and Samuel Williams—suggests that some of these men experienced difficulties fitting back into the routines they had known. Ironically, captivity experiences gave these men skills in woodcraft that they probably did not have before and in all likelihood instilled in them the desire to use those skills as hunters of Indians. All of them went out on scouts during the war. Jonathan Hoyt was described as a "skillful woodsman, scout and officer." Baker, the Kelloggs, and Samuel Williams received commissions as officers in the provincial troops; Hoyt obtained a commission in the militia. The Kelloggs and Samuel Williams also found government employment as interpreters, thanks to their language skills.[19]

Thomas Baker, an outspoken man who was "somewhat rough in manner," gained recognition and a wife as a direct result of his captivity and subsequent military service. After returning from captivity, this former garrison soldier rose to the rank of captain in the provincial forces. While accompanying John Williams and John Stoddard on their mission to Canada in 1713, the thirty-two-year-old bachelor met and fell in love with the widow Christine Le Beau, an English captive who had been born Margaret Otis in Dover, New Hampshire, and married a Frenchman. Despite the resistance of French authorities and her Canadian family, she returned to New England with Baker, leaving behind her children and property. They married in Northampton in 1715 and moved to Brookfield, Massachusetts, where Thomas became a prominent resident. In 1721 they returned to New France in an unsuccessful effort to retrieve Margaret's children. Sometime in the late 1720s, the Bakers lost their lands in Brookfield and found themselves in difficult circumstances financially. They moved to Mendon, Massachusetts, and then on to Newport, Rhode Island, before settling in Dover, New Hampshire. in 1735. Thomas died the same year, but Margaret lived until 1773 supporting herself during her widowhood as a tavernkeeper.[20]

For Joseph Kellogg the unintended acquisition of skills in war and knowledge of Native culture helped him rise further than he probably would have, based on family connections alone. In 1714 at twenty-three he married Rachel Devotion, daughter of the minister of Suffield, Massachusetts. He was posted to Northfield in 1716, where he began as a "Serjeant of the Guard" and "Interpreter to the Indians." By 1723 he had obtained a captain's commission. Three years later New York authorities attempted to lure him away from Massachusetts, offering liberal pay and congenial service if he would settle in Albany. He declined. Soon after this offer, he took over command of Fort Dummer, upriver from Northfield, where he established a government trading post. In 1729 the Massachusetts governor appointed Kellogg a justice of the peace, an office usually held by members of the region's more prominent families such as the Wellses or Williamses. He was now Captain Joseph Kellogg, Esquire, a considerable achievement for a man from a family of modest means. He would be remembered as a particularly good interpreter, "the best in his day, that New England had, and was employed upon every occasion." Captain Kellogg continued to serve Massachusetts as a soldier, diplomat, interpreter, and magistrate, spending most of his time along the frontier of western Massachusetts, until he died in "a broken state of health" on a relief expedition to Fort Oswego in 1756. His wife, Rachel, and their five children lived in Suffield, which lay along the Massachusetts-Connecticut border—far from the dangers of border raids.[21]

Joseph's older brother Martin also achieved a certain prominence and position that might not have been possible without the experience he gained in New France. He would be remembered as "a very remarkable man for his courage and bodily strength." His frontier experiences became something of a legend in New England, where "Many stories were related of his feats and exploits in early life," especially of when he "was several times captured and carried to Canada." After returning from his second captivity, he continued to serve in the provincial military, attaining a lieutenancy by 1712. Two years later he accompanied John Williams and John Stoddard on their mission to Canada. Settling in Wethersfield, Connecticut, in 1716, he married Dorothy Chester, a member of the town's leading family. He was elected to important local offices and represented the town in the Connecticut legislature. For Martin as for his younger brother Joseph, captivity had forged a close bond with members of the Williams family, and Martin in particular appears to have used this connection to advance himself. In 1751 he joined the teaching staff of the mission in Stockbridge, Massachusetts, where members of the Williams family exercised a great deal of influence. Captain Martin Kellogg died a prominent and wealthy man in 1753.[22]

Less dramatic were the changes in the lives of other returned captives who came from and returned to more humble lives. For former captives Ebenezer Nims and his wife Sarah Hoyt, their dramatic marriage in Lorette was the prelude to a rather unexceptional life on a farm in Wapping, a hamlet a couple of miles south of the village of Deerfield. They had six children, all sons, and lived until around 1760, dying in their mid-seventies. Briefly after their return in 1714, they had shared a house on the street with Ebenezer's brother John, who had been captured in 1703. John had married his stepsister, Elizabeth Hull, who had also been taken captive in 1704. They had twelve children. Like the Nimses, members of the Brooks, Sheldon, and Stebbins families returned to Deerfield and settled into the routines of yeoman farmers whose world was shaped by the rhythms of family births, marriages, and deaths and the cycles of the season. They were not men who served in important town offices; they did not acquire much wealth. Nor is there much evidence in the outward patterns of their lives suggesting any lasting impact of the raid and captivity.[23]

The most significant legacy for many former captives may have been religious. Their outward adherence to the established congregational church suggests that inwardly they may have shared their pastor's interpretation of their ordeal as a time of spiritual testing and a confirmation of their faith. Of the twenty-five captives who lived out their lives in Deerfield, at least twenty-one of them joined the local church. The four remaining individuals may have joined before they died, but whether they did cannot be determined because of a gap in the church records. This proportion was high even for a town in the Connecticut valley, where the percentage of residents who joined local churches was usually higher than elsewhere in New England. It is quite possible that these former captives took to heart John Williams's injunction to "let not your outward freedom put away the sense of Deplorableness and Dangerousness of an Unconverted State; and the Depths of Misery they are in, that are Captives to Sin and Satan, and Condemned already by a Holy God, for not believing in the Name of the Son of God" and to "make all Haste to get into a Converted State." And even though he did not do so hastily, forty-three-year-old Ebenezer Sheldon was finally "taken into full communion" on February 24, 1734, the Sunday before the thirtieth anniversary of his capture.[24]

Former captives appear to have passed on to their children their devotion to the congregational church. During the religious revivals of 1734–1735 and 1741–1742 the children of former captives were more likely than others to join the church. While two-thirds of the town's young people over the age of fifteen joined during the revivals, 75 percent of the children of former captives joined compared with only 41 percent of those children who lacked such a parent. Again, former captives may have heeded the call of their former pastor John

Williams to "Tell others, how great a Privilege they enjoy, that have the Scriptures and so many Days in God's Courts. And at your Return, beware lest you forget your own judgment, whilst in Captivity, of the Precariousness of such a choice of Mercy." They also had before them examples of unredeemed captives, such as Eunice Williams, who had lost this privilege, and they may have felt more acutely the threat to the immortal souls of their offspring. Like John Williams, these parents would have been in a position to provide powerful personal testimonies about faith and salvation. Because of their experiences and fears, their children may have been particularly well prepared for the revival's message of salvation by faith alone and the importance of a conversion experience.[25]

Two of the more dramatic conversions by children of former captives appear to have played roles in promoting heightened religious concern in the town. In Deerfield the 1734–1735 revival began in the town's Green River section (today Greenfield) and among the first converts there was Aaron Denio (an anglicanization of De Noyon), who joined the church in April 1734. He had been born and baptized in Canada. He came to Deerfield as a ten-year-old after the war but had not bound himself to the church. Another Deerfield resident stirred by the awakening of religious concern was Ebenezer Nims Jr., who had been born to captives in Lorette and baptized there. He had Deerfield's Parson Ashley rebaptize him in 1737, "Being dissatisfied with his Baptism, he consented to the articles of the Christian faith, entered into Covenant, was baptized and admitted to the fellowship of the church." The same day the Reverend Ashley preached two sermons "showing that the church of Rome is the mother of harlots spoke of by St. Paul, [and] none of her administrations can be valid." Here is clear evidence that the legacy of captivity did affect former captives and their offspring.[26]

Elsewhere former captives or their offspring played similarly didactic roles during this period of religious concern. In Northampton the first stirrings of the 1734–1735 revival came in the little hamlet of Pascommuck that had been attacked French and Indians in May 1704. Among those converted was one, probably Elisha Searle, who had "been taken captive in his childhood, was trained up in Canada in the popish religion" before returning and being in some measure "brought off from popery." However, he remained "very awkward and dull of receiving any true and clear notion of the Protestant scheme, till he was converted; and then was remarkably altered in this respect."[27]

The most powerful example of the association made between captivity and conversion was unknowingly provided by Eunice Williams, an unredeemed captive. In July 1741 at the height of the Great Awakening, Eunice and her family arrived from Canada to visit her relatives. On August 4 during a visit to her brother, the Reverend Eliezer Williams of Mansfield, Connecticut, she became an object lesson in a revival sermon preached by her cousin, the Reverend

Solomon Williams. He used Eunice as a living symbol of the bondage and slavery to sin in which the unconverted find themselves. Solomon assured his audience that while many of them rightly felt compassion for the *"poor Captive"* still in the "Thickness of *popish* Darkness & Superstition," they were "themselves no better off if they remained *out of Christ,* and destitute of true *Faith in* him" and "unrenewed, & unsanctified." Only by accepting their dependence on Christ and his faith alone would they be spared a fate worse than Eunice's "pittiable and sorrowful Condition." As Eunice, who no longer understood a word of English, was unmoved by Solomon's extended metaphor on her plight, other fallen children were awakened and sought admission to her brother Eliezer's church.[28]

For those outside of her family, Eunice had ceased to be a real person and had become a symbol, a trophy to be won in the cultural struggle for North America. When Eunice returned again in the fall of 1743 with her husband and children she saw her relatives once more and for the first and only time revisited Deerfield. She also traveled to Boston with her family and met with officials of the Massachusetts government. The legislature voted that "the sum of twelve pounds ten shillings be allowed to be paid . . . to Tarraige (An Indian of the Cagnawaga Tribe who hath marryed an English Woman). His Wife and Children now in Town as a Present." In Deerfield lore this would be remembered as an offer of land to entice Eunice and her family to resettle in New England, when in fact it was the offer of a relatively modest sum to a Kahnawake man, Tarraige, and "an English woman"—no name given—who had married him in order to further secure his ties to English America.[29]

THOUGH New England continued to grow and expand in the quarter century after 1712, Deerfield remained a town whose significance was defined by Native interests and actions. During the late 1710s and early 1720s, Natives often visited Deerfield. The first party came in 1714, bringing with them young Aaron de Noyon, son of Jacques de Noyon and his wife, Abigail Stebbins, who had journeyed south to visit his grandfather John Stebbins. Upon arriving Aaron had decided to stay, changed his name to Aaron Denio and, as related above, joined the Deerfield church in 1734. In 1716, members of the Iroquois League used Deerfield as a gathering place for recruits, some of them probably from Canada, to fight against the Catawbas in the Carolinas. Two years later one of John Williams's Abenaki masters visited him. He allegedly did so because he "was so deeply impressed . . . that Mr. Williams was more than a common man." In later years captives, such as Mary Field, Joanna Kellogg, and Eunice Williams, who had become members of Native communities returned to New England to visit their families.[30]

Not all contacts between Deerfield residents and Natives were peaceful. When fighting between English colonists and Abenakis broke out on the Maine frontier in 1722, residents of the Connecticut valley expected once again to be on the front line. For Deerfield, this war—the Fourth Anglo-Abenaki War—differed from past conflicts. Northfield, twelve miles beyond Deerfield, provided a more inviting target for raiding parties. Since Northfield was more exposed, it was garrisoned by a company of forty to fifty men. Deerfield had only a dozen or at most two dozen garrison soldiers. To further shield the valley, Massachusetts built a blockhouse on the west bank of the Connecticut River near present-day Brattleboro, Vermont. Fort Dummer, as it came to be known, was garrisoned with soldiers and Native scouts paid by the province. Despite the presence of these more northerly posts, Deerfield residents remained concerned and complained that "the difficulties of war lie so hard upon us, that several families, & also several young men have drawn off from us, & several more are going in a little time, to the great discouragement of those who are left behind." Around this time, William Belding and his wife, Margaret, both of whom had survived the 1704 attack, moved to Norwalk, Connecticut, and Moses Nash a newcomer to Deerfield, and his wife headed for West Hartford, Connecticut.[31]

Deerfield was once again on the defensive. The town's fortifications were strengthened and companies of Indians from Connecticut were stationed in town. These Mohegan, Pequot, and Niantic allies and English scouts operated out of Deerfield ranging far to the north. In February 1725 eight men "at Deerfield, several of whom are men of estate and have been prisoners with the Indians and know their manners" proposed to go out on a scout and lie in wait for Native raiding parties. That March a party of sixty-five men under Captain Thomas Wells Jr., of Deerfield scouted as far as the frontiers of New France but returned with little to show for their effort. During the course of the war about two dozen men from Deerfield served as scouts or rangers among them former captives Joseph Kellogg, Joseph Clesson, and John Catlin Jr., and at least ten men who as boys had come through the 1704 attack unscathed. Another of these soldiers was James Corse, son and brother of Deerfield captives, and "a noted hunter and scout" who served in the military through the end of the French and Indian wars in 1763.[32]

Despite the inability of Massachusetts soldiers to inflict a defeat on Western Abenakis comparable to the attack on Norridgewock in the east, they did keep the western frontiers relatively safe. The weight of English numbers made itself felt as garrisons were strengthened and scouts kept constantly in the field. Casualties in the Connecticut valley were relatively light. No Deerfield resident was killed, only three wounded, and just one captured. All of these casualties were adult males. Lacking the numbers mobilized during the War of the Spanish Succession and the additional punch provided by active French participation, Native raiding parties avoided direct assaults on English towns or houses.[33]

When the Fourth Anglo-Abenaki War ended, peaceful visits resumed. The Huron captor of Jonathan Hoyt, presumably Thaovenhosen, and the Kahnawake Mohawk captors of Ebenezer Sheldon and his sister Mary Sheldon Clapp came to visit. But these Mohawk visitors made such demands that Sheldon petitioned the Massachusetts government for reimbursement. In the 1730s, two other Deerfield residents petitioned for reimbursement for time and money spent caring for sick members of the Iroquois League. By this time, Massachusetts authorities had lit a council fire at Deerfield, designating it as a place to negotiate with Mohawk representatives of the League in 1723 and with Kahnawake Mohawks, Schaghticokes, and Odanak Abenakis in the mid-1730s.[34]

Peaceful contacts kept alive the hopes of current and former Deerfield residents that they could secure the return of relatives still in Canada. Joseph Kellogg was among the more persistent. Sometime during the late 1710s Joseph had attempted unsuccessfully to secure the return of his younger sisters Joanna and Rebecca. Both lived at Kahnawake and had apparently married into the community. In 1729 Joseph tried again and "with much Persuasion" brought the thirty-four year-old Rebecca back to Massachusetts. To win her confidence he had been "obliged to take an Indian Man & Boy, with whom she lived, to make her easy, & to promise that he would use no Force with her to keep her from returning to Canada, she being bigotted to the Roman Catholik Religion." He got around his promise by petitioning the Massachusetts legislature and "Praying that the said Indians may be sent away in such manner as may be for their Satisfaction, & the Court [the General Court, the legislature of Massachusetts] would use their Authority to prevent his Sister's Return." The legislature obliged and sent the man and the boy off on a mission to either Kahnawake or Odanak. It also paid them £40 "to make the Messengers content and easy." Rebecca remained behind and not long after became the second wife of Benjamin Ashley of Westfield. Joseph's contact with Natives in Canada and in the years since his own return had done nothing to shake his own preference for the life he knew in New England, and he went to great lengths to secure it for, possibly impose it on, his sister.[35]

Stephen Williams also maintained his contacts with Natives and his belief in the superiority of an English way of life (figure 22). After his return from captivity he stayed with relatives in Roxbury while preparing for Harvard, which he entered in 1709, graduating in the class of 1713. He was ordained in 1716 as the minister in Longmeadow, Massachusetts, and settled into the routine of life in his parish. His captivity, however, had marked him. He fought French Catholicism in word and deed for the rest of his life, preaching sermons against the Catholic faith as a member of the 1745 expedition that captured Louisbourg and while serving with New England forces at the Battle of Lake George in 1755. He also remained "solicitous for the welfare of the poor Heathen, ever since I was a Prisoner with them." While ministering to his Longmeadow congregation, he maintained close ties with local Natives and those further afield, and regularly

FIGURE 22. The Reverend Stephen Williams (1693–1782). Oil painting, circa 1755, attributed to Joseph Badger. Because of his capture in 1704 and later service as a chaplain on military expeditions in 1745, 1755, and 1756, Williams became something of a symbol of New England's decades-long contest with the Catholic French in Canada. He also maintained a life-long interest in the Protestant missionary efforts among Natives in the Northeast. Photograph courtesy of the Pocumtuck Valley Memorial Association, Memorial Hall Museum, Deerfield, Massachusetts.

prayed that God "would have mercy on them & delight in their welfare & bring these poor heathens to a serveing acquaintance with Christ." Though clearly rooted in his own religion's sense of righteousness, his concern was unusual at a time when indifference or outright hostility greeted most missionary activity in New England. In 1730 he drew up "a memorial respecting the condition of the poor Indians." In the mid-1730s he took several Native boys into his home to educate them. At the same time he collected stories about Deerfield "in the warrs with the Indians," which he saw as "remarkable providences of God towards the people of that place." Indians had a place in Stephen's world—even in his home—but it was one ordained and directed by a Protestant God.[36]

During the early and mid-1730s Stephen Williams's activities and the interest of Governor Jonathan Belcher of Massachusetts launched an ambitious missionary project directed at the Mahicans living along the Housatonic River. After an initial approach by one of the Mahicans, Williams and another western Massachusetts minister met with them in July 1734 and made a formal proposal to establish a mission on the banks of the Housatonic. The ministers secured the support of the governor and the Massachusetts Commissioners of the Edinborough Society for Propagating the Gospel. After the Mahicans accepted the proposal, Williams recruited a minister and a teacher for the mission. The actual ordination of the missionary, John Sergeant, and the formal launching of the mission took place at a conference held in Deerfield in August 1735. No doubt, Massachusetts authorities used the occasion in the hope that other Native participants at the conference might be inspired to follow the Mahicans' example.[37]

The 1735 Deerfield conference was called to reaffirm the peace secured in 1727 at the end of the Fourth Anglo-Abenaki War. To renew pledges of peace, Massachusetts authorities wanted to meet with representatives of the Iroquois League and Schaghticokes from New York and with Mohawks from Kahnawake and Abenakis from Odanak. By the early 1730s, there was cause for concern as both the French and the English sought to increase their influence and presence in the Champlain valley. In 1730 French soldiers had chased English traders out of the region and begun constructing a fort at Crown Point. Zacharie-François Hertel oversaw construction of this new fort; his brother Pierre Hertel de Moncours, a probable veteran of the Deerfield raid, commanded the new post; and, their nephew Pierre-Joseph Hertel de Beaubassin, who was fluent in Abenaki, served as interpreter at the post. The English countered by sending James Corse of Deerfield to explore a route from the Connecticut River to Otter Creek, a possible site for an English settlement and fort in the mid-Champlain valley. The ostensible purpose of Corse's journey from Fort Dummer to Otter Creek and on to New France was to search for his sister Elizabeth, who remained in Canada. At Fort Dummer itself, Captain Joseph Kellogg and a small garrison remained on guard.[38]

For the English as for the French, the region's Natives held the key to controlling the Champlain valley. Massachusetts authorities undertook a series of initiatives to strengthen their ties with them. Governor Belcher of Massachusetts sought to use treaty conferences, improved trade, and missionaries to lure Natives from the French and bind them to the English. To enhance the attractiveness of the trading post at Fort Dummer, the governor appointed the ill-starred Ebenezer Hinsdale as post chaplain and missionary to the Natives. He hoped that the presence of an English missionary might counter the activities of French missionaries and entice Schaghticokes, Abenakis, and Kahnawake Mohawks who traded at the post to settle in the area. The new mission to the Mahicans offered another possible location for settling Natives who would ally themselves with the English for military calculations, which, along with religious concerns, lay behind this missionary undertaking. The English undoubtedly wanted to reap strategic benefits similar to those that the French gained from the establishment of Kahnawake, La Montagne, and Odanak.[39]

Late August of 1735, therefore, saw the largest gathering of Natives and colonists in Deerfield since the 1704 attack. Governor Belcher, attended by most of his Council and members of the legislature's lower house, as well as the region's ministers and other local notables, and 170 Indians—women and children as well as men—arrived in the village. Among these Natives were in all likelihood some participants of the 1704 raid. The governor met first with the Schaghticokes and assured them that they could trade with Captain Kellogg at Fort Dummer without fear of being cheated. He also encouraged them to receive instruction from the Reverend Hinsdale so that they could lead "better lives than ever yet you have done." They thanked the governor for his words and drank a toast to the king. Belcher said much the same to the Kahnawake Mohawks, who also thanked him for his words, and reaffirmed the treaty made eleven years ago in Albany. The Abenakis from Odanak echoed the Mohawks' desire to see peace maintained. On the following days, the governor exchanged speeches with the Mahicans as they ceremonially affirmed the relationship that would place them under the protection of the Massachusetts government and the spiritual care of its missionary.[40]

The conference closed on Sunday, August 31, with a church service in Deerfield's meeting house attended by both English and Natives. Governor Belcher formally proposed to send John Sergeant as missionary to the Mahicans and Sergeant accepted the charge. The assembled ministers then ordained him. For their part, the Mahicans publicly agreed to receive their new pastor. This auspicious beginning marked the commencement of a half-century of missionary activity among the Mahicans in Stockbridge, Massachusetts, that would conclude with the Natives' loss of their lands and their removal to western New York.

Kinsmen of the Reverends John and Stephen Williams would play a prominent role in taking the Natives' land. Joseph Kellogg, his brother Martin, and their sister Rebecca were also employed at the mission during the early 1750s in an unsuccessful effort to encourage members of the Iroquois League to settle in Stockbridge.[41]

Only Rebecca Kellogg appears to have had any real affinity for the Native peoples with whom she worked. A minister who met her in 1753 described her as a "very good sort of woman, and an extraordinary interpreter in the Iroquois language." That year she made a difficult journey west from New England to New York to serve as the minister's interpreter to the Iroquois at Ouquaga. She was evidently a religious woman, and her husband, Benjamin Ashley, was an evangelical man. He accompanied her to Ouquaga, where she died at the age of sixty-one, in August 1757, only months after her older brother Joseph. The Iroquois called her Wausania, which may be a corruption of Waskonhon, meaning "the bridge." They much lamented her death. They had lost a valuable go-between with the English, and Deerfield lost a connection to Native communities in the Northeast.[42]

The last direct link between Deerfield and a Native community was Eunice Williams, and she remained in touch with her relatives in western Massachusetts until her death. In June 1761, Eunice, her husband, her daughter Katharine and Katherine's son Thomas visited her brother Stephen in Longmeadow. They had a hard time communicating because there was no interpreter. The family stayed for ten days before returning to Canada. After all her years at Kahnawake, Stephen still prayed that "God w[oul]d touch their hearts and encline them to turn their faces to their Friends and to embrace the religion of Jesus Christ," a hope that a devout Catholic such as Eunice would have found perplexing. Stephen last heard from Eunice in 1781 when he received a letter in which she informed him that she was "still in the land of the living" but expected that this was probably "the last time you may hear from me." When she died four years later, in 1785, at the age of eighty-nine, she was probably the last surviving captive.[43]

E VEN though several current and former residents of Deerfield, such as the Kelloggs and the Williamses, remained in contact with particular groups of Natives into the 1750s, the village of Deerfield ceased to play a prominent role in such relations. After 1750, Deerfield became less central to the trade, diplomacy, and wars of the New England frontier. As their families continued to produce ever more children demanding ever more land to farm, English settlers pushed farther up the Connecticut River beyond Northfield. Others moved along the Merrimack River to Pennacook, which they renamed Concord. Most of the surviving Pennacooks retreated north to Canada, though small groups remained in and around their homeland. To the west, Schaghticokes migrated north to Odanak, the last residents leaving in 1754. After the abortive attempt to move east to the Mahican mission village at Stockbridge, League Mohawks retreated farther west or lived uneasily in ever closer proximity to encroaching New Yorkers. As these people, both Native and English, moved, the frontier shifted north and west, leaving Deerfield a relatively isolated English village. And, as the survivors of the Deerfield raid gradually died off, the memories of its days as a frontier outpost faded. Natives and French came to be seen as intruders who played only a peripheral and antagonistic role in the village's history. New Englanders started to see themselves as native Americans and forgot that once things had been quite different.

REMEMBERING FEBRUARY 29, 1704

ACH year on the weekend closest to that rarest of anniversaries, February 29, costumed re-enactors gather at a site known as the Indian House Memorial in Deerfield. Over the course of two days, New England's unpredictable weather permitting, hundreds of visitors come to see faux English colonists, French soldiers, Canadian militiamen, and Indian warriors. They all come to mark the 1704 raid on Deerfield, now a museum-village and educational center preserving the material heritage of early America.

Today's annual gatherings are relentlessly peaceful. The commemoration is intended "to educate visitors about the cultures of the Indians and settlers rather than focus on the battle." Re-enactors portraying English colonists demonstrate candle making, beer brewing, and hearth cooking and offer visitors "opportunities to try out spinning, carding and weaving on old equipment." A fashion show explains "who wore what and why . . . to show the different cultures of that time and to get across the idea that they were co-existing at the same time that each was vying for control." Native Americans talk about Native dress, regalia, and hairstyles. The emphasis is on showing "our home life, our love of children and of games, . . . the things that make us human beings." Espousing uncharacteristically martial sentiments, a solitary figure in the gray-white dress coat of an enlisted man in the *troupes de la marine* informs visitors that these French fighting men were the era's equivalent of "the United States Marines, the Army's rangers, the Special Forces." It is a rare reminder of the violent clash of opposing empires and peoples three centuries ago. Overall, the current commemoration seeks to bring people together by helping them understand the cultures—English, Native, and French—that converged in what one organizer once referred to rather blandly as "the Deerfield Incident." For the organizer of these annual events "massacre is a dirty word."[1]

Massacre also was not the word used by the English colonists themselves to describe what happened on February 29, 1704. Colonial New Englanders, though shocked and outraged by the raid, did not call it a massacre. What impressed them at the time was the general devastation. Almost half of the village was burned and left in ruins. Had Deerfield not been turned into a military post, it most likely would have been abandoned for the remainder of the War of the

Spanish Succession. For almost a century afterward, the raid was usually characterized as "the assault on" "the destruction of" or "mischief at" Deerfield.[2]

Throughout that century, the English empire grew exponentially more powerful than the French, especially in North America. Instead of forcing New Englanders to re-evaluate their membership in the English empire, the Deerfield raid drove them to embrace it all the more fervently. Whether serving as musketmen on military scouts or preachers on larger expeditions, the men of Deerfield did everything within their power to carry the war to their French and Indian enemies. After 1708 English forces began to mount counterattacks that put the French on the defensive. In 1710 they conquered Acadia. In 1745 New Englanders captured the fortress of Louisbourg. In 1760 the British conquered New France. Thereafter Canada became a part of the British empire—just as New England was about to leave it.

It was, however, the memory of "the destruction of Deerfield"—at a time when New France was strong and dangerous and New England weak and divided—that prevailed among the English colonists rather than their imperial victories over the French and their Native allies. At Deerfield in 1704 the English were hapless victims, amateur soldiers, innocent women and children—not the stuff out of which mighty empires are made. As New England towns became part of the vigorous, expansive United States, memory of the event grew ever stronger. As the United States dispossessed and removed Indians, many white Americans preferred to remember the times when their actual or metaphorical ancestors were the victims of the French and Indians. The story of the raid became part of what Tom Engelhardt has called "the American war story," in which Indians "by the ambush, the atrocity, and the capture of the white woman (or even of the frontiersman himself) . . . became the aggressors and so sealed their own fate."[3] The invaded were portrayed as the invader, and the intruders became the victims. Memories of many other colonial raids—on Haverhill, Northampton, Casco, and Salmon Falls—would fade, replaced by Custer's Last Stand and other stories from the American West. But the Deerfield raid continued to be remembered, in part because of John Williams's *The Redeemed Captive* and in part because it had acquired a distinctive name: the Deerfield Massacre.

It took the founding of the United States to turn the "destruction of Deerfield" into a massacre. The word *massacre* first appeared in print in 1804, when the Reverend John Taylor of Deerfield used the word five times in his centennial sermon commemorating the "Destruction of the Town."[4] Taylor's sermon evoked the memory of the raid as a key moment in the village's history and helped ensure that this became a cornerstone of the village's identity in the new republic. After this sermon, some nineteenth-century writers occasionally spoke of "the massacre of the Inhabitants of Deerfield" or "the Deerfield Massacre," but other writers continued to identify the attack as "the sack of Deerfield" or "the destruction of Deerfield."[5]

The killing of Deerfield's residents became the predominant motif of the village's historical memory in the early 1900s. At this point, local preservers and promoters of "Old Deerfield" were working to maintain the village's aging homes and fading history as positive assets in the age of industrialization, urbanization, and immigration. They began speaking more regularly of "the Deerfield Massacre" and the name stuck. On July 29, 1903, the local historical association met to commemorate "the Bi-centennial of the Massacre at Deerfield by the French and Indians" and to dedicate a memorial stone for "the Dead of 1704." In his keynote address, the local historian George Sheldon spoke of "the Deerfield Massacre."[6] Three years later another local historian, Emma Coleman, published a guidebook for tourists that mentions "the massacre of Feb. 29, 1704," and "the massacre."[7]

Preservation and dissemination of the memory of "the massacre" received a helping hand in the late 1940s when Henry and Helen Flynt of Greenwich, Connecticut, financed and directed a multi-million-dollar restoration of Deerfield's surviving colonial houses and founded Historic Deerfield, Inc., to maintain the village as "a living monument . . . to the early Americans and their reassuringly civilized way of life." Popular magazines of the period, such as *Antiques, Ford Times,* and *National Geographic,* introduced national audiences to Historic Deerfield and to "the Deerfield Massacre" or simply, "the Massacre."[8] For Henry Flynt, the message of colonial Deerfield's struggles remained relevant, for "this village heard the beat of the tom-tom two-and-a-half centuries ago, and met the challenge as we are meeting it in Korea today, with the lives of brave young men and women."[9] He correctly assumed that the Deerfield Massacre had meaning for the citizens of a superpower fighting on the frontiers of the Cold War. As the United States projected its power throughout the world, there were Americans who still identified themselves with the beleaguered victims of frontier Deerfield.

The descendants of the raiders remembered things quite differently. In fact, they have not preserved as strong a memory of the Deerfield raid as have Anglo-Americans. The Hurons of Lorette have no living memory of the raid. Their participation had to be rediscovered in period documents. As for the Mohawks, French, and Abenakis, each has preserved some sort of account to justify their ancestors' decision to join the Deerfield raid. In none of these communities does Deerfield play anything like the symbolic role it does in the United States. For them, the attack on Deerfield was but one small incident in a much larger struggle against English expansion.

Canadian historians are fundamentally ambivalent about the legacy of raids such as the one on Deerfield. Most are disturbed by the loss of civilian lives inflicted during these raids and readily point to the large numbers of Indians present to account for this ostensible breach of European codes of conduct. Many French Canadians look back to the period as one of independence and heroism. Since the nineteenth century, they have found reassurance in the fate of those Deerfield captives who became French. As François-Xavier Garneau, one of the first and most influential French Canadian historians, wrote, they "were treated tenderly by the Canadians and often ended up embracing the Catholic religion and settling down in the country." Their choice to stay in Canada thus seems like an endorsement of French Canadian culture and religion, if not an acknowledgment of its superiority. If the growing genealogical interest in New England captives is any indication, French Canadians are prouder than ever of this heritage.[10]

But the imperial wars that brought in captives ultimately brought on the conquest of New France. How and why Canada was conquered remains a hotly debated issue. Was it French imperial neglect? British aggression? Or something else? Anglo-Canadians are left with the task of reconciling these issues with the traditions of the British conquerors. As a result of the conquest, all Canadians have to wrestle with questions rarely debated in the United States: Who was right during the colonial wars? Was the conquest good or bad for Canadian society? Their answers often have reflections in contemporary Canadian politics.[11]

Kahnawake Mohawks contend with a different set of questions. They were no more conquered by the British than the French, but they have struggled to maintain their community through centuries of colonialism. This is the framework within which they have remembered the attack. Deerfield was not located within their homeland, so their role in the raid cannot be portrayed as retaliation for losing lands to the English. Instead, it is explained in the form of a captivity narrative. The captive in this story is a bell, originally cast in Europe for the mission church at Kahnawake. According to a nineteenth-century version of the story, the bell was taken from the ship transporting it to Canada by a New England privateer. It was subsequently purchased by John Williams, who had the bell brought to Deerfield. Upon learning of its fate, the mission priest, Père Nicolas, "assembled the Indians together and recounted to them the unhappy situation of the bell, retained in purgatory in the hands of heretics and he begged them to go recover it." The Mohawks, led by their priest, joined the Deerfield raid, liberated their bell, and carried it triumphantly to Kahnawake. There is, however, no contemporary evidence for this story, and when asked, "How much of this legend is historically true?" Alexandre, a nineteenth-century resident of Kahnawake who retold this particular version of the story in 1882, responded, "But very little I fear."[12]

Nevertheless, this story of the bell does bring out themes found in several Mohawk accounts of the raid. As in French and Anglo-Canadian accounts, there is ambivalence about the raid. The Kahnawake Mohawks' motivations are presented as just, pious, and very Catholic. Much emphasis is also placed on the collective action and the community's loss and restoration, which echo the concerns of the mourning war. Still, in these accounts the Mohawks do not initiate the raid; a French priest and the French governor play important roles in initiating it. Little is said of the actual fighting. Later versions assert that the Mohawks "went directly to the church and secured the bell. They then withdrew through the village with the bell and retired from the fight," implying that the French and the Abenakis were chiefly responsible for the killing and destruction.[13]

The Deerfield raid played a different role in Abenaki memory. The Abenakis of Odanak, some of them descendants of the original inhabitants of the Connecticut valley, never forgot their association with their ancestral lands. In the nineteenth century, long after the wars were over, some came to visit Deerfield, claiming to be descendants of Eunice Williams. In the early twentieth century an Abenaki woman named Elizabeth Mary Sadoques, whose ancestors had lived in central Massachusetts in the days before Deerfield was founded, explained to Deerfield's local historical society how her Abenaki forebears were descended from Eunice. It was they, not Mohawks, who had taken her captive. Her ancestors had attacked Deerfield "to regain their lands" at the prompting of the French, who used "them for their own purposes." After Eunice supposedly married into their community, her family preferred to think of Deerfield as Williamsecook, the home of their Williams ancestors. In short, the Abenakis belonged there as much as—if not more than—the members of Deerfield's local historical society.[14]

Stories such as those told by Elizabeth Sadoques, John Williams, François-Xavier Garneau, and others have reflected the historical experience and the cultural concerns of the group telling the story. These stories can tell us as much, if not more, about the storytellers as they do about the event itself. Though the stories change over time, the core structures of the stories remain, reflecting subtle, and not so subtle, cultural differences. For three centuries now, amateur and professional historians in Deerfield, Montreal, Kahnawake, and Odanak have recalled the 1704 raid on Deerfield in ways that have strengthened the identity of their communities. But they have done so at a cost. The broader problems and ambiguities of empire and alliance that helped produce the raid are obscured along with the presence of Pennacooks, Hurons, and Iroquois of the Mountain. Furthermore, the challenges confronting each individual get lost in accounts that prefer to talk about the clash of cultures and empires rather than individuals and the choices that they faced.

Our focus on the many different stories of the individual captors and captives has sought to draw out the complex motives and actions of individuals caught up in the events of 1704. In doing this, we have attempted to reassess the ways in which historians, both amateur and professional, have characterized the peoples and places associated with the Deerfield raid. Out of the many different and often antagonistic stories we have tried to tell one. It is our hope that our history helps readers to understand better the problems and pressures confronting the inhabitants of colonial America by recovering what brought them together as well as what drove them apart.

APPENDIX A

Identities of Native Peoples

	Odanak Abenakis	Pennacooks	Kahnawake Mohawks	Iroquois of the Mountain	Hurons
Williams's name	Indians	Eastern Indians	Maquas	Maquas	Maquas
Alternative names	Canada Indians North Indians Sokokis	Penikokes Penaski Openangos	Iroquois of the Sault French Mohawks	Iroquois of the Mountain French Mohawks	Lorettans French Mohawks Wendat
Modern cultural and linguistic categories	Algonquian Mostly Western Abenakis	Algonquian Western Abenakis	Iroquoian Iroquois	Mostly Iroquoian Iroquois, Huron	Iroquoian Huron
Location	St. Francis River	Vermont New Hampshire Southeastern Maine	Near Montreal	Montreal Island	Near Quebec
Principal villages	Odanak	Pennacook Pigwacket Cowass	Kahnawake	La Montagne Sault-au-Récollet Lac des Deux Montagnes	Lorette

SOURCE: Identities of Indians from John Williams's *The Redeemed Captive*. Adapted from Calloway, *The Western Abenakis of Vermont*, 8–9.

APPENDIX B

Status of Deerfield Residents

Name	Share[a]	Real[b]	Personal[c]	K[d]	D[e]	E[f]	R07[g]	R14[h]	F[i]	I[j]	UK[k]
Mr. John Williams	8		300	2	1		5			1	
Sgt. Benoni Stebbins	26	300		1							
Mehuman Hinsdale	26		100	1			2				
Samson Frary	20	250		3	1						
Ens. John Sheldon	18		100	2			3				
Mr. John Catlin	16	250		2			2				
Capt. Jonathan Wells	16										
Godfrey Nims	14	250		4	1		1	1	1		
Thomas French	10		100	1	1		3		2	1	
William Arms											
Samuel Carter	13	100		1	3		1		2	1	
Simon Beamon	12	100					2				
John Hawks Jr.	13	70		5							
Daniel Belding	10	150			1						
Eleazer Hawks	10										
John Stebbins	8	100					3		4		
Ebenezer Brooks	8	70									
Nathaniel Brooks		70			1		1		1		1
Lt. David Hoyt			50		3		2	1			
Ebenezer Smead											
Ebenezer Severance											
Samuel Smead	3	50		4							
John Hawks Sr.		50		1	1						
Mr. John Richards		50			1						
John Field		50		1			2			1	
Joseph Petty			50			1	1				
Martin Kellogg			40	1		1	1	1		1	
David Hoyt Jr.			50	1							
Philip Mattoon			50	3							
Benjamin Burt			40				3				
Edward Allen	5								1		
John Allen											
Widow Sarah Hurst	4		20		1		1	1	3	1	1
The Allisons	10		20								

Name	Share[a]	Real[b]	Personal[c]	K[d]	D[e]	E[f]	R07[g]	R14[h]	F[i]	I[j]	UK[k]
Ebnezer Warner	20				1		2				1
Michael Mitchell											
Widow Sarah Williams											
Widow Sarah Mattoon							1				
John Sheldon Jr.	20						1				
John Smead											
Joseph Catlin Jr.	20			1							
William Belding											
David Alexander	20			1	1	1	1				
Benjamin Munn	20										
Widow Elizabeth Corse	20				1				1		
Andrew Stevens	20			1					1		
Pomroys	20				1		2				
Jacques de Noyon	20								4		
Joseph Brooks	10										
Samuel Price	10			1				1			
John Wilton							1				
Slaves				1	1						
Orphans									2	1	1
Soldiers				5	1	2	2	1			
Militia				5			1				
Others				2			3				

[a]Share: Number of propriety shares reflects current real estate holdings.

[b]Real: Value in £ of real property—housing and barns—lost in 1704 attack.

[c]Personal: Value in £ of personal property—animals, household furnishings—lost in 1704 attack.

[d]K: Number from family or category that were killed in attack.

[e]D: Number from family or category that died on march to Canada.

[f]E: Number from family or category that escaped.

[g]R07: Number from family or category that returned by 1707.

[h]R14: Number from family or category that returned by 1714.

[i]F: Number from family or category that stayed with French.

[j]I: Number from family or category that stayed with Indians.

[k]UK: Number from family or category whose fate is unknown.

APPENDIX C

Identities of French Raiders

Known participants

Lieutenant Jean-Baptiste Hertel de Rouville, 1668–1722

Ensign René Boucher de la Perrière, 1668–1742

Ensign François-Marie Margane de Batilly, 1672–1704

Charles Legardeur de Croisille, 1677–1749

Jacques-René Gaultier de Varennes, 1677–1757

Pierre Gaultier de Varennes et de la Vérendrye, 1685–1749

Likely participants

René Hertel de Chambly, 1675–1708

Lambert Hertel, 1677–?

Michel Hertel de Cournoyer, 1685–?

Pierre Hertel de Moncours, 1687–1739

APPENDIX D

List of the 1704 Deerfield Captives

Name	Age	Fate
Mary Alexander	36	Returned to Deerfield
Mary Alexander	2	Killed on the march
Joseph Alexander	23	Escaped on the march
Sarah Allen	12	Naturalized[a] 1710, married 1710, remained in New France
Mary Allis	22	Returned to Deerfield
Thomas Baker	21	Escaped from New France
Simon Beamon	47	Returned to Deerfield
Hannah Beamon	36	Returned to Deerfield
Hepzibah Belding	54	Killed on the march
John Bridgman	30	Escaped in the Meadows
Nathaniel Brooks	39	Returned to Deerfield
Mary Brooks	40	Killed on the march
Mary Brooks	7	Naturalized 1710, remained in New France?
William Brooks	6	Fate Unknown
Abigail Brown	25	Returned to Deerfield
Benjamin Burt	23	Returned to New England
Sarah Burt	22	Returned to New England
John Burt	21	Returned to Deerfield
Hannah Carter	29	Killed on the march
Hannah Carter	7 mo.	Killed on the march
Mercy Carter	10	Married, remained in Kahnawake
Samuel Carter Jr.	12	Remained in New France
John Carter	8	Naturalized 1710, married 1718, remained in New France
Ebenezer Carter	6	Returned to New England
Marah Carter	3	Killed on the march
John Catlin	17	Returned to Deerfield
Ruth Catlin	20?	Returned to Deerfield
Elizabeth Corse	32?	Killed on the march
Elizabeth Corse	8	Naturalized 1710, married 1712, remained in New France
Daniel Crowfoot	3	Fate unknown
Jacques De Noyon	36	Remained in New France

Name	Age	Fate
Abigail Stebbins De Noyon	17	Naturalized 1710, remained in New France
Sarah Dickinson	24	Returned to New England
Joseph Eastman	20	Returned to New England
Mary Field	28	Returned to New England
Mary Field	6	Married, remained in Kahnawake
John Field	3	Returned to New England
"Marguerite Field"	3	Married, 1722, remained in New France
Mary Frary	64?	Killed on the march
Thomas French	47	Returned to Deerfield
Mary French	40	Killed on the march
Thomas French. Jr.	14	Returned to Deerfield
Mary French	17	Returned to New England
Freedom French	11	Naturalized 1710, married 1713, remained in New France
Martha French	8	Naturalized 1710, married 1711, remained in New France
Abigail French	6	Remained in Kahnawake
Mary Harris	9	Married, remained in Kahnawake
Samuel Hastings	20	Naturalized 1710, returned to New England
Elizabeth Hawks	6	Killed on the march
Mehuman Hinsdale	31	Returned to Deerfield
Mary Hinsdale	23	Returned to Deerfield
Jacob Hickson	?	Died of starvation in VT
David Hoyt	52	Died of starvation in VT
Abigail Hoyt	44	Returned to Deerfield
Sarah Hoyt	17	Married 1712, returned to Deerfield
Jonathan Hoyt	15	Returned to Deerfield
Ebenezer Hoyt	8	Killed on the march
Abigail Hoyt	2	Killed on the march
Elizabeth Hull	15	Returned to Deerfield
Sarah Hurst	40	Naturalized 1710, married 1710, returned to New England
Sarah Hurst	18	Returned to New England
Elizabeth Hurst	16	Naturalized 1710, married 1712, returned to New England
Thomas Hurst	12	Naturalized 1710, married 1718, remained in New France
Ebenezer Hurst	10	Naturalized 1710, probably returned to New England
Hannah Hurst	8	Naturalized 1710, married 1712, remained with the Iroquois of the Mountain
Benjamin Hurst	2	Killed on the march
Martin Kellogg	45	Returned to New England
Martin Kellogg, Jr.	17	Escaped from New France
Joseph Kellogg	12	Naturalized 1710, returned to New England
Joanna Kellogg	11	Married, remained at Kahnawake

Name	Age	Fate
Rebecca Kellogg	8	Married, returned to New England
John Marsh	24	Returned to New England
Sarah Mattoon	17	Returned to Deerfield
Mehitable Nims	36	Killed on the march
Ebenezer Nims	17	Married 1712, returned to Deerfield
Abigail Nims	3	Married 1715, remained in New France
Joseph Petty	31	Escaped from New France
Sarah Petty	31	Returned to Deerfield
Lydia Pomroy	20	Returned to New England
Joshua Pomroy	28	Returned to New England
Esther Pomroy	27?	Killed on the march
Samuel Price	18?	Naturalized 1710, returned to New England
Jemima Richards	10	Killed on the march
Josiah Rising	9	Married 1715, remained in New France
Hannah Sheldon	23	Returned to Deerfield
Mary Sheldon	16	Returned to Deerfield
Ebenezer Sheldon	12	Returned to Deerfield
Remembrance Sheldon	11	Returned to New England
John Stebbins	56	Returned to Deerfield
Dorothy Stebbins	42	Returned to Deerfield
John Stebbins, Jr.	19	Returned to Deerfield
Samuel Stebbins	15	Returned to New England
Thankful Stebbins	12	Naturalized 1710, married 1711, remained in New France
Ebenezer Stebbins	9	Naturalized 1710, remained in New France
Joseph Stebbins	4	Married 1734?, remained in New France
Elizabeth Price Stevens	20	Naturalized 1710, married 1706, remained in New France
Ebenezer Warner	27	Returned to Deerfield
Waitstill Warner	24	Killed on the march
Sarah Warner	4	Returned to Deerfield
Waitstill Warner	2	Fate Unknown
John Williams	39	Returned to Deerfield
Eunice Williams	39	Killed on the march
Samuel Williams	15	Returned to Deerfield
Esther Williams	13	Returned to New England
Stephen Williams	10	Returned to New England
Eunice Williams	7	Married 1713, remained in Kahnawake
Warham Williams	4	Returned to New England
Frank	?	Killed on the march
John Wilton	39	Returned to New England
Judah Wright	26	Returned to Deerfield

NOTE: Two additional French men whose names are unknown were taken and returned to New France.

[a]Indicates that the individual in question became a naturalized French subject.

French and Indian Raids on New England, 1703–1712

Date	Place	Raid[a]	Raiders[b]	K[c]	W[d]	C[e]	KC[f]	Sources[g]
1703								
8/10	Wells, Me.	Att	20F;500I[h]	22		17[i]		IW:5;C,1:41
8/10	Cape Porpoise, Me.	Att				10[i]		IW:5;C,2:9
8/10	Winter Harbor, Me.	Att						IW:5–6
8/10	Saco, Me.	Att		11		24		IW:6;C,2:13–15
8/10	Spurwink, Me.	Att		13[i]		9[i]		IW:6;C,2:25–29
8/10	Scarborough, Me.	Att						IW:6
8/10	Perpooduck, Me.	Att		25		8		IW:6
8/10	Casco, Me.	Att		2		1		IW:6–7
8/17	Hampton, N.H.	Att	30I	5				IW:8;P:135
10/6	Scarborough, Me.	Amb	120I	16		3		IW:9;P:136
10/8	Deerfield, Mass.	Amb				2		IW:9
10/13	York, Me.	House		6		2		IW:9;P:136
10/30	Salmon Falls, N.H.	Amb		1				P:136
?	Berwick, Me.	Amb						IW:10
12/20	Saco, Me.	Amb		3		2		P:137
12/24	Casco, Me.	Amb		4	2			IW:10
1704								
1/28	Berwick, Me.	Att	30–40I	1	1			IW:10;P:137
?	Exeter, N.H.	Att						IW:10
?	Worcester, Mass.	House		1		6		C,1:313–17
2/8	Haverhill, Mass.	Att	6I			13	5	P:137
2/29	Deerfield, Mass.	Att	50F;200+I	49		112	21	S,1:308–09
4/25	Oyster River, N.H.	Att		1				IW:14;P:138
4/26	Exeter, N.H.	Amb		1		2		IW:14;P:138
4/28	Cochecho, N.H.	Amb			1			IW:14;P:138
5/11	Wells, Me.	Amb		2		1		IW:15;P:138
5/11	Deerfield, Mass.	Amb		1		1	1	W:156
5/13	Pascommuck, Mass.	Att	20F;50I	1		37	20	P:15;S,1:318–19
5/28	Cochecho, N.H.	Amb	4I					P:138
6/1	Oyster River, N.H	Amb	8–9I	1				P:138
6/?	Dover, N.H.	House		3		7–8		P:138
7/15	Hatfield, Mass.	Amb		1				W:157
7/20	Deerfield, Mass.	Skirm		1				W:157

Date	Place	Raid[a]	Raiders[b]	K[c]	W[d]	C[e]	KC[f]	Sources[g]
7/20	Casco, Me.	Amb				1	1	P:138
7/20	Hadley, Me.	Amb			1			W:157
7/29	Worcester, Mass.	Amb		1				IW:24
7/31	Westfield, Mass.	Skirm		2				IW:24;S,1:322
7/31	Brookfield, Mass.	Amb		1	1			IW:24;W:157
7/31	Lancaster, Mass.			4				P:139
8/?	Groton, Mass.					2		IW:24
8/4	Nashaway, Mass.							IW:24
8/4	Haverhill, Mass.	Amb		2				P:139
8/8	Marlborough, Mass.	Amb				4		IW:n9;C,1:342
8/8	Exeter, N.H.	Amb		1				P:139
8/9	Amesbury, Mass.	Amb				3		P:139,C,1:365
8/10	Wells, Me.			2				P:139
8/11	Dover, N.H.	Amb	7–8I	2				IW:25;P:139
8/11	York, Me.	Amb		1				IW:25;P:139
8/19	Oyster River, N.H.	Amb		1+				IW:25;P:139
1705								
5/4	Kittery, Me.	Amb	10–12I	5		5		IW:31;P:140
5/21	Kittery, Me.	Amb		1	1			IW:31;P:140
10/15	Cape Neddick, Me.	Att	18I	2		4	2	IW:31;P:141
10/15	Lancaster, Mass.					3		IW:n11:C,1:330
11/4	Oyster River, N.H.					1		P:141
1706								
4/27	Oyster River, N.H.	House		8–10	2			IW:32;P:142
6/6	Kittery, Me.	Amb		1		1		IW:32–33;P:142
6/4	Cochecho, N.H.	Amb		2		1		P:142
7/3	Haverhill, Mass.			1				P:142
7/3	Dunstable, Mass.	Att		9	5	1		IW:34–35;P:142
7/4	Amesbury, Mass.	Att	40I	8–10				IW:35;P:143
7/4	Kingston, N.H.	Cattle						IW:36
7/6,8	Reading, Mass.	House		4		4		IW:365;P:143
7/27	Chelmsford, Mass.	Amb		1		1		IW:35;P:143
7/?	Sudbury, Mass.							IW:36
7/21,27	Groton, Mass.	Amb		2		1	1	IW:36;P:143
7/23	Exeter, N.H.	Amb	20I	4	1	3		IW:36–37;P:143
7/31	Chicopee, Mass.	Amb		1				W:157
7/31	Brookfield, Mass.	Amb		1				W:157
8/1	Wells, Me.	Amb		2				P:143
8/1	Hampton, N.H.	Amb	7–8I	1		1		P:143
8/10	Dover, N.H.	Amb		1		1		IW:40
1707								
5/22	Oyster River, N.H.					2		IW:45;P:145
6/11	Groton, Mass.	Amb		1				P:145
6/11	Cambridge, Mass.	Amb		1				P:145

Date	Place	Raid[a]	Raiders[b]	K[c]	W[d]	C[e]	KC[f]	Sources[g]
6/16	Kittery, Me.		7I	5–6				IW:44;P:145
7/8	Oyster River, N.H.	Amb	20–30I			2		IW:44;P:145
7/16	Lancaster, Mass.			1				IW:n15
7/?	Westfield, Mass.			1				J:268
7/20	Groton, Mass.	Amb				3		C,1:293–294
7/?	Casco, Me.	Amb		3		2		IW:44
7/22	Exeter N.H.	Amb	7I		1			IW:44;P:145
8/10	York-Wells, Me.	Amb	40–50	4		1		IW:44;P:146
8/?	Marlborough, Mass.	Amb	24?	2	2	1		IW:44
8/18	Northborough, Mass.	Amb		2		1		IW:n15
9/13	Exeter, N.H.	Amb		1				IW:45;P:146
9/15	Kingston, N.H.	Amb		1				IW:45,n15
9/17	Oyster River, N.H.	Amb	30I	8				IW:45;P:146
9/21	Winter Harbor, Me.	Amb	150I	1				IW:45–46;P:146
9/28	Berwick, Me.	Amb		2	1			IW:46;P:146
9/30	Dover, N.H.	Amb				1		P:146
1708								
4/22	Wells, Me.	Amb				1		IW:45;C,1:435
7/9	Northampton, Mass.	Amb			2			W:157
7/26	Chicopee, Mass.	House	7–8I	3	2	1	1	W:157
8/29	Haverhill, Mass.	Att	100F;60I	16		17		P:148
?	Amesbury, Mass.			1				IW:48
9/18	Oyster River, N.H.	House						P:148
9/19	Kittery, Me.	Amb		2				IW:48;P:148
10/26	Deerfield, Mass.	Amb		1				W:158
10/30	Brookfield, Mass.	Skirm		1	3	1		W:158
1709								
4/12	Deerfield, Mass.	Amb				1		IW:48;W:158–59
5/6	Exeter, N.H.	Amb				4		IW:48
5/?	Oyster River, N.H.			1				IW:n16
6/2	Dunstable, Mass.					1		C,1:330
6/11	Exeter, N.H.	Amb		1				P:149
6/24	Deerfield, Mass.	Amb	40F;140I	2		2		S,1:372–73
6/30	Oyster River, N.H.	Amb		1				P:149
8/8	Brookfield, Mass.			2				W:160
8/?	Wells, Me.			1		1		IW:49
1710								
?	York, Me.			1				IW:58
6/23	Epping, N.H.	Amb		3		2		IW:58
6/23	Exeter, N.H.	Amb		1		5		IW:59
6/23	Kingston, N.H.	Amb		2		2		IW:n18
6/?	Dover, N.H.			1				D:264
7/?	Waterbury, Conn.			3				IW:59
7/?	Simsbury, Conn.			1				IW:59

Date	Place	Raid[a]	Raiders[b]	K[c]	W[d]	C[e]	KC[f]	Sources[g]
7/20	Brookfield, Mass.	Amb		6				W:161
7/?	Marlborough, Mass.	Amb		1				IW:59
7/?	Chelmsford, Mass.			1				IW:59
8/ 2	Winter Harbor, Me.	Att	40–50F&I	1		2		IW:59
8/ 9	Winter Harbor, Me.	Att		3		6		IW:59
?	Cochecho, N.H.			1				IW:59
1711								
?	Winter Harbor, Me.					1		IW:61
4/?	Cochecho, N.H.	Amb		4				IW:61
4/?	York, Me.	Amb		1	1			IW:61
4/29	Wells, Me.	Amb		2				IW:61
?	Cochecho, N.H.	Amb		1		1		IW:61
8/10	Northampton, Mass.	Amb		1		1		W:161
1712								
4/16	Exeter, N.H.	Amb		1				IW:71
4/?	York, Me.	Amb		1				IW:71
4/?	Wells, Me.	Amb		3	3	2		IW:71
4/?	Kittery, Me.			1		1		IW:71
4/?	Oyster River, N.H.			1				IW:72
4/?	Dover, N.H.			1	1			IW:72
5/14	York, Me.	Skirm	30F&I	1		7		IW:72
6/1	Kittery, Me.	House		1	2			IW:72
6/2	Kingston, N.H.				1	1		IW:72
6/2	Berwick, Me.			1				IW:72
7/18	Wells, Me.			1		1		IW:72
7/?	Dover, N.H.			2				IW:72
7/29	Chicopee, Mass.	House				1		W:161
7/30	Deerfield area	Amb		1		2		W:161
9/1	Wells, Me.	Amb		1	1			IW:73
9/?	Wells, Me.	Amb		3		1		IW:73

[a] Amb: ambush outside of home or village
Att: attack on village or group of houses
Cattle: only cattle killed and wounded
House: attack on an individual house
Skirm: a skirmish

[b] F: French; I: Indians

[c] Number killed

[d] Number wounded

[e] Number captured

[f] Killed after capture

[g] Sources used to identify raid and determine casualties
    C: Coleman, *New England Captives Carried to Canada*
    D: Drake, *Border Wars of New England*

IW: Penhallow, *History of the Indian Wars*
J: Judd, *History of Hadley*
P: Pike, "Journal of the Rev. John Pike"
S: Sheldon, *History of Deerfield*
W: Williams, "An Account of Some Ancient Things"

[h] 20 Frenchmen and 500 Indians participated in the attacks on 8/10.

[i] These figures are estimated using Penhallow, Pike, and Coleman.

APPENDIX F

Fates of the 1704 Deerfield Captives

	Females			Males			
	Over 21	20–13	Under 13	Over 21	20–13	Under 13	Total
Numbers taken	23	12	24	24[a]	12	17	112[a]
Died on march	10		6	3		2	21
Escaped				4	1		5
Returned by 1707	12	8	1	14	7	5	47
Returned by 1714	1	2			3	2	8
Returned Later			1		1		2
With French		2	8	3[a]		6	19[a]
With Natives			7				7
Fate Unknown			1			2	3
While in Canada							
Converts		3	11	3	5		22[b]
Naturalized	1	3	7	2	5		18
Married	1	3[c]	14[c]		1[c]	4[c]	23

SOURCES: Coleman, *New England Captives Carried to Canada;* Fournier, *De la Nouvelle-Angleterre à la Nouvelle France.*

[a] Includes 3 Frenchmen who "had lived in Deerfield for some time."

[b] This is an underestimate. It includes only those captives for whom a record of baptism exists and those captives at Kahnawake—Abigail French, Mary Field, and Eunice Willams—for whom other evidence of their embrace of Catholicism exists. It excludes three other females known to have been at Kahnawake and four people who were naturalized but for whom no record of baptism exists.

[c] Includes a captive who married another Deerfield captive.

APPENDIX G

Fates of New England Captives Taken between 1703 and 1712

	Females				Males				
	Over 21	20–13	Under 13	UK	Over 21	20–13	Under 13	UK	Total
Numbers taken	42	23	56	2	66[a]	28	53	16	286[a]
Died before 1713	13	16	8		9	1	3		35
Escaped					6	1			7
Returned	28	6	10		44	18	23	2	141
With French		6	23		3[a]	5	14	1	52[a]
With Kahnawake Mohawks			6				4		10
With Iroquois of the Mountain			3				1		4
With Abenakis at Odanak								3[b]	3[b]
Fate Unknown	1		6	2	4	3	8	10	34

SOURCES: See sources cited for appendixes E and F.

NOTE: A total of 372 captives were taken in New England between 1703 and 1713. The table above includes the 286 on whom we have the most information. It is known that of the remaining 86, 26 were killed almost immediately after they were captured, leaving 60 additional individuals unaccounted for.

[a]Includes 3 Frenchmen who "had lived in Deerfield for some time."

[b]Three individuals, presumably children, who remained at Odanak after the 1714 trip by John Stoddard and John Williams.

ABBREVIATIONS

ANF Archives Nationales de France, Paris.

ANQM Archives Nationale de Quebec, Montreal.

Baxter Manuscripts James Phinney Baxter, ed. *Baxter Manuscripts: Documentary History of the State of Maine.* 24 vols. Portland: Maine Historical Society, 1869–1916.

CSP Calendar of State Papers. Colonial series. *America and West Indies.* 39 vols. London: Hereford Times, 1860–1969.

DCB Dictionary of Canadian Biography. 14 vols. Toronto: University of Toronto Press, 1967–1998.

JR Ruben Gold Thwaites, ed. *The Jesuit Relations and Allied Documents: Travels and Explorations of the Jesuit Missionaries in New France, 1610–1791.* 73 vols. Cleveland, Ohio: Burrows Brothers, 1896–1901.

MA Massachusetts Archives, Boston, Massachusetts.

NAC National Archives of Canada, Ottawa.

NYCD E. B. O'Callaghan, ed. *Documents Relative to the Colonial History of the State of New York.* 15 vols. Albany, N.Y.: Weed, Parsons, 1853–1887.

PPNH Nathaniel Bouton, ed. *New Hampshire Provincial Papers: Documents relating to the Province of New Hampshire.* 7 vols. Concord, Nashua, Manchester, N.H.: 1867–1873.

RAPQ Rapport de l'archiviste de la province de Québec. Québec: A. Proulx, 1920–.

WP Winthrop Papers. Collections of the Massachusetts Historical Society. 6th ser., vol. 3. Boston: Massachusetts Historical Society, 1889.

NOTES

Introduction: War and Captivity

1. The English still used the Julian calendar, which was eleven days behind the Gregorian used by most western European countries, including France (and is the calendar that we use today). According to the Julian calendar the new year began on March 25 instead of January 1, thus dates in English documents between January 1 and March 25 were often written with both years. Hence the English recorded the date of the raid as February 29, 1703/04; for the French, the raid occurred on March 11, 1704. In the text and in all English documents cited in the notes we have retained the use of the Julian or Old Style dates except we give the year as beginning on January 1. The dates in French documents cited in the notes are Gregorian, or New Style.

2. Francis Parkman, *Half Century of Conflict,* vol. 2 of *France and England in North America* (New York: Library of America, 1983), 373.

3. [Samuel Sewall], *Diary of Samuel Sewall* in *Collections of the Massachusetts Historical Society,* 5th series (Boston, 1879), 5:87.

4. Peter MacLeod, *The Canadian Iroquois and the Seven Years' War* (Toronto: Dundurn Press, 1996), 36.

5. Richard White, *The Middle Ground: Indians, Empires, and Republics in the Great Lakes Region, 1650–1815* (New York: Cambridge University Press, 1991), esp. x, 50–53.

6. Andrew R. L. Cayton and Fredrika J. Teute, eds., *Contact Points: American Frontiers from the Mohawk Valley to the Mississippi, 1750–1830* (Chapel Hill: University of North Carolina Press, 1998), 2, 3; James H. Merrill, "Shamokin, 'the very seat of the Prince of darkness': Unsettling the Early American Frontier," in Clayton and Teute, *Contact Points,* 21.

7. Most notably C. Alice Baker, *True Stories of New England Captives Carried to Canada during the Old French and Indian Wars* (1897; reprint, Bowie, Md.: Heritage Books, 1990); Emma Lewis Coleman, *New England Captives Carried to Canada between 1677 and 1760 during the French and Indian Wars,* 2 vols. (Portland, Maine: Southworth Press, 1925); John Demos, *The Unredeemed Captive: A Family Story from Early America* (New York: Knopf, 1994).

Chapter 1: Frontier Town

1. MA, 113:57a; the classical statement of this mythic understanding of the frontier is Frederick Jackson Turner, "The Significance of the Frontier in American History" (1894; Readex Microprint, 1966), 199–227.

2. Gloria L. Main, *Peoples of a Spacious Land: Families and Cultures in Colonial New England* (Cambridge: Harvard University Press, 2001), 62.

3. Russel G. Handsmen, "Illuminating History's Silence in the 'Pioneer Valley,'" *Ar-*

tifacts 19, no. 2 (fall 1991): 19–21; Claire C. Carlson, "Native American Presences in Deerfield, Massachusetts: An Essay and Resource Guide," June 1995, 9–22. For the story of Wequamps, see George Sheldon, *A History of Deerfield, Massachusetts* (Deerfield: privately printed, 1895–1896), 1:29.

4. Richard I. Melvoin, *New England Outpost: War and Society in Colonial Deerfield* (New York: Norton, 1989), 26–32; Peter Allen Thomas, "In the Maelstrom of Change: The Indian Trade and Cultural Process in the Middle Connecticut River Valley, 1635–1665" (Ph.D. diss., University of Massachusetts, 1979), 29–44, 96–120. For general discussions, see Kathleen J. Bragdon, *Native People of Southern New England, 1500–1650* (Norman: University of Oklahoma Press, 1996), 71–74, 80–129; William Cronon, *Changes in the Land: Indians, Colonists, and the Ecology of New England* (New York: Hill and Wang, 1983), 19–53.

5. Chief Sachem, September 1659, quoted in Sheldon, *History of Deerfield*, 1:67. See Melvoin, *New England Outpost*, 32–36; Thomas, "In the Maelstrom of Change," 121–202, 261–333.

6. Sheldon, *History of Deerfield*, 1:49–68; Melvoin, *New England Outpost*, 36–43; Thomas, "In the Maelstrom of Change," 203–244.

7. Sheldon, *History of Deerfield*, 1:68–70; Melvoin, *New England Outpost*, 43–47; Thomas, "In the Maelstrom of Change," 244–260.

8. Quotations from Sheldon, *History of Deerfield*, 1:8; see Sheldon, *History of Deerfield*, 1:7–13; Melvoin, *New England Outpost*, 49–58; Cronon, *Changes in the Land*, 54–81.

9. Sheldon, *History of Deerfield*, 1:1–7; Melvoin, *New England Outpost*, 51–69; John Frederick Martin, *Profits in the Wilderness: Entrepreneurship and the Founding of New England Towns in the Seventeenth Century* (Chapel Hill: University of North Carolina Press, 1991), 131–148, 186–216, 239–240.

10. Sheldon, *History of Deerfield*, 9–22; Melvoin, *New England Outpost*, 58–69; Martin, *Profits in the Wilderness*, 31.

11. Sheldon, *History of Deerfield*, 1:13–19, 24, 39, 42; Melvoin, *New England Outpost*, 62–63; J. Ritchie Garrison, *Landscape and Material Life in Franklin County, Massachusetts, 1770–1860* (Knoxville: University of Tennessee Press, 1991), 18–21.

12. Garrison, *Landscape and Material Life*, 18–21.

13. Joseph Wood, *The New England Village* (Baltimore, Md.: Johns Hopkins University Press, 1997), 13–16, 32–37, 43–54, 118–119; Cronon, *Changes in the Land*, 127–156.

14. Quoted in Sheldon, *History of Deerfield*, 1:191.

15. Kevin Sweeney, "The Children of the Covenant: The Formation and Transformation of a Second Generation New England Community" (paper prepared for Historic Deerfield Summer Fellowship Program, 1971), 4, 11. See also Melvoin, *New England Outpost*, 79–80.

16. Sweeney, "Children of the Covenant," 10–12. See also Melvoin, *New England Outpost*, 77–79.

17. Sweeney, "Children of the Covenant," 12. See also Melvoin, *New England Outpost*, 75–77.

18. Sweeney, "Children of the Covenant," 12–13. These points are also forcefully made in Melvoin, *New England Outpost*, 81–91.

19. Quotations from Sheldon, *History of Deerfield*, 1:37, 2:136. Sheldon puts the population at 125, while Melvoin puts it at 200. Melvoin's estimate is more accurate. See Sheldon, *History of Deerfield*, 1:92; Melvoin, *New England Outpost*, 75.

20. Douglas Edward Leach, *Flintlock and Tomahawk: New England in King Philip's War* (New York: Norton 1966), 1–72; James D. Drake, *King Philip's War: Civil War in New England, 1675–1676* (Amherst: University of Massachusetts Press, 1999), 57–108. See also Jill Lepore, *The Name of War: King Philip's War and the Origins of American Identity* (New York: Knopf, 1998).

21. See n. 20. The best discussion of the fighting in the Connecticut Valley is in Melvoin, *New England Outpost*, 92–128.

22. Increase Mather quoted in Sheldon, *History of Deerfield*, 1:101. Melvoin, *New England Outpost*, 97–107. Sheldon claims that seventeen residents of Deerfield were killed but gives only fourteen names. Melvoin says fourteen were killed. See Sheldon, *History of Deerfield*, 1:103, 108, and Melvoin, *New England Outpost*, 103.

23. Sheldon, *History of Deerfield*, 1:111–128; Melvoin, *New England Outpost*, 105–111; Leach, *Flintlock and Tomahawk*, 87–88, 94–102, 112, 116, 119, 184, 200, 205–207.

24. Melvoin, *New England Outpost*, 111–123; Sheldon, *History of Deerfield*, 1:128–178.

25. Sheldon, *History of Deerfield*, 1:179–188; Melvoin, *New England Outpost*, 124–128.

26. The primary source for the raid is [Quentin Stockwell], "Quentin Stockwell's Relation of His Captivity and Redemption," reported by Increase Mather, in *Puritans among the Indians: Accounts of Captivity and Redemption, 1676–1724*, ed. Alden T. Vaughan and Edward W. Clark (Cambridge: Harvard University Press, 1981), 79–89. See also Sheldon, *History of Deerfield*, 1:179–188; Melvoin, *New England Outpost*, 124–128.

27. Sweeney, "Children of the Covenant," 18–19.

28. Sweeney, "Children of the Covenant," 20; Melvoin, *New England Outpost*, 131–135.

29. Sheldon, *History of Deerfield*, 2:854–857, 104–105, 167–168, 214, 293, 356–357; J. H. Temple and George Sheldon, *A History of the Town of Northfield, Massachusetts, for 150 Years* (Albany, N.Y.: Joel Munsell, 1875), 115–116. In Deerfield the average age of first service as a selectman was 34.5 years. The average age for a typical board of selectmen was 43 years. Both figures are about 10 years younger than those found in parts of eastern Massachusetts. Sweeney, "Children of the Covenant," 36.

30. Sheldon, *History of Deerfield*, 1:71, 2:318; James Russell Trumbull, *History of Northampton, Massachusetts from Its Settlement in 1654* (Northampton: privately printed, 1898–1902), 1:180–181.

31. Quotations from Sheldon, *History of Deerfield*, 2:318. See also Sheldon, *History of Deerfield*, 1:196, 2:854–857, 318; Trumbull, *History of Northampton*, 1:290–291.

32. Sweeney, "Children of the Covenant," 34–37; Melvoin, *New England Outpost*, 165–168.

33. Quotation from the Town Book of Deerfield (microfilm, Memorial Libraries, Deerfield), 60; Melvoin, *New England Outpost*, 159–170; Sweeney, "Children of the Covenant," 31–33, 37.

34. Melvoin, *New England Outpost*, 170–177.

35. Stephen Foster, *The Long Argument: English Puritanism and the Shaping of New England Culture* (Chapel Hill: University of North Carolina Press, 1991), 156, 185, 281; Paul Lucas, *Valley of Discord: Church and Society along the Connecticut River, 1636–1725* (Hanover, N.H.: University Press of New England, 1976), 53–57, 133–135, 141–142.

36. Sheldon, *History of Deerfield*, 1:197–199, 436, 455–456, 2:377.

37. Quotations from John Williams, "The Redeemed Captive Returning to Zion," in Vaughan and Clark, *Puritans among the Indians*, 175; Sheldon, *History of Deerfield*, 1:198.

38. Sheldon, *History of Deerfield*, 2:888–890; Ira Berlin, *Many Thousands Gone: The*

First Two Centuries of Slavery in North America (Cambridge: Harvard University Press, 1998), 17–63.

39. Isaac Chauncey, *A Blessed Manumission of Christ's Faithful Ministers, when they have finish'd their Testimony: A Sermon Preach'd at the Funeral of the Reverend John Williams* (Boston: D. Henchman and Thomas Hancock, 1729), 21.

40. Sweeney, "Children of the Covenant," 31–33, 37.

41. "Examination of Micah Mudge of Northfield aged 38 . . . taken 15th October 1688," MA, 129:243; *NYCD*, 3:562; Temple and Sheldon, *History of Northfield*, 111–119; Evan Haefeli and Kevin Sweeney, "Revisiting *The Redeemed Captive*: New Perspectives on the 1704 Attack on Deerfield," *William and Mary Quarterly*, 3rd ser., 52, no. 1 (January 1995): 23–24.

42. Quotations from Sheldon, *History of Deerfield*, 1:220, 228. See also Susan McGowan and Amelia F. Miller, *Family and Landscape: Deerfield Homelots from 1671* (Deerfield: Pocumtuck Valley Memorial Association, 1996), 16–17, 43, 174.

43. Sheldon, *History of Deerfield*, 1:222–243; James Spady, "As If in a Great Darkness: Native American Refugees of the Middle Connecticut Valley in the Aftermath of King Philip's War," *Historical Journal of Massachusetts* 23, no. 2 (summer 1995): 184–185, 189–196; Haefeli and Sweeney, "Revisiting *The Redeemed Captive*," 25.

44. Quotations from John Pynchon and Samuel Partridge to the earl of Bellomont, July 6, 1698, in *The Pynchon Papers,* ed. Carl Bridenbaugh and Juliette Tomlinson (Boston: Colonial Society of Massachusetts, 1982), 1:305–307; Sheldon, *History of Deerfield*, 1:222, 228. See also Spady, "As If in a Great Darkness," 190–196.

45. John Pynchon to Robert Treat Esq., Springfield June 19, 1690, Judd Manuscripts Miscellaneous, 8:219–224, Forbes Library, Northampton, Mass.

46. Quotation from John Pynchon to Robert Treat Esq., Springfield June 19, 1690, Judd Manuscripts Miscellaneous, 8:219–224. See also Spady, "As If in a Great Darkness," 188–190.

47. Sheldon, *History of Deerfield*, 1:243–264; Melvoin, *New England Outpost*, 182–204. Quotation from Sheldon, *History of Deerfield*, 1:222, 228.

48. *Acts and Resolves, Public and Private of the Province of Massachusetts Bay* (Boston: Wright and Potter, 1869–1922), 1:194–195; Melvoin, *New England Outpost*, 152.

49. Sweeney, "Children of the Covenant," 31–33, 37.

50. Cotton Mather, *Decennium Luctuosum: Or, the Remarkables of the Long War with Indian Salvages* in *Narratives of the Indian Wars*, ed. Charles H. Lincoln (New York: C. Scribner's Sons, 1913), 271.

51. Sheldon, *History of Deerfield*, 1:199; 2:104–105, 293–295.

52. Sheldon, *History of Deerfield*, 2:31, 219, 268–269, 265; Emma Lewis Coleman, *New England Captives Carried to Canada between 1677 and 1760 during the French and Indian Wars* (Portland, Maine: Southworth Press, 1925), 2:118–120.

53. The three widows were Elizabeth Corse, Sarah Hurst, and Sarah Mattoon. For the estates of their husbands see Hampshire County Probate Records (microfilm edition), Historic Deerfield Library, 3:22, 27, 90. The orphans were Daniel Crowfoot, "Marguerite" French, Mary Harris, and Jacob Rising. Jacob Rising's mother had died, but his father, who was not dead, sent his young son to live with his wife's Hinsdale relatives in Deerfield. See Coleman, *New England Captives*, 2:74–75, 77, 78–80, 87–88, 91–92, 107–108; Melvoin estimates the population at 260, in *New England Outpost*, 152.

54. Quoted in Sheldon, *History of Deerfield*, 1:289.

Chapter 2: New France

1. For an overview of New France on the eve of the raid on Deerfield, see Guy Frégault, "La Nouvelle-France, territoire et population," in *Le XVIIIè Siècle canadien: Études* (Montreal: HMH, 1968), 13–57. For French fears of the (very real) English ambitions for continental hegemony, see also Frégault, "L'Empire britannique et la conquête du Canada (1700–1713)," in *Le XVIIIè Siècle*, 58–85. For evidence of English ambition, see *CSP* 1702, no. 1009, 20:628–629; *NYCD*, 4:1067–1069.

2. For the shift in French policy, see William Eccles, *Canada under Louis XIV* (Toronto: McClelland and Stewart, 1964), 240–242; Eccles, "Fur Trade and Imperialism," in *Essays on New France* (Toronto: Oxford University Press, 1987), 75–95; Eccles, "La Mer de l'Ouest," in *Essays*, 96–109; Eccles, "Military Establishment," in *Essays*, 110, 122–123; Dale Miquelon, *New France, 1701–1744: "A Supplement to Europe"* (Toronto: McClelland and Stewart, 1987), 1–2, 53–54.

3. Eccles, *Canada under Louis XIV,* 46–48, 59–76, 99–118, 250–252.

4. Eccles, *Canada under Louis XIV,* 202–204, 244–245; Miquelon, *New France,* 15–18, 56–66, 127–128; Yves F. Zoltvany, *Philippe de Rigaud de Vaudreuil: Governor of New France, 1703–1725* (Toronto: McClelland and Stewart, 1974), 37–38; Guy Frégault, "La Compagnie de la colonie," in *Le XVIIIè Siècle,* 242–269.

5. Richard White, *The Middle Ground: Indians, Empires, and Republics in the Great Lakes Region, 1650–1815* (New York: Cambridge University Press, 1991), esp., 33–40, 98–120, 142–151.

6. Governor Vaudreuil quoted in Gilles Havard, *The Great Peace of Montreal of 1701: French-Native Diplomacy in the Seventeenth Century,* trans. Phyllis Arnoff and Howard Scott (Montreal and Kingston: McGill-Queen's University Press, 2001), 169–173, 179–183, 193; Frégault "La Compagnie de la Colonie," 276–280.

7. White, *Middle Ground,* 116–120, 142–151; Francis H. Hammang, *The Marquis de Vaudreuil: New France at the Beginning of the Eighteenth Century: Part I—New France and the English Colonies* (Bruges and Louvain: Louvain University, 1938), 83–105; Havard, *Great Peace of Montreal,* 31–34, 39–43, 79–90, 171–173, 252–253. Most contemporaries and subsequent historians concluded that the English could offer cheaper prices. See Pierre-François-Xavier de Charlevoix, *History and General Description of New France,* trans. and ed. John Gilmary Shea (1870; reprint, Chicago: Loyola University Press, 1962) 5:157–158; [Louis Armand de Lom d'Arce, baron de Lahotan], *New Voyages to North-America by the Baron de Lahontan,* ed. Reuben Gold Thwaites (Chicago: A. C. McClurg, 1905), 1:58–59, 98–99, 326, 394; Eccles, *Canada under Louis XIV,* 220; White, *Middle Ground,* 119. Even Matthew Laird, who has challenged this assumption, is forced to admit that Albany merchants as a rule paid higher prices for beaver and that the prices for trade goods increased in New France during war years, a not infrequent occurrence. See Laird, "The Price of Empire: Anglo-French Rivalry for the Great Lakes Fur Trades, 1700–1760" (Ph.D. diss., College of William and Mary, 1995), 141, 148–150, 179–180.

8. Dudley to the Council of Trade and Plantations, August 5, 1702, *CSP,* 1702–1703, no. 810, 20:501–505; Brouillan à Pontchartrain, 21 octobre, 1703, NAC, C14 D 4: 212; Zoltvany, *Vaudreuil,* 42.

9. *DCB,* 2:116; Hammang, *Vaudreuil,* 111–113; Miquelon, *New France,* 27–29; Zoltvany, *Vaudreuil,* 41–42.

10. *DCB,* 2:116; Hammang, *Vaudreuil,* 113–115. For figures on French manpower see

René Chartrand, *Canadian Military Heritage, 1000–1754* (Montreal: Art Global, 1993), 74, 111; Jay Cassel, "The Troupes de la Marine in Canada, 1683–1760: Men and Materiel" (Ph.D. diss., University of Toronto, 1988), 67. Estimates of New England manpower are based on data for Connecticut, Massachusetts, and New Hampshire drawn from Evarts B. Greene and Virginia D. Harrington, *American Population before the Federal Census of 1790* (New York: Columbia University Press, 1931), 48, 49, 14, 71. For Callière's intention to send the Natives against the Connecticut River settlements, see "Propositions made by the River Indians to his Excell^{cy} Edward Cornbury Captn General & governor in Cheiffe &c in Albany the 13 of August 1702," *NYCD*, 4:996. For lack of resources, see NAC, C11A, 20:160.

11. *DCB*, 2:565–568.

12. Governor Vaudreuil quoted in Havard, *Great Peace of Montreal*, 181; Vaudreuil à Pontchartrain, 17 novembre, 1704, NAC, C11A 22:37; Hammang, *Vaudreuil*, 118–120; Zoltvany, *Vaudreuil*, 46–53.

13. Hammang, *Vaudreuil*, 111–113, 139; Zoltvany, *Vaudreuil*, 45–46. The comments by Champigny on a dispatch from Vaudreuil and the Intendant Beauharnois dated 17, novembre, 1703, NAC, C11A 21:51, have been erroneously attributed to Pontchartrain because of a misleading version of the memorandum published in *NYCD*, 9:755. Pontchartrain's own comments, which were not reproduced in the version in *NYCD*, make it clear that he disagreed with Champigny's critical assessment of Vaudreuil's actions. Pontchartrain disagreed with Champigny and supported Vaudreuil. See Pontchartrain à Vaudreuil, 20 juin, 1703, NAC, B 23:210–211. Among those historians who have been misled by the version in *NYCD* are Francis Parkman and George Sheldon. See Francis Parkman, *Half-Century of Conflict, vol. 2 of France and England in North America* (New York: Library of America, 1983), 404, George Sheldon, *A History of Deerfield, Massachusetts* (Deerfield: privately printed, 1895–1896), 1:286–287. For more on this confusion, see Hammang, *Vaudreuil*, 121–122.

14. Ian K. Steele, *Warpaths: Invasions of North America* (New York: Oxford University Press, 1994), 77. Estimate of Canadian losses in Jóse António Brandâo, *"Your fyre shall burn no more": Iroquois Policy toward New France and Its Native Allies to 1701* (Lincoln: University of Nebraska Press, 1997), 93; Robert Larin, *Brève Histoire du peuplement européen en Nouvelle-France* (Sillery: Septentrion, 2000), 148.

15. Lorraine Gadoury, *La Noblesse de Nouvelle-France: Familles et alliances,* (Montreal: Hurtubise HMH, 1991), 7–52, 64–71, 156; Miquelon, *New France,* 240–241; Jay Cassel, "Troupes de la Marine," 142–151. In France nobles appear to have constituted .75 percent to 1.5 percent of the population. See Gail Bossenga, "Society," in *Old Regime France, 1648–1788,* ed. William Doyle (New York: Oxford University Press, 2001), 57; Pierre Goubert, *The Ancien Régime,* trans. Steve Cox (New York: Harper & Row, 1973), 167; Fernand Braudel and Ernest Labrousse, eds., *Histoire économique et sociale de la France* (Paris: Presses Universitaires de France, 1970–1980), 2:607.

16. For the presence of De Rouville and three or four of his brothers, see Charlevoix, *History,* 5:161; [François Hertel] "Mémoire des services du Sr. Hertel père et de ses enfants," *Canadian Antiquarian and Numismatic Journal,* 2nd. ser. 1, no. 1 (July 1889): 8. The specific identities of De Rouville's brothers are surmised from their ages and subsequent military service. For the presence of Boucher, see *DCB,* 3:81–82. For the presence of the Gaultiers, see NAC, D2C57:28; Estelle Mitchell, *Messire Pierre Boucher (écuyer) Seigneur de*

Boucherville, 1622–1717 (Montreal: Librairie Beauchemin, 1967), 294–295. For the presence of Legardeur, see "Memoire," NAC, E 199:150–151.

17. Eccles, "Military Establishment," 115; Cassel, "Troupes de la Marine," 57–58, 79–81, 136, 145–146; Chartrand, *Canadian Military Heritage,* 84–86, 144–145; C. J. Russ, "Les Troupes de la Marine, 1683–1713" (master's thesis, McGill University, 1973), 133–143. For the characterization of the appointment of cadets as welfare, see Cassel, "Troupes de la Marine," 146 n. 7; Russ, "Troupes de la Marine," 141. Ignace Boucher served for seven years in the *troupes* and spent 900 livres of his own money on one company after another without receiving a regular commission. Eventually he resigned. See [Pierre Boucher], "Memoires de feu Monsieur Boucher, Seigneur de Boucherville, et ancien gouverneur des Trois-Rivières," *Bulletin des recherches historiques,* 1926, 404.

18. Hammang, *Vaudreuil,* 30 n. 7; Zoltvany, *Vaudreuil,* 99n; Charlevoix, *History,* 5:20–21; Cassel, "Troupes de la Marine," 57–58, 75–79, 105–106, 517 n. 1; Russ, "Troupes de la Marine," 133–143. See also John A. Lynn, *Giant of the Grand Siècle: The French Army, 1610–1715* (New York: Cambridge University Press, 1997), 227–228.

19. The identities of 94 of the officers in the *troupes* in 1701 and their places of birth were obtained from Pierre-Georges Roy, *Les Petites Choses de nôtre histoire,* 3rd. ser. (Lévis, 1922), 154–172. This list does not include the approximately 28 *enseignes en second.* Cassel cites 30 percent for the proportion of Canadian-born officers during the period 1701 to 1705, but his calculation apparently does not take into account the *enseignes en second,* who were overwhelmingly Canadian born. See Cassel, "Troupes de la Marine," 77, table 2. See also Russ, "Troupes de la Marine," 144–145. For France, see John Charles Roger Childs, *Armies and Warfare in Europe, 1648–1789* (New York: Holmes and Meier, 1982), 81. For Spanish comparisons, see Max L. Moorhead, *The Presidio: Bastion of the Spanish Borderlands* (Norman: University of Oklahoma Press, 1975), 182; Vito Alessio Robles, ed., *Diario y Derrotero de lo Caminado, Visito y Observado en la Visita que hizo a los Presidios de la Nueva Espana Septentrional el Bridagier Pedro de Rivera,* Archivo Historico Militar Mexicano, no. 2 (Mexico: Taller Autografico, 1946), 200–201. For English comparison, see Stanley Pargellis, "The Four Independent Companies of New York," in *Essays in Colonial History Presented to Charles McLean Andrews* (New Haven, Conn.: Yale University Press, 1931), 99, 101; Chartrand, *Canadian Military Heritage,* 165–166. The ratio of officers to men in a rifle company in the United States Army today is about 1 to 30. We are indebted to Captain Evan Wollen, U.S. Army, for this information. On soldiers' inability to name their officers see Cassel, "Troupes de la Marine," 132.

20. On the 1708 Haverhill raid there were six *enseignes en pied* and six *enseignes en second* and at least three cadets. In addition there were two other officers and one hundred men. Cassel also believes that "of all groups in the colony, both marines and militia, these men [the cadets] probably had the most experience in guerila warfare and the greatest familiarity with the territory." Cassel, "Troupes de la Marine," 136. For a later period, see Theodore G. Corbett, *A Clash of Cultures on the Warpath of Nations: The Colonial Wars in the Hudson-Champlain Valley* (Fleichmanns, N.Y.: Purple Mountain Press, 2002), 129.

21. Hammang, *Vaudreuil,* 83, 89–108. On the economy, see Robin Briggs, *Early Modern France, 1560–1725,* 2nd ed. (New York: Oxford University Press, 1998), 71; Miquelon, *New France,* 3, 55–76, 127–128, 261; Gadoury, *Noblesse de Nouvelle-France,* 33–36, 71–73, 85, 154, 167; Allan Greer, *The People of New France* (Toronto: University of Toronto Press, 1997), 51–52. On the role of seniority, see Cassel, "Troupes de la Marine," 76, 107–109.

22. The total of eleven ennobled Canadian families is from Gadoury, *Noblesse de Nouvelle-France*, 29–32, 167.

23. [Boucher], "Memoires," 398–400; *DCB*, 2:82–86. Such intermarriage was very rare in the Laurentian heartland. See Louise Dechêne, *Habitants and Merchants in Seventeenth Century Montreal*, trans. Liana Vardi (Montreal and Kingston: McGill-Queen's University Press, 1992), 14–15.

24. [Boucher], "Memoires," 401; *DCB*, 2:85.

25. Peter N. Moogk, *La Nouvelle France: The Making of French Canada—A Cultural History* (East Lansing: Michigan State University Press, 2000), 53–86; Jack Verney, *The Good Regiment: The Carignan-Salières Regiment in Canada, 1665–1668* (Montreal and Kingston: McGill-Queen's University Press, 1991), 110.

26. Richard Colebrook Harris, *The Seigneurial System in Early Canada: A Geographical Study* (Madison: University of Wisconsin Press, 1966), 79–97, 169; Miquelon, *New France*, 194–197; Greer, *People of New France*, 37–40. On rank and economic status, see Dechêne, *Habitants and Merchants*, 233–34; Moogk, *La Nouvelle France*, 160, 173; Yves F. Zoltvany, *The Government of New France: Royal, Clerical, or Class Rule* (Scarborough, Ont.: Prentice-Hall of Canada, 1971), 101. See also Louis Lavallée, *La Prairie en Nouvelle-France, 1647–1760* (Montreal and Kingston: McGill-Queen's University Press, 1992), 105–106.

27. Harris, *Seigneurial System*, 81–97, 169; Miquelon, *New France*, 197; Moogk, *La Nouvelle France*, 211–212; Dechêne, *Habitants and Merchants*, 216, 234. For the tightening of the seigneurial system in the eighteenth century, see Dechêne, *Habitants and Merchants*, 142–143, Lavallée, *La Prairie*, 96–101; Allan Greer, *Peasant, Lord, and Merchant: Rural Society in Three Quebec Parishes, 1740–1840* (Toronto: University of Toronto Press, 1985), 89–139.

28. *DCB*, 2:86. The identity of the original settlers and the genealogical data on which our calculations were based came from G. Robert Gareau, *Premières Concessions d'habitations, 1673, Boucherville* (Montreal: Société d'histoire des Îles Percées, 1973); *Pionniers et pionnières des débuts de Boucherville jusqu'à 1700* (Boucherville: Société d'histoire des Îles Percées, 1992); René Jetté, *Dictionnaire généalogique des familles du Québec* (Montreal: Les Presses de l'Université de Montréal, 1983). On immigration to New France, see Moogk, *La Nouvelle France*, 87–120; Hubert Charbonneau, *The First Canadians: Pioneers in the St. Lawrence Valley* (Newark: University of Delaware Press, 1993), esp. 31–40, 70, 97–98. See also Larin, *Brève Histoire*, 92, 105. For 1698 population figures, see *Censuses of Canada, 1665 to 1871* (Ottawa: I. B. Taylor, 1876), 4:40. For the assessment of Boucherville, see Harris, *Seigneurial System*, 104, 113; *DCB*, 2:86. For the characterization of the Bouchers as "quite well-to-do," see William Bennett Munro, *The Seignorial System in Canada: A Study in French Canadian Policy* (New York: Longmans, Green, 1907), 173n. 4.

29. Pierre Boucher, *True and Genuine Description of New France, Commonly Called Canada, and of the Manners and Customs and Productions of that Country*, trans. and ed. E. L. Montizambert (1881), 81. Dechêne, *Habitants and Merchants*, 144–151; Greer, *Peasant, Lord, and Merchant*, 8–13, 25, 88, 97–103; Harris, *Seigneurial System*, 196; "La Commune," 25 août, 1698, Familles Boucher, Archives du Séminaire de Trois-Rivières.

30. Jetté, *Dictionnaire généalogique*, 136–140; *DCB*, 1:109, 326–327, 2:86–87.

31. *DCB*, 3:81.

32. [Hertel], "Mémoire des services," 6; *DCB*, 2:282.

33. [Hertel], "Mémoire des services," 7–8; Charlevoix, *History*, 4:145–147; Char-

trand, *Canadian Military Heritage*, 90–105; *DCB*, 2:283–284; Jetté, *Dictionnaire généalogique*, 566–567.

34. Memoire à Frontenac, 21 mai, 1698, *RAPQ*, 1928–1929, 359; *DCB*, 2:283. For the characterization of the Hertels as poor, see Munro, *Seignorial System*, 173–174. See also Cassel, "Troupes de la Marine," 150–151; Gadoury, *Noblesse de Nouvelle-France*, 36.

35. *DCB*, 2:284–286.

36. Guy Frégault, *Canadian Society in the French Regime* (Ottawa: Canadian Historical Association, 1981), 8. See also, Steele, *Warpaths*, 77; However, one should not exaggerate their influence on policy; see Cassel, "Troupes de la Marine," 495–497. One hundred and twenty-six of the 170 nobles who arrived in New France and remained were officers or soldiers. See Gadoury, *Noblesse de Nouvelle-France*, 51.

37. Armstrong Starkey, *European and Native American Warfare, 1675–1815* (Norman: University of Oklahoma Press, 1998), 43.

38. William J. Eccles, *The French in North America, 1500–1783*, rev. ed. (Markham, Ont.: Fitzhenry & Whiteside, 1998), 123. On irregular or partisan warfare in late seventeenth-century Europe and the use of *compagnies franches* or independent companies, see Brent Nosworthy, *The Anatomy of Victory: Battle Tactics, 1689–1763* (New York: Hippocrene, 1990), 210–216; Lynn, *Giant of the* Grand Siècle, 538–546.

39. Champigny quoted in William J. Eccles, *Frontenac, the Courtier Governor* (1959; Toronto: McClelland and Stewart, 1968), 215; Cassel, "Troupes de la Marine," 57–58, 99, 103, 131–135, 197, 492; Russ, "Troupes de la Marine," 200–201; Chartrand, *Canadian Military Heritage*, 186.

40. Eccles, *Frontenac*, 214–22, 252; Cassel, "Troupes de la Marine," 135. Thirty of the one hundred men on Iberville's expedition were enlisted men from the *troupes;* see George F. Stanley, *Canada's Soldiers: The Military History of an Unmilitary People* (Toronto: Macmillan, 1974), 33. Nineteen of the 110 Frenchmen on the Schenectady raid were men from the *troupes;* see Lawrence H. Leder, ed., *The Livingston Indian Records, 1666–1723* (Gettysburg: Pennsylvania Historical Association, 1956), 158. On French recruiting for raids at this time, see also Hubert Charbonneau, "Du Saint-Laurent au Mississippi: Les compagnons d'Iberville," *Mémoires de la Société Généalogique Canadienne-Française* 51–1, no. 223 (2000): 41–67.

41. Charlevoix, *History*, 5:9; Cassel, "Troupes de la Marine," 524–526; Jay Cassel, "The Militia Legend: Canadians at War, 1665–1760," in *Canadian Military History since the Seventeenth Century*, ed. Yves Temblay (Ottawa, 2001), 3–5.

42. *DCB*, 2:283; Chartrand, *Canadian Military Heritage*, 96; [Lahontan], *New Voyages*, 1:51. For the destination of captives, see Emma Lewis Coleman, *New England Captives Carried to Canada between 1677 and 1760 during the French and Indian Wars* (Portland, Maine: Southworth Press, 1925), 2:68, 71, 74, 83, 125, 127.

43. Chartrand, *Canadian Military Heritage*, 91–100; Cassel, "Canadian Militia Legend," 4; Dechêne, *Habitants and Merchants*, 119–122; 370n. 134. Dechêne suggests that one-third of the men in western New France may have participated in the fur trade (120). For estimate for all of New France of 18 percent, see Miquelon, *New France*, 156. See also Hubert Charbonneau, Bertrand Desjardins, and Pierre Beauchamp, "Le Comportement démographique des voyageurs sous le régime français," *Histoire sociale / Social History* 21 (1978): 120–133.

44. Vaudreuil's biographers also conclude that his primary purpose was to retain the support of New France's allies; see Hammang, *Vaudreuil*, 105; Zoltvany, *Vaudreuil*, 78.

CHAPTER 3: NATIVES AND MISSIONS

1. Quotation from Samuel Penhallow, *History of the Indian Wars,* ed. Edward Whee-lock (1726; 1924; reprint, Williamstown, Mass.: Corner House, 1973), 29. On the relative autonomy of the mission villages, see Dennis Delâge, "Hurons de Lorette," in *Les Hurons de Lorette,* ed. Denis Vaugeois (Sillery: Septentrion, 1996), 109–110; Allan Greer, *The People of New France* (Toronto: University of Toronto Press, 1997), 79–80; Gilles Havard, *The Great Peace of Montreal of 1701: French-Native Diplomacy in the Seventeenth Century,* trans. Phyllis Aronoff and Howard Scott (Montreal and Kingston: McGill-Queen's University Press, 2001), 37; Peter N. Moogk, *La Nouvelle France: The Making of French Canada—A Cultural History* (East Lansing: Michigan State University Press, 2000), 43–44.

2. Marc Jetten, *Enclaves amérindiennes: Les 'reductions' du Canada, 1637–1701* (Sillery: Septentrion, 1994), 34–45.

3. This paragraph is a crude summary of an increasingly sophisticated literature on conversion in New France. Among the most relevant works we have consulted are François-Marc Gagnon, *La Conversion par l'image: Un Aspect de la mission des Jésuites auprès des Indiens du Canada au XVIIème siècle* (Montreal: Bellarmin, 1975); James Axtell, *The Invasion Within: The Contest of Cultures in Colonial North America* (New York: Oxford University Press, 1985), 91–127; Bruce Trigger, *The Children of Aataentsic: A History of the Huron People to 1660* (Montreal and Kingston: McGill-Queen's University Press, 1987), 2:699–704; Kenneth M. Morrison, "Towards a History of Intimate Encounters: Algonkian Folklore, Jesuit Missionaries, and Kiwakwe, the Cannibal Giant," *American Indian Culture and Research Journal* 3, no. 4 (1979): 51–80; Kenneth M. Morrison, "Montagnais Missionization in Early New France: The Syncretic Imperative," *American Indian Culture and Research Journal* 10, no. 3 (1986): 1–23; Kenneth M. Morrison, "Baptism and Alliance: The Symbolic Mediations of Religious Syncretism," *Ethnohistory* 37, no. 4 (1990): 416–437; Jocelyn "Tehatarongantase" Paul, "Croyances religieuses et changement social chez les Hurons de Lorette" (master's thesis, University of Montreal, 1991); John Steckley, "The Warrior and the Lineage: Jesuit Use of Iroquoian Images to Communicate Christianity," *Ethnohistory* 39, no 4 (1992): 478–507; Jetten, *Enclaves amérindiennes,* 89–121.

4. Cornelius J. Jaenen, *Friend and Foe: Aspects of French-Amerindian Culture Contact in the Sixteenth and Seventeenth Centuries* (Toronto: McClelland and Stewart, 1976), 41–83; Trigger, *Children of Aataentsic,* 2:699–723; Paul, "Croyances religieuses," 5–22. For another use of this critique from beyond the grave, see John Williams, "The Redeemed Captive Returning to Zion," in *Puritans among the Indians: Accounts of Captivity and Redemption, 1676–1724,* ed. Alden T. Vaughan and Edward W. Clark (Cambridge: Harvard University Press, 1981), 201.

5. Anne Marie Blouin, "Histoire et iconographie des Hurons de Lorette du XVIIè au XIXè siècle" (Ph.D. thesis, University of Montreal, 1987), 93–107; Trigger, *Children of Aataentsic,* 2:725–797, 820–825.

6. Daniel Richter, "War and Culture: The Iroquois Experience," *William and Mary Quarterly,* 3rd ser., 40 (1985): 528–559.

7. Richter, "War and Culture," 528–559.

8. Blouin, "Histoire et iconographie," 217–255; Trigger, *Children of Aataentsic,* 2:797–820. For differences between Algonkians and Hurons in the Sillery mission, see Léon

Gérin, "La Seigneurie de Sillery et les Hurons de Lorette," *Bulletin des recherches historiques* 13, no. 10 (1907): 73–115, esp. 96–97.

9. James P. Ronda "The Sillery Experiment: A Jesuit-Indian Village in New France, 1637–1663," *American Indian Culture and Research Journal* 3, no. 1 (1979): 1–18; Blouin, "Histoire et iconographie," 217–277; Lucien Campeau, "Roman Catholic Missions in New France," in *History of Indian-White Relations*, ed. Wilcomb E. Washburn, vol. 4 of *Handbook of North American Indians*, ed. William C. Sturtevant (Washington, D.C.: Smithsonian Institution, 1988), 468–469.

10. Le Roy Bacqueville de la Pothèrie, *Histoire de l'Amérique Septentrionale: Relation d'un séjour en Nouvelle-France* (1722; reprint, Monaco: Rocher, 1997), 2:486.

11. Campeau, "Roman Catholic Missions," 468–469. On the Hurons' Lorette, see Blouin, "Histoire et iconographie," 255–307; Gérin, "La Seigneurie de Sillery," 73–115; Christian Morisonneau, "Huron of Lorette," in *Northeast*, ed. Bruce Trigger, vol. 15 of Sturtevant, *Handbook of North American Indians*, 389–393; Cornelius J. Jaenen, "Some Unresolved Issues: Lorette Hurons in the Colonial Context," in *Essays in French Colonial History: Proceedings of the 21st Annual Meeting of the French Colonial Historical Society*, ed. A. J. B. Johnston (East Lansing: Michigan State University Press, 1997), 111–125. For the Sulpicians' Lorette, see Campeau, "Roman Catholic Missions," 468–469; Julia Boss, "'To honor there the holy house': Creating a Place of Pilgrimage at Notre Dame de Lorette" (paper presented at the annual conference of the Omohundro Institute for Early American History and Culture, Austin, Texas, June 12, 1999); Louise Tremblay, "La Politique missionnaire des Sulpiciens au XVIIè et début du XVIIIè siècle, 1668–1735" (master's thesis, University of Montreal, 1981), 57.

12. *JR*, 66:147–153, 157.

13. *JR*, 66:153; Paul, "Croyances religieuses," 42–67, 83–97. On the Jesuits' efforts to render Christianity compatible with Iroquoian cultural concerns, see Steckley, "Warrior and the Lineage," 478–507. On the Huron Feast of the Dead, see *JR*, 10, pt. 2:265–305.

14. *JR*, 66:173. On Louis D'Avaugour's career, which took him to the Illinois country and then to Paris as procurator for the Jesuits in Canada and Louisiana after his service at Lorette (1705–c.1720), see *DCB*, 2:40–41.

15. *JR*, 66:165–171. The name Thaovenhosen most likely resulted from mishearing and a faulty transcription. There is no "v" in the Huron language. Thaovenhosen is probably a variant of Tsaouenhohoui, Saouhenhohi, or Isawanhoni. These were the names of Huron leaders from later periods of the community's history. See Blouin, "Histoirie et iconographie," 249, 270; Colin Coates, *The Metamorphoses of Landscape and Community in Early Quebec* (Montreal and Kingston: McGill-Queen's University Press, 2000), 162.

16. *JR*, 66:159–161, 169.

17. Morisonneau, "Huron of Lorette," 389–390; Gédéon de Catalogne, "Report on the Seigniories and Settlements in the Districts of Quebec, Three Rivers, and Montreal," in *Documents Relating to the Seignorial Tenure in Canada 1598–1854*, ed. William Bennett Munro (Toronto: Champlain Society, 1908), 132; Alain Beaulieu, "Les Hurons de Lorette, le 'traité Murray' et la liberté de commerce," in *Les Hurons de Lorette*, ed. Denis Vaugeois (Sillery: Septentrion, 1996), 266–260; Marcel Trudel, "Les Hurons et Murray en 1760," in Vaugeois, *Les Hurons de Lorette*, 141–145.

18. An observer noted that there were "about thirty warriors" at Lorette in 1709. *Letters from North America*, trans. Ivy Alice Dickson (Belleville, Ont.: Mika, 1980), 218.

19. Axtell, *Invasion Within*, 40; Moogk, *La Nouvelle France*, 255–256; Patricia Simpson, *Marguerite Bourgeoys and Montreal, 1640–1665* (Montreal and Kingston: McGill-Queen's University Press, 1997), 66–185; Louise Dechêne, *Habitants and Merchants in Seventeenth Century Montreal*, trans. Liana Vardi (Montreal and Kingston: McGill-Queen's University Press, 1992), 7, 47–67, 90–96.

20. *JR*, 63:181, 60:277–87. On the settlement of La Montagne, see Gretchen Green, "A New People in an Age of War: The Kahnawake Iroquois, 1667–1760" (Ph.D. diss., College of William and Mary, 1991)," 42–44; William N. Fenton and Elizabeth Tooker, "Mohawk," in *Northeast*, ed. Bruce Trigger, vol. 15 of *Handbook of North American Indians*, ed. William C. Sturtevant (Washington, D.C.: Smithsonian Institution); 472–73 and Dechêne, *Habitants and Merchants*, 6–10; Tremblay, "La Politique missionnaire," 48–60, 158; Jan Grabowski, "The Common Ground: Settled Natives and French in Montreal, 1667–1760" (Ph.D. diss., University of Montreal, 1993), app. 1, 330–358. For Grey Lock living near Mount Royal in the early 1700s, see Josiah H. Temple and George Sheldon, *A History of the Town of Northfield, Massachusetts for 150 Years* (Albany, N.Y.: Joel Munsell, 1875), 194.

21. Both quotations from Dechêne, *Habitants and Merchants*, 9; Campeau, "Roman Catholic Missions," 468–469; Grabowski, "Common Ground," 288–296. On the weakening of the assimilationist program at Jesuit missions, see Greer, *People of New France*, 80–84. Not all Sulpicians agreed with Belmont. See Tremblay, "La Politique missionnaire," 61–70.

22. Campeau, "Roman Catholic Missions," 468–469. On Marguerite Bourgeoys and the Congregation de Notre Dame in the seventeenth century, see *DCB*, 1:115–119; William Henry Foster III, "Women at the Centers, Men at the Margins: The Wilderness Mission of the Secular Sisters of Early Montreal Reconsidered," in *Women and Religion in Old and New Worlds*, ed. Susan E. Dinan and Debra Myers (New York: Routledge, 2001), 93–112. On the Sulpician missions and the Congrégation de Notre-Dame's involvement with them, see Dechêne, *Habitants and Merchants*, 10–13; Charles-P. Beaubien, *Le Sault-au-Récollet: Ses rapports avec les premiers temps de la colonie* (Montreal: C. O. Beauchemin & Fils, 1898), 93–224.

23. Quoting l'abbé Cuoq, *Mémoires*, in Beaubien, *Le Sault-au-Récollet*, 154. See also Tremblay, "La Politique missionnaire," 70–74. On the Cult of the Virgin's popularity, especially among Iroquoians, see William B. Hart, "'The Kindness of the Blessed Virgin': Faith, Succour, and the Cult of Mary among Christian Hurons and Iroquois in Seventeenth-Century New France," in *Spiritual Encounters: Interactions between Christianity and Native Religion in Colonial America*, ed. Nicholas Griffiths and Fernando Cervantes (Lincoln: University of Nebraska Press, 1999), 65–90.

24. Catalonge, "Report on the Seigniories," 101; Dechêne, *Habitants and Merchants*, 10–13; Tremblay, "La Politique missionnaire," 50–51, 94, 159.

25. Tremblay, "La Politique missionnaire," 94–98. Campeau, "Roman Catholic Missions," 468–469; Boss, "'To honor there the holy house'"; Tremblay, "La Politique missionnaire," 57. On the Sulpician priests, see *DCB*, 2:641–642, 3:542–543.

26. Tremblay, "La Politique Missionnaire," 89–98.

27. Green, "New People," 177; *DCB*, 2:241; *Letters from North America*, 219, reports forty Iroquois and thirty Algonkin warriors at the Sault-au-Récollet in 1709. See also Tremblay, "La Politique missionnaire," 70–74.

28. John Demos, *The Unredeemed Captive: A Family Story from Early America* (New York: Knopf, 1994), 137–138; Grabowski, "Common Ground," 65–66.

29. Quotation from Vaudreuil et Radot au ministre, 13 novembre, 1708, NAC, C11A 28:62. The number of warriors is from *Letters from North America*, 219. On the complex relations among Kahnawake, the League Iroquois, the French, and the English in the 1680s and 1690s, see Green, "New People," 68–168; Daniel K. Richter, *The Ordeal of the Longhouse: The Peoples of the Iroquois League in the Era of European Colonization* (Chapel Hill: University of North Carolina Press, 1992), 144–213.

30. Catalonge, "Report on the Seigniories," 108–109; Demos, *Unredeemed Captive*, 160–161, 131–134. On the Albany-Montreal fur trade, see Jan Grabowski, "Les Amérindiens domiciliés et la 'contrebande' des fourreures en Nouvelle France," *Recherches amérindiennes au Québec* 24, no. 3 (1994): 45–52; Jean Lunn, "The Illegal Fur Trade out of New France, 1713–1760," *Canadian Historical Association Annual Report*, (1939), 61–76; Francis H. Hammang, *The Marquis de Vaudreuil: New France at the Beginning of the Eighteenth Century Part I* (Bruges and Louvain: Louvain University, 1938), 182–183; Gerald R. Alfred, *Heeding the Voices of Our Ancestors: Kahnawake Mohawk Politics and the Rise of Native Nationalism* (Toronto: Oxford University Press, 1995), 43–47. See also Peter MacLeod, *The Canadian Iroquois and the Seven Years' War* (Toronto: Dundurn Press, 1996), 16, 19–20.

31. Catalonge, "Report on the Seigniories," 108–109; Demos, *Unredeemed Captive*, 120–131; Alfred, *Heeding the Voices*, 25, 38; Dechêne, *Habitants and Merchants*, 13; Jetten, *Enclaves amérindiennes*, 92–93; Greer, *People of New France*, 80–84; David Blanchard, ". . . To the Other Side of the Sky: Catholicism at Kahnawake, 1667–1700," *Anthropologica* 24 (1982): 90, 92–97; James Smith, "Of the Remarkable Occurrences in the Life and Travels of Colonel James Smith," in *Indian Captivities; or, Life in the Wigwam*, ed. Samuel G. Drake (1851; reprint, Bowie, Md.: Heritage Books, 1995), 206, 255.

32. *JR*, 63:167; Pierre-François-Xavier de Charlevoix, *History and General Description of New France*, trans. and ed. John Gilmary Shea (1870; reprint, Chicago: Loyola University Press, 1962), 4:123; Alfred, *Heeding the Voices*, 33–43.

33. Green, "New People in an Age of War," 82–91, 112–113, 121–122, 132–135, 141–143, 149, 166.

34. See sources cited in n. 33.

35. Green, "New People," 98–108; Peter Mancall, *Deadly Medicine: Indians and Alcohol in Early America* (Ithaca, N.Y.: Cornell University Press, 1995); George F. G. Stanley, "The Indians and the Brandy Trade during the French Regime," *Revue d'histoire de l'Amerique française* 6, no. 4 (1953): 489–505. For an excellent discussion of the liquor trade and its consequences in Montreal, see Grabowski, "Common Ground," 193–245.

36. George Sheldon, *A History of Deerfield, Massachusetts* (Deerfield: privately printed, 1895–1896), 1:254–256.

37. Vaudreuil à Pontchartrain, 3 avril, 1704, NAC, C11A 22:32. See also Zoltvany, *Vaudreuil*, 48, 76–77; Richter, *Ordeal of the Longhouse*, 218.

38. Charles B. de Saileville, "A History of the Life and Captivity of Miss Eunice Williams, Alias, Madam De Roguers, Who Was Styled 'The Fair Captive,'" [1842], Neville Public Museum (microfilm, State Historical Society of Wisconsin, Area Research Center, Green Bay), reel 7, 27–29.

39. Evan Haefeli and Kevin Sweeney, "Revisting *The Redeemed Captive:* New Perspectives on the 1704 Attack on Deerfield," *William and Mary Quarterly,* 3rd ser., 52, no. 1 (January 1995): 41; *Letters from North America,* 219, finds "about 190 warriors" at Kahnawake.

40. On the identity of the Abenakis on the Deerfield raid, see Haefeli and Sweeney, "Revisiting *The Redeemed Captive,*" 10–30.

41. Colin Calloway, *The Western Abenaki of Vermont, 1600–1800: War, Migration, and the Survival of an Indian People* (Norman: University of Oklahoma Press, 1990), 55–75.

42. Gordon M. Day, "The Identity of the Saint Francis Indians," Canadian Ethnology Service Paper no. 71, Ottawa, 1981, 1–5, 16–21.

43. Day, "Identity of the Saint Francis Indians," 21–25; Haefeli and Sweeney, "Revisiting *The Redeemed Captive,*" 10–15, 19–21, 25–26.

44. Williams, "Redeemed Captive," 185–186; Haefeli and Sweeney, "Revisiting *The Redeemed Captive,*" 18–19.

45. Thomas Charland, *Les Abénakis d'Odanak* (Montreal: Lévrier, 1964), 32–36, 50; Cotton Mather, "New Assaults from the Indians," in Vaughan and Clark, *Puritans among the Indians,* 137. On the importance of personal relationships, see Kenneth M. Morrison, *The Embattled Northeast: The Elusive Ideal of Alliance in Abenaki-Euroamerican Relations* (Berkeley: University of California Press, 1984), 31, 70–71, 102, 127, 136.

46. Day, "Identity of the Saint Francis Indians," 31–33; "Concession par Madame Crevier et son fils aux sauvages Abenakis et Sokokis," 23 août, 1700, Henri Vassal Collection, F249/D4/2/1, and Accord, February 29, 1712, Henri Vassal Collection, F249/D3/10/10, Archives du Séminaire de Nicolet; [Stephen Williams], *Narrative of the Captivity of Stephen Williams,* ed. George Sheldon (Deerfield, Mass., 1889), 10; Jeremy Belknap, *The History of New Hampshire,* 2nd ed. (Dover, N.H.: O. Crosby and J. Varncy, 1813), 1:204. See also Emma Lewis Coleman, *New England Captives Carried to Canada between 1677 and 1760 during the French and Indian Wars* (Portland, Maine: Southworth Press, 1925), 1:168.

47. *Letters from North America,* 218.

48. For characterization of missions as "strongholds surrounded by stones," see *Letters from North America,* 218.

CHAPTER 4: BETWEEN EMPIRES

1. Gordon Day, "Western Abenaki," in *Northeast,* ed. Bruce Trigger, vol. 15 of *Handbook of North American Indians,* ed. William C. Sturtevant (Washington, D.C.: Smithsonian Institution, 1978), 148–159; Colin G. Calloway, "Wanalancet and Kancagamus [*sic*]: Indian Strategy on the New Hampshire Frontier," *Historical New Hampshire* 43 (winter 1988): 264–270. The most recent treatment of the Pennacooks is David Stewart-Smith, "The Pennacook Indians and the New England Frontier, circa 1604–1733" (Ph.D. diss., Union Institute, Cincinnati, Ohio, 1998). In this book the Pigwackets, who are often treated as a distinct people, are considered to be Pennacooks whose home village was Pigwacket. In this we follow David Stewart-Smith, who considers the Western Abenaki-speaking peoples at Pennacook, Pigwacket, Ossipee, and Winnipesaukee to be an identifiable group that he calls the Central Abenaki. We refer to them as Pennacooks to provide clarity and because we believe it is more in line with period usage. Stewart-Smith, "Pennacook Indians," 1–45. We also include Cowass or Cowassuck in this group of Pen-

nacook villages. Even though Sokokis (who were Western-Abenaki-speakers) or the Mahicans (who were not Abenaki-speakers) may have established this village that was located near present-day Newbury, Vermont, it was primarily if not exclusively a Pennacook community from at least 1690 to 1710. On this categorization of Cowass, see Evan Haefeli and Kevin Sweeney, "Revisiting *The Redeemed Captive:* New Perspectives on the 1704 Attack on Deerfield," *William and Mary Quarterly,* 3rd. ser., 52, no. 1 (January 1995): 29.

2. For the identification of Wattanummon as the captor of Stephen Williams, who was taken prisoner at Deerfield in 1704, and for evidence of the presence of Pennacooks on the Deerfield raid, see George Sheldon, *A History of Deerfield, Massachusetts* (Deerfield: privately printed, 1895–1896), 1:381; Haefeli and Sweeney "Revisiting *The Redeemed Captive,*" 19–30.

3. Abiel Abbot, *History of Andover from Its Settlement to 1829* (Andover, Mass.: Flagg and Gould, 1829), 44; Daniel Gookin, *Historical Collections of the Indians in New England* (1792; reprint, New York: Arno Press, 1972), 8–9; Neal Salisbury, *Manitou and Providence: Indians, Europeans, and the Making of New England, 1500–1643* (New York: Oxford University Press, 1982), 105–106; Calloway, "Wanalancet and Kancagamus," 265–270.

4. Jere Daniell, *Colonial New Hampshire: A History* (Millwood, N.Y.: KTO, 1981), 3, 8–10; Gordon Day, "The Ouragie War: A Case History in Iroquois-New England Indian Relations," in *Extending the Rafters: Interdisciplinary Approaches to Iroquoian Studies,* ed. Michael K. Foster, Jack Campisi, and Marianne Mithun (Albany: State University of New York Press, 1984), 35–50; Neal Salisbury, "Toward the Covenant Chain: Iroquois and Southern New England Algonquians, 1637–1884," in *Beyond the Covenant Chain: The Iroquois and Their Neighbors in Indian North America,* ed. Daniel K. Richter and James H. Merrill (Syracuse, N.Y.: Syracuse University Press, 1987), 68; Peter Allen Thomas, "In the Maelstrom of Change: The Indian Trade and Cultural Process in the Middle Connecticut River Valley, 1635–1665" (Ph.D. diss., University of Massachusetts, 1979), 395.

5. Daniel Gookin, *An Historical Account of the Doings and Sufferings of the Christian Indians of New England, in the Years 1675, 1676, 1677* (1836; reprint, New York: Arno Press, 1972), 462–463; [William Hubbard], *The History of the Indian Wars in New England from the First Settlement to the Termination of the War with King Philip in 1677, from the Original Work by the Rev. William Hubbard,* Samuel Drake, ed. (1865; reprint, New York: Burt Franklin, 1971), 1:148, 2:209; Calloway, "Wanalancet and Kancagamus," 273–275; Colin Calloway, *The Western Abenakis of Vermont, 1600–1800: War, Migration, and the Survival of an Indian People* (Norman: University of Oklahoma Press, 1990), 81.

6. Mary Beth Norton, *In the Devil's Snare: The Salem Witchcraft Crisis of 1692* (New York: Knopf, 2002), 89–90; Samuel A. Drake, *The Border Wars of New England* (1897; reprint, Williamstown, Mass.: Corner House, 1973), 17–20; Calloway, "Wanalancet and Kancagamus," 275. In 1704 the Reverend John Williams of Deerfield would meet a Jesuit priest who "justified the Indians in what they did against us, rehearsing some things done by Major Waldron above thirty years ago, and how justly God retaliated them in the last war, and inveighed against us for beginning this war with the Indians. And said we had before the last winter, and in the winter, been very barbarous and cruel in burning and killing Indians." John Williams, "The Redeemed Captive Returning to Zion," in *Puritans among the Indians: Accounts of Captivity and Redemption, 1676–1724,* ed. Alden T. Vaughan and Edward W. Clark (Cambridge: Harvard University Press, 1981), 183. See also *CSP* 1704–1705, no. 120, 22:52.

7. Gordon Day, "The Identity of the St. Francis Indians," (Canadian Ethnology Service Paper no. 71, Ottawa, 1981), 16–25; Harald E. L. Prins, "Amesokanti: Abortive Tribeformation on the Colonial Frontier" (paper read at the annual meeting of the American Society for Ethnohistory, Williamsburg, Va., 1988, 4, 5–6; Calloway, "Wanalancet and Kancagamus," 270, 273–277, 281, 283; Peter S. Leavenworth, "'The Best Title That Indians Can Claime': Native Agency and Consent in the Transferral of Penacook-Pawtucket Land in the Seventeenth Century," New England Quarterly 72, no. 2 (June 1999): 293–300; Calloway, Western Abenakis, 81–83; Louis Armand de Lom d'Arce, Baron de Lahontan, New Voyages to North-America by Baron de Lahontan, ed. Reuben Gold Thwaites (Chicago: A. C. McClurg, 1905), 1:327–328. For the presence of the father of Kancamagus, who was a Pennacook living with the Androscoggins, and of Nescambiouit (Asacambuit), who was a Pigwacket living at Norridgwock, see Calloway, "Wanalancet and Kancagamus," 276; Drake, Border Wars of New England, 105n.1.

8. Gookin, Doings and Sufferings, 463, 520–521; Drake, Indian Wars of New England, 2:208–209; Calloway, "Wanalancet and Kancagamus," 270, 274–277, 283; Calloway, Western Abenakis, 81; Abbot, History of Andover, 44.

9. Calloway, "Wanalancet and Kancagamus, 276–282; PPNH, 1:583–585, 588–589.

10. Kenneth A. Morrison, The Embattled Northeast: The Elusive Ideal of Alliance in Abenaki-Euroamerican Relations (Berkeley: University of California Press, 1984), 113–114.

11. NYCD, 3:561–62; MA, 30:310–311, 119:243. See also Josiah H. Temple and George Sheldon, A History of the Town of Northfield, Massachusetts for 150 Years (Albany, N.Y.: Joel Munsell, 1875), 111–116.

12. Baxter Manuscripts, 6:429–430, 436, 440–442, 499; Calloway, "Wanalancet and Kancagamus," 282–283; DCB, 2:25; Jeremy Belknap, The History of New Hampshire (Dover N.H.: O. Crosby and J. Varncy, 1813), 1:198–201; Norton, In the Devil's Snare, 82–32; Drake, Border Wars of New England, 17–20; Emma Lewis Coleman, New England Captives Carried to Canada during the French and Indian Wars (Portland, Maine: Southworth Press, 1925), 1:137–164.

13. Morrison, Embattled Northeast, 115–117; Andros Tracts, ed. W. H. Whitemore, (Boston: Prince Society, 1867–1874), 1:41, 104, 151; Calloway, "Wanalancet and Kancagamus," 283. The two Pennacooks may very well have been referring to an actual transaction during the winter of 1675–1676 when Andros, then governor of New York, had enlisted the Mohawks' aid in the New England colonists' war with the followers of King Philip.

14. Baxter Manuscripts, 5:376–377; MA, 37:325; Calloway, "Wanalancet and Kancagamus," 285–286.

15. Morrison, Embattled Northeast, 128, 140–141; Drake, Border Wars of New England, 107–108, 111–112; PPNH, 2:110–112, 299–300; Baxter Manuscripts, 5:164–166; Calloway, "Wanalancet and Kancagamus," 284–285.

16. Abbot, History of Andover, 43–45; Claude Fuess, Andover: Symbol of New England— The Evolution of a Town (Portland, Maine: Anthoensen Press, 1959), 75–77.

17. MA, 30: 426, 450; CSP, 1700, nos. 167iii, 167x, 345, 1:95–96, 179–187; Baxter Manuscripts, 10:43–45, 63–65, 68–69; Calloway, Western Abenakis, 98–101. Calloway, noting that the confederates apparently planned to fight the English in 1700, claims that the "conspiracy proved abortive and the Indian gathering was probably never as large nor as hostile as the rumors suggested" ("Wanalancet and Kancagamus," 287). In principle he is probably right, but three years later the confederacy did play a role in pulling its

members into the War of the Spanish Succession. See also Morrison, *Embattled Northeast*, 147–148.

18. MA, 30:459, 476a–477, 480–483; *CSP*, 1700, no. 330, 18:171–172; *Baxter Manuscripts*, 10:87–95; Dale Miquelon, *New France, 1701–1744: "A Supplement to Europe"* (Toronto: McClelland and Stewart, 1987), 101.

19. *CSP*, 1702, nos. 810ii, 1009ii, 20:502–504, 642–43; *NYCD*, 4:996–997; Yves F. Zoltvany, *Philippe de Rigaud de Vaudreuil: Governor of New France, 1703–1725*, (Toronto: McClelland and Stewart, 1974), 41–42; Calloway, *Western Abenakis*, 101.

20. *Baxter Manuscripts*, 10:87–95; *CSP*, 1702, nos. 633, 810ii, 1061, 20:404, 504, 673; *CSP*, 1702–1703, no. 432, 21:246; MA, 30:459, 476a–477, 480–483.

21. *CSP*, 1702–1703, nos. 625, 694, 21:385, 421.

22. *CSP*, 1702–1703, no. 694, 21:421; Williams, "Redeemed Captive," 184; Morrison, *Embattled Northeast*, 154–158.

23. Samuel Penhallow, *History of the Indian Wars*, ed. Edward Wheelock (1726; 1924; reprint, Williamstown, Mass.: Corner House, 1973), 2–4; [Samuel Sewall], *Diary of Samuel Sewall*, in *Collections of the Massachusetts Historical Society*, 5th ser. (Boston, 1879), 6:85–87.

24. Penhallow, *Indian Wars*, 4–5 [Sewall], *Diary*, 6:87; *CSP*, 1702–1703, no. 898, 21:542–543. There is nothing in Governor Dudley's report on the conference or in the report in Samuel Sewall's diary that alludes to the plot later recounted by Penhallow.

25. Morrison, *Embattled Northeast*, 152–159; William Cronon, *Changes in the Land: Indians, Colonists, and the Ecology of New England* (New York: Hill and Wang, 1983), 94.

26. *Baxter Manuscripts*, 23:33–34; *CSP*, 1702–1703, nos. 898, 969, 996, 1025, 21:543, 583, 601, 640; Morrison, *Embattled Northeast*, 152–159.

27. Broullion quoted in Zoltvany, *Vaudreuil*, 42; *Baxter Manuscripts*, 23:33.

28. Morrison, *Embattled Northeast*, 146–156; Miquelon, *New France*, 26, 29; [Stephen Williams], *Narrative of the Captivity of Stephen Williams*, ed. George Sheldon (Deerfield, Mass., 1889), 10. Colin Calloway overstates the situation when he claims, "The influence of French priests was still predominant among the Pennacooks in 1700." Calloway, *Western Abenakis*, 48.

29. John G. Reid, "Unorthodox Warfare in the Northeast, 1703," *Canadian Historical Review* 73, no. 2 (1992): 211–220; Morrison, *Embattled Northeast*, 129; Williams, "Redeemed Captive," 184.

30. Vaudreuil et Beauharnois à Pontchartrain, 15 novembre 1703, NAC, C11, 21:51; Zoltvany, *Vaudreuil*, 45; Williams, "Redeemed Captive," 184. Ian K. Steele also sees the intervention by the Natives from Canada as playing a critical role. Steele, *Warpaths: Invasions of North America* (New York: Oxford University Press, 1994), 155. The presence of Abenakis from Odanak in Maine in summer 1703 is confirmed by John Williams, who saw at St. Francis in 1704, "several poor children who had been taken from the Eastward the summer before." Williams, "Redeemed Captive," 183.

31. Penhallow, *Indian Wars*, 5–9. The lower report of casualties is from Penhallow, *Indian Wars*, 5–8; the higher is from John Pike, "Journal," *Massachusetts Historical Society Proceedings, 1875–1876*, (1876), 135. Penhallow and others estimate that "upwards of five hundred Indians," besides the French, participated in these attacks. All sources agree that 200 Indians accompanied Beaubassin from Canada. Subtracting these 200 from the combined force of 500 leaves 300, which would be approximately two-thirds of the estimated "four hundred and fifty fighting Men from Penobscot, Westward." The estimate

of 450 fighting men is also from Penhallow, *History of the Indian Wars*, 60. Kenneth Morrison's assessment that "these Frenchmen, along with Micmac allies, found a few willing warriors among the Abenakis tribes" seriously underestimates involvement of Pennacooks and Eastern Abenakis in these raids during the summer of 1703. See Morrison, *Embattled Northeast*, 158.

32. Joseph Dudley, *A Declaration Against the Pennicooke and Eastern Indians, August 18, 1703* (Boston, 1703); Penhallow, *Indian Wars*, 8–10; *CSP*, 1702–1703, no. 1142, 21:726; Drake, *Border Wars of New England*, 165–166; Williams, "Redeemed Captive," 183. The Reverend John Pike indicates that the second expedition "towards Pegwakket" returned on October 30, 1703, and "brought in 6 Indian scalps & 5 Captives, all squaws and children (both killed and taken) except one old man." Pike, "Journal," 136.

33. Williams, "Redeemed Captive," 188; [Williams], *Narrative of the Captivity of Stephen Williams*, 6–9.

CHAPTER 5: WARNINGS

1. Samuel Penhallow, *History of the Indian Wars*, ed. Edward Wheelock (1726; 1924; reprint, Williamstown, Mass.: Corner House, 1973), 12; Thomas Hutchinson, *The History of the Colony and Province of Massachusetts-Bay*, ed. Lawrence Shaw Mayo (Cambridge: Harvard University Press, 1936), 2:103.

2. Joseph Dudley to Fitz-John Winthrop, Boston, May 27, 1703, *WP*, 129; Lord Cornbury to the Earl of Nottingham, New York, June 22, 1704, *NYCD*, 4:1099–1100. See also "Minutes of Council in Assembly of the Massachusetts Bay," May 26, 1703, *CSP*, 1702–1703, no. 739, 21:454; Patricia U. Bonomi, *The Lord Cornbury Scandal: The Politics of Reputation in British America* (Chapel Hill: University of North Carolina Press, 1998), 168–170.

3. Joseph Dudley to Fitz-John Winthrop, Boston, May 27, 1703, *WP*, 129; George Sheldon, *A History of Deerfield, Massachusetts* (Deerfield: privately printed, 1895–1896), 1:285; Everett Kimball, *The Public Life of Joseph Dudley: A Study of the Colonial Policy of the Stuarts in New England, 1660–1715* (New York: Longmans, Green, 1911), 134–135, 138–140, 143–151.

4. Fitz-John Winthrop to Joseph Dudley, June 9, 1703, *WP*, 131.

5. "Minutes of Council in Assembly of the Massachusetts Bay," July 29, 1703, *CSP*, 1702–1703, no. 969, 21:583.

6. Joseph Dudley to Fitz-John Winthrop, Boston, ult July 1703, *WP*, 137.

7. Samuel Partridge to Fitz-John Winthrop, Hatfield, August 10, 1703, Henry N. Flynt Library, Historic Deerfield, Inc.

8. Fitz-John Winthrop to John Chester, New London, August 12, 1703, *WP*, 138; John Chester to Fitz-John Winthrop, Wethersfield, August 16, 1703, *WP*, 140–141; Fitz-John Winthrop to Joseph Dudley, New London, August 19, 1703, *WP*, 145; John Chester to Fitz-John Winthrop, Wethersfield, August 10, 1703, *WP*, 147–148.

9. Sheldon, *History of Deerfield*, 1:220–221, 283–284. See also Susan McGowan and Amelia F. Miller, *Family and Landscape: Deerfield Homelots from 1671* (Deerfield, Mass.: Pocumtuck Valley Memorial Association, 1996), 16–17, 43, 174.

10. Steven Charles Eames, "Rustic Warriors: Warfare and the Provincial Soldier on the Northern Frontier, 1689–1748" (Ph.D. diss., University of New Hampshire, 1989), 43–55.

11. Eames, "Rustic Warriors," 91–93.

12. For insight into Vaudreuil's reasons for maintaining such a large force of French and Native allies near Montreal see Vaudreuil et Beauharnois à Pontchartrain, Quebec, 17 novembre 1704, *RAPQ*, 1938–1939, 56.

13. Lord Cornbury to the Lords of Trade, New York, June 30, 1703, *NYCD*, 4:1061; Yves F. Zoltvany, *Philippe de Rigaud de Vaudreuil: Governor of New France, 1703–1725* (Toronto: McClelland and Stewart, 1974), 45.

14. Le Roy Bacqueville de la Pothèrie, *Histoire de l'Amérique Septentrionale: Relation d'un séjour en Nouvelle-France* (1722; reprint, Monaco: Rocher, 1997), 2:606; Ramezay au ministre 14 novembre 1704, ANF, C11A 22:77. On the meeting, see Zoltvany, *Vaudreuil*, 46–48; *NYCD*, 9:746–751.

15. Pontchartrain à Vaudreuil, 20 juin, 1703, NAC, B 23:210–211; Vaudreuil au ministre, 3 avril, 1704, ANF, C11A 22:32.

16. Evan Haefeli and Kevin Sweeney, "Revisiting *The Redeemed Captive:* New Perspectives on the 1704 Attack on Deerfield," *William and Mary Quarterly*, 3rd. ser., 52, no. 1 (January 1995): 3–46; Dale Miquelon, *New France, 1701–1744: "A Supplement to Europe"* (Toronto: McClelland and Stewart, 1987), 40; For similar reluctance to characterize such a raid as guerilla warfare, see Jay Cassel, "The Troupes de la Marine in Canada, 1683–1760: Men and Materiel" (Ph.D. diss., University of Toronto, 1987), 500–501.

17. Pierre François Xavier Charlevoix, *History and General Description of New France*, trans. and ed. John Gilmary Shea (New York: privately printed, 1870), 4:121, 130, 133.

18. Peter MacLeod, *The Canadian Iroquois and the Seven Years War* (Toronto: Dundurn Press, 1996), 19, 27.

19. Both statements by the Kahnawke Mohawks and Iroquois of the Mountain are quoted in MacLeod, *Canadian Iroquois*, 21, x, 5–22.

20. James Smith, "Of the Remarkable Occurrences in the Life and Travels of Colonel James Smith," in *Indian Captivities; or, Life in the Wigwam*, ed. Samuel G. Drake (1851; reprint, Bowie, Md.: Heritage Books, 1995), 24; "1696 Mémoire," NAC C11 A 125:161–169; Brent Nosworthy, *The Anatomy of Victory: Battle Tactics, 1689–1763* (New York: Hippocrene, 1990), 210–216; John A. Lynn, *Giant of the Grand Siècle: The French Army, 1610–1715* (New York: Cambridge University Press, 1997), 538–546.

21. MacLeod, *Canadian Iroquois*, 5–22; Geoffrey Parker, "Early Modern Europe," in *The Laws of War: Constraints on Warfare in the Western World*, ed. Michael Howard, George J. Andreopoulos, and Mark R. Shulman (New Haven, Conn.: Yale University Press, 1994), 40–58; Harold E. Selesky, "Colonial America," in Howard, Andreopoulos, and Shulman, *Laws of War*, 59–85; John Charles Roger Childs, *Armies and Warfare in Europe, 1648–1789* (New York: Holmes and Meier, 1982), 2–4, 150–155; Frank Tallett, *War and Society in Early Modern Europe, 1495–1715* (New York: Routledge, 1992), 163, 172–173.

22. MacLeod, *Canadian Iroquois*, 5–22.

23. Douglass Edward Leach, *Arms for Empire: A Military History of the British Colonies in North America, 1607–1763* (New York: Macmillan, 1973), 130. See also Guy Chet, "Degeneration and Regeneration of European Warfare in Colonial New England: The Response of Colonial and British Forces to the Challenges of Wilderness Warfare (Ph.D. diss., Yale University, 2001), 161–163.

24. It took approximately three weeks to reach Schenectady, New York, two months to reach Salmon Falls, New Hampshire, and four months to reach Casco, Maine. Charlevoix, *History*, 4:122–124, 130, 132–137.

25. *Letters from North America*, trans. Ivy Alice Dickson (Belleville, Ont.: Mika, 1980),

65; John Bartlett, "Narrative," in Joshua Coffin, *A Sketch of the History of Newbury, Newburyport, and West Newbury from 1636 to 1845,* (Boston: Samuel G. Drake, 1845), 332.

26. René Chartrand, *Canadian Military Heritage, 1000–1754* (Montreal: Art Global, 1993), 96; Louise Dechêne, *Habitants and Merchants in Seventeenth Century Montreal* (Montreal and Kingston: McGill-Queen's University Press, 1992), 119–120; [Pierre Boucher], "Memoires de feu Monsieur Boucher, Seigneur de Boucherville, et ancien gouverneur des Trois-Rivières," *Bulletin des recherches historiques,* 1926, 398.

27. Roland Viau, *Enfants du néant et mangeurs d'ames; Guerre, culture et société en Iroquoisie ancienne* (Cap-Saint-Ignace: Boréal, 1997), 39, 89–90; *JR,* 66:163–171.

28. William Eccles, *Frontenac, Courtier Governor* (1959; reprint, Toronto: McClelland and Stewart, 1968), 257n.; Gretchen Green, "A New People in an Age of War: The Kahnawake Iroquois, 1667–1760" (Ph.D. diss., College of William and Mary, 1991), 153.

29. Penhallow, *Indian Wars,* 13.

30. Sheldon, *History of Deerfield,* 1:285; Emma Lewis Coleman, *New England Captives Carried to Canada between 1677 and 1760 during the French and Indian Wars* (Portland, Maine: Southworth Press, 1925), 2:118–120.

31. *DCB,* 3:493–494; Marine Leland, "A Canadian Explorer in Deerfield: Jacques de Noyon (1668–1745)," *William's Scrapbook,* Connecticut Valley Historical Museum, Autumn 1955, 3–5.

32. On most settling down in their late twenties, Miquelon, *New France,* 156; Louis Lavallée, *La Prairie en Nouvelle-France, 1647–1760* (Montreal and Kingston, 1992), 228–230.

33. "Information furnished by Samuel York respecting the Western Indians," September 2, 1700, *NYCD,* 4:748–750; Memorial of Two French Bushrangers to the Earl of Belmont, *NYCD,* 4:797; Earl of Bellomont to the Lords of Trade, November 28, 1700, *NYCD,* 4:482; Leland, "Jacques de Noyon," 5–8; E-Z Massicotte, "Jacques de Noyon: Nouveaux Détails sur sa carrière," *Bulletin des recherches historiques* 48 (1942): 122–123. On the situation in the Upper Country, see Richard White, *The Middle Ground: Indians, Empire, and Republics in the Great Lakes Region, 1650–1815* (New York: Cambridge University Press, 1991) 99–109, 116–117.

34. Leland, "Jacques de Noyon," 8–9; Coleman, *New England Captives,* 2:118–126.

35. Historians assume that few Indian-white marriages occurred in seventeenth-century New England. See Yasuhide Kawashima, *Puritan Justice and the Indian: White Man's Law in Massachusetts, 1630–1763* (Middletown, Conn.: Wesleyan University Press, 1986), 98–99. For an example of an Englishman who had spent time with Native captors but returned on his own to an English colony after the Peace of Ryswick, see "Information furnished by Samuel York," 749.

36. Coleman, *New England Captives,* 1:169, 173–175, 2:402.

37. Lord Cornbury to the Lords of Trade, September 9, 1703, *NYCD,* 4:1070; William Whiting to Fitz-John Winthrop, Hartford, September 27, 1703, *WP,* 155–156; Sheldon, *History of Deerfield,* 1:287. The September report of the diversion of men to Quebec may have been a garbled and delayed report of the diversion of men to Quebec in mid-May or early June.

38. Solomon Stoddard to Joseph Dudley, Northampton, October 22, 1703, and John Williams to Joseph Dudley, Deerfield, October 21, 1703, in Sheldon, *History of Deerfield,* 1:291, 289.

39. Sheldon, *History of Deerfield,* 1:287–292; Richard I. Melvoin, *New England Outpost: War and Society in Colonial Deerfield* (New York: Norton, 1989), 213–215.

40. Samuel Partridge to Fitz-John Winthrop, Hatfield, February 21, 1704, *WP*, 171; Sheldon, *History of Deerfield*, 1:287, 292. On the autumn end to raiding, see Penhallow, *Indian Wars*, 28.

41. Samuel Partridge and John Pynchon to Fitz-John Winthrop, Hatfield, January 18, 1704, *WP*, 168–169; Samuel Partridge to Fitz-John Winthrop, Hatfield, February 21, 1704, *WP*, 170–171. The information in Schuyler's report was probably similar to that contained in a letter Governor Cornbury sent to Dudley on January 21, 1704. In this letter Cornbury informs Dudley, "I have ordered Collonell Schuyler to send to your upper towns if occasion require." Schuyler was undoubtedly the source of information Cornbury conveyed to Dudley, and it was imprecise regarding the timing and location of the impending French attack. See Cornbury to Dudley, New York, January 21, 1703/04, Cornbury Box, folder 1, New York Historical Society.

42. Cornbury to Dudley, New York, January 21, 1703/04, Cornbury Box, folder 1, Cornbury Correspondence, New York Historical Society; Joseph Dudley to [?], February 16, 1704, no. 1727, Emmet Collection, New York Public Library; Penhallow, *Indian Wars*, 10–11; Samuel Partridge to Fitz-John Winthrop, Hatfield, February 21, 1704, *WP*, 170–171; Isaac Addington to Fitz-John Winthrop, Boston, March 6, 1704, *WP*, 180. For evidence of raiders as far west as Worcester, see Coleman, *New England Captives*, 1:313–317.

43. Lord Cornbury to the Earl of Nottingham, New York, June 22, 1704, *NYCD*, 4:1099. Less than a year after the Deerfield raid, Northampton residents appeared to be "the most carelish pepell in the world; hardly such a thing as a watch in the towne, nor had a scoute all this winter." John Livingston to his father-in-law, Northampton, January 10, 1705, quoted in the *WP*, 321n. For additional examples of a failure to be on guard, see Eames, "Rustic Warriors," 94–97.

CHAPTER 6: ASSAULT

1. For reasons unknown, George Sheldon suggests that they "would doubtless have surrendered to the English at discretion had the attack on the town been unsuccessful." George Sheldon, *A History of Deerfield Massachusetts* (Deerfield: privately printed, 1895–1896), 1:295.

2. Samuel Penhallow, *History of the Indian Wars*, ed. Edward Wheelock (1726; 1924; reprint, Williamstown, Mass.: Corner House, 1972), 11–12. For De Rouville's exhortation at Haverhill in 1708, see Pierre-François-Xavier de Charlevoix, *History and General Description of New France*, trans. and ed. John Gilmary Shea (1870; reprint, Chicago: Loyola University Press, 1902), 5:206. For an exhortation by the Christian Mohawk leader Kryn, see Charlevoix, *History*, 4:123.

3. On "Mimicking gusts of wind," see [Lucy Watson], "Mrs. Lucy Watson's memory & Account of New Settlers in the American Woods 1762, Chiefly Walpole, n [ew] H [amp shire]. . . . Lucy Watson's Acct of New Settlers of Walpole, N.H. were related to her son John F. Watson, in the year 1825 when in her 71st year of her age," 2–3, Watson Family Papers, box 2, Winterthur Museum, Winterthur, Dela.; On "drift of snow," see William Whiting to Fitz-John Winthrop, Hartford, March 4, 1704, *WP*, 176; Penhallow, *Indian Wars*, 12. For the height of the palisade, see Susan McGowan and Amelia F. Miller, *Family and Landscape: Deerfield Homelots from 1671* (Deerfield, Mass.: Pocumtuck Valley Memorial Association, 1996), 43.

4. Charlevoix, *History*, 4:124–126, 130–132; Thomas E. Burke Jr., *Mohawk Frontier: The Dutch Community of Schenectady, New York, 1661–1710* (Ithaca, N.Y.: Cornell University Press, 1991), 104–108. Simultaneous assaults were also used by eighteen parties of Abenakis at Oyster Bay (Durham) in 1692. See Samuel A. Drake, *The Border Wars of New England* (1897, 1910; reprint, Williamstown, Mass.: Corner House, 1973), 96–110.

5. John Williams, "The Redeemed Captive Returning to Zion," in *Puritans among the Indians: Accounts of Captivity and Redemption, 1676–1764*, ed. Alden T. Vaughan and Edward W. Clark (Cambridge: Harvard University Press, 1981), 172; "An Account of the Destruction at Deerfield, February 29, 1703–04," quoted in Sheldon, *History of Deerfield*, 1:302. A letter from Isaac Addington, the secretary of Massachusetts Bay Colony, to Governor Winthrop of Connecticut also attributes the surprise to "the watches being negligent of their duty." Isaac Addington to Fitz-John Winthrop, Boston, March 6, 1704, *WP*, 180. For the French and Indian reliance on swords and axes during De Rouville's 1708 attack on at Haverhill, see Charlevoix, *History*, 5:206.

6. Williams, "Redeemed Captive," 172–173; Drake, *Border Wars of New England*, 178; Emma Lewis Coleman, *New England Captives Carried to Canada between 1677 and 1760 during the French and Indian Wars* (Portland, Maine: Southworth Press, 1925), 2:78.

7. Interpretation is based on Fitz John Winthrop's Table of Losses, reprinted in Sheldon, *History of Deerfield*, 1:304–305, and the tribal identity of the captors of specific captives.

8. Interpretation is based on sources cited in n. 7.

9. John Williams to Stephen Williams, Deerfield, March 11, 1728/29, Gratz Collection, Historical Society of Pennsylvania, and sources cited in n. 7.

10. See sources cited in n. 9 and Sherman W. Adams and Henry R. Stiles, *The History of Ancient Wethersfield, Connecticut* (New York: Grafton Press, 1904), 2:463. During the 1708 Haverhill raid, some residents escaped by hiding in their cellars. See Drake, *Border Wars of New England*, 244–246.

11. "Destruction at Deerfield," 302.

12. Sheldon, *History of Deerfield*, 1:311–312. For the flight of Ensign John Sheldon and the militiaman, see John Williams to Stephen Williams, March 11, 1728/29, the Reverend John Williams and Family Papers, Gratz Collection, Historical Society of Pennsylvania.

13. Williams, "The Redeemed Captive," 172–174; "Destruction at Deerfield," 303.

14. Sheldon, *History of Deerfield*, 1:302–303, 312–313. On small shot, see Guy Chet, "Degeneration and Regeneration of European Warfare in Colonial New England: The Response of Colonial and British Forces to the Challenges of Wilderness Warfare" (Ph.D. diss., Yale University, 2001), 70–71, 106–107.

15. "Destruction at Deerfield," 302–303.

16. Charlevoix, *History*, 4:126, 132, 5:206–207; Drake, *Border Wars of New England*, 247–249.

17. "Destruction at Deerfield," 301, for petition quoted, 301; William Whiting to Fitz-John Winthrop, Hartford, March 4, 1704, *WP*, 176; *JR*, 66:159.

18. "Destruction at Deerfield," 301, 302.

19. Sheldon, *History of Deerfield*, 1:297–299, 300–303, 306–307. Richard Billing and Samuel Field received a bounty for a scalp. See *Acts and Resolves, Public and Private of the Province of Massachusetts Bay* (Boston: Wright and Potter, 1869–1922), 8:462.

20. MA, 71:44; "Destruction at Deerfield," 301, 303.

21. May 31, 1704, petition in MA, 71:46.

22. "[K]illed 5," in William Whiting to Fitz-John Winthrop, Hartford, March 4, 1704, *WP*, 176. For Marsh, see Sheldon, *History of Deerfield*, 1:298, 308, Coleman, *New England Captives*, 2:102.

23. "Destruction at Deerfield," 303; William Whiting to Fitz-John Winthrop, Hartford, March 4, 1704, *WP*, 176–177. On the pursuit of raiders and the likelihood of success, see Steven Charles Eames, "Rustic Warriors: Warfare and the Provincial Soldier on the Northern Frontier, 1689–1748" (Ph.D. diss., University of New Hampshire 1989), 57–63.

24. "Destruction at Deerfield," 303.

25. Sheldon, *History of Deerfield*, 1:304–309. We use the figure 50 killed. There were the nine soldiers killed in the Meadow Fight. In addition to the thirty-eight people listed by name in Sheldon, *History of Deerfield*, 1:308, we add Philip Mattoon among those killed in the village, an unnamed garrison soldier and an unnamed child in the Frary household. Two contemporary sources claim that Mattoon was killed in the village, the Table of Losses and a record produced in February 1729 by Daniel White, the town clerk of Hadley, Massachusetts. The latter record is located in the Reverend John Williams and Family, case 8, folder 12, Papers Relating to the 1704 Attack on Deerfield, Gratz Collection, Historical Society of Pennsylvania. Previous body counts have overlooked the fact that the Table of Losses claims that five garrison soldiers were killed. See Sheldon, *History of Deerfield*, 1:305. Two are listed by name as dying in the Meadows Fight, Sergeant Samuel Boltwood and Samuel Field, and two are listed by name among those who died in the village, Joseph Ingersoll and Thomas Selden (Sheldon, *History of Deerfield*, 1:308–309). This leaves one soldier and a child in the Frary household unaccounted for, making a total of 50 deaths.

26. Sheldon, *History of Deerfield*, 1:306–309. John Bridgman's escape accounts for the discrepancy between the figures of 111 and 112 captives that one finds in different accounts of the Deerfield raid. Some use the figure 109, which counts Bridgman but does not count the three Frenchmen, who were in fact residents of Deerfield and treated as captives by the attackers. The traditional accounting also includes Philip Mattoon among those killed in the attack but excludes "Marguerite" Field, who is not on Sheldon's list but is included among Emma Coleman's accounting of Deerfield captives. See Coleman, *New England Captives*, 2:78–80.

27. Fitz John Winthrop's Table of Losses, 304–305, 313. None of those killed and only one of the houses lost to fire can be located south of the stockade. A house belonging to Nathaniel Brooks stood just south of the stockade and was probably ignited when the raiders torched the houses at the southern end of the palisade. Only two of the captives came from households south of the stockade, and, as Sheldon suggests (1:313), Sarah Allen and Sarah Mattoon were probably away from home at the time of the attack. For the fate of Nathaniel Brooks's house and for the number and fate of houses north of stockade, we have relied up information in McGowan and Miller, *Family and Landscape*, 10, 11, 22, 73, 164, 169, 176.

28. Williams, "The Redeemed Captive," 174; [François Hertel], "Mémoire des services du Sr. Hertel Pére et de ses enfants," *Canadian Antiquarian and Numismatic Journal*, 2nd. ser. 1, no. 1 (July 1889): 8. The amounts of plunder collected by the English after the battle included eight guns, eight blankets, seven hatchets, and one bayonet, suggesting that the bodies of seven Indians and one Frenchman were stripped. See Sheldon, *History of Deerfield*, 1:300. For "30 dead," see Joseph Dudley to the Council of Trade and Plantations, April 20, 1704, *CSP*, no. 260, 22:100; "40 dead" in William Whiting to Fitz-John

Winthrop, Hartford, March 4, 1704, *WP*, 176, and in Williams, "Redeemed Captive," 174; "50 dead," but only twelve to fifteen wounded in "Destruction." 303 and Colonel Robert Quary to the Council of Trade and Plantations, Virginia, May 30, 1704, *CSP*, 1704–1705, no. 353, 22:140. On Haverhill, see Charlevoix, *History*, 5:204–207, and Penhallow, *Indians Wars*, 47, who gives the French and Indians losses at Haverhill as nine dead and several wounded. It is worth noting that both Abenakis and Iroquois made a point of trying to remove the bodies of fallen comrades. See Penhallow, *Indian Wars*, 25; Alice Nash, "The Abiding Frontier: Family, Gender, and Religion in Wabanaki History, 1600–1763" (Ph.D. diss., Columbia University, 1997), 132; Roland Viau, *Enfants du néant et mangeurs d'ames: Guerre, culture et société en Iroquoisie ancienne* (Cap-Saint-Ignace: Boréal, 1997), 109.

29. [Hertel], "Mémorial," 8; Vaudreuil au ministre, 3 avril, 1704, ANF, C11A, 22:32–33; Ramezay au ministre, 14 novembre, 1704, ANF C11A 22:77; Charles Legardeur de Croisille [1747], NAC, E 91:150–151.

30. Vaudreuil to Brouillan, Quebec, March 15, 1704, translation by Isaac Addington, *WP*, 257.

31. Samuel Partridge to Fitz-John Winthrop, Hatfield, March 13, 1704, *WP*, 183; Governor Dudley to the Council of Trade and Plantations, July 13, 1704, *CSP*, 1704–1705, no. 455, 22:214.

CHAPTER 7: RETREAT

1. John Williams, "The Redeemed Captive Returning to Zion," in *Puritans among the Indians: Accounts of Captivity and Redemption, 1676–1724*, ed. Alden T. Vaughan and Edward W. Clark (Cambridge: Harvard University Press, 1981), 174–175; George Sheldon, *A History of Deerfield, Massachusetts* (Deerfield: privately printed, 1895–1896), 1:308, 314–315.

2. Williams, "Redeemed Captive," 174–175; Theodore G. Corbett, *A Clash of Cultures on the Warpath of Nations: The Colonial Wars in the Hudson-Champlain Valley* (Fleischmanns, N.Y.: Purple Mountain Press, 2002), 137; Emma Lewis Coleman, *New England Captives Carried to Canada between 1677 and 1760 during the French and Indian Wars* (Portland, Maine: Southworth Press, 1925), 1:370.

3. Jeremy Belknap, *The History of New Hampshire* (Dover, N.H.: O. Crosby and J. Varncy, 1813), 1:227; Thomas E. Burke Jr., *Mohawk Frontier: The Dutch Community of Schenectady, New York, 1661–1710* (Ithaca, N.Y.: Cornell University Press, 1991), 123–124, 131; Corbett, *Clash of Cultures*, 96, 117; See also Ian K. Steele, "Surrendering Rites: Prisoners on Colonial North American Frontiers," in *Hanoverian Britain and Empire: Essays in Memory of Philip Lawson*, ed. Stephen Taylor, Richard Connors, and Clyve Jones (Rochester, N.Y.: Boydell Press, 1998), 139.

4. Williams, "Redeemed Captive," 174–175; John Gyles, "Memoirs of Odd Adventures, Strange Deliverances, etc.," in Vaughan and Clark, *Puritans among the Indians*, 105; "Capt. Benjamin Wright's Scout," in Sheldon, *History of Deerfield*, 1:371.

5. Williams, "Redeemed Captive," 174; *NYCD*, 3:708.

6. [Stephen Williams], *Narrative of the Captivity of Stephen Williams*, ed. George Sheldon (Deerfield, Mass., 1889), 5. See also Sheldon, *History of Deerfield*, 1:318–319.

7. [Williams], *Narrative of the Captivity of Stephen Williams*, app., 15–16; Coleman, *New England Captives*, 2:36–38.

8. Williams, "Redeemed Captive," 176–177, 179–180.

9. Thomas Hutchinson, *The History of the Colony and Province of Massachusetts-Bay,* ed. Lawrence Shaw Mayo (Cambridge: Harvard University Press, 1936), 2:104n; [Williams], *Narrative of the Captivity of Stephen Williams,* 5, 6. On the pacing of the march and the killings, see Samuel Carter, "The Route of the French and Indian Army That Sacked Deerfield February 29th, 1703–4, on Their Return March to Canada with the Captives," *Pocumtuck Valley Memorial Association History and Proceedings,* (1898), 132.

10. Williams, "Redeemed Captive," 175–176.

11. Williams, "Redeemed Captive," 174, 177, 181; [Williams], *Narrative of the Captivity of Stephen Williams,* 5. Whereas the word is "Distributed" in the printed version, it is clearly "disturbed" in the manuscript. The original untitled manuscript is in the Williams Family Papers, box 1, folder 10, Pocumtuck Valley Memorial Association. The only further insight that we have into these discussions is provided by Father D'Avaugour's account of the Hurons, which indicates that these discussions over the fate of captives were intratribal, not intertribal. See *JR,* 66:169–171.

12. Williams, "Redeemed Captive," 172, 177; Gyles, "Memoirs of Odd Adventures," 124.

13. Coleman, *New England Captives,* 2:68–69, 118–128. On the French taking captives, see Steele, "Surrendering Rites," 153, and for later troubles over captives in the French-Native alliance, see Steele, *Betrayals: Fort William Henry and the "Massacre"* (New York: Oxford University Press, 1990).

14. Williams, "Redeemed Captive," 173–174; Sheldon, *History of Deerfield,* 1:307; Daniel K. Richter, *The Ordeal of the Longhouse: The Peoples of the Iroquois League in the Era of European Colonization* (Chapel Hill: University of North Carolina Press, 1992), 66–67; William Starna and Ralph Watkins, "Northern Iroquoian Slavery," *Ethnohistory* 39, no. 4 (1992): 44–45.

15. Williams, "Redeemed Captive," 177. On the identity of the intended victim, see Evan Haefeli and Kevin Sweeney, "Revisiting *The Redeemed Captive:* New Perspectives on the 1704 Attack on Deerfield," *William and Mary Quarterly* 3rd. ser. 52, no. 1 (January 1995): 43–45.

16. Williams, "Redeemed Captive," 174; *JR,* 66:169.

17. *JR,* 66:169.

18. *JR,* 66:169–171.

19. *JR,* 66:171.

20. Williams, "Redeemed Captive," 177; [Williams], *Narrative of the Captivity of Stephen Williams,* 6; Carter, "Route of the Captives," 132–133.

21. Williams, "Redeemed Captive," 174–179.

22. Williams, "Redeemed Captive," 174–179, 180.

23. Williams, "Redeemed Captive," 177–178.

24. [Williams], *Narrative of the Captivity of Stephen Williams,* 6; Williams, "Redeemed Captive," 178; Carter, "Route of the Captives," 134.

25. [Williams], *Narrative of the Captivity of Stephen Williams,* 6; Williams, "Redeemed Captive," 180; Carter, "Route of the Captives," 135.

26. [Williams], *Narrative of the Captivity of Stephen Williams,* 6–7; Carter, "Route of the Captives," 135–136.

27. Williams, "Redeemed Captive," 179; Carter, "Route of the Captives," 136–137.

28. Williams, "Redeemed Captive," 180.

29. Williams, "Redeemed Captive," 181–182; Carter, "Route of the Captives," 137–143.

30. [Williams], *Narrative of the Captivity of Stephen Williams,* 6–7; Carter, "Route of the Captives,"143–144.

31. [Williams], *Narrative of the Captivity of Stephen Williams,* 6–7.

32. [Williams], *Narrative of the Captivity of Stephen Williams,* 7–8.

33. [Williams], *Narrative of the Captivity of Stephen Williams,* 7–8; Carter, "Route of the Captives," 145–146, 148–149.

34. Vaudreuil à Pontchartrain, 16 novembre, 1704, NAC, C11A 22:34. A Speech of the Abenaki Indians at Cowasuck to the Governor-General, 13 juin 1704, NAC, F3, 2:407–410.

35. [Williams], *Narrative of the Captivity of Stephen Williams,* 7–8; Carter, "Route of the Captives," 147–149; Sheldon, *History of Deerfield,* 1:319–320.

36. [Williams], *Narrative of the Captivity of Stephen Williams,* 8; Carter, "Route of the Captives," 149–151.

CHAPTER 8: ADOPTING CAPTIVES

1. John Williams, "The Redeemed Captive Returning to Zion," in *Puritans among the Indians: Accounts of Captivity and Redemption, 1676–1724,* ed. Alden T. Vaughan and Edward W. Clark (Cambridge: Harvard University Press, 1981), 182–183.

2. [Stephen Williams], *Narrative of the Captivity of Stephen Williams,* ed. George Sheldon (Deerfield, Mass., 1889), 8.

3. [Williams], *Narrative of the Captivity of Stephen Williams,* 8–9.

4. Williams, "Redeemed Captive," 196. See also J. M. Bumsted, "'Carried to Canada!': Perceptions of the French in British Colonial Captivity Narratives, 1690–1760," *American Review of Canadian Studies* 13, no. 1 (1983): 80–81, 86–88, 90.

5. Ian Steele, "Surrendering Rites: Prisoners on Colonial North American Frontiers," in *Hanoverian Britain and Empire: Essays in Memory of Philip Lawson,* ed. Stephen Taylor, Richard Connors, and Clyve Jones (Rochester, N.Y.: Boydell Press, 1998), 139–140.

6. [Williams], *Narrative of the Captivity of Stephen Williams,* 9–10.

7. [Williams], *Narrative of the Captivity of Stephen Williams,* 9–10.

8. [Williams], *Narrative of the Captivity of Stephen Williams,* 10–11.

9. Roland Viau, *Enfants du néant et mangeurs d'âmes: Guerre, culture et société en Iroquoisie ancienne* (Cap-Saint-Ignace: Boreal, 1997), 161–199.

10. George Sheldon, *A History of Deerfield, Massachusetts* (Deerfield: privately printed, 1885–1896), 1:371; Emma Lewis Coleman, *New England Captives Carried to Canada between 1677 and 1760 during the French and Indian Wars* (Portland, Maine: Southworth Press, 1925), 1:65.

11. Evan Haefeli, "Ransoming New England Captives in New France" *French Colonial History* 1 (2002):115–119.

12. Peter N. Moogk, *La Nouvelle France: The Making of French Canada—A Cultural History* (East Lansing: Michigan State University Press, 2000), 100; Marcel Trudel, *L'Escalavage au Canada Français: Histoire et conditions de l'escalavage* (Quebec: Presses Universitaires Laval, 1960), 84, 89. During the same period, the presence of only six black slaves can be documented in New France.

13. Pierre-François Xavier de Charlevoix, *Journal of a Voyage to North-America* (London: R. and J. Dodsley, 1761), 1:371; Viau, *Enfants du néant,* 193–199.

14. Haefeli, "Ransoming New England Captives," 118–121.

15. Williams, "Redeemed Captive," 188; Coleman, *New England Captives,* 2:49–51, 63–64. For Agathe de Saint-Père, see *DCB,* 3:580–581; for Jacques Le Ber, see *DCB,* 2:374–376.

16. Peter MacLeod, *The Canadian Iroquois and the Seven Years' War* (Toronto: Dundurn Press, 1996), 9.

17. William A. Starna and Ralph Watkins, "Northern Iroquoian Slavery," *Ethnohistory* 38, no. 1 (1991): 34–35, 41–46; Alice K. Nash, "The Abiding Frontier: Family, Gender, and Religion in Wabanaki History" (Ph.D. diss., Columbia University, 1997), 95–106, 253–260.

18. Williams, "Redeemed Captive," 189; Coleman, *New England Captives,* 2:58, 106, 107; Viau, *Enfants du néant,* 150; Starna and Watkins, "Northern Iroquoian Slavery," 41, 47–49.

19. Williams, "Redeemed Captive," 183, 191.

20. [Williams], *Narrative of the Captivity of Stephen Williams,* 9–10; Joseph Kellogg, "When I was Carryed to Canada, . . ." verso, the Reverend John Williams and Family, case 8, box 28, folder "Papers Relating to the 1704 Attack on Deerfield," Gratz Collection, Historical Society of Pennsylvania.

21. Steele, "Surrendering Rites," 140; [Williams], *Narrative of the Captivity of Stephen Williams,* 10–11.

22. Coleman, *New England Captives,* 2:58, 78, 106; James Smith, "Of the Remarkable Occurrences in the Life and Travels of Colonel James Smith," in *Indian Captivities; or, Life in the Wigwam,* ed. Samuel G. Drake (1851; reprint, Bowie, Md.: Heritage Books, 1995), 199. We are indebted to Kanatakta, executive director of the Kanien'kehaka Raotitiohkwa Cultural Center at Kahnawake, for bringing to our attention the likely meaning of James Smith's Mohawk name.

23. Williams, "Redeemed Captive," 185–186.

24. Charles B. de Saileville, "A History of the Life and Captivity of Eunice Williams, Alias Madam De Roguers, Who Was Styled 'The Fair Captive,'" [1842], Neville Public Museum (microfilm, State Historical Society of Wisconsin, Area Research Center, Green Bay), reel 7, 27–29. For Eunice's full story, see John Demos, *The Unredeemed Captive: A Family Story from Early America* (New York: Knopf, 1994).

25. De Saileville, "Life and Captivity," 56–57, 65, 97–98. See also Demos, *Unredeemed Captive,* 151–54.

26. Williams, "Redeemed Captive," 189.

27. Williams, "Redeemed Captive," 189.

28. [Williams], *Narrative of the Captivity of Stephen Williams,* 10; Kellogg, "When I was Carryed," verso.

29. Louise Dechêne, *Habitants and Merchants in Seventeenth Century Montreal,* trans. Liana Vardi (Montreal and Kingston: McGill-Queen's University Press, 1992), 48.

30. Coleman, *New England Captives,* 2:68; Bumsted, "Carried to Canada," 86–87, 90–92; Leslie Choquette, *Frenchmen into Peasants* (Cambridge: Harvard University Press, 2000); Dechêne, *Habitants and Merchants,* 20–43.

31. *DCB,* 2:385–386; 3:580–581; William Henry Foster II, "Agathe Saint-Père and Her Captive New England Weavers: Technical Transference and Cultural Exchange in

One Woman's Enterprise in Colonial French Canada," *French Colonial History* (2002): 129–141.

32. Kellogg, "When I was Carryed," verso.

33. *DCB*, 2:467–68; Coleman, *New England Captives*, 1:40; Alice C. Baker, *True Stories of New England Captives Carried to Canada during the Old French and Indian Wars* (1897; reprint, Bowie, Md.: Heritage Books, 1990), 320–326.

34. For Mary Sayward, see William Henry Foster, "The Captor's Narrative: Catholic Women and Their Puritan Men on the Early North American Frontier, 1635–1760" (Ph.D. diss., Cornell University, 2000), 119–145; *DCB*, 2:601–602; Coleman, *New England Captives*, 1:239. For Dubuisson, see *DCB*, 3:532–533; Williams, "Redeemed Captive," 207–208.

35. Jacque Le Ber, *DCB*, 2:374–376 (includes Jeanne); Pierre Le Ber, *DCB*, 2:377–378; Charles Le Moyne de Longueuil, Baron de Longueuil, *DCB*, 2:401–403; Paul Le Moyne de Maricourt, *DCB*, 2:403–405.

36. Coleman, *New England Captives*, 2:113–116, 91–92; Williams, "Redeemed Captive," 206–208, 210, 219, 220.

37. Williams, "Redeemed Captive," 221; Esther Williams to [Stephen ?] Williams, Deerfield, February 28, 1709/1710, The Reverend John Williams and Family, case 8, box 28, Gratz Collection, Historical Society of Pennsylvania; Coleman, *New England Captives*, 1:398, 350–351, 424–435, 2:7–8, 91; Marcel Fournier, *De la Nouvelle-Angleterre à la Nouvelle-France: L'histoire des captifs anglo-américans au Canada entre 1675 et 1760* (Montreal: Société généalogique canadienne-française, 1992), 116–119, 150, 175.

38. Kellogg, "When I was Carryed," recto.

39. Kellogg, "When I was Carryed," recto.

40. Kellogg, "When I was Carryed," recto.

41. Kellogg, "When I was Carryed," recto, verso.

42. Williams, "Redeemed Captive," 204–220.

43. Cotton Mather, *Good Fetch'd Out of Evil* (Boston: B. Green, 1706), 29–33; Esther Williams to [Stephen ?] Williams, February 28, 1709/1710.

44. Williams, "Redeemed Captive," 197–198.

CHAPTER 9: DIPLOMACY AND SCANDAL

1. Ian K. Steele, "Surrendering Rites: Prisoners on Colonial American Frontiers," in *Hanoverian Britain and Empire: Essays in Memory of Philip Lawson,* ed. Stephen Taylor, Richard Connors, and Clyve Jones (Rochester, N.Y.: Boydell Press, 1998), 145; Emma Lewis Coleman, *New England Captives Carried to Canada between 1677 and 1760 during the French and Indian Wars* (Portland, Maine: Southworth Press, 1925), 1:72–76, 78–79, 123–124.

2. C. Alice Baker, *True Stories of New England Captives Carried to Canada during the Old French and Indian Wars* (1897; reprint, Bowie, Md.: Heritage Books, 1990), 172–173; Coleman, *New England Captives*, 1:402.

3. Coleman, *New England Captives*, 1:79–80; George Sheldon, *A History of Deerfield, Massachusetts* (Deerfield: privately printed, 1895–1896), 1:324–325.

4. Yves F. Zoltvany, *Philippe de Rigaud de Vaudreuil: Governor of New France, 1703–1725* (Toronto: McClelland and Stewart, 1974), 59.

5. Coleman, *New England Captives*, 1:79–81; Sheldon, *History of Deerfield*, 1:324–326;

Francis H. Hammang, *The Marquis de Vaudreuil: New France at the Beginning of the Eighteenth Century, Part 1—New France and the English Colonies* (Bruges and Louvain: Louvain University, 1938), 125–126; *DCB*, 2:449–50.

6. John Williams, "The Redeemed Captive Returning to Zion," in *Puritans among the Indians: Accounts of Captivity and Redemption, 1676–1724*, ed. Alden T. Vaughan and Edward W. Clark (Cambridge: Harvard University Press, 1981), 198; Sheldon, *History of Deerfield*, 1:327–329. George Sheldon claims that one of Ensign Sheldon's children returned with him. Both Sheldon and Coleman claim that his daughter Mary and his son Remembrance returned in 1706, which would leave Ebenezer as the child who returned in 1705, though Sheldon also lists him with a question mark as returning in 1706.

7. Hammang, *Vaudreuil*, 126–127.

8. Joseph Petty to Stephen Williams, Deerfield, n.d., reprinted in Sheldon, *History of Deerfield*, 1:353.

9. Joseph Petty to Stephen Williams, in Sheldon, *History of Deerfield*, 1:353–354.

10. Quoted in C. Alice Baker, "The Adventures of Baptiste, Part II," *Pocumtuck Valley Memorial Association History and Proceedings* 4 (1905):462–463.

11. Everett Kimball, *The Public Life of Joseph Dudley* (New York: Longmans, 1911), 104–105.

12. Pierre-François-Xavier de Charlevoix, *History and General Description of New France*, ed. and trans. John Gilmary Shea (1870; reprint, Chicago: Loyola University Press, 1962), 5:176; Kimball, *Joseph Dudley*, 112–114; G. M. Waller, *Samuel Vetch, Colonial Enterpriser* (Chapel Hill: University of North Carolina Press, 1960), 79–83; Zoltvany, *Vaudreuil*, 62–63.

13. Coleman, *New England Captives*, 1:81–82, 2:91. George Sheldon incorrectly claims that Samuel Williams returned in 1705, though "The Redeemed Captive" makes it clear that Samuel was still in Canada in March 1706. See Sheldon, *History of Deerfield*, 1: 330; Williams, "Redeemed Captive," 200–201, 219–220.

14. Dudley à Vaudreuil, 4 juillet, 1705, *Collection de manuscrits, . . . relatifs à la Nouvelle*-France (Quebec: A. Coté, 1883–1885), 2:435–438; Traité fait et conclue pour la restauration des prisonniers, 1705, NAC, F3 8:380–383; Vaudreuil à Pontchartrain 10 octobre, 1705, NAC, C11A 22:246–247; Dudley's proposed treaty, NAC, C11A 22:286–288; Vaudreuil's counter proposal, NAC, C, C11A 22:282–285; Hammang, *Vaudreuil*, 130; Zoltvany, *Vaudreuil*, 61–62.

15. Vaudreuil to Ponchartrain, June 8, 1708, *NYCD*, 9:813; Hammang, *Vaudreuil*, 130–131; Zoltvany, *Vaudreuil*, 62; Kimball, *Joseph Dudley*, 104.

16. Coleman, *New England Captives Carried to Canada*, 1:81–82; Kimball, *Joseph Dudley*, 115; Zoltvany, *Vaudreuil*, 62–63, 65–66, 71–75; Richard R. Johnson, *John Nelson, Merchant Adventurer: A Life between Empires* (New York: Oxford University Press, 1991), 108–109; Cadillac à Pontchartrain 28 octobre, 1705, NAC, C11A 23:163. See also Jack S. Radabaugh, "The Military System of Colonial Massachusetts, 1690–1740" (Ph.D. diss., University of Southern California, 1965), 236–243.

17. Cadillac à Pontchartrain 28 octobre, 1705, NAC, C11A 23:163; Charlevoix, *History of New France*, 5:176; Hammang, *Vaudreuil*, 133–138; Zoltvany, *Vaudreuil*, 62–63, 65–66.

18. Coleman, *New England Captives*, 1:83–85; Sheldon, *History of Deerfield*, 1:332–333; David Odell Damerall, "Modernization of Massachusetts: The Transformation of Public Attitudes and Institutions, 1689 to 1715" (Ph.D. diss., University of Texas at Austin, 1981), 197–198.

19. Williams, "Redeemed Captive," 223–224; Hammang, *Vaudreuil*, 132; Sheldon, *History of Deerfield*, 1:333.

20. Williams, "Redeemed Captive," 223–224; Coleman, *New England Captives*, 1:83–85; Hammang, *Vaudreuil*, 132.

21. Thomas Hutchinson, *The History of the Colony and Province of Massachusetts-Bay*, ed. Lawrence Shaw Mayo (Cambridge: Harvard University Press, 1936), 2:114–121; Philip S. Haffenden, *New England in the English Nation, 1689–1713* (Oxford: Clarendon Press, 1974), 238–241; Richard R. Johnson, *Adjustment to Empire: The New England Colonies, 1675–1715* (New Brunswick, N.J.: Rutgers University Press, 1981), 342–347; Hammang, *Vaudreuil*, 132; Kimball, *Joseph Dudley*, 114–119; Waller, *Samuel Vetch*, 83–88.

22. Coleman, *New England Captives*, 1:85; Sheldon, *History of Deerfield*, 1:336–337.

23. Coleman, *New England Captives*, 1:85; Sheldon, *History of Deerfield*, 1:337.

24. Williams, "Redeemed Captive," 224; Coleman, *New England Captives*, 1:83–86; Damerall, "Modernization of Massachusetts," 199–201; MA, 71:272. George Sheldon incorrectly identifies Warham as the Williams son to whom this offer was made. It was, however, Samuel who lived with Jacques Le Ber, one of the wealthiest men in New France. See Sheldon, *History of Deerfield*, 1:337; Coleman, *New England Captives*, 2:49–51; *DCB*, 2:374–376.

25. [Cotton Mather], *Diary of Cotton Mather* (Boston: Massachusetts Historical Society, 1911–1912), 1:565, 581, 589–90; *A Modest Enquiry into the Grounds and Occasions of the Late Pamphlet Intitled A Memorial of the Deplorable State of New-England By a disinterested hand* (London, 1707), reprinted in *Collections of the Massachusetts Historical Society*, 5th ser., 6 (1879): 87.

26. *Andros Tracts*, ed. W. H. Whitemore, (Boston: Prince Society, 1867–1874), 1:160; Michael G. Hall, *The Last Puritan: The Life of Increase Mather* (Middletown, Conn.: Wesleyan University Press, 1988), 306–310; Johnson, *Adjustment to Empire*, 333–342; William Pencak, *War, Politics, and Revolution in Provincial Massachusetts* (Boston: Northeastern University Press, 1981), 42–47; Samuel Eliot Morison, *Harvard College in the Seventeenth Century* (Cambridge: Harvard University Press, 1936), 2:539–540; Kenneth Silverman, *The Life and Times of Cotton Mather* (New York: Columbia University Press, 1985), 202–212; [Cotton Mather], *Selected Letters*, comp. Kenneth Silverman (Baton Rouge: Louisiana State University Press, 1971), 67–68, 71–72.

27. *A Memorial of the Present Deplorable State of New-England, with the Many Disadvantages it Lyes under, by the Maleadministration of their Present Governour, Joseph Dudley, Esq. and His son Paul, Boston, 1707* [sic] (London, 1707), reprinted in *Collections of the Massachusetts Historical Society*, 5th. ser., 6 (1879): 40–42; [Samuel Sewall], *Diary of Samuel Sewell* in *Collections of the Massachusetts Historical Society*, 5th ser., (Boston, 1879), 6:200, 201–202, 203; Silverman, *Cotton Mather*, 207–221. Silverman assumes Cotton Mather was the author (213), as does Kimball, *Joseph Dudley*, 183.

28. *Memorial of the Present Deplorable State*, 44, 36–39, 40, 43–46, 47–50, 49, 64; Richard L. Bushman, "Corruption and Power in Provincial America," in *The Development of a Revolutionary Mentality: Library of Congress Symposium on the American Revolution* (Washington, D.C., 1972), 71. The term "politics of scurrility" comes from Patricia U. Bonomi, *The Lord Cornbury Scandal: The Politics of Reputation in British America* (Chapel Hill: University of North Carolina Press, 1998), 10, 147–158. For suspicions, see the statements by the prisoner, probably Joseph Bartlett, interviewed by Vaudreuil, NAC, C11A 28:151–152. See also *NYCD*, 9:817.

29. [Mather], *Diary,* 1:593; Cotton Mather, *The Frontiers Well-Defended* (Boston: T. Green, 1707) 9, 24–25, 27–28, 29–39, 33, 50.

30. [Mather], *Diary,* 1:575.

31. Williams, "Redeemed Captive," 169. There are many discussions of this text. Among those we have consulted are Rosalie Murphy Baum, "John Williams's Captivity Narrative: A Consideration of Normative Ethnicity," in *A Mixed Race: Ethnicity in Early America,* ed. Frank Shuffleton (New York: Oxford University Press, 1993), 56–76; Gary L. Ebersole, *Captured by Texts: Puritan to Post-Modern Images of Indian Captivity* (Charlottesville: University Press of Virginia, 1995), 72–76; Kenneth M. Morrison, "The Wonders of Divine Mercy: A Review of John Williams' *The Redeemed Captive," American Review of Canadian Studies* 9, no. 1 (1979): 56–62; June Namias, *White Captives: Gender and Ethnicity on the American Frontier* (Chapel Hill: University of North Carolina Press, 1993), 53–58; Richard VanDerBeets, *The Indian Captivity Narrative: An Early American Genre* (Lanham, M.D.: University Press of America, 1984), 13–23.

32. Thomas Foxcroft, *Eli, the Priest Dying Suddenly* (Boston: S. Gerrish, 1729), 38. Vaughan and Clark also make the point that Williams "did not dwell on the Lord's rebukes." Vaughan and Clark, *Puritans among the Indians,* 1. See also, Pauline Turner Strong, *Captive Selves, Captivating Others: The Politics and Poetics of Colonial American Captivity Narratives* (Boulder, Colo.: Westview, 1999), 139.

33. Williams, "Redeemed Captive," 170. This is only one of two instances of a gubernatorial imprimatur cited in Hellmut Lehmann-Haupt, *The Book in America: A History of the Making and Selling of Books in the United States,* 2nd ed. (New York: Bowker, 1951), 43. Several scholars have found Williams's fulsome dedication of *The Redeemed Captive* to Governor Dudley perplexing and embarrassing. Alden Vaughan and Edward Clark are quick to point out that "Williams, of course, was grateful for Dudley's help in redeeming New England captives." Vaughan and Clark, *Puritans among the Indians,* 169, n1. Rosalie Murphy Baum, in contrast, finds the dedication to be a "very worldly opening, even a politically expedient opening" and "particularly puzzling given our awareness that Dudley was so disliked by many prominent Puritan families (eg. Mathers and the Sewells)." She does not pursue her insight into the dedication's obvious political content. See Baum, "John Williams's Captivity Narrative," 64.

34. Williams "Redeemed Captive," 170, 190, 223–224. John Demos dismisses the dedication as being "quite standard—even formulaic" in *The Unredeemed Captive: A Family Story from Early America* (New York: Knopf, 1994), 67.

35. Williams, "Redeemed Captive," 202, 221, 203–295, 191.

36. Williams, "Redeemed Captive," 190, 204–220; Isaac Chauncey, *A Blessed Manumission of Christ's Faithful Ministers, when they have finish'd their Testimony: A Sermon Preach'd at the Funeral of the Reverend John Williams* (Boston: D. Henchman and T. Hancock, 1729), 22.

37. Demos, *Unredeemed Captive,* 74; John Williams, *God in the Camp* (Boston: B. Green, 1707), 14–15, 15, 16–20.

38. Hall, *Last Puritan,* 319; Richard Bushman, *King and People in Provincial Massachusetts* (Chapel Hill: University of North Carolina Press, 1985),109; Massachusetts Council quoted in Kimball, *Joseph Dudley,* 185, n. 4; Johnson, *Adjustment to Empire,* 387–388; Morison, *Harvard College,* 2:548–556; Pencak, *War, Politics, and Revolution,* 49–51; Silverman, *Cotton Mather,* 207–221; [Mather], *Selected Letters,* 74–76.

39. Declaration of the Hampshire Clergy, Northampton, November 11, 1707, Trea-

sury 1/103 fol. 189, Public Record Office. We want to thank Professor Margaret Hunt for obtaining a copy of this petition. All of the county's ministers signed, except for the Reverend Edward Taylor of Westfield.

40. Quoted in Kimball, *Joseph Dudley,* 186n. 4; *Calendar of Treasury Papers, 1702–1707* (London: Longman & Co., 1874), 3:547–550; *CSP,* 1706–1708, no. 1186, 23:587–596.

41. Bushman, *King and People,* 67; Hutchinson, *History,* 2:160, 111; Pencak, *War, Politics, and Revolution,* 49. Haffenden, *New England,* 211–242; Johnson, *Adjustment to Empire,* 347–350, 354–362, 377–378, 384–389, 405; Pencak, *War, Politics, and Revolution,* 45–53.

42. Quoted in Sheldon, *History of Deerfield,* 1:340.

43. Sheldon, *History of Deerfield,* 1:338–342.

44. Sheldon, *History of Deerfield,* 1:339–340, 348–349; Hammang, *Vaudreuil,* 1:177–178; Kimball, *Joseph Dudley,* 102–104. Vaudreuil à Pontchartrain, 8 novembre, 1707, NAC, C11A 26:201; Subercase à Pontchartrain, 26 juin, 1707, in *Collection de manuscrits,* 2:469; Vaudreuil à Pontchartrain, 28 juin, 1708, NAC, C11A 28:90. As several historians have pointed out, the reasons for New York's de facto neutrality were complicated and the neutrality of the Iroquois League played a central role, but historians such as G. M. Waller and Patricia Bonomi have not recognized the degree to which Cornbury actively sought to reassure Vaudreuil of his pacific intentions. On this point, the French sources are more revealing than the English sources. See G. M. Waller, "New York's Role in Queen Anne's War, 1702–1713," *New York History* 33 (January 1952): 40–53; Bonomi, *Lord Cornbury Scandal,* 168–170.

45. Sheldon, *History of Deerfield,* 1:340–342; MA, 71:236–238, 239–240, 438.

46. Coleman, *New England Captives,* 2:73.

CHAPTER 10: IMPERIAL AND PARALLEL WARS

1. Howard H. Peckham, *The Colonial Wars, 1689–1762* (Chicago: University of Chicago Press, 1964), 74.

2. Vaudreuil to Brouillan, Quebec, March 15, 1704, *WP,* 257n; Samuel Penhallow, *History of the Indian Wars,* ed. Edward Wheelock, (1726; 1924; reprint, Williamstown, Mass.: Corner House, 1973), 15–16. See also George Sheldon, *A History of Deerfield, Massachusetts* (Deerfield: privately printed, 1895–1896), 1:318–319.

3. Vaudreuil et Beauharnois à Pontchartrain, 17 novembre, 1704, *RAPQ,* 1938–1939, 56; Penhallow, *Indian Wars,* 23.

4. Vaudreuil et Beauharnois à Pontchartrain, 17 novembre, 1704, *RAPQ,* 1938–1939, 56; William Whiting to Fitz-John Winthrop, July 28, 1704, *WP,* 244–248. Penhallow identifies the raiders' destination as Northampton, Williams as merely the Connecticut River. Penhallow, *Indian Wars,* 23–24; John Williams, "The Redeemed Captive Returning to Zion," in *Puritans among the Indians: Accounts of Captivity and Redemption, 1676–1724,* ed. Alden T. Vaughan and Edward W. Clark (Cambridge: Harvard University Press, 1981), 191; Pierre-François-Xavier de Charlevoix, *History and General Description of New France,* trans. and ed. John Gilmary Shea (1870; reprint, Chicago: Loyola University Press, 1962), 5:166; Gretchen Green, "A New People in an Age of War: The Kahnawake Iroquois, 1667–1760" (Ph.D. diss., College of William and Mary, 1991), 171–175; Francis H. Hammang, *The Marquis de Vaudreuil: New France at the Beginning of the Eighteenth Century: Part I—New France and the English Colonies* (Bruges and Louvain: Louvain University, 1938), 121.

5. William Whiting to Fitz-John Winthrop, July 28, 1704, *WP,* 244–248. Newgate told the English that he was sent to New France as a servant, but Vaudreuil refers to him as a *"soldat,"* not a *habitant,* indicating that he was a member of the *troupes,* rather than a member of the militia. See Vaudreuil et Beauharnois au ministre, 17 novembre, 1704, *RAPQ,* 1938–1939, 56.

6. Penhallow, *Indian Wars,* 24–25; Vaudreuil et Beauharnois au ministre, 17 novembre 1704, *RAPQ,* 1938–1939, 56; Ramezay à Pontchartrain, 14 novembre, 1704, NAC, C11A 22:69, 77; *NYCD,* 9:764; Williams, "Redeemed Captive," 191–192; Sheldon, *History of Deerfield,* 1:320–322.

7. Pontchartrain à Vaudreuil 17 juin 1705, NAC, B 27:47. See also Daniel Richter, *The Ordeal of the Longhouse: The Peoples of the Iroquois League in the Era of European Colonization* (Chapel Hill: University of North Carolina Press, 1992), 218; Dale Miquelon, *New France, 1701–1744: "A Supplement to Europe"* (Toronto: McClelland and Stewart, 1987), 41.

8. *JR,* 67:30–32; Gordon Day, "Western Abenaki," in *Northeast,* ed. Bruce Trigger, vol. 15 of *Handbook of North American Indians,* ed. William C. Sturtevant (Washington, D.C.: Smithsonian Institution, 1978), 151; Vaudreuil et Beauharnois à Pontchartrain, 17 novembre, 1704, *NYCD,* 9:762, 764–765; Charlevoix, *History,* 5:166–167; *NYCD,* 4:1164; Green, "New People," 173–175.

9. Richard L. Bushman, *King and People in Provincial Massachusetts* (Chapel Hill: University of North Carolina Press, 1985), 123n. 103; Governor Dudley to the Council of Trade and Plantations, July 13, 1704 *CSP,* 1704–1705, no. 455, 22:214; Fitz-John Winthrop to Joseph Dudley, New London, June 8, 1704, *WP,* 216–217; Penhallow, *Indian Wars,* 40; The Committee of War to Fitz-John Winthrop, July 3, 1704, *WP,* 235–236; William Whiting to Fitz-John Winthrop, Northampton, August 21, 1704, *WP,* 260; John M. Murrin, "Anglicizing an American Colony: The Transformation of Provincial Massachusetts" (Ph.D. diss., Yale University, 1966), 79–82; William Pencak, *War, Politics, & Revolution in Provincial Massachusetts* (Boston: Northeastern University Press, 1981), 36–38.

10. Bushman, *King and People,* 123n. 103; Governor Dudley to the Council of Trade and Plantations, July 13, 1704, CSP, 1704–1705, no. 455, 22:214; Fitz-John Winthrop to Joseph Dudley, New London, June 8, 1704, *WP,* 216–217; Penhallow, *Indian Wars,* 40; The Committee of War to Fitz-John Winthrop, July 3, 1704, *WP,* 235–236; Ian K. Steele, *Warpaths: Invasions of North America* (New York: Oxford University Press, 1994), 142–145.

11. Fitz-John Winthrop to Lord Cornbury, New London, April 22, 1704, *WP,* 192; Joseph Dudley to W. Popple, Boston, November 27, 1704, CSP, 1704–1705, no. 680, 22:325; Lord Cornbury to the Lords of Trade, New York, November 6, 1704, *NYCD,* 4:1121; Penhallow, *Indian Wars,* 16–19; Peckham, *Colonial Wars,* 54.

12. Penhallow, *Indian Wars,* 20–23.

13. Jay Cassel, "The Troupes de la Marine in Canada, 1683–1760: Men and Materiel" (Ph.D. diss., University of Toronto, 1988), 76, 107–109; Vaudreuil et Beauharnois au ministre, 14 juin 1704, *RAPQ,* 1938–1939, 42; Lorraine Gadoury, *La Noblesse de Nouvelle-France: Familles et alliances* (Quebec: Hurtubise HMN, 1992), 71–73.

14. Vaudreuil et Beauharnois au Ministre, 17 novembre, 1704, *RAPQ,* 1938–1939, 60.

15. Vaudreuil et Beauharnois au Ministre, 17 novembre, 1704, *RAPQ,* 1938–1939, 58, 62.

16. *DCB,* 3:81–82, 422; 2:285–286.

17. For Vaudreuil's reputation, see *DCB,* 2:573.

18. Vaudreuil to Pontchartrain quoted in Emma Lewis Coleman, *New England Cap-*

tives Carried to Canada between 1677 and 1760 during the French and Indian Wars (Portland, Maine: Southworth Press, 1925), 1:355; Penhallow, *Indian Wars,* 9, 40; Richard R. Johnson, *Adjustment to Empire: The New England Colonies, 1675–1715* (New Brunswick, N.J.: Rutgers University Press, 1981), 239.

19. Samuel A. Drake, *The Border Wars of New England* (1897; 1910; reprint, Williamstown, Mass.: Corner House, 1973), 225–226, 224–237.

20. Penhallow, *Indian Wars,* 32; Murrin, "Anglicizing an American Colony," 77–90; Kenneth M. Morrison, *The Embattled Northeast: The Elusive Ideal of Alliance in Abenaki-Euroamerican Relations* (Berkeley: University of California Press, 1984), 159–161; Jack S. Radabaugh, "The Military System of Colonial Massachusetts, 1690–1740" (Ph.D. diss., University of Southern California, 1965), 196–206; Steven Charles Eames, "Rustic Warriors: Warfare and the Provincial Soldier on the Northern Frontier, 1689–1748" (Ph.D. diss., University of New Hampshire, 1989), 135, 145–150, 165–173.

21. Sheldon, *History of Deerfield,* 1:358–384.

22. Yves F. Zoltvany, *Philippe de Rigaud de Vaudreuil: Governor of New France, 1703–1725* (Toronto: McClelland and Stewart, 1974), 77–79.

23. Lawrence Leder, ed., *The Livingston Indian Records, 1666–1723,* (Gettysburg: Pennsylvania Historical Association, 1956), 201; Zoltvany, *Vaudreuil,* 78–79; Green, "New People," 174–175.

24. Hammang, *Vaudreuil,* 175–203; Zoltvany, *Vaudreuil,* 75–77; Green, "New People," 233; Jan Grabowski, "The Common Ground: Settled Natives and French in Montreal, 1667–1760" (Ph.D., University of Montreal, 1993), 247n. 5; in *Collections de manuscrits . . . relatifs à la Nouvelle-France* (Quebec: A. Coté, 1883–1885), 2:245–246; Colin Calloway, *The Western Abenakis of Vermont, 1600–1800: War, Migration, and the Survival of an Indian People* (Norman: University of Oklahoma Press, 1990), 106; Pontchartrain to Raudot, June 6, 1708, *NYCD,* 9:811.

25. Hammang, *Vaudreuil,* 147–153.

26. C. H. McIlwain, ed., *Peter Wraxall's Abridgement of the New York Indian Records* (Cambridge: Harvard University Press, 1915), 56; Vaudreuil au ministre, Quebec, 5 novembre, 1708, *RAPQ,* 1939–1940, 426–441; Vaudreuil et Raudot au ministre, Quebec, 14 novembre, 1708, *RAPQ,* 1939–1940, 444–463; Charlevoix, *History,* 5:204–08. For Deschaillons, see *DCB,* 3:578–579, and his father, Saint-Ours, *DCB,* 2:592–593.

27. William Eccles, *Canadian Society during the French Regime* (Montreal: Harvest House, 1968), 73–74; Guy Frégault, *Le XVIIIe Siècle canadien: Études* (Montreal: HMH, 1968), 180. On the acquisition of horses, see Louise Dechêne, *Habitants and Merchants in Seventeenth Century Montreal,* trans. Liana Vardi (Montreal and Kingston: McGill-Queen's University Press, 1992), 179–180.

28. Vaudreuil au ministre, 5 novembre, 1708, *RAPQ,* 1939–1940, 430–432; [François Hertel], "Mémoires des Services du Sr. Hertel perè et de ses enfants," *Canadian Antiquarian and Numismatic Journal,* 2nd ser., 1, no. 1 (July 1889), 9; Charlevoix, *History,* 5:204; "Liste des officers qui ont été dans le parti commandé par mrs. Deschaillons et de Rouville," in *Collections de manuscrits,* 1:503–504.

29. Vaudreuil au ministre, 5 novembre, 1708, *RAPQ,* 1939–1940, 430–432; McIlwain, *Wraxall's Abridgement,* 53, 56, 61–62; Charlevoix, *History,* 5:205, 208; Leder, *Livingston Indian Records,* 201; Green, "New People," 174–177.

30. Vaudreuil au ministre, 5 novembre, 1708, *RAPQ,* 1939–1940, 430–432; Vaudreuil et Raudot, 13 novembre, 1708, NAC, C11A 28:38–42; Charlevoix, *History,* 5:206–207; *CSP,*

1708–1709, no. 511, 24:239–240; Joseph Bartlett, "Narrative," in Joshua Coffin, *A Sketch of the History of Newbury, Newburyport, and West Newbury from 1636 to 1845* (Boston: Samuel G. Drake, 1845), 331–332; Drake, *Border Wars of New England*, 238–249; Coleman, *New England Captives*, 1:352–360.

31. Vaudreuil au ministre, 5 novembre, 1708, *RAPQ*, 1939–1940, 430–432.

32. "Resumé d'une lettre de Monsieur de Subercase au ministre," Port-Royal, le 25 et 30 décembre 1708, in *Collections de manuscrits*, 2:499–500.

33. Vaudreuil au ministre, 14 novembre, 1709, *RAPQ*, 1942–1943, 429. Examination and Intelligence of some Indians, June 21, 1709, *NYCD*, 5:85–87; [Stephen Williams], *Narrative of the Captivity of Stephen Williams*, ed. George Sheldon (Deerfield, Mass., 1889), 17–18; Sheldon, *History of Deerfield*, 1:368–372.

34. "Examination and Intelligence of some Indians," June 21, 1709, *NYCD*, 5:85–87; de Rouville et de la periere à Vaudreuil, 5 juillet, 1709, C 11A 31:106–109; Penhallow, *Indian Wars*, 49; Sheldon, *History of Deerfield*, 1:372–373.

35. De Rouville et de la periere à Vaudreuil, 5 juillet 1709, NAC, C11A 31:106–109; Vaudreuil au Ministre, 14 novembre, 1709, *RAPQ*, 1942–1943, 429; Sheldon, *History of Deerfield*, 1:373.

36. [Williams], *Narrative of the Captivity of Stephen Williams*, 18; Coleman, *New England Captives*, 2:89.

37. [Williams], *Narrative of the Captivity of Stephen Williams*, 19–20; John Demos, *The Unredeemed Captive: A Family Story from Early America* (New York: Knopf, 1994), 88–91.

38. Vaudreuil et Raudot à Pontchartrain, 2 novembre, 1710 NAC, C11A 31:26; At a Meeting of the Commissioners, Albany, July 17, 1709, in Leder, *Livingston Indian Records*, 212; McIlwain, *Wraxall's Abridgement*, 80.

39. Vaudreuil au ministre, 14 novembre, 1709, *RAPQ*, 1942–1943, 428; Charlevoix, *History*, 5:218–219; Francis Parkman, *Half Century of Conflict*, vol. 2 of *England and France in North America* (New York: Library of America, 1983), 430–431.

40. Vaudreuil au ministre, 14 novembre, 1709, *RAPQ*, 1942–1943, 428; "Parolles des Sauvages," 2 aout 1709, NAC, C11A, 30:128–130; Charlevoix, *History*, 5:218–219; "Memoire sur le Canada," in *Collections de manuscrits*, 2:617–618.

41. Claude de Ramezay au ministre, 1 novembre, 1711 NAC, C11A 32:107, 132–133.

42. On the English invasion plans, see Geoffrey Plank, *An Unsettled Conquest: The British Campaign against the Peoples of Acadia* (Philadelphia: University of Pennsylvania Press, 2001), 40–67. On the Abenakis' refusal to fight, see Hammang, *Vaudreuil*, 157–161; Morrison, *Embattled Northeast*, 159–161.

43. Vaudreuil au ministre, 1 mai, 1710, *RAPQ*, 1942–1943, 442.

44. Sheldon, *History of Deerfield*, 1:373, 376.

45. Penhallow, *Indian Wars*, 60–61; Hammang, *Vaudreuil*, 157–161; Morrison, *Embattled Northeast*, 159–161.

46. Penhallow, *Indian Wars*, 32. See also Murrin, "Anglicizing an American Colony," 77–90; [Williams], *Narrative of the Captivity of Stephen Williams*, 23–25.

47. [Williams], *Narrrative of the Captivity of Stephen Williams*, 21; Nathaniel Bouton, ed. *New Hampshire Provincial Papers: Documents Relating to the Province of New Hampshire*, (Concord, Nashua, Manchester, 1867–1873), 2:635n; *Collections de manuscrits*, 2:483–484, 493; Calloway, *Western Abenakis*, 107; Richter, *Ordeal of the Longhouse*, 226.

48. Penhallow, *Indian Wars*, 75, 76, 77; Dale Miquelon, *New France*, 102–108.

49. For Acadian life under British rule, see Plank, *An Unsettled Conquest*.

CHAPTER 11: NATIVE VILLAGES

1. These figures derive from Emma Lewis Coleman, *New England Captives Carried to Canada between 1677 and 1760 during the French and Indian Wars* (Portland, Maine: Southworth Press, 1925), and Marcel Fournier, *De la Nouvelle-Angleterre à la Nouvelle-France: l'Histoire des captifs anglo-américains au Canada entre 1675 et 1760* (Montreal: Société généalogique canadienne-française, 1992). Neither author was able to account for every captive taken. Some captives remain anonymous and their fates unknown, but the fates of three-quarters of those taken prisoner can be recovered. In particular, the fates of all but 10 percent of those who made it to Canada can de determined. The numbers quoted, then, though rough and incomplete, provide a reasonably good sense of the scale of the phenomenon. A study of the populations of Native communities in Canada also concludes that most captives were repatriated or died. See John A. Dickinson and Jan Grabowski, "Les Populations amérindiennes de la Vallée Laurentienne, 1608–1765," in *Annales de démographie historique 1993* (Société de démographie historique, E.H.E.S.S., Paris), 1993, 60.

2. Coleman, *New England Captives*, 1:91–93.

3. Coleman, *New England Captives*, 1:93–94; George Sheldon, *A History of Deerfield, Massachusetts* (Deerfield: privately printed, 1895–96), 1:381–383.

4. [John Stoddard], "Stoddard's Journal," *New England Historical and Genealogical Register* 5 (January 1851): 26–28; Coleman, *New England Captives*, 1:94–95; Sheldon, *History of Deerfield*, 1:386–387.

5. Stoddard, "Journal," 28, 29, 32.

6. John Williams to Samuel Sewell, June 1, 1714, *WP*, 5:295.

7. Stoddard, "Journal," 37–38, 40–41.

8. Stoddard, "Journal," 30, 33; Coleman, *New England Captives*, 1:96; Sheldon, *History of Deerfield*, 1:387; Fournier, *De la Nouvelle-Angleterre*, 141, 146, 150, 192.

9. Stoddard, "Journal," 40–41; Coleman, *New England Captives*, 2:103.

10. Coleman, *New England Captives*, 2:91. Two other Deerfield captives, Samuel Hastings and Ebenezer Warner, lived near Quebec, suggesting that they too may have been taken by the Hurons. But, if this was true, neither remained very long at Lorette.

11. Coleman, *New England Captives*, 2:103.

12. Coleman, *New England Captives*, 1:158; Peter Kalm, *Peter Kalm's Travels in North America: The English Version of 1770*, ed. Adolph B. Benson (1937; reprint, New York: Dover, 1964), 2:456–457.

13. Kalm, *Travels in North America*, 2:456–457, 462–463; Serge Goudreau, "Le Village huron de Lorette: Une crèche pour les enfants canadiens du XVIIIè siècle," *Mémoires de la société généalogique canadienne-française* 223 (spring 2000): 7–12. For a collection of essays on the contested identity of Lorette's Hurons, see Dennis Vaugeois, ed., *Les Hurons de Lorette* (Sillery: Septentrion, 1996), esp. 43–47, 53, 184, 187–188, 270–271.

14. A "Huron chief of Lorette" died in an attack on Rutland, Massachusetts, in August 1723. See Sheldon, *History of Deerfield*, 1:397. For the importance of alliances with their Native neighbors in particular, see Huwennuwanenhs L. K. Picard-Sioui, "Le Cas du statut des Wendats domiciliés: Réflexion sur l'imaginaire colonial et ses utilizations contemporaines" (unpublished paper, 2000, in the authors' possession).

15. Other English captives who also took up lands at Riviéres-des-Prairies were John Dicker, Mathias Farnsworth, and Adonjah Rice—all captives taken during the War of

the Spanish Succession. On Sulpician land policy and the mission, see Louise Tremblay, "La Politique missionnaire des Sulpiciens au XVIIè et debut de XVIIIè siècle, 1668–1735" (master's thesis, University of Montreal, 1981), 89–117.

16. Joseph Kellogg, "When I was Carryed to Canada . . . ," verso, the Reverend John Williams and Family, case 8, box 28, folder "Papers Relating to the 1704 Attack on Deerfield," Gratz Collection, Historical Society of Pennsylvania.

17. Coleman, *New England Captives*, 2:107–108.

18. Coleman, *New England Captives*, 2:107–108; Kellogg, "When I was Carryed," verso.

19. Coleman, *New England Captives*, 2:108–111; Denise Chopin, "Abigail Nims (Elizabeth Nims)," trans. Rosemaire Belise, *Okami: Journal de la Société d'histoire d'Oka* 25, no. 2 (2000): 5–10; Denise Chopin, "La descendance d'Abigail (Elizabeth) Nims," trans. Rosemarie Belise, *Okami: Journal de la Société d'histoire d'Oka* 26, no. 1 (2001): 14–22.

20. Coleman, *New England Captives*, 2:96–97.

21. Coleman, *New England Captives*, 2:96–97.

22. Coleman, *New England Captives*, 2:78.

23. Sheldon, *History of Deerfield*, 1:357; Coleman, *New England Captives*, 2:26–27.

24. Sheldon, *History of Deerfield*, 1:308–309; Father Gabriel Sagard, *The Long Journey to the Country of the Hurons,* ed. George M. Wrong, trans. H. H. Langton (Toronto: Champlain Society, 1939), 132–134; John Demos, *The Unredeemed Captive: A Family Story from Early America* (New York: Knopf, 1994), 159–162.

25. Alden T. Vaughan and Daniel K. Richter, "Crossing the Cultural Divide: Indians and New Englanders, 1605–1763," *American Antiquarian Society Proceedings* 90 (1980): 64; J. Norman Head, *White into Red: A Study of the Assimilation of White Persons Captured by Indians* (Metuchen, N.J.: Scarecrow Press, 1973); 119–137; Susan M. Socolow, "Spanish Captives in Indians Societies: Cultural Contact along the Argentine Frontier, 1600–1835," *Hispanic American Historical Review* 72, no. 1 (1992): 73–99; Vaudreuil à Saint-Pierre, 6 juillet, 1707, NAC, C11A, 26:66.

26. Coleman, *New England Captives*, 2:87. Plessis's remark does not make a whole lot of sense, unless Abigail was quite fit. He says he recognized her "by her tall figure and gait." The earliest he could have seen her would have been in the 1770s or 1780s when she would have been in her seventies or eighties. On family size and family limitation among Iroquoians, see Pierre-François-Xavier de Charlevoix, *Journal of a Voyage to North America* (London: R. and J. Dodsley, 1761), 2:20; Dickinson and Grabowski, "Les Populations amerindiennes," 54, 57; Dean R. Snow, *The Iroquois* (Cambridge: Blackwell, 1994), 71–74; Demos, *Unredeemed Captive*, 157–159.

27. Coleman, *New England Captives*, 2:87–88, 100.

28. Demos, *Unredeemed Captive*, 162–163.

29. Coleman, *New England Captives*, 2:70, 87–88; Gerald R. Alfred, *Heeding the Voices of Our Ancestors: Kahnawake Mohawk Politics and the Rise of Native Nationalism* (Toronto: Oxford University Press, 1995), 46.

30. Coleman, *New England Captives*, 2:87–88; Robert Eastburn, "A Faithful Narrative of the Many Dangers and Sufferings, as well as Wonderful Deliverances of Robert Eastburn," in *Held Captive by Indians: Selected Narratives, 1642–1836*, ed. Richard VanDerBeets (Knoxville: University of Tennessee Press, 1994), 167–168. On Native migration to the Ohio Country, see Richard White, *The Middle Ground: Indians, Empires, and Republics in the Great Lakes Region, 1650–1815* (New York: Cambridge University Press), 186–189.

31. Alfred, *Heeding the Voices,* 43–47; Gretchen Lynn Green, "A New People in an Age of War: The Kahnawake Iroquois, 1667–1760" (Ph.D. diss., College of William and Mary, 1991), 228–301; Jean Lunn, "The Illegal Fur Trade out of New France, 1713–1760," *Canadian Historical Association Annual Report,* 1939, 61–67; Jan Grabowski, "Les amérindiens domiciliés et la 'contrebande' des fourreures en Nouvelle France," *Recherches amérindiennes au Québec* 24, no. 3 (1994): 45–52; Demos, *Unredeemed Captive,* 177–213, 226–229; Esther Williams to Stephen Williams, February 28, 1709, Reverend John Williams and Family, case 8, box 28, Gratz Collection, Historical Society of Pennsylvania; Elizabeth M. Sadoques, "History and Traditions of Eunice Williams and Her Descendants," *Pocumtuck Valley Memorial Association History and Proceedings* (1929): 126–131; Gordon Day, "The Identity of the Saint Francis Indians," Canadian Ethnology Service Paper no. 71, Ottawa: 1981, 46–49.

32. Stoddard, "Journal," 41.

33. *DCB,* 2:25–26; "Sauvages Abenakis," report of Ramezay et Begon, 7 novembre, 1715, NAC, C11A 36:.225–229. For postwar Acadia, see Geoffrey Plank, *An Unsettled Conquest: The British Campaign against the Peoples of Acadia* (Philadelphia: University of Pennsylvania Press, 2001), 68–105. For postwar Abenakis, see Kenneth M. Morrison, *The Embattled Northeast: The Elusive Ideal of Alliance in Abenaki-Euroamerican Relations* (Berkeley: University of California Press, 1984), 165–168; David L. Ghere, "The 'Disappearance' of the Abenaki in Western Maine: Political Organization and Ethnocentric Assumptions," *American Indian Quarterly* 17, no. 2 (1993): 193–198; Harald Prins and Bruce Bourque, "Norridgewock: Village Translocation on the New England-Acadian Frontier," *Man in the Northeast* 33 (1986), 137–158.

34. Morrison, *Embattled Northeast,* 164–183; William Pencak, *War, Politics, and Revolution in Provincial Massachusetts* (Boston: Northeastern University Press, 1981), 62–80.

35. Morrison, *Embattled Northeast,* 182–185.

36. Morrison, *Embattled Northeast,* 182, 184; *DCB,* 2:669; Stephen Williams, Diary, August 10, 1722, microfilm edition of typescript transcription, 1:371, Storrs Library, Longmeadow, Mass., quoted in Josiah H. Temple and George Sheldon, *A History of the Town of Northfield, Massachusetts, for 150 Years* (Albany, N.Y.: Joel Munsell, 1875), 189. For D'Abbadie, see *DCB,* 3:3.

37. Yves F. Zoltvany, *Philippe de Rigaud de Vaudreuil: Governor of New France, 1703–1725* (Toronto: McClelland and Stewart, 1974), 196–201.

38. Colin Calloway, *The Western Abenakis of Vermont, 1600–1800: War, Migration, and the Survival of an Indian People* (Norman: University of Oklahoma Press, 1990), 113–131; Fannie Hardy Eckstrom, "Who Was Paugus?" *New England Quarterly* 12 (1939): 203–226; C. H. McIlwain, ed., *Peter Wraxall's Abridgement of the New York Indian Records* (Cambridge: Harvard University Press, 1915), 152n. 1, 175–176.

39. David L. Ghere, "Diplomacy and War on the Maine Frontier, 1678–1759," in *Maine: The Pine Tree State from Prehistory to Present,* ed. Richard W. Judd, Edwin A. Churchill, and Joel W. Eastman (Orono: University of Maine Press, 1995), 130–134; Morrison, *Embattled Northeast,* 185–190; Sheldon, *History of Deerfield,* 1:393–453; Coleman, *New England Captives,* 2:133–170.

40. Zoltvany, *Vaudreuil,* 207–209; Calloway, *Western Abenakis,* 127–130; Morrison, *Embattled Northeast,* 188–190.

41. Coleman, *New England Captives,* 2:147–151, 156, 164–166; Vaughan and Richter, "Crossing the Cultural Divide," 71.

42. James H. Merrell, "'Their Very Bones Shall Fight': The Catawba-Iroquois Wars," in *Beyond the Covenant Chain: The Iroquois and Their Neighbors in Indian North America, 1600–1800*, ed. Daniel K. Richter and James H. Merrell, (Syracuse, N.Y.: Syracuse University Press, 1987), 115–133; Green, "New People," 228–301.

CHAPTER 12: NOBLES AND HABITANTS

1. There is much evidence of these trends in Cameron Nish, *Les Bourgeois-Gentilshommes de la Nouvelle-France, 1729–1748* (Montreal: Fides, 1968), though we do not accept his underlying argument that these families were part of a colonial bourgeoisie.

2. *DCB*, 2:285–286; René Jetté, *Dictionnaire généalogique des familles du Québec* (Montreal: Les Presses de l'Université de Montréal, 1983), 567.

3. Pierre-Georges Roy, *Lettres de noblesse, généalogies, érections de comtes et baronnies insinuées par le Conseil Souverain de la Nouvelle-France* (Beauceville: L'Éclaireur, 1920), 2:164; *DCB*, 2:283, 286; Jay Cassel "The Troupes de la Marine in Canada, 1683–1760: Men and Materiel" (Ph.D. diss., University of Toronto, 1987), 157–158; Dale Miquelon, *New France, 1701–1744, "A Supplement to Europe"* (Toronto: McClelland and Stewart, 1987), 326n. 31.

4. *DCB*, 3:288–289, 2:284; François Daniel, *Histoire des grandes familles françaises du Canada* (Montreal: Eusèbe Sénécal, 1867), 408–409; Jean-Baptiste-Melchoir Hertel de Rouville, "Généalogie de la famille Hertel," *Nova Francia* 5 (1930): 160. On the noblesse and the fur trade in the Upper Country during this period, see Nish, *Bourgeois-Gentilshommes*, 77–98; Gratien Allaire, "Officiers et marchands: Les Sociétés de commerce des fourreures, 1715–1760," *Revue d'histoire de l'Amérique française* 40, no. 3 (winter 1987): 409–428.

5. Jetté, *Dictionnaire*, 4–5, 509–510, 566–567, 817; Cassel, "Troupes de la Marine," 157–158; Lorraine Gadoury, *La Noblesse de Nouvelle-France: Familles et alliances* (Montreal: Hutubise HMH, 1991), 60–62, 74–77, 117–123, 149–154. See also Nish, *Bourgeois-Gentilshommes*, 113–115, 157–172.

6. The other brothers whose sons served as officers were Beaulac, Cournoyer, Moncours, and Joseph de St. François. *DCB*, 2: 284, 286, 3:83, 288–289, 289–290; Daniel, *Histoire des grandes familles*, 408, 141–415; De Rouville, "Généalogie de la famille Hertel," 160; Gadoury, *Noblesse de Nouvelle-France*, 117. The information on officers serving in the *troupes* during the Seven Years' War is drawn from Cassel, "Troupes de la Marine," app. H, 555–600. No other family came close to rivaling the record of the Bouchers and the Hertels, though four families—Céloron, Drouet, Godefroy, and Le Gardeur—provided six officers each during this war.

7. The nephew was Ensign Pierre Boucher de Boucherville. *DCB*, 3:80, 81–82.

8. *DCB*, 3:245–246.

9. *DCB*, 3:246–253; Gaultier de La Vérendrye, NAC, E, 199:6.

10. *DCB*, 3:374; Memoir, NAC, 99:150–151; Nish, *Bourgeois-Gentilshommes*, 107, 118–119.

11. Miquelon, *New France*, 240–243, 262; Peter N. Moogk, *La Nouvelle France: The Making of French Canada—A Cultural History* (East Lansing: Michigan State University Press, 2000), 158–159; Cassel, "Troupes de la Marine," 494.

12. Sixteen lived out their lives in New France: Sarah Allen, Mary Brooks, "Marguerite" Field, John Carter, Samuel Carter, Elizabeth Corse, Abigail Stebbins de Noyon,

Freedom French, Martha French, Thomas Hurst, Abigail Nims, Jacob Rising, Ebenezer Stebbins, Joseph Stebbins, Thankful Stebbins, and Elizabeth Price Stevens. We also discuss in this chapter several individuals who left New France after living in Canada for almost a decade: Sarah Hurst Perkins, Ebenezer Hurst, Elizabeth Hurst, Joseph Kellogg, Samuel Hastings, and Samuel Price. In addition there was Samuel Stebbins, who remained until the late 1720s. We include Sarah Allen, the daughter of Edward and Mercy Allen, who became Marie-Françoise Allen and lived out her life in New France. Sarah Allen, the daughter of John and Elizabeth Allen, who died in Deerfield on May 14, 1715, has been misidentified as the captive. See Marcel Fournier, *De la Nouvelle-Angleterre à la Nouvelle-France: L'Histoire des captifs anglo-américains au Canada entre 1675 et 1760* (Montreal: Société généalogique canadienne-française, 1992), 102.

13. Micheline Dumont, "Les Femmes de la Nouvelle-France Etaient-Elles Favorisées?" *Atlantis* 8, no. 1 (fall 1982): 120.

14. Moogk, *La Nouvelle France,* 167–168.

15. Emma Lewis Coleman, *New England Captives Carried to Canada between 1677 and 1760 during the French and Indian Wars* (Portland, Maine: Southworth Press, 1925), 2:70, 88, 97, 116. Fournier, *De la Nouvelle-Angleterre,* 146, 181. Coleman gives no indication of Ebenezer's life after his baptism but assumes that he lived out his life in New France. Fournier claims Hurst returned in 1713. Coleman also loses track of Hastings after his naturalization. Again, Fournier assumes that he returned with the last batch of prisoners at the war's end. He clearly wanted to return in 1709–1710, for Esther Williams remarked that he "would come home if he could." See Esther Williams to Stephen Williams, February 28, 1709–1710, the Reverend John Williams and Family, case 8, box 28, Gratz Collection, Historical Society of Pennsylvania.

16. *DCB,* 3:324–325.

17. Coleman, *New England Captives,* 2:72.

18. Coleman, *New England Captives,* 2:123, 125.

19. Coleman, *New England Captives,* 2:126–127; Fournier, *De la Nouvelle-Angleterre,* 207, 208. Fournier claims that Ebenezer Stebbins returned, but in this instance, we tend to discount his conclusion.

20. Coleman, *New England Captives,* 2:127; Fournier, *De la Nouvelle-Angleterre,* 208–209. For Thankful's marriage contract, see M. Tailhandier dit LaBeaume, 4 février 1711. M. Lepailleur de LaFerté, 14 mars, 1717, for Chambly land. Daughter's marriages: to F. Simonnet, 19 novembre, 1738 (Marguerite to a blacksmith at Chambly), and G. Hodiesne, 5 février, 1742 (Charlotte to a man from Beaumont, near Quebec), ANQM.

21. Coleman, *New England Captives,* 2:118–124; *DCB,* 3:493–494.

22. Moogk, *La Nouvelle France,* 64, 229–233; Allan Greer, *The People of New France* (Toronto: University of Toronto Press 1997), 69–71; Catherine L. Stebbins, "Jacques De-Noyon" (Historic Deerfield Library, n.d.), 224–230.

23. Stebbins, "Jacques DeNoyon," 224–230. For Abigail's business transactions see M. Tailhandier dit LeBeaume, 10 avril, 1713, 11 avril, 1716, and 20 juin and 20 août, 1719, ANQM. Most of these documents take care to note that she is separated from Jacques in terms of goods.

24. Greer, *People of New France,* 20–23; Moogk, *La Nouvelle France,* 219; Gloria L. Main, *Peoples of a Spacious Land: Families and Cultures in Colonial New England* (Cambridge: Harvard University Press, 2001), 80–81, 210; Coleman, *New England Captives,* 2:67.

25. Moogk, *La Nouvelle France,* 113–114. Robert Larin's estimates suggest that captives provided almost 3 percent of the gross immigration of thirty-six thousand to Canada during the French colonial period. See Larin, *Brève Histoire du peuplement européen en Nouvelle-France* (Sillery: Septentrion, 2000), 82.

26. Moogk, *La Nouvelle France,* 178, 199–206.

27. Coleman, *New England Captives,* 2:68, 75–76; Jetté, *Dictionnaire,* 822.

28. Coleman, *New England Captives,* 1:148–154, 240–243, 303–304, 383–388, 410, 2:113–116, 166–167; Fournier, *De la Nouvelle-Angleterre,* 190, 192.

29. Coleman, *New England Captives,* 113–116; Fournier, *De la Nouvelle-Angleterre,* 190.

30. Coleman, *New England Captives,* 1:123, 128–129; 2:93; Marc-André Bédard, *Les Protestants en Nouvelle-France* Cahiers d'histoire no. 31 (Quebec: Société historique de Québec, 1978), 46, 54–56.

31. Coleman, *New England Captives,* 2:91–92. Fournier, *De la Nouvelle-Angleterre,* 181, claims that the Perkinses returned to New England in September 1713. He also claims that Sarah's son Ebenezer returned as well (155). For Samuel Price, see Fournier, *De la Nouvelle-Angleterre,* 192.

32. Coleman, *New England Captives,* 1:123, 129, 358–360, 374–375, 2:92–93. Fournier, *De la Nouvelle-Angleterre,* 147, claims that Elizabeth and her husband returned to New England at the end of the war.

33. Coleman, *New England Captives,* 2:79–80; *DCB,* 2:579–580.

34. For links between La Prairie and Kahnawake, see Linda Breuer Gray, "Narratives and Identities in the Saint Lawrence Valley, 1667–1720" (Ph.D. diss., McGill University, 1999).

35. Coleman, *New England Captives,* 2:83–84. G. Hodiesne, 2 juin, 1762, is Pierre Roy's marriage contract at age forty and lists him as a master stone-cutter; J.-B. Adhémar dit Saint-Martin, 15 août, 1740, is Jacques Roy's marriage contract at age twenty-two and lists him as a master-mason and stone-cutter; J.-B. Adhemer dit Saint-Martin, 21 juin, 1736, lists their sister Marie-Joseph as married at age twenty-two to Pierre Achambault from Pointe-aux-Trembles (a *habitant,* according to A. Foucher, 3 mars, 1753); F. Simonnet, 21 avril, 1748, is Laurent Roy's marriage contract; A. Foucher, 29 octobre, 1752, lists Laurent as a shoemaker, ANQM.

36. Coleman, *New England Captives,* 2:85–87; Fournier, *De La Nouvelle-Angleterre,* 133–134. L.-C. Danré de Blanzy, 18 janvier, 1757, lists Jean-Louis as a weaver; J.-B. Adhémar dit Saint-Martin, 3 mai, 1733, is the marriage contract; F. Simonnet, 29 février, 1742, lists Jean-Louis as a militia lieutenant; F. Simonnet, 25 juin, 1752, lists him as a militia captain; A. Foucher, 13 mars, 1757, mentions Marie-Anne and Potdevin Perrot, a carpenter; A. Foucher, 23 juillet, 1752, is the marriage contract between Joseph Plessis and Marie-Louise Menard; L.-C. Danré de Blanzy, 18 janvier, 1757, is Marie-Marguerite's marriage contract; Martha is alive on 19 février, 1763 (P. Panet de Meru), but on 11 juin Jean-Louis is a widower (G. Hodiesne), ANQM. On Bishop Plessis, see "A Scion of the Church in Deerfield: Joseph Octave Plessis," in C. Alice Baker, *True Stories of New England Captives Carried to Canada during the Old French and Indian Wars* (1897; reprint, Bowie, Md.: Heritage Books, 1990), 272–303.

37. Coleman, *New England Captives,* 1:231; 2:71, 82–85, 93, 95; Fournier, *De la Nouvelle-Angleterre,* 133.

38. Her second husband was named Pierre Monet. Coleman, *New England Captives,* 74–76, 84; Fournier, *De la Nouvelle-Angleterre,* 116–117, 124.

39. Coleman, *New England Captives*, 2:93–97; Fournier, *De la Nouvelle-Angleterre*, 147–148. See also Charles-P. Beaubien, *Le Sault-au-Récollet: Ses rapports avec les premiers temps de la colonie* (Montreal: C. O. Beauchemin & Fils, 1898). For the difficult lives of urban widows, who made up most of the urban poor, see André Lachance, *La Vie urbaine en Nouvelle France* (Montreal: Boreal, 1987), 60–65.

40. Coleman, *New England Captives*, 2:70–71; J-B. Adhémar dit Saint-Martin, 27 octobre, 1718, is a marriage contract; P. Raimbault, 20 decembre, 1718, is a first grant of land; P. Raimbault, 24 mars, 1721, is a second grant of land at Rivières-des-Prairies; in J. David, 18 mai, 1722, Jean Chartier buys more land in the same place, ANQM.

41. Fournier, *De la Nouvelle-Angleterre*, 112; Coleman, *New England Captives*, 2:72; M. Lepailleur de LaFerté, 24 septembre, 1725, records Zacharie-François's grant to John, here noted as "anglais de nation"; in M. Lepailleur de LaFerté, 22 mars, 1730, John returns the land to Zacharie-François; in M. Lepailleur de LaFerté, 27 juin, 1732, John obtains land at Contrecoeur; in M. Lepailleur de LaFerté, 4 juin, 1734, John obtains more land at Contrecoeur in the name of all his children. For John's land sales on Montreal Island, see J. David, 17 février, 1726, 11 mars, 1726 (two land sales in one day), and J.-B. Adhémar dit Saint-Martin, 3 février, 1727, 12 novembre, 1727, 15 janvier, 1733, ANQM. For François-Antoine de Pecuady de Contreceour, see *DCB*, 3:505.

42. For Carter's land sales in Rivières-des-Prairies, see J. David, 15 février and 11 mars, 1726, and J.-B. Adhémar dit Saint-Martin, 15 janvier, 1733. For his credit relationships with Montreal merchants, see J.-B. Adhémar dit Saint-Martin, 26 février, 1738, 17 and 18 janvier, 1745, 14 février, 1749, AMQM. For Carter's engagement as a *voyageur*, see L.-C. Danré de Blanzy, 20 juillet and 2 août, 1742 (where he is referred to as "Langlois"). For his partnership with Louise de Ramezay, see G. Hodiesne, 29 août, 1746, and 25 novembre, 1755, ANQM. For Françoise-Louise de Ramezay's entrepreneurial efforts, see *DCB*, 2:548.

43. For the marriages of Carter's children, see L. C. Danré de Blanzy, 16 septembre, 1750 (Marie), J. Crevier-Duvernay, 31 mai, 1751 (Joseph), J.-B. Daguilhe, 19 février, 1753 (Jean-Baptiste), L.-C. Danré de Blanzy, 6 mars, 1756 (Theodore); for his donation to his children, see J. Crevier-Duvernay, 6 octobre, 1751; for his sons' disposal of some of the Contrecoeur land in 1755, see J. Crevier-Duvernay, 13 octobre, 1755; for his residence at Beaujeu and land transactions at Longueuil, see G. Hodiesne, 7 septembre, 1754; Fournier, *De la Nouvelle-Angleterre*, 112; for Carter's last land deals see A. Grise dit Villefranche, 10 aoûts and 4 novembre, 1763, 20 août, 1764, 20 novembre, 1765, 12 mars, 1770, 2 mars, 1771, ANQM.

CHAPTER 13: NEW ENGLAND IMPERIALISM

1. Richard I. Melvoin, *New England Outpost: War and Society in Colonial Deerfield* (New York: Norton, 1989), 250; Gloria L. Main, *Peoples of a Spacious Land: Families and Cultures in Colonial New England* (Cambridge: Harvard University Press, 2001), ix.

2. Town Book to 1762, Town of Deerfield, microfilm, 47, Historic Deerfield Library.

3. Fitz John Winthrop's Table of Losses puts the total property loss at 3,015 pounds, or 60,300 shillings. The average daily wage in colonial New England was 2 shillings. The loss of 3,015 pounds is, therefore, the equivalent of roughly 30,150 days work. See George Sheldon, *A History of Deerfield, Massachusetts* (Deerfield: privately printed, 1895–1896), 1:304–305.

4. Sheldon, *History of Deerfield,* 1:317; Petition by Jonathan Wells, MA, 71:166–167. Melvoin follows Sheldon in assuming that the women and children left Deerfield. Melvoin, *New England Outpost,* 231. On Choate, see *Acts and Resolves, Public and Private of the Province of Massachusetts Bay* (Boston: Wright and Potter, 1869–1922), 8:404.

5. Sheldon, *History of Deerfield,* 2:101, 189, 157, 293, 265, 301–302.

6. Sheldon, *History of Deerfield,* 2:240, 239, 268–269, 97, 101, 214, 157, 226–227, 265, 263, 377–380. An earlier study that concludes that only twenty-five captives returned to Deerfield counts only those who lived out their lives in Deerfield and does not include eight individuals who moved away after initially returning to Deerfield. Four of these individuals would move to Northfield in the late 1710s or 1720s. Ann E. McCleary, "The Child against the Devil: The Effects of Indian Captivity on the Redeemed Captives and the Puritan Zion" (paper prepared for Historic Deerfield Summer Fellowship Program, 1975), 16. Melvoin also uses the figure thirty-three. See Melvoin, *New England Outpost,* 250. See our appendix C.

7. Sheldon, *History of Deerfield,* 1:337–338, 359–360, 460–462, 2:377–378; Issac Chauncey, *A Blessed Manumission of Christ's Faithful Ministers, when they have finish'd their Testimony: A Sermon Preach'd at the Funeral of the Reverend John Williams* (Boston: D. Henchman and T. Hancock, 1729), 24.

8. Those moving to Deerfield were John Amsden, weaver; Joseph Atherton; Samuel Bardwell; Thomas Bardwell, sadler; Timothy Childs, weaver; Samuel Childs, blacksmith; Joseph Clesson; James Corse, hunter; Aaron Denio, shoemaker; Samuel Field, tavernkeeper; Benoni Moors; Moses Nash, schoolteacher; Jonathan Patterson, tailor; George Swan; Thomas Taylor, sadler; Samuel Taylor, storekeeper; James Tute; and Judah Wright, weaver. See Sheldon, *History of Deerfield,* 1:498–499, 506–507, 2:29, 51, 57, 58, 110–111, 127, 133–134, 139, 157, 242, 247, 260, 336–337, 348, 393. See also Melvoin, *New England Outpost,* 250–251.

9. Melvoin, *New England Outpost,* 252–253, 255–256. The sons and daughters had 6.6 children, whereas their parents had had 7.1. See Kevin Sweeney, "Children of the Covenant" (paper prepared for Historic Deerfield Summer Fellowship Program, 1971), 23–25.

10. The eight who signed and eventually moved to Northfield were Joseph Alexander, Peter Evans, Zechariah Field, Eleazer Mattoon, Isaac Mattoon, Joseph Petty, Joseph Severance, and Thomas Taylor. With the exception of Joseph Severance, they all moved to Northfield. The following Deerfield residents also moved to Northfield: Edmund Grandy, Eleazer Mattoon, Nathaniel Mattoon, Benoni Moors, Jonathan Patterson, and Joseph Stebbins. See Josiah H. Temple and George Sheldon, *A History of the Town of Northfield, Massachusetts, for 150 Years* (Albany, N.Y.: Joel Munsell, 1875), 133–135, 138, 150, 454, 533, 541. See also Melvoin, *New England Outpost,* 252, 254.

11. Sheldon, *History of Deerfield,* 487–489; Melvoin, *New England Outpost,* 267–269; Sweeney, "Children of the Covenant," 26–28.

12. Sweeney, "Children of the Covenant," 29.

13. Sheldon, *History of Deerfield,* 2:855–857; Melvoin, *New England Outpost,* 258–262; Sweeney, "Children of the Covenant," 39–40, 46–48.

14. Sheldon, *History of Deerfield,* 1:486; *Boston Evening Post,* October 7, 1754.

15. Sheldon, *History of Deerfield,* 1:307, 2:857, 393; Sylvester Judd, *The History of Hadley including the Early History of Hatfield, South Hadley, Amherst and Granby, Massachusetts* (Springfield, Mass.: H. R. Huntting, 1905), 448–449, "Genealogies," 47, 91–92.

The captive John Marsh of Hatfield (born November 6, 1672) has been confused with twenty-four-year-old John Marsh of Hadley (born March 9, 1679 and died September 2, 1725). The latter John Marsh was a prominent Hadley resident but could not have been the captive because he married Joanna Porter in Hadley on June 27, 1704, long before any captives returned from Canada. We, therefore, follow Coleman, *New England Captives*, 2:102.

16. Sheldon, *History of Deerfield*, 2:855–857, 168, 105, 214, 379–380.

17. Coleman, *New England Captives*, 2:89; Sheldon, *History of Deerfield*, 2:203–204; Births, Intentions, Marriages, and Deaths, 1722, Town of Deerfield, microfilm, [3, 16], Historic Deerfield Library.

18. Clifford K. Shipton, *Sibley's Harvard Graduates* (Cambridge: Harvard University Press, 1933–1975), 8:141–148. On Hinsdale's dismissal from the ministry, see "To the Reverend Gentlemen Assembled in Deerfield July 11, 1750, to hear a Complaint Exhibited against Mr. Ebenezer Hinsdale," Thomas Williams Papers, 17, New York Historical Society; Deposition by Oliver Partridge, July 7, 1750, Timothy Childs, Timothy Childs Jr., John Catlin 2nd, Thomas Williams, Statement by Committee of the Deerfield Church, July 11, 1750, Deerfield Family Papers, box 103, Pocumtuck Valley Memorial Association. On his uncertain paternity, see Sheldon, *History of Deerfield*, 2:204.

19. Sheldon, *History of Deerfield*, 1:359–384, 2:214.

20. James Russell Trumbull, *History of Northampton, Massachusetts from Its Settlement in 1654* (Northampton: privately printed, 1898–1902), 1:486–490.

21. E. B. O'Callaghan, ed. *The Documentary History of the State of New York* (Albany: Weed, Parsons, 1849–1851), 3:1037; Coleman, *New England Captives*, 2:99–100; Sheldon, *History of Deerfield*, 2:227; *DCB*, 3:324–325.

22. O'Callaghan, *Documentary History*, 3:1037; Sherman W. Adams and Henry R. Stiles, *The History of Ancient Wethersfield, Connecticut* (New York: Grafton Press, 1904), 1:776–781; Coleman, *New England Captives*, 2:97–99; Sheldon, *History of Deerfield*, 2:226–227.

23. Sheldon, *History of Deerfield*, 2:251, 90–91, 294–295, 319.

24. John Williams, in Cotton Mather, *Good Fetch'ed out of Evil* (Boston: B. Green, 1706), 13. McCleary, "Child against the Devil," 17; Records of the First Church of Deerfield, microfilm, Historic Deerfield, Library. The four who died before the earliest surviving list of church members was drawn up were Simeon Beaman, John Burt, John Stebbins, and Samuel Williams. Between one-third and two-thirds of adult males were members of the churches in Hampshire County in the 1730s. See Kevin M. Sweeney, "Unruly Saints: Religion and Society in the River Towns of Massachusetts, 1700–1735" (senior honors thesis, Williams College, 1972), 53–55.

25. Williams in Mather, *Good Fetched out of Evil*, 26; McCleary, "Child against the Devil," 37.

26. Jonathan Edwards, "A Faithful Narrative," in *The Great Awakening*, ed. C. C. Goen, vol. 4 of *The Works of Jonathan Edwards* (New Haven, Conn.: Yale University Press, 1972), 153; quoted in Sheldon, *History of Deerfield*, 2:139; McCleary, "Child against the Devil," 34–36.

27. Edwards, "Faithful Narrative," 147–148, 184–185.

28. Solomon Williams, *The Power and Efficacy of the Prayers of the People of God, when rightly offered to him; and the Obligation and Encouragement thence arising to be much in*

Prayer: A Sermon Preached at Mansfield, Aug. 4, 1741 (Boston: S. Kneeland and T. Green, 1742), 25.

29. Quotations from Coleman, *New England Captives*, 2:387–388; John Demos, *The Unredeemed Captive: A Family Story from Early America* (New York: Knopf, 1994), 207–213.

30. Sheldon, *History of Deerfield*, 2:139; Daniel Richter, *The Ordeal of the Longhouse: The Peoples of the Iroquois League in the Era of European Colonization* (Chapel Hill: University of North Carolina Press, 1992), 239–240; John Williams to Stephen Williams, May 24, 1718, Fisher Howe Miscellaneous Letters, folder 1, Williams College Archives, Williamstown, Mass.; Annotation to handwritten copy of "The Redeemed Captive Returning to Zion," 25, in Eleazer Williams Papers, 1634–1964, microfilm edition, State Historical Society of Wisconsin, Area Research Center, Green Bay; Coleman, *New England Captives*, 2:78, 100–101; Demos, *Unredeemed Captive*, 188–213.

31. To Governor Dummer, April 6, 1724, quoted in Sheldon, *History of Deerfield*, 1:409; see also Sheldon, *History of Deerfield*, 1:420; 2:81, 247.

32. John Stoddard to Governor Dummer, February 3, 1725, quoted in Sheldon, *History of Deerfield*, 1:438; see also Sheldon, *History of Deerfield*, 1:433, 442, 452–453.

33. Melvoin, *New England Outpost*, 263–266; Sheldon, *History of Deerfield*, 1:392–453.

34. For Hoyt, see [Stephen Williams], *Narrative of the Captivity of Stephen Williams*, ed. George Sheldon (Deerfield, Mass,: Pocumtuck Valley Memorial Association, 1889), 33n. 38. For the Sheldons, see *Acts and Resolves*, 11:324–25, 504. Sheldon, *History of Deerfield*, 1:527; MA, 29:147.

35. Quotations from Coleman, *New England Captives*, 2:101.

36. Stephen Williams to Benjamin Coleman, in Nathaniel Appleton, *Gospel Ministers Must be fit for The Master's Use and Prepared to every Good Work if they would be Vessels unto Honour* (Boston: S. Kneeland & T. Green, 1735), vii. Stephen Williams, Diary, December 31, 1718, December 29, 1730, January 6, 1729, microfilm edition, Longmeadow Public Library, Longmeadow, Mass. For taking Indian lads into his home, see Stephen Williams, Diary, December 20, 1735, December 15, 1738, January 9, 1740.

37. Stephen Williams, Diary, May 24, July 7–9, 19, 23, 27, 29, August 12–22, 1722; Patrick Frazier, *The Mohicans of Stockbridge* (Lincoln: University of Nebraska Press, 1992), 1–38.

38. Colin Calloway, *The Western Abenakis of Vermont, 1600–1800: War, Migration, and the Survival of an Indian People* (Norman: University of Oklahoma Press, 1990), 133–136; Sheldon, *History of Deerfield*, 1:522, 2:133

39. Calloway, *Western Abenakis*, 137–138.

40. "Indian Treaties," *Collections of the Maine Historical Society* 4 (1856): 129–130, 131–132; Calloway, *Western Abenakis*, 138–140; Frazier, *Mohicans of Stockbridge*, 32–56, 69–123, 138–245; Sheldon, *History of Deerfield*, 1:522–525.

41. "Indian Treaties," 142–144; Coleman, *New England Captives*, 2:101–102; Lion G. Miles, "The Red Man Dispossessed: The Williams Family and the Alienation of Indian Land in Stockbridge, Massachusetts, 1736–1818," *New England Quarterly* 66, no. 1 (March 1994): 46–76.

42. O'Callaghan, *Documentary History,* 3:1037–1038; Demos, *Unredeemed Captive*, 237.

43. Quotations from Coleman, *New England Captives,* 2:62–63. See also Demos, *Unredeemed Captive*, 214–241.

Afterword: Remembering February 29, 1704

1. *Greenfield Recorder,* February 2, 1989; *Springfield Union News,* February 25, 1993; *Springfield Sunday Republican,* February 28, 1993; Kevin M. Sweeney, personal recollections of February 28, 1993.

2. Samuel Penhallow, *The History of the Wars,* ed. Edward Wheelock (1726; 1924, reprint, Williamstown, Mass.: Corner House, 1973), 12; George Sheldon, *A History of Deerfield, Massachusetts* (Deerfield: privately printed, 1895–1896), 1:300–301, 302–305, 343; Coll. Partridge and Major Pynchon about The Mischeif at Deerfield, Winthrop Papers, Massachusetts Historical Society.

3. Tom Englehardt, *The End of Victory Culture: Cold War America and the Disillusioning of a Generation* (Amherst: University of Massachusetts Press, 1998), 5, 23.

4. John Taylor, *A Century Sermon Preached at Deerfield, February 29, 1804: In Commemoration of the Destruction of the Town by the French and Indians* (Greenfield, Mass.: John Denio, 1804), 7, 15, 18, 20, 21.

5. Epaphras Hoyt, *Antiquarian Researches* (Greenfield, Mass.: A. Phelps, 1824), viii, says "sacks and destroys"; Henry Trumbull, *History of the Discovery of America . . . and of their Most Remarkable Engagements with the Indians . . .* (Boston: George Clark, 1836), writes of the "massacre of the Inhabitants of Deerfield" (80); Stephen West Williams, "Ancient History of Pocomptuck or Deerfield" (manuscript, 1836), app. 19, 21, refers to the "sacking & burning of the town" and "the massacre at the outset" of the attack. Williams Family Papers, box 12, folder 3, Pocumtuck Valley Memorial Association. See also John W. Barber, *Historical Collections, Being a General Collection of Interesting Facts, Traditions, Biographical Sketches, Anecdotes, &c., Relating to the History and Antiquities of Every Town in Massachusetts* (Worcester, Mass.: Dorr, Howland, 1841), 251, calls it simply "the attack;" George Bancroft, *History of the United States: From the Discovery of the American Continent* (Boston: Little, Brown, 1852–1878), 3:213, calls it the "burning of Deerfield"; Henry M. Burt, *Burt's Illustrated Guide of the Connecticut Valley* (Springfield, Mass.: New England Publishing Company, 1866), 108–112, has an entry entitled "Deerfield—Indian Massacres"; Louis H. Everts, ed., *History of the Connecticut Valley in Massachusetts* (Philadelphia: Lippincott, 1879), 1:62, 64, describes the attack as "the Burning of Deerfield" and the "sacking of Deerfield"; John G. Palfrey, *History of New England* (Boston: Little, Brown, 1859–1890), 3:241, calls it the "sack of Deerfield"; *Collections of the Massachusetts Historical Society,* 6th ser., Winthrop Papers 3 (1889): 176 has a reference in a footnote to "the well-known Deerfield Massacre"; Edward Channing, *A History of the United States* (New York: Macmillan, 1908), 2:539, calls it the "attack on Deerfield"; Sheldon, *History of Deerfield,* 1:316, calls it "the catastrophe of February 29, 1704"; and Edwin M. Bacon, *The Connecticut River and the Valley of the Connecticut* (New York: G. P. Putnam's Sons, 1906), 164, calls it "the destruction of Deerfield."

6. [George Sheldon], "Field Meeting—1903," *History and Proceedings of the Pocumtuck Valley Memorial Association* 4 (1905): 379–423; *History and Proceedings of the Pocumtuck Valley Memorial Association* 4 (1905): 379, 381.

7. Emma Lewis Coleman, *A Historic and Present Day Guide to Old Deerfield* (Boston: 1907), 87, 92.

8. R. W. Hatch, "Old Deerfield, Mass." *Ford Times* 41, no. 3 (March 1949): 2–9; "The Deerfield Issue," *Antiques Magazine* 70, no. 3 (September 1956): 223–267; Bart McDow-

ell, "Deerfield Keeps a Truce with Time," *National Geographic* 135, no. 6 (June, 1969): 780–809.

9. Samuel Chamberlain and Henry N. Flynt, *Frontier of Freedom: The Soul and Substance of America Portrayed in One Extraordinary Village, Old Deerfield, Massetts.* (New York: Hastings House, 1952), 1.

10. Francois-Xavier Garneau, *Histoire du Canada,* 8th ed., revised and expanded by Hector Garneau (Montreal: L'Arbre, 1944–1946), 4:56–57. For the growing French-Canadian genealogical interest in New England captives, see Marcel Fournier, *De la Nouvelle Angleterre à la Nouvelle-France: L'Histoire des captifs anglo-américains au Canada entre 1675 et 1760* (Montreal: Société généalogique canadienne-française, 1992), as well as several Web sites referring specifically to Deerfield captives.

11. Ian K. Steele, *Guerrillas and Grenadiers: The Struggle for Canada, 1688–1760* (Toronto: Ryerson, 1969), 1–2. See also Michel Brunet, "The British Conquest: Canadian Social Scientists and the Fate of the *Canadiens,*" in *Approaches to Canadian History,* ed. Carl Burger (Toronto: University of Toronto Press, 1967), 84–98; Carl Berger, *The Writing of Canadian History* (Toronto: Oxford University Press, 1976), 19–20, 126–127, 185–186.

12. Mrs. E. A. Smith, Collector, "Caughnewage Legends,"American Bureau of Ethnology manuscript (1882), [3–4, 13]. For a discussion and critique of the bell story, see Geoffrey E. Buerger, "Out of Whole Cloth: The Tradition of the St. Regis Bell" (paper presented at the Mid-Atlantic Conference for Canadian Studies, Bucknell University, 1986; copy in the Pocumtuck Valley Memorial Association Library, Deerfield, Mass.).

13. David Blanchard, *Seven Generations: A History of the Kanienkehaka* (Kahnawake, 1980), 208–209.

14. Elizabeth M. Sadoques, "History and Traditions of Eunice Williams and Her Descendants," in *Pocumtuck Valley Memorial Association History and Proceedings* 6 (1929): 127–129. For evidence of close contact between Abenakis and Kahnawake Mohawks that would have given Sadoques a very likely connection to Eunice's descendants, see Jack Frisch, "The Abenakis Among the St. Regis Mohawks," *Indian Historian* 4, no. 1 (1971): 27–29; Colin Calloway, *The Western Abenakis of Vermont, 1600–1800: War, Migration, and the Survival of the Indian People* (Norman: University of Oklahoma Press, 1990), 163–164, 197–201, 243; Gordon Day, "The Identity of the Saint Francis Indians," Canadian Ethnology Service paper no. 71 (Ottawa, 1981), 76, 83, 85, 94, 97, see 86, 130, for Elizabeth's ancestor Shattoockquis from Quaboag, today Brookfield.

BIBLIOGRAPHY

MANUSCRIPT PRIMARY SOURCES

Archives du Séminaire de Nicolet, Nicolet, Quebec
   Henri Vassal Collection
Archives du Séminaire de Trois-Rivières, Trois-Rivières, Quebec
    Compilation de documents re: Familles Boucher, Montarville
    Boucher de la Bruére
Archives Nationales de Québec, Montreal
   Archives Judiciaires de Montréal, Montreal
     Jean-Baptiste Adhémar dit Saint-Martin, 1714–1754
     Jacques Crevier-Duvernay, 1748–1760
     Jean-Baptiste Daguilhe, 1749–1783
     Louis-Claude Danré de Blanzy, 1738–1760
     Jacques David, 1719–1726
     Antoine Foucher, 1746–1800
     Antoine Grise, dit Villefranche, 1756–1785
     Gervais Hodiesne, 1740–1764
     Michel Lepailleur de LaFerté, 1703–1732
     Pierre Panet de Meru, 1755–1778
     Pierre Raimbault, 1697–1727
     François Simonnet, 1737–1778
     Marien Tailhandier dit Le Beaume, 1699–1730
Canadian National Archives, Ottawa
    Série B, Lettres envoyées
    Série C11A, Correspondence générale, Canada
    Série D2, Troupes colonials
    Série E Dossiers personnels
    Série F3, Collection Moreau Saint-Méry
Archives Nationales, Paris
    Série C11A, Correspondence générale, 1540–1784
Forbes Library, Northampton, Massachusetts
   Judd Manuscripts
Historic Deerfield Library, Deerfield, Mass.
    Births, Intentions, Marriages, and Deaths, 1722, Town of Deerfield, microfilm
    Hampshire County Probate Records, 1662–1820, 32 vols. microfilm.
    Records of the First Church of Deerfield, microfilm
    Town Book to 1762, Town of Deerfield, microfilm

Historical Society of Pennsylvania, Philadelphia
  Gratz Collection
Massachusetts Historical Society, Boston
  Winthrop Papers
Massachusetts State Archives, Boston
  Massachusetts Archives
Pocumtuck Valley Memorial Association, Deerfield, Mass.
  Williams Family Papers
New York Historical Society, New York City
  Cornbury Correspondence
  Thomas Williams Papers
New York Public Library, New York City
  Emett Collection
Storrs Library, Longmeadow, Mass.
  Stephen Williams Diary, typescript
Williams College Archives, Williamstown, Mass.
  Fisher Howe Miscellaneous Letters
Winterthur Museum, Winterthur, Del.
  Watson Family Papers
Wisconsin State Historical Society, Area Research Center, Green Bay
  Eleazer Williams Papers

PUBLISHED PRIMARY SOURCES

Acts and Resolves, Public and Private of the Province of Massachusetts Bay. 21 vols. Boston: Wright and Potter, 1869–1922.

Andros Tracts. Edited by W. H. Whitemore. 3 vols. Boston: Prince Society, 1867–1874.

Appleton, Nathaniel. *Gospel Ministers Must be Fit for the Master's Use and Prepared to Every Good Work if They Would be Vessels Unto Honour.* Boston: S. Kneeland and T. Green, 1735.

Bartlett, Joseph. "Narrative." In Joshua Coffin, *A Sketch of the History of Newbury, Newburyport, and West Newbury from 1636 to 1845,* 331–334. Boston: Samuel G. Drake, 1845.

Baxter, James Phinney, ed. *Baxter Manuscripts: Documentary History of the State of Maine.* 24 vols. Portland: Maine Historical Society, 1869–1916.

[Boucher, Pierre]. "Memoires de feu Monsieur Boucher, Seigneur de Boucherville, et ancien gouverneur des Trois-Rivières." *Bulletin des recherches historiques,* 1926, 398–404.

Boucher, Pierre. *True and General Description of New France, Commonly Called Canada, and of the Manners and Customs and Productions of that Country.* Translated and edited by Edward Louis Montizambert. 1664. Reprint, Paris: Florentin Lambert, 1881.

Bouton, Nathaniel, ed. *New Hampshire Provincial Papers: Documents Relating to the Province of New Hampshire.* 7 vols. Concord, Nashua, Manchester, 1867–1873.

Bridenbaugh, Carl, and Juliette Tomlinson, eds. *The Pynchon Papers.* 2 vols. Boston: Colonial Society of Massachusetts, distributed by University Press of Virginia, 1982.

Calendar of State Papers. Colonial Series, *America and West Indies.* 39 vols. London: Hereford Times, 1860–1969.

Calendar of Treasury Papers. Vol. 3, *1702–1707.* London: Longman & Co., 1874.

Catalogne, Gédéon de. "Report on the Seigniories and Settlements in the Districts of Quebec, Three Rivers, and Montreal." In *Documents Relating to the Seignorial Tenure in Canada, 1598–1854,* edited by William Bennett Munro, 94–151. Toronto: Champlain Society, 1908.

Censuses of Canada, 1665 to 1871. 4 vols. Ottawa: I. B. Taylor, 1876.

Charlevoix, Pierre-François-Xavier de. *History and General Description of New France.* 6 vols. Translated and edited by John Gilmary Shea. 1870. Reprint, Chicago: Loyola University Press, 1962.

———. *Journal of a Voyage to North-America.* 2 vols. London: R. and J. Dodsley, 1761.

Chauncey, Isaac. *A Blessed Manumission of Christ's Faithful Ministers, when they have finish'd their Testimony: A Sermon Preach'd at the Funeral of the Reverend John Williams.* Boston: D. Henchman and T. Hancock, 1729.

Collection de manuscrits, contenant lettres, mémoires, et autres documents historiques relatifs à la Nouvelle-France. 4 vols. Quebec: A. Coté, 1883–1885.

Dudley, Joseph. *A Declaration Against the Pennicooke and Eastern Indian, August 18, 1703.* Boston, 1703.

Eastburn, Robert. "A Faithful Narrative of the Many Dangers and Sufferings, as well as Wonderful and Surprizing Deliverances of Robert Eastburn." In *Held Captive by Indians: Selected Narratives, 1642–1836,* edited by Richard VanDerBeets, 151–176. Knoxville: University of Tennessee Press, 1994.

Edwards, Jonathan. "A Faithful Narrative." In *The Great Awakening,* edited by C. C. Goen, 111–211. Vol. 4 of *The Works of Jonathan Edwards.* New Haven, Conn.: Yale University Press, 1972.

Foxcroft, Thomas. *Eli, the Priest Dying Suddenly.* Boston: S. Gerrish, 1729.

Gookin, Daniel. *An Historical Account of the Doings and Sufferings of the Christian Indians of New England, in the Years 1675, 1676, 1677.* 1835. Reprint, New York: Arno Press, 1972.

Gyles, John. "Memoirs of Odd Adventures, Strange Deliverances, etc." In *Puritans among the Indians: Accounts of Captivity and Redemption, 1676–1724,* edited by Alden T. Vaughan and Edward W. Clark, 91–131. Cambridge: Harvard University Press, 1981.

[Hawley, Gideon]. "A Letter from Rev. Gideon Hawley of Mashpee containing a Narrative of his Journey to Onohoghgwage in 1753." *Collections of the Massachusetts Historical Society,* 1st ser., 4 (1795): 1033–1046.

[Hertel, Joseph François]. "Mémoires des services du Sr. Hertel père et de ses Enfants." *Canadian Antiquarian and Numismatic Journal,* 2nd ser., 1, no. 1 (July 1889): 5–9.

[Hubbard, William]. *The History of the Indian Wars in New England from the First Settlement to the Termination of the War with King Philip in 1677, from the Original Work by the Rev. William Hubbard.* 2 vols. Edited by Samuel Drake. 1865. Reprint, New York: Burt Franklin, 1971.

"Indian Treaties." *Collections of the Maine Historical Society,* 4 (1856): 123–144.

Kalm, Peter. *Peter Kalm's Travels in North America: The English Version of 1770.* 2 vols. Edited by Adolph B. Benson. 1937. Reprint, New York: Dover, 1964.

[Lahontan, Louis Armand de Lom d'Arce, Baron de]. *New Voyages to North-America by the Baron de Lahontan.* 2 vols. Edited by Reuben Gold Thwaites. Chicago: A. C. McClurg, 1905.

La Potherie, Le Roy Bacqueville de. *Histoire de l'Amérique Septentionale: Relation d'un séjour en Nouvelle-France.* 2 vols. 1722. Reprint, Monaco: Rocher, 1997.

Leder, Lawrence H., ed. *Livingston Indian Records, 1666–1723.* Gettysburg: Pennsylvania Historical Association, 1956.

Letters from North America. Translated by Ivy Alice Dickson. Belleville, Ont.: Mika, 1980.

Mather, Cotton. *Decennium Luctuosum: Or, the Remarkables of the Long War with Indian Salvages.* In *Narratives of the Indian Wars,* edited by Charles H. Lincoln, 169–299. New York: C. Scribner's Sons, 1913.

[Mather, Cotton]. *Diary of Cotton Mather.* 2 vols. Boston: Massachusetts Historical Society, 1911–1912.

Mather, Cotton. *The Frontiers Well-Defended.* Boston: T. Green, 1707.

———. *Good Fetch'd out of Evil.* Boston: B. Green, 1706.

———. "New Assaults from the Indians." In *Puritans among the Indians: Accounts of Captivity and Redemption, 1676–1724,* edited by Alden T. Vaughan and Edward W. Clark, 133–144. Cambridge: Harvard University Press, 1981.

[Mather, Cotton]. *Selected Letters of Cotton Mather.* Compiled by Kenneth Silverman. Baton Rouge: Louisiana State University Press, 1971.

McIlwain, C. H., ed. *Peter Wraxall's Abridgement of the New York Indian Records.* Cambridge: Harvard University Press, 1915.

A Memorial of the Present Deplorable State of New-England, with the Many Disadvantages it Lyes under, by the Maleadministration of their Present Governour, Joseph Dudley, Esq. and His son Paul, Boston, 1707 [sic]. London, 1707. Reprinted in *Collections of the Massachusetts Historical Society,* 5th. ser., 6 (1879): 31–64.

A Modest Inquiry into the Grounds and Occasions of the Late Pamphlet Intitled A Memorial of the Deplorable State of New-England By a disinterested hand. London, 1707. Reprinted in *Collections of the Massachusetts Historical Society,* 5th. ser., 6 (1879): 65–95.

O'Callaghan, E. B. *The Documentary History of the State of New York.* 4 vols. Albany: Weed, Parsons, 1849–1851.

———, ed. *Documents Relative to the Colonial History of the State of New York.* 15 vols. Albany: Weed, Parsons, 1853–1887.

Pagent of Old Deerfield on the Grounds of the Allen Homestead, Deerfield, 1910. Deerfield, Mass.: Village Improvement Society of Deerfield, 1910.

Pagent of Old Deerfield on the Grounds of the Allen Homestead, Deerfield, 1913. Deerfield, Mass.: Village Improvement Society of Deerfield, 1913.

Penhallow, Samuel. *History of the Indian Wars.* Edited by Edward Wheelock. 1726. 1924. Reprint, Williamstown, Mass.: Corner House, 1973.

Pike, John. "Journal of the Rev. John Pike." *Proceedings of the Massachusetts Historical Society, 1875–1876,* 1876, 117–151.

Rapport de l'archiviste de la province de Quebec. Quebec: Proulx, 1920–.

Robles, Vito Alessio, ed. *Diario y Derrotero de lo Caminado, Visito y Observado en la Visita que hizo a los Presidios de la Nueva Espana Septentrional el Brigadier Pedro de Rivera.* Archivo Historico Militar Mexicano, no. 2. Mexico: Taller Autografico, 1946.

Roy, Pierre-Georges. *Lettres de noblesse, généalogies, érections de comtes et baronnies insinuées par le Conseil Souverain de la Nouvelle-France.* 2 vols. Beauceville: L'Eclaireur, 1920.

———. *Les Petites Choses de nôtre histoire.* 3rd ser. Lévis, 1922.

Sagard, Father Gabriel. *The Long Journey to the Country of the Hurons.* Edited by George M. Wrong. Translated by H. H. Langton. Toronto: Champlain Society, 1939.

[Sewall, Samuel]. *Diary of Samuel Sewall.* In *Collections of the Massachusetts Historical Society,* 5th ser. 3 vols. Boston, 1879.

Smith, James. "Of the Remarkable Occurrences in the Life and Travels of Colonel James Smith." In *Indian Captivities; or, Life in the Wigwam*, edited by Samuel G. Drake, 178–264. 1851. Reprint, Bowie, Md.: Heritage Books, 1995.

Stockwell, Quentin. "Quentin Stockwell's Relation of His Captivity and Redemption." Reported by Increase Mather. In *Puritans among the Indians: Accounts of Captivity and Redemption, 1676–1724*, edited by Alden T. Vaughan and Edward W. Clark, 79–89. Cambridge: Harvard University Press, 1981.

[Stoddard, John]. "Stoddard's Journal." *New England Historical and Genealogical Register* 5 (January 1851): 21–42.

Thwaites, Ruben Gold, ed. *The Jesuit Relations and Allied Documents: Travels and Explorations of the Jesuit Missionaries in New France, 1610–1791*. 73 vols. Cleveland, Ohio: Burrows Brothers, 1896–1901.

Williams, John. *God in the Camp*. Boston: B. Green, 1707.

———. "The Redeemed Captive Returning to Zion." In *Puritans among the Indians: Accounts of Captivity and Redemption, 1676–1724*, edited by Alden T. Vaughan and Edward W. Clark, 167–226. Cambridge: Harvard University Press, 1981.

Williams, Solomon. *The Power and Efficacy of the Prayers of the People of God, when rightly offered to him; and the Obligation and Encouragement thence arising to be much in Prayer: A Sermon Preach'd at Mansfield*. Boston: S. Kneeland and T. Green, 1742.

Williams, Stephen. "An Account of Some Ancient Things." In John Williams, *The Redeemed Captive Returning to Zion*, edited by Stephen West Williams, 156–161. 1853. Reprint, Cambridge, Mass.: Applewood Books, 1987.

[Williams, Stephen]. *Narrative of the Captivity of Stephen Williams*. Edited by George Sheldon. Deerfield, Mass.: Pocumtuck Valley Memorial Association, 1889.

Winthrop Papers. Massachusetts Historical Society Collections, 6th ser., 3 (1889).

Published Secondary Sources

Abbot, Abiel. *History of Andover from Its Settlement to 1829*. Andover, Mass.: Flagg and Gould, 1829.

Adams, Sherman W., and Henry R. Stiles. *The History of Ancient Wethersfield, Connecticut*. 2 vols. New York: Grafton Press, 1904.

Alfred, Gerald R. *Heeding the Voices of Our Ancestors: Kahnawake Mohawk Politics and the Rise of Native Nationalism*. Toronto: Oxford University Press, 1995.

Allaire, Gratien. "Officiers et marchands: Les Sociétés de commerce des fourreures, 1715–1760." *Revue d'histoire de l'Amérique française* 40, no. 3 (winter 1987): 409–428.

Altman, Morris. "Economic Growth in Canada, 1695–1739." *William and Mary Quarterly*, 3rd ser., 45, no. 4 (October 1988): 684–711.

———. "Seignorial Tenure in New France, 1688–1739: An Essay on Income Distribution and Retarded Economic Development." *Historical Reflections/Réflections Historiques* 10, no. 3 (fall 1983): 335–375.

Axtell, James. *The Invasion Within: The Contest of Cultures in Colonial North America*. New York: Oxford University Press, 1985.

Bacon, Edwin M. *The Connecticut River and the Valley of the Connecticut*. New York: Putnam, 1906.

Baker, C. Alice. *True Stories of New England Captives Carried to Canada during the Old French and Indian Wars*. 1897. Reprint, Bowie, Md.: Heritage Books, 1990.

Bancroft, George. *History of the United States: From the Discovery of the American Continent.* 10 vols. Boston: Little, Brown, 1852–1878.

Barber, John W. *Historical Collections, Being a General Collection of Interesting Facts, Traditions, Biographical Sketches, Anecdotes, &c., Relating to the History and Antiquities of Every Town in Massachusetts.* Worcester, Mass.: Dorr, Howland, 1841.

Baum, Rosalie Murphy. "John Williams's Captivity Narrative: A Consideration of Normative Ethnicity." In *A Mixed Race: Ethnicity in Early America,* edited by Frank Shuffleton, 56–76. New York: Oxford University Press, 1993,.

Beaubien, Charles-P. *Le Sault-au-Récollet: Ses rapports avec les premiers temps de la colonie.* Montreal: C. O. Beauchemin & Fils, 1898.

Beaulieu, Alain. "Les Hurons de Lorette, le 'traité Murray' et la liberté de commerce." In *Les Hurons de Lorette,* edited by Denis Vaugeois, 254–295. Sillery: Septentrion, 1996.

Bédard, Marc-André. *Les Protestants en Nouvelle-France.* Cahiers d'histoire, no. 31. Quebec: Société historique de Québec, 1978.

Belknap, Jeremy. *The History of New Hampshire.* 2nd ed. 3 vols. Dover, N.H.: O. Crosby and J. Varncy, 1813.

Berger, Carl. *The Writing of Canadian History.* Toronto: Oxford University Press, 1976.

Berlin, Ira. *Many Thousands Gone: The First Two Centuries of Slavery in North America.* Cambridge: Harvard University Press, 1998.

Berthet, Thierry. *Seigneurs et colons de Nouvelle France: L'Emergence d'une société distincte au XVIIIème siècle.* Cachan: L'E.N.S., 1992.

Blanchard, David. *Seven Generations: A History of the Kanienkehaka.* Kahnawake, 1980.

———. ". . . To the Other Side of the Sky: Catholicism at Kahnawake, 1667–1700." *Anthropologica* 24 (1982): 77–102.

Bonomi, Patricia U. *The Lord Cornbury Scandal: The Politics of Reputation in British America.* Chapel Hill: University of North Carolina Press for the Omohundro Institute of Early American History and Culture, Williamsburg, Va., 1998.

Bossenga, Gail. "Society." In *Old Regime France, 1648–1788,* edited by William Doyle. New York: Oxford University Press, 2001.

Bouton, Nathaniel. *The History of Concord . . . with a History of the Ancient Penacooks.* Concord, N.H.: B. W. Sanborn, 1856.

Bragdon, Kathleen J. *Native People of Southern New England, 1500–1650.* Norman: University of Oklahoma Press, 1996.

Brandão, Jóse António. *"Your fyre shall burn no more": Iroquois Policy toward New France and Its Native Allies to 1701.* Lincoln: University of Nebraska Press, 1997.

Braudel, Fernand, and Ernest Labrousse, eds. *Histoire économique et sociale de la France.* 4 vols. Paris: Presses Universitaires de France, 1970–1980.

Briggs, Robin. *Early Modern France, 1560–1725.* 2nd ed. New York: Oxford University Press, 1998.

Brunet, Michael. "The British Conquest: Canadian Social Scientists and the Fate of the *Canadiens.*" In *Approaches to Canadian History,* edited by Carl Berger, 84–98. Toronto: University of Toronto Press, 1967.

Bumsted, J. M. "'Carried to Canada!': Perceptions of the French in British Colonial Captivity Narratives, 1690–1760." *American Review of Canadian Studies* 13, no. 1 (1983): 79–96.

Burke, Thomas E. Jr. *Mohawk Frontier: The Dutch Community of Schenectady, New York, 1661–1710.* Ithaca, N.Y.: Cornell University Press, 1991.

Burt, Henry M. *Burt's Illustrated Guide of the Connecticut Valley.* Springfield, Mass.: New England Publishing Company, 1866.

Bushman, Richard L. "Corruption and Power in Provincial America." In *The Development of a Revolutionary Mentality: Library of Congress Symposium on the American Revolution,* 62–91. Washington, D.C.: Library of Congress, 1972.

———. *King and People in Provincial Massachusetts.* Chapel Hill: University of North Carolina Press for the Institute of Early American History and Culture, Williamsburg, Va., 1985.

Calloway, Colin G. "Wanalancet and Kancagamus [*sic*]: Indian Strategy on the New Hampshire Frontier." *Historical New Hampshire* 43 (winter 1988): 264–290.

———. *The Western Abenakis of Vermont: War, Migration, and the Survival of an Indian People, 1600–1800.* Norman: University of Oklahoma Press, 1990.

Campeau, Lucien. "Roman Catholic Missions in New France." In *History of Indian-White Relations,* edited by Wilcomb Washburn, 465–470. Vol. 4 of *Handbook of North American Indians,* edited by William C. Sturtevant. Washington, D.C.: Smithsonian Institution, 1988.

Carter, Samuel. "The Route of the French and Indian Army That Sacked Deerfield February 29th, 1703–4, on Their Return March to Canada with the Captives." In *Pocumtuck Valley Memorial Association History and Proceedings* 2 (1898): 126–151.

Cassel, Jay. "The Militia Legend: Canadians at War, 1665–1760." In *Canadian Military History since the Seventeenth Century,* edited by Yves Trembly, 59–67. Ottawa, 2001.

Cayton, Andrew R. L., and Fredrika J. Teute, eds. *Contact Points: American Frontiers from the Mohawk Valley to the Mississippi, 1750–1830.* Chapel Hill. N.C.: University of North Carolina Press for the Omohundro Institute of Early American History and Culture, Williamsburg, Va., 1998.

Chamberlain, Samuel, and Henry N. Flynt. *Frontier of Freedom: The Soul and Substance of America Portrayed in One Extraordinary Village, Old Deerfield, Massetts.* New York: Hastings House, 1952.

Champagne, Antoine. *La Vérendrye et le poste de l'ouest.* Québec: Laval: Presses de l'Université Laval, 1968.

Channing, Edward. *A History of the United States.* 7 vols. New York: Macmillan, 1908.

Charbonneau, Hubert. "Du Saint-Laurent au Mississippi; les compagnons d'Iberville." *Mémoires de la Société généalogique canadienne-française* 51–1, no. 223 (2000): 41–67.

———. *The First French Canadians: Pioneers in the St. Lawrence Valley.* Newark: University of Delaware Press, 1993.

Charbonneau, Hubert, Bertrand Desjardins, and Pierre Beauchamp, "Le Comportement démographique des voyageurs sous le régime français." *Histoire sociale/Social History* 21 (1978): 120–133.

Charland, Thomas. *Les Abénakis d'Odanak.* Montreal: Lévrier, 1964.

Chartrand, René. *Canadian Military Heritage, 1000–1754.* Montreal: Art Global, 1993.

Childs, John Charles Roger. *Armies and Warfare in Europe, 1648–1789.* New York: Holmes and Meier, 1982.

Chopin, Denise. "Abigail (Elizabeth) Nims." Translated by Rosemaire Belise. *Okami: Journal de la Société d'histoire d'Oka* 25, no. 2 (2000): 5–10.

———. "La descendance d'Abigail (Elizabeth) Nims." Translated by Rosemaire Belise. *Okami: Journal de la Société d'histoire d'Oka* 26, no. 1 (2001): 14–22.

Choquette, Leslie. "Center and Periphery in French North America." In *Negotiated Em-*

pires: Centers and Peripheries in the Americas, 1500–1820, edited by Christine Daniels and Michael V. Kennedy, 193–206. New York: Routledge, 2002.

———. *Frenchmen into Peasants.* Cambridge: Harvard University Press, 2000.

Coates, Colin. *The Metamorphoses of Landscape and Community in Early Quebec.* Montreal and Kingston: McGill-Queen's University Press, 2000.

Coleman, Emma Lewis. *A Historic and Present Day Guide to Old Deerfield.* Boston, 1907.

———. *New England Captives Carried to Canada between 1677 and 1760 during the French and Indian Wars.* 2 vols. Portland, Maine: Southworth Press, 1925.

Corbett, Theodore, G. *A Clash of Cultures on the Warpath of Nations: The Colonial Wars in the Hudson-Champlain Valley.* Fleischmanns, N.Y.: Purple Mountain Press, 2002.

Cronon, William. *Changes in the Land: Indians, Colonists, and the Ecology of New England.* New York: Hill and Wang, 1983.

Daniel, François. *Histoire des grandes familles françaises du Canada.* Montreal: Eusèbe Sénécal, 1867.

Daniell, Jere. *Colonial New Hampshire: A History.* Millwood, N.Y.: KTO, 1981.

Day, Gordon. "The Identity of the Saint Francis Indians." Canadian Ethnology Service Paper no. 71, Ottawa, 1981.

———. "The Ouragie War: A Case History in Iroquois-New England Indian Relations." In *Extending the Rafters: Interdisciplinary Approaches to Iroquoian Studies,* edited by Michael K. Foster, Jack Campisi, and Marianne Mithun, 35–50. Albany: State University of New York Press, 1984.

———. "Western Abenaki." In *Northeast,* edited by Bruce Trigger, 148–159. Vol. 15 of *Handbook of North American Indians,* edited by William C. Sturtevant. Washington, D.C.: Smithsonian Institution, 1978

Dechêne, Louise. *Habitants and Merchants in Seventeenth Century Montreal.* Translated by Liana Vardi. Montreal and Kingston: McGill-Queen's University Press, 1992.

"The Deerfield Issue." *Antiques Magazine* 70, no. 3 (September 1956): 223–267.

Delâge, Denis. "Hurons de Lorette." In *Les Hurons de Lorette,* edited by Denis Vaugeois, 96–131. Sillery: Septentrion, 1996.

Demos, John. *The Unredeemed Captive: A Family Story from Early America.* New York: Knopf, 1994.

Desbarats, Catherine M. "Agriculture within the Seigneurial Régime of Eighteenth-Century Canada: Some Thoughts on the Recent Literature." *Canadian Historical Review* 73, no. 1 (March 1992): 1–29.

———. "The Cost of Canada's Native Alliances: Reality and Scarcity's Rhetoric." *William and Mary Quarterly,* 3rd. ser., 5, no. 4 (October 1995): 609–630.

Devine, E. J., *Historic Caughnawaga.* Montreal: Messenger Press, 1922.

Dickinson, John A., and Jan Grabowski. "Les Populations amérindiennes de la Vallée Laurentienne, 1608–1765." *Annales de démographie historiques 1993* (Société de démographie historique, E.H.E.S.S., Paris), 1993, 51–65.

Dictionary of Canadian Biography. 14 vols. Toronto: University of Toronto Press, 1967–1998.

Drake, James D. *King Philip's War: Civil War in New England, 1675–1676.* Amherst: University of Massachusetts Press, 1999.

Drake, Samuel A. *The Border Wars of New England.* 1897. 1910. Reprint, Williamstown, Mass.: Corner House, 1973.

Dumont, Micheline. "Les Femmes de la Nouvelle-France Etaient-Elles Favorisées?" *Atlantis* 8, no. 1 (fall 1982): 118–124.

Ebersole, Gary L. *Captured by Texts: Puritan to Post-Modern Images of Indian Captivity.* Charlottesville: University Press of Virginia, 1995.

Eccles, William J. *Canada under Louis XIV.* Toronto: McClelland and Stewart, 1964.

———. *The Canadian Frontier, 1534–1760.* Rev. ed. Albuquerque: University of New Mexico Press, 1974.

———. *Canadian Society during the French Regime.* Montreal: Harvest House, 1968.

———. *Essays on New France.* Toronto: Oxford University Press, 1987.

———. *The French in North America, 1500–1783.* Rev. ed. Markham, Ont.: Fitzhenry & Whiteside, 1998.

———. *Frontenac, the Courtier Governor.* 1959. Reprint, Toronto: McClelland and Stewart, 1968.

Eckstrom, Fannie Hardy. "Who Was Paugus?" *New England Quarterly* 12 (1939): 203–226.

Englehardt, Tom. *The End of Victory Culture: Cold War America and the Disillusioning of a Generation.* Amherst: University of Massachusetts Press, 1998.

Everts, Louis H., ed. *History of the Connecticut Valley in Massachusetts.* 2 vols. Philadelphia: Lippincott, 1879.

Fenton, William N., and Elizabeth Tooker. "Mohawk." In *Northeast,* edited by Bruce Trigger, 466–480. Vol. 15 of *Handbook of North American Indians,* edited by William C. Sturtevant. Washington, D.C.: Smithsonian Institution, 1978.

Foster, Stephen. *The Long Argument: English Puritanism and the Shaping of New England Culture.* Chapel Hill: University of North Carolina Press for the Institute of Early American History and Culture, Williamsburg, Va., 1991.

Foster, William Henry III. "Agathe Saint-Père and Her Captive New England Weavers: Technical Transference and Cultural Exchange in One Woman's Enterprise in Colonial French Canada." *French Colonial History* 1 (2002): 129–141.

———. "Women at the Centers, Men at the Margins: The Wilderness Mission of the Secular Sisters of Early Montreal Reconsidered." In *Women and Religion in Old and New Worlds,* edited by Susan E. Dinan and Debra Myers, 93–112. New York: Routledge, 2001.

Fournier, Marcel. *De la Nouvelle-Angleterre à la Nouvelle-France: L'Histoire des captifs anglo-américains au Canada entre 1675 et 1760.* Montreal: Société généalogique canadienne-française, 1992.

Frazier, Patrick. *The Mohicans of Stockbridge.* Lincoln: University of Nebraska Press, 1992.

Frégault, Guy. *Canadian Society in the French Regime.* Ottawa: Canadian Historical Association, 1981.

———. *Le XVIIIè Siècle canadien: Études.* Montreal: HMH, 1968.

Frisch, Jack. "The Abenakis among the St. Regis Mohawks." *Indian Historian* 4, no. 1 (spring 1971): 27–29.

Fuess, Claude. *Andover: Symbol of New England—The Evolution of a Town.* Portland, Maine: Anthoensen Press, 1959.

Gadoury, Lorraine. *La Noblesse de Nouvelle-France: Familles et alliances.* Montreal: Hurtubise HMH, 1991.

Gagnon, François-Marc. *La Conversion par l'image: Un Aspect de la mission des Jésuites auprès des Indiens du Canada au XVIIème siècle.* Montreal: Bellarmin, 1975.

Gareau, G. Robert. *Pionniers et pionnières des débuts de Boucherville jusqu'à 1700.* Boucherville: Société d'histoire des Îles Percées, 1992.

———. *Premières Concessions d'habitations, 1673, Boucherville.* Montreal: Société d'histoire des Îles Percées, 1973.

Garneau, François-Xavier. *Histoire du Canada,* 8th ed. Revised and expanded by Hector Garneau. 9 vols. Montreal: L'Arbe, 1944–1946.

Garrison, J. Ritchie. *Landscape and Material Life in Franklin County, Massachusetts, 1770–1860.* Knoxville: University of Tennessee Press, 1991.

Gérin, Léon. "La Seigneurie de Sillery et les Hurons de Lorette." *Bulletin des recherches historiques* 13, no. 10 (1907): 73–115.

Ghere, David L. "Diplomacy and War on the Maine Frontier, 1678–1759." In *Maine: The Pine Tree State, from Prehistory to Present,* edited by Richard W. Judd, Edwin A. Churchill, and Joel W. Eastman, 120–142. Orono: University of Maine Press, 1995.

———. "The 'Disappearance' of the Abenaki in Western Maine: Political Organization and Ethnocentric Assumptions." *American Indian Quarterly* 17, no. 2 (1993): 193–207.

Gookin, Daniel. *Historical Collections of the Indians in New England.* 1792. Reprint, New York: Arno Press, 1972.

Goubert, Pierre. *The Ancien Régime.* Translated by Steve Cox. New York: Harper & Row, 1973.

Goudreau, Serge. "Le Village huron de Lorette: Une Crèche pour les enfants canadiens du XVIIIè siècle." *Mémoires de la Société généalogique canadienne-française* 223 (spring 2000): 7–12.

Grabowski, Jan. "Les Amérindiens domiciliés et la 'contrebande' des fourreures en Nouvelle France." *Recherches amérindiennes au Québec* 24, no. 3 (1994): 45–52.

Greene, Evarts B., and Virginia D. Harrington. *American Population before the Federal Census of 1790.* New York: Columbia University Press, 1931.

Greer, Allan. *Peasant, Lord, and Merchant: Rural Society in Three Quebec Parishes, 1740–1840.* Toronto: University of Toronto Press, 1985.

———. *The People of New France.* Toronto: University of Toronto Press, 1997.

Haefeli, Evan. "Ransoming New England Captives in New France." *French Colonial History* 1 (2002): 113–128.

Haefeli, Evan, and Kevin Sweeney. "Revisiting *The Redeemed Captive:* New Perspectives on the 1704 Attack on Deerfield." *William and Mary Quarterly,* 3rd ser., 52, no.1 (January 1995): 3–46.

———. "Wattanummon's World: Personal and Tribal Identity in the Algonquian Diaspora, c. 1660–1712." In *Actes du Vingt-Cinquième Congrès des Algonquinistes,* edited by William Cowan, 212–224. Ottawa: Carleton University, 1994.

Haffenden, Philip S. *New England in the English Nation, 1689–1713.* Oxford: Clarendon Press, 1974.

Hall, Michael G. *The Last Puritan: The Life of Increase Mather.* Middletown, Conn.: Wesleyan University Press, 1988.

Hammang, Francis H. *The Marquis de Vaudreuil: New France at the Beginning of the Eighteenth Century: Part I: New France and the English Colonies.* Bruges and Louvain: Louvain University, 1938.

Handsmen, Russel G. "Illuminating History's Silence in the 'Pioneer Valley.'" *Artifacts* 19, no. 2 (fall 1991): 14–25.

Harris, Richard Colebrook. *The Seigneurial System in Early Canada: A Geographical Study.* Madison: University of Wisconsin Press, 1966.

Hart, William B. "'The Kindness of the Blessed Virgin': Faith, Succour, and the Cult of Mary among Christian Hurons and Iroquois in Seventeenth-Century New France." In *Spiritual Encounters: Interactions between Christianity and Native Religion in Colonial America,* edited by Nicholas Griffiths and Fernado Cervantes, 65–90. Lincoln: University of Nebraska Press, 1999.

Hatch, R. W. "Old Deerfield, Mass." *Ford Times* 41, no. 3 (March 1949): 2–9.

Havard, Gilles. *The Great Peace of Montreal of 1701: French-Native Diplomacy in the Seventeenth Century.* Translated by Phyllis Aronoff and Howard Scott. Montreal and Kingston: McGill-Queen's University Press, 2001.

Head, J. Norman. *White into Red: A Study of the Assimilation of White Persons Captured by Indians.* Metuchen, N.J.: Scarecrow Press, 1973.

Hoyt, Epaphras. *Antiquarian Researches.* Greenfield, Mass.: A. Phelps, 1824.

Hutchinson, Thomas. *The History of the Colony and Province of Massachusetts-Bay.* 2 vols. Edited by Lawrence Shaw Mayo. Cambridge: Harvard University Press, 1936.

Jaenen, Cornelius J. *Friend and Foe: Aspects of French-Amerindian Culture Contact in the Sixteenth and Seventeenth Centuries.* Toronto: McClelland and Stewart, 1976.

———. "Some Unresolved Issues: Lorette Hurons in the Colonial Context." In *Essays in French Colonial History: Proceedings of the 21st Annual Meeting of the French Colonial Historical Society,* edited by A. J. B. Johnston, 111–125. East Lansing: Michigan State University Press, 1997.

Jennings, Francis. *The Ambiguous Iroquois Empire: The Covenant Chain Confederation of Indian Tribes with English Colonies from Its Beginnings to the Lancaster Treaty of 1744.* New York: Norton, 1984.

Jetté, René. *Dictionnaire généalogique des familles du Québec.* Montreal: Les Presses de l'Université de Montréal, 1983.

Jetten, Marc. *Enclaves amérindiennes: Les 'réductions' du Canada, 1637–1701.* Sillery: Septentrion, 1994.

Johnson, Richard R. *Adjustment to Empire: The New England Colonies, 1675–1715.* New Brunswick, N.J.: Rutgers University Press, 1981.

———. *John Nelson, Merchant Adventurer: A Life between Empires.* New York: Oxford University Press, 1991.

Judd, Sylvester. *The History of Hadley including the Early History of Hatfield, South Hadley, Amherst and Granby, Massachusetts.* Springfield, Mass.: H. R. Huntting, 1905.

Kawashima, Yashuide. *Puritan Justice and the Indian: White Man's Law in Massachusetts, 1630–1763.* Middletown, Conn.: Wesleyan University Press, 1986.

Kimball, Everett. *The Public Life of Joseph Dudley: A Study of the Colonial Policy of the Stuarts in New England, 1660–1715.* New York: Longmans and Green, 1911.

Lachance, André. *La Vie urbaine en Nouvelle France.* Montreal: Boreal, 1987.

Lamarche, Hélène. "Les Habitants de Lachine et le massacre de 1689." *Memoires de la Société généalogique canadienne-française* 50, no. 3, cahier 221 (fall 1999): 189–228.

Larin, Robert. *Brève histoire du peuplement europeén en Nouvelle-France.* Sillery: Septentrion, 2000.

Lavallée, Louis. *La Prairie en Nouvelle-France, 1647–1760.* Montreal and Kingston: McGill-Queen's University Press, 1992.

Leavenworth, Peter S. "'The Best Title That Indians Can Claime': Native Agency and Consent in the Transferral of Penacook-Pawtucket Land in the Seventeenth Century." *New England Quarterly* 72, no. 2 (June 1999): 275–300.

Leach, Douglas Edward. *Arms for Empire: A military history of the British Colonies in North America, 1607–1763*. New York: Macmillan, 1973.

———. *Flintlock and Tomahawk: New England in King Philip's War*. New York: Norton, 1966.

Lehmann-Haupt, Hellmut. *The Book in America: A History of the Making and Selling of Books in the United States*. 2nd ed. New York: Bowker, 1951.

Leland, Marine. "A Canadian Explorer in Deerfield: Jacques de Noyon (1668–1745)." *William's Scrapbook* (Connecticut Valley Historical Museum), autumn 1955, 3–5.

Lepore, Jill. *The Name of War: King Philip's War and the Origins of American Identity*. New York: Knopf, 1998.

Lucas, Paul. *Valley of Discord: Church and Society along the Connecticut River, 1636–1725*. Hanover, N.H.: University Press of New England, 1976.

Lunn, Jean. "The Illegal Fur Trade out of New France, 1713–1760." *Canadian Historical Association Annual Report*, 1939, 61–76.

Lynn, John A. *Giant of the* Grand Siècle: *The French Army, 1610–1715*. New York: Cambridge University Press, 1997.

MacLeod, Peter. *The Canadian Iroquois and the Seven Years' War*. Toronto: Dundurn Press, 1996.

Main, Gloria L. *Peoples of a Spacious Land: Families and Cultures in Colonial New England*. Cambridge: Harvard University Press, 2001.

Mancall, Peter. *Deadly Medicine: Indians and Alcohol in Early America*. Ithaca, N.Y.: Cornell University Press, 1995.

Marion, Séraphin. *Un Pionnier canadien: Pierre Boucher*. Quebec: Proulx, 1927.

Martin, John Frederick. *Profits in the Wilderness: Entrepreneurship and the Founding of New England Towns in the Seventeenth Century*. Chapel Hill: University of North Carolina Press for the Institute of Early American History and Culture, Williamsburg, Va., 1991.

Massicote, E-Z. "Jacques de Noyon: Nouveaux Details sur sa carriére." *Bulletin des recherches historiques* 48 (1942): 122–123.

McDowell, Bart. "Deerfield Keeps a Truce with Time." *National Geographic* 135, no. 6 (June 1969): 780–809.

McGowan, Susan, and Amelia F. Miller. *Family and Landscape: Deerfield Homelots from 1671*. Deerfield, Mass.: Pocumtuck Valley Memorial Association, 1996.

Melvoin, Richard I. *New England Outpost: War and Society in Colonial Deerfield*. New York: Norton, 1989.

Merrell, James H., "Shamokin, 'the very seat of the Prince of darkness': Unsettling the Early American Frontier." In *Contact Points: American Frontiers from the Mohawk Valley to the Mississippi, 1750–1830*, edited by Andrew R. L. Cayton and Fredrika J. Teute, 60–87. Chapel Hill: University of North Carolina Press for the Omohundro Institute of Early American History and Culture, Williamsburg, Va., 1998.

———. "'Their Very Bones Shall Fight': The Catawba-Iroquois Wars." In *Beyond the Covenant Chain: The Iroquois and Their Neighbors in Indian North America, 1600–1800*, edited by Daniel K. Richter and James H. Merrell, 115–133. Syracuse, N.Y.: Syracuse University Press, 1987.

Miles, Lion G. "The Red Man Dispossessed: The Williams Family and the Alienation of Indian Land in Stockbridge, Massachusetts, 1736–1818." *New England Quarterly* 67, no.1 (March 1994): 46–76.

Miquelon, Dale, *New France, 1701–1744: "A Supplement to Europe."* Toronto: McClelland and Stewart, 1987.

Mitchell, Estelle. *Messire Pierre Boucher (écuyer) Seigneur de Boucherville, 1622–1717.* Montreal: Librairie Beauchemin, 1967.

Moogk, Peter N. *La Nouvelle France: The Making of French Canada—A Cultural History.* East Lansing: Michigan State University Press, 2000.

Moorhead, Max L. *The Presidio: Bastion of the Spanish Borderlands.* Norman: University of Oklahoma Press, 1975.

Morison, Samuel Eliot. *Harvard College in the Seventeenth Century.* 2 vols. Cambridge: Harvard University Press, 1936.

Morisonneau, Christian. "Développement et population de la réserve indienne du village-huron, Lorretteville." In *Les Hurons de Lorette,* edited by Denis Vaugeois, 80–94. Sillery: Septentrion, 1996.

———. "Huron of Lorette." In *Northeast,* edited by Bruce Trigger, 389–393. Vol. 15 of *Handbook of North American Indians,* edited by William C. Sturtevant. Washington, D.C.: Smithsonian Institution, 1978.

Morrison, Kenneth M. "Baptism and Alliance: The Symbolic Mediations of Religious Syncretism." *Ethnohistory* 37, no. 4 (1990): 416–437.

———. *The Embattled Northeast: The Elusive Ideal of Alliance in Abenaki-Euramerican Relations.* Berkeley: University of California Press, 1984.

———. "Montagnais Missionization in Early New France: The Syncretic Imperative." *American Indian Culture and Research Journal* 10, no. 3 (1986): 1–23.

———. "Towards a History of Intimate Encounters: Algonkian Folklore, Jesuit Missionaries, and Kiwakwe, the Cannibal Giant." *American Indian Culture and Research Journal* 3, no. 4 (1979): 51–80.

———. "The Wonders of Divine Mercy: A Review of John Williams' *The Redeemed Captive." American Review of Canadian Studies* 9, no. 1 (1979): 56–62.

Munro, William Bennett. *The Seignorial System in Canada: A Study in French Canadian Policy.* New York: Longmans, Green, 1907.

Namias, June. *White Captives: Gender and Ethnicity on the American Frontier.* Chapel Hill: University of North Carolina Press, 1993.

Nish, Cameron. *Les Bourgeois-Gentilshommes de la Nouvelle-France, 1729–1748.* Montreal: Fides, 1968.

Noel, Jan. "New France: Les Femmes Favorisées." In *Rethinking Canada: The Promise of Women's History,* edited by Veronica Strong-Boag and Anita Clarir Fellman, 23–44. Toronto: Copp Clark Pitman, 1985.

Norton, Mary Beth. *In the Devil's Snare: The Salem Witchcraft Crisis of 1692.* New York: Knopf, 2002.

Nosworthy, Brent. *The Anatomy of Victory: Battle Tactics, 1689–1763.* New York: Hippocrene Books, 1990.

Palfrey, John G. *History of New England.* 5 vols. Boston: Little, Brown, 1859–1890.

Pargellis, Stanley. "The Four Independent Companies of New York." In *Essays in Colonial History Presented to Charles McLean Andrews.* New Haven, Conn.: Yale University Press, 1931.

Parker, Geoffrey. "Early Modern Europe." In *The Laws of War: Constraints on Warfare in the Western World,* edited by Michael Howard, George J. Andreopoulos, and Mark R. Shulman, 40–58. New Haven, Conn.: Yale University Press, 1994.

Parkman, Francis. *Half Century of Conflict.* Vol. 2 of *France and England in North America.* New York: Library of America, 1983.

Peckham, Howard H. *The Colonial Wars, 1689–1762.* Chicago: University of Chicago Press, 1964.

Pencak, William. *War, Politics, and Revolution in Provincial Massachusetts.* Boston: Northeastern University Press, 1981.

Plank, Geoffrey. *An Unsettled Conquest: The British Campaign against the Peoples of Acadia.* Philadelphia: University of Pennsylvania Press, 2001.

Prins, Harald, and Bruce Bourque. "Norridgewock: Village Translocation on the New England-Acadian Frontier." *Man in the Northeast* 33 (1986): 137–158.

Reid, John G. "Unorthodox Warfare in the Northeast, 1703." *Canadian Historical Review* 73, no. 2 (1992): 211–220.

Richter, Daniel. *The Ordeal of the Longhouse: The Peoples of the Iroquois Leage in the Era of European Colonization.* Chapel Hill: University of North Carolina Press for the Institute of Early American History and Culture, Williamsburg, Va., 1992.

———. "War and Culture: The Iroquois Experience." *William and Mary Quarterly,* 3rd ser., 40 (1985): 528–559.

Ronda, James P. "The Sillery Experiment: A Jesuit-Indian Village in New France, 1637–1663." *American Indian Culture and Research Journal* 3, no.1 (1979): 1–18.

Rouville, Jean-Baptiste-Melchior Hertel de. "Généalogie de la famille Hertel." *Nova Francia* 5 (1930): 156–169.

Sadoques, Elizabeth M. "History and Traditions of Eunice Williams and Her Descendants." *Pocumtuck Valley Memorial Association History and Proceedings* 6 (1929): 126–131.

Salisbury, Neal. *Manitou and Providence: Indians, Europeans, and the Making of New England, 1500–1643.* New York: Oxford University Press, 1982.

———. "Toward the Covenant Chain: Iroquois and Southern New England Algonquians, 1637–1684." In *Beyond the Covenant Chain: The Iroquois and Their Neighbors in Indian North America,* edited by Daniel K. Richter and James H. Merrell, 61–73. Syracuse, N.Y.: Syracuse University Press, 1987.

Scalberg, Daniel A. "The French-Amerindian Religious Encounter in Seventeenth- and Early Eighteenth-Century New France." *French Colonial History* 1 (2002): 101–112.

Selesky, Harold E. "Colonial America." In *The Laws of War: Constraints on Warfare in the Western World,* edited by Michael Howard, George J. Andreopoulos, and Mark R. Shulman, 59–85. New Haven, Conn.: Yale University Press, 1994.

Sévigny, P. André. *Les Abénaquis: Habitat et migrations (17è et 18è siècles) Saint Laurent.* Montreal: HDI Library, 1976.

[Sheldon, George]. "Field Meeting—1903." *History and Proceedings of the Pocumtuck Valley Memorial Association* 4 (1905): 379–423.

Sheldon, George. *A History of Deerfield, Massachusetts.* 2 vols. Deerfield: privately printed, 1895–1896.

Shipton, Clifford. *Sibley's Harvard Graduates.* 13 vols. Cambridge: Harvard University Press, 1933–1975.

Silverman, Kenneth. *The Life and Times of Cotton Mather.* New York: Columbia University Press, 1985.

Simpson, Patricia. *Marguerite Bourgeoys and Montreal, 1640–1665.* Montreal and Kingston: McGill-Queen's University Press, 1997.

Snow, Dean R. *The Iroquois.* Cambridge: Blackwell, 1994.

Socolow, Susan M. "Spanish Captives in Indian Societies: Cultural Contact along the Argentine Frontier, 1600–1835." *Hispanic American Historical Review* 72, no. 1 (1992): 73–99.

Spady, James. "As if in a Great Darkness: Native American Refugees of the Middle Connecticut Valley in the Aftermath of King Philip's War." *Historical Journal of Massachusetts* 23, no. 2 (summer 1995): 183–197.

Stanley, George F. *Canada's Soldiers: The Military History of an Unmilitary People.* Toronto: Macmillan, 1974.

———. "The Indians and the Brandy Trade during the French regime." *Revue d'histoire de l'Amerique francaise* 6, no. 4 (1953): 489–505.

Starkey, Armstrong. *European and Native American Warfare, 1675–1815.* Norman: University of Oklahoma Press, 1998.

Starna, William, and Ralph Watkins. "Northern Iroquoian Slavery." *Ethnohistory* 38, no. 1 (winter 1991): 34–57.

Steckley, John. "The Warrior and the Lineage: Jesuit Use of Iroquoian Images to Communicate Christianity." *Ethnohistory* 39, no. 4 (1992): 478–507.

Steele, Ian. K. *Betrayals: Fort William Henry and the "Massacre."* New York: Oxford University Press, 1990.

———. *Guerrillas and Grenadiers: The Struggle for Canada, 1688–1760.* Toronto: Ryerson, 1969.

———. "Surrendering Rites: Prisoners on Colonial North American Frontiers." In *Hanoverian Britain and Empire: Essays in Memory of Philip Lawson,* edited by Stephen Taylor, Richard Connors, and Clyve Jones, 126–151 . Rochester, N.Y.: Boydell Press, 1998.

———. *Warpaths: Invasions of North America.* New York: Oxford University Press, 1994.

Strong, Pauline Turner. *Captive Selves, Captivating Others: The Politics and Poetics of Colonial American Captivity Narratives.* Boulder, Colo.: Westview Press, 1999.

Sulte, Benjamin. *Histoire des Canadiens-Français 1608–1880: Origine, histoire, religion, guerres, découvertes, colonisation, coutumes, vie domestique, sociale et politique, dévelopment, avenir; par Benjamin Sulte.* 8 vols. Montreal: Wilson, 1882–1884.

Tallett, Frank. *War and Society in Early Modern Europe: 1495–1715.* New York: Routledge, 1992.

Tanguay, Cyprien. *Dictionnaire genealogique des familles canadiennes.* 7 vols. Quebec: Eusébe Senêcal, 1871–1890.

Taylor, John. *A Century Sermon Preached at Deerfield, February 29, 1804: In Commemoration of the Destruction of the Town by the French and Indians.* Greenfield, Mass.: John Denio, 1804.

Temple, Josiah H., and George Sheldon. *A History of the Town of Northfield, Massachusetts for 150 Years.* Albany, N.Y.: Joel Munsell, 1875.

Trigger, Bruce. *The Children of Aataentsic: A History of the Huron People to 1660.* 2 vols. Montreal and Kingston: McGill-Queen's University Press, 1987.

Trudel, Marcel. *L'Esclavage au Canada Français: Histoire et conditions de l'esclavage.* Quebec: Presses Universitaires Laval, 1960.

———. "Les Hurons et Murray en 1760." In *Les Hurons de Lorette,* edited by Denis Vaugeois, 132–159. Sillery: Septentrion, 1996.

———. *Introduction to New France.* 1968. Reprint, Pawtucket, R.I.: Quitin, 1997.

Trumbull, Henry. *History of the Discovery of America . . . and of their Most Remarkable Engagements with the Indians . . .* Boston: George Clark, 1836.

———. *History of the Indian Wars.* 1846. Reprint, Toronto: Cole, 1972.

Trumbull, James Russell. *History of Northampton, Massachusetts, from Its Settlement in 1654.* 2 vols. Northampton: privately printed, 1898–1902.

Turner, Frederick Jackson. *The Significance of the Frontier in American History* 1894. Readex Microprint, 1966, 199–227.

VanDerBeets, Richard. *The Indian Captivity Narrative: An Early American Genre.* Lanham, Md.: University Press of America, 1984.

Vaughan, Alden T., and Edward W. Clark, eds. *Puritans Among the Indians: Accounts of Captivity and Redemption, 1676–1724.* Cambridge: Harvard University Press, 1981.

Vaughan, Alden, and Daniel K. Richter. "Crossing the Cultural Divide: Indians and New Englanders, 1605–1763." *American Antiquarian Society Proceedings* 90 (1980): 23–99.

Verney, Jack. *The Good Regiment: The Carignan-Salieres Regiment in Canada, 1665–1668.* Montreal and Kingston: McGill-Queen's University Press, 1991.

Viau, Roland. *Enfants du néant et mangeurs d'âmes: Guerre, culture et société en Iroquoisie ancienne.* Cap-Saint-Ignace: Boréal, 1997.

Waller, G. M. "New York's Role in Queen Anne's War, 1702–1713. *New York History* 33 (January 1952): 40–53.

———. *Samuel Vetch, Colonial Enterpriser.* Chapel Hill: University of North Carolina Press for the Early American Institute of History and Culture, Williamsburg, Va., 1960.

White, Richard. *The Middle Ground: Indians, Empires, and Republics in the Great Lakes Region, 1650–1815.* New York: Cambridge University Press, 1991.

Wood, Joseph. *The New England Village.* (Baltimore, Md.: Johns Hopkins University Press, 1997.

Wrong, George A. *The Conquest of New France: A Chronicle of the Colonial Wars.* New Haven: Yale University Press, 1918.

———. *The Rise and Fall of New France,* 2 vols. New York: Macmillan, 1928.

Zoltvany, Yves F. *The Government of New France: Royal, Clerical, or Class Rule.* Scarborough, Ont.: Prentice-Hall of Canada, 1971.

———. *Philippe de Rigaud de Vaudreuil: Governor of New France, 1703–1725.* Toronto: McClelland and Stewart, 1974.

UNPUBLISHED SECONDARY SOURCES

Buerger, Geoffrey. "Out of Whole Cloth: The Tradition of the St. Regis Bell." Paper presented at the Mid-Atlantic Conference for Canadian Studies, Bucknell University, 1986. Copy in the Pocumtuck Valley Memorial Association Library, Deerfield, Mass.

———. "Pavillion'd upon Chaos: The History and Historiography of the Deerfield Massacre." Master's thesis, Dartmouth College, 1985.

Blouin, Anne Marie. "Histoire et iconographie des Hurons de Lorette du XVIIè au XIXè siècle." Ph.D. diss., University of Montreal, 1987.

Boss, Julia. "'To honor there the holy house': Creating a Place of Pilgrimage at Notre Dame de Lorette." Paper presented at the annual conference of the Omohundro Institute for Early American History and Culture, Austin, Tex., June 12, 1999.

Carlson, Claire C. "Native American Presences in Deerfield, Massachusetts: An Essay and Resource Guide." June 1995. Copy at Historic Deerfield, Inc.

Cassel, Jay. "The Troupes de la Marine in Canada, 1683–1760: Men and Materiel." Ph.D. diss., University of Toronto, 1988.

Chet, Guy. "Degeneration and Regeneration of European Warfare in Colonial New England: The Response of Colonial and British Forces to Challenges of Wilderness Warfare." Ph.D. diss., Yale University, 2001.

Damerall, David Odell. "Modernization of Massachusetts: The Transformation of Public Attitudes and Institutions, 1689 to 1715." Ph.D. diss., University of Texas at Austin, 1981.

Eames, Steven Charles. "Rustic Warriors: Warfare and the Provincial Soldier on the Northern Frontier, 1689–1748." Ph.D. diss., University of New Hampshire, 1989.

Foster, William Henry. "The Captor's Narrative: Catholic Women and Their Puritan Men on the Early North American Frontier, 1653–1760." Ph.D. diss., Cornell University, 2000.

Grabowski, Jan. "The Common Ground: Settled Natives and French in Montreal, 1667–1760." Ph.D. diss., University of Montreal, 1993.

Gray, Linda Breuer. "Narratives and Identities in the Saint Lawrence Valley, 1667–1720." Ph.D. diss., McGill University, 1999.

Green, Gretchen. "A New People in an Age of War: The Kahnawake Iroquois, 1667–1760." Ph.D. diss., College of William and Mary, 1991.

Laird, Matthew Robert. "The Price of Empire: Anglo-French Rivalry for the Great Lakes Fur Trades, 1700–1760." Ph.D. diss., College of William and Mary, 1995.

McCleary, Ann E. "The Child against the Devil: The Effects of Indian Captivity on the Redeemed Captives and the Puritan Zion." Paper prepared for Historic Deerfield Summer Fellowship Program, 1975.

Murrin, John M. "Anglicizing an American Colony: The Transformation of Provincial Massachusetts." Ph.D. diss., Yale University, 1966.

Nash, Alice. "The Abiding Frontier: Family, Gender, and Religion in Wabanaki History, 1600–1763." Ph.D. diss., Columbia University, 1997.

Paul, Jocelyn, Tehatarongantase. Croyances religieuses et changement social chez les Hurons de Lorette." Master's thesis, University of Montreal, 1991.

Picard-Sioui, Huwennuwanenhs L. K. "Le Cas du statut des Wendats domiciliés: Réflexion sur l'imaginaire colonial et ses utilizations contemporains." Unpublished paper, 2000, in the authors' possession.

Prins, Harald E. L. "Amesokanti: Abortive Tribeformation on the Colonial Frontier." Paper read at the annual meeting of the American Society for Ethnohistory, Williamsburg, Va., 1988.

Radabaugh, Jack S. "The Military System of Colonial Massachusetts, 1690–1740." Ph.D. diss., University of Southern California, 1965.

Russ, Christopher J. "Les Troupes de la Marine, 1683–1713." Master's thesis, McGill University, 1973.

Saileville, Charles B. de. "A History of the Life and Captivity of Miss Eunice Williams, Alias, Madam De Roguers, Who Was Styled 'The Fair Captive.'" [1842]. Neville

Public Museum. Microfilm, State Historical Society of Wisconsin, Area Research Center, Green Bay.

Scalberg, Daniel Allen. "Religious Life in New France under the Laval and Saint-Vallier Bishoprics: 1659–1727." Ph.D. diss., University of Oregon, 1990.

Smith, Mrs. E. A., collector. "Caughnewage Legends." American Bureau of Ethnology manuscript. 1882.

Stebbins, Catherine. "Jacques DeNoyon." Historic Deerfield Library, n.d.

Stewart-Smith, David. "The Pennacook Indians and the New England Frontier, circa 1604–1733." Ph.D. diss., Union Institute, Cincinnati, Ohio, 1998.

Sweeney, Kevin. "The Children of the Covenant: The Formation and Transformation of a Second Generation New England Community." Paper prepared for Historic Deerfield Summer Fellowship Program, 1971.

———. "Unruly Saints: Religion and Society in the River Towns of Massachusetts, 1700–1750." Senior honors thesis, Williams College, 1972.

Thomas, Peter Allen. "In the Maelstrom of Change: The Indian Trade and Cultural Process in the Middle Connecticut River Valley, 1635–1665." Ph.D. diss., University of Massachusetts, 1979.

Tremblay, Louise. "La Politique missionaire des Sulpiciens au XVIIè et début du XVIIIè siècle, 1668–1735." Master's thesis, University of Montreal, 1981.

INDEX

References to illustrations are in italics

Abbadie, Jean-Vincent d' (Baron de Saint-Castin), 88

Abenakis, 14, *60, 73–77, 126, 130, 228;* economy, 89–90, 148; English relations, 37–38, 74–75, 85, 89, 92, 185, 207, 211, 227–29, 269 (*See also* Anglo-Abenaki Wars); French alliance, 14, 37–38, 39, 73, 74–75, 229; French relations, 87, 89–92, 186, 203; motivations for joining Deerfield raid, 1, 2, 102; parallel wars, 185, 201; participation in Deerfield raid, 113, 115–17, 119; peace, desire for, 2, 84, 86–87, 88–89, 90, 190, 205; raids on New England, 37, 82, 127, 191, 194, 198, 205, 229; reestablishment in New England, 225, 227; refuge in New France, 55, 190; religion, 90; treatment of captives, 126–27, 130, 132, 146–47, 148, 150–51, 153, 225; warnings of Deerfield raid, 89. *See also* Koessek Abenakis; Odanak Abenakis; Pennacooks; Sokokis

Acadia, 34, 37, 54, 85; English attacks on *188–89, 191–92,* 194, 203; French loss of, 204, 207, 227. *See also* Port Royal

African Americans, 7, 27, 30, 126, 320n12

Agawams, 12, 14; village of, *13,* 14, 15

Albany (New York), *13, 37,* 68, 72, 196–97, 299n7

Alexander, David, 281

Alexander, Joseph, 126, 254, 283, 337n10

Alexander, Mary, 252, 283

Alexander, Mary (daughter), 135, 283

Alexandre (Kahnawake resident), 275

Algonkins, 55, 56, 64

Allen, Edward, 182, 251, 280

Allen, Elizabeth, 251

Allen, John, 251, 280

Allen, Sarah, 283, 317n27

alliances, English-Native, 195, 201

alliances, French-Native, 1–2; Abenakis, 14, 37–38, 39, 73, 74–75, 229; breakdown of, 185, 190; fragility of, 55–56; fur trade and, 35–38; Kahnawake Mohawks, 1, 69–72, 186–87; Native motivations for, 5, 62, 63; Pennacooks, 100; Western Natives, 36–37

Allis, Mary, 283

Allison, John, 116, 280

Allison, Thomas, 116, 280

Amerindians. *See* Natives

Amesokanti, village of, *13, 60, 75,* 80

Amsden, John, 337n8

Andover (Massachusetts), 84–85

Andros, Sir Edmund, 83, 310n13

Androscoggins, 88

Anenharison, Michel, 220

Anglo-Abenaki Wars: First Anglo-Abenaki War (*See* King Philip's War); Fourth Anglo-Abenaki War, 215, 227–30, 240, 250, 265–66, 268; Second Anglo-Abenaki War, 28, 81–85, 89; Third Anglo-Abenaki War, 2, 91, 102

Anjou, Philippe d', 35

Appleton, Samuel, 174

Arms, John, 200

Arms, William, 32, 280

Arosen (Kahnawake Mohawk), 225. *See also* Arousent

Arousent, (League Mohawk), 202. *See also* Arosen

Arsikantegouk, village of, 73. *See also* Odanak

Ashley, Benjamin, 266, 270

Ashley, Jonathan, 255, 263

EVAN HAEFELI was born and raised on Long Island, New York. While attending Hampshire College in Amherst, Massachusetts, he spent a summer studying French in Chicoutimi, Quebec, an experience that enhanced his awareness of that country's complex role in early American history. Under the supervision of Kevin Sweeney, he wrote a senior thesis at Hampshire on representations of the 1704 French and Indian attack on Deerfield. Thus began the collaboration that saw him through graduate school at Princeton University and led ultimately to the completion of this book eleven years later. He taught at Princeton University for two years before starting his current job at Tufts University. At present he is working on a book about religious toleration in colonial America.

KEVIN SWEENEY is Professor of History and American Studies at Amherst College, where he has taught since 1989. Born in Saratoga Springs, New York, he majored in history at Williams College and obtained his doctorate in history from Yale. A 1971 Historic Deerfield Summer Fellow, he served as Director of Academic Programs at Historic Deerfield from 1986 to 1989. He has also worked at the Webb-Deane-Stevens Museum in Wethersfield, Connecticut, and the Winterthur Museum in Delaware. He currently lives in Greenfield, Massachusetts, with his wife, Margaret, and their sons, Michael and Jamie.